The Blessed Place
of Freedom

Also by Dean B. Mahin

One War at a Time: The International Dimensions of the American Civil War

Olive Branch and Sword: The United States and Mexico, 1845–1848

The Blessed Place
of Freedom

Europeans in Civil War America

DEAN B. MAHIN

BRASSEY'S, INC.
Washington, D.C.

Library of Congress Cataloging-in-Publication Data

Mahin, Dean B., 1925–
       The blessed place of freedom : Europeans in Civil War America / Dean B. Mahin.—1st ed.
           p.   cm.
Includes bibliographical references (p.   ) and index.
     ISBN 1–57488–484–0 (acid-free paper)
   1. United States—History—Civil War, 1861–1865—Social aspects.   2. United States—History—Civil War, 1861–1865—Participation, Immigrant.
3. Immigrants—United States—History—19th century.   4. Immigrants—Southern States—History—19th century.   5. Europeans—United States—History—19th century.   6. Europeans—Southern States—History—19th century.   7. United States—Foreign public opinion, European.   8. Public opinion—Europe.   9. United States—History—Civil War, 1861–1865—Personal narratives.   I. Title.
     E468.9   .M2145   2002
     937.7'1—dc21   2002007996

ISBN 1-57488-484-0   (alk. paper)

Printed in the United States of America on acid-free paper that meets the American National Standards Institute Z39-48 Standard.

Brassey's, Inc.
22841 Quicksilver Drive
Dulles, Virginia 20166

First Edition

10 9 8 7 6 5 4 3 2 1

CONTENTS

We Germans . . . are prepared to defend our American home as the blessed place of freedom.

—*Staats-Zeitung, St. Paul, Minnesota, newspaper, May 4, 1861*

PREFACE

My earlier book on international dimensions of the American Civil War, *One War at a Time*, focused on the reactions of the Union, Confederate, and European governments to diplomatic issues during the Civil War. During research for that book, I was often reminded that there was another broad spectrum of international dimensions of the war—the reactions of individual Europeans who were in the North or South during the war as immigrants, volunteers, or observers. This book focuses on these reactions.

Most books about immigrants during the Civil War have been written by ethnic authors eager to demonstrate the military contribution of their ethnic group to the Union or the Confederacy. My goal has been to provide a balanced view of the roles and reactions of each major ethnic group in each region.

Each of a series of "ethnic" chapters (Chapters 2 through 6 and 8 through 12) focuses on a major immigrant group in North or South. These chapters cover the reasons the immigrants volunteered for the Union or Confederate army, estimates of the number who served, efforts by some of the immigrants or residents to avoid or escape from military service, major controversies involving the group, and individuals from their home country who came to America during the war as volunteers, correspondents, or other observers. Chapter 7 examines the flow of immigrants to the North during the war.

A series of "topical" chapters (Chapters 1 and 13 through 24) focuses on the reactions of European immigrants in North and South and of volunteers and visitors from Europe to the major phases of the war and to other major topics including the election of 1860, secession, the Union and Confederate presidents, the two armies, naval dimensions of the war, slavery and emancipation, Union and Confederate relations with Britain and France, the election of 1864, Lee's surrender at Appomattox, and the death of Lincoln.

Although a flood of diaries, letters, and memoirs by participants in the Civil War have been published, only a few of these were written by immigrants and most of them focused on camp life and military events with only rare comments on major Civil War issues and personalities. Generalizations about the reactions of immigrants to many important issues must therefore be approached with great caution. I have used tightly edited quotes from European immigrants and visitors to show the pattern of their reactions. On most topics, I have preferred to let Europeans speak for themselves, rather than to attempt to generalize about their reactions. The evidence regarding immigrant reactions is often too limited to permit broad generalizations. Moreover, even in cases when clear reactions were recorded by a number of immigrants, it is rarely possible to establish that these were the views of the majority of the members of any group.

My goal was to provide a comprehensive sampling of the reactions of Europeans who were in America during the Civil War, plus those generalizations and conclusions that can be derived from the available evidence. A "reported" reaction is usually by a journalist reporting to his newspaper or an official military observer reporting to the military authorities in his country. A "recorded" reaction is usually an entry in a diary or journal. A "recalled" account or comment is from a memoir or recollection written some years later. The source of each quote is indicated in the notes.

I also cite some of the conclusions of other authors who studied the reactions of Europeans in America or commented on immigrant reactions in a study of a particular topic or issue. As with Europeans, I preferred to quote scholars directly rather than summarize their conclusions. This gives them full credit for their work and full responsibility for their generalizations, and clearly separates their conclusions from those based on my research.

Many Europeans came to the North or South during the war as newspaper correspondents, other civilian observers, official and unofficial military observers, and officers serving as volunteers in the Union and Confederate armies. The reactions of many of these European visitors were recorded in articles and books written during or shortly after the war. I was especially interested in the reactions of these international visitors because during three Cold War decades (1950 to 1980) most of my professional work was with international visitors invited to the United States by the U.S. Department of State.

The reactions of European observers in America during the Civil War usually reflected public reactions to the war in their own countries. My research for this book produced extensive evidence concerning European reactions to the war that supports conclusions in my previous book, *One War at a Time*. Many of my conclusions in this book regarding international reactions are based on research for the two books over a period of more than five years.

During the two years of research for this book, I made full use of the excellent facilities of the Charlotte-Mecklenburg Public Library and the Atkins Library at the University of North Carolina at Charlotte. Through their efficient interlibrary loan services, I consulted many books from other libraries. I also made extensive use of the Official Records of the Union and Confederate Armies on the compact disc published by Guild Press, the Official Records of the Union and Confederate Navies available on-line from Cornell University, and the Collected Works of Abraham Lincoln available on-line from the Abraham Lincoln Association. These searchable records have provided evidence of disaffection and efforts to avoid military service by immigrants that was not readily available to earlier scholars. Important information was obtained from Internet web sites; the URLs of those sites are listed in the bibliography.

I am very grateful for information and advice provided by many individuals in America and Europe. Information or advice regarding Germans was provided by Geoff Blankenmeyer, Erich W. Bright, Bret Coulson, Jim Epperson, Ed Frank, Sevilla Finley, Dave Hamisch, Ray Nagel, Joseph R. Reinhart, Dale Rosengarten, George B. Shealy, Dave Smith, John A. Stovall, Rodman L. Underwood, Wilhelm Van der Heydt, and Scott Williams in America and by Tim Engelhart, Wolfgang Hochbruck, and Martin Kuehn in Germany. Help with the Irish was provided by Joe Bilby, Jim Creed, Joe Hourigan, Dave Matthews, Kevin O'Beirne, Kevin O'Malley, David O'Keefe, Ronnie Ranew, Bill Rose, Michael Ruddy, Chris Samito, Kenneth Womack in America and by Michael MacNamara in Ireland. Information and advice concerning Britons was provided by William Beard, John Black, Roger Hughes, Gordon Jones, Jerri Linke, and William Van Vugt in America and from John Bennett, Leonard Boardman, Jane Carpenter, Gordon Clifford, John Collier, Norman Creaser, James Falkner, Jason Faxackarley, Brian Gardner, Jerry Hunter, Anne Knowles, J. Basil Larkins, Michael Hammerson, Allan Mitchell, Tony Powell, and Roy Rawlinson in Britain. Data on other Europeans came from Guy Gallez (Belgians), Philip Katz and David Lockmiller (French), Stephen Beszedits (Hungarians), Scott A. MacKenzie (Italians), Bo Backstrom, Bertil Haggman, Michael Ruddy, Joan Schuette, and Edi Thorstensson (Swedes), and Wilhelm Von der Heyte (Swiss).

I especially appreciate the help of Rodman L. Underwood, who read Chapters 2 and 9 and made a number of suggestions for the improvement of these chapters, and Brigadier General Larry Garrett (USMC, ret.), who reviewed the military terminology and conclusions in Chapter 17. I am extremely grateful for the support and help of my wife, Ursula, including her eagle-eyed editing of the final manuscript, and for the effective and considerate teamwork of Don McKeon, David Arthur, Dorothy Smith, and their colleagues at Brassey's, Inc., and Larry Goldberg and his production team at Shepherd, Inc.

Dean B. Mahin

Chapter 1

DECISIVE ELEMENTS IN THE COMING STRUGGLE

Europeans in the North: 1856–1861

The census of 1860 indicated that 4,138,697 residents of the United States—about 12 percent of the total population of 34.3 million—were born in other countries. Nearly 98 percent of them came from Europe or Canada; only 83,026 immigrants were from Latin America, Asia, or Africa. The European immigrants were strongly concentrated in Northeastern and Midwestern cities and in agricultural and forested areas in the upper Midwest. Only 233,455 persons born in other countries—5.7 percent of the foreign-born population in the United States—lived in states that would form the Confederacy the following year.

The 1,611,304 Irish immigrants, the largest ethnic group, accounted for 39 percent of the foreign-born in the United States. Many factors contributed to the massive Irish migration to America in the late 1840s and 1850s; the most significant of these was the terrible famine in Ireland in the late 1840s after the potato crops failed.

In 1860 the great majority of Irish immigrants in America—1,526,541 persons—lived in Northern states, with only 84,763 in future Confederate States. Nearly 60 percent of the Irish in the North were in three states: New York (498,072), Pennsylvania (201,939), and Massachusetts (185,434). Most of these Irish were in New York City, Philadelphia, and Boston. There were also many Irish in other urban areas in the Northeast and Midwest, including 87,573 Irish in Illinois and 76,826 in Ohio. Irish immigrants rarely had sufficient funds to travel farther than the port city at which they arrived. Most of them were fleeing from a disastrous experience with farming in Ireland and did not have the inclination, skills,

1

or capital to go into farming in America. During the 1850s the Irish took over most of the jobs as laborers, stevedores, coachmen, draymen, waiters, cooks, barbers, and servants in Northeastern port cities. Most of the Irish living in nonurban areas were employed in the construction of canals or railroads or in the mining industry.

Kirby A. Miller, who studied Irish emigration, wrote that "Irish emigrants were disproportionately concentrated in the lowest-paid, least-skilled, and most dangerous and insecure employment. With few exceptions, they also displayed the highest rates of transience, residential density and segregation, inadequate housing and sanitation, commitments to prisons and charity institutions, and excess mortality."[1] A French journalist, Ernest Duvergier de Hauranne, described the Irish district in New York in 1864: "Between Broadway and the Hudson River there exists a filthy, run-down neighborhood inhabited by Irish immigrants and colored people exclusively. It is impossible to imagine anything more depressingly poor than these wooden shacks and long muddy avenues."[2]

The 1,301,136 U.S. residents born in one of the thirty-four German-speaking states of central Europe accounted for 31 percent of the foreign-born in the United States. The emigration of Germans had been stimulated in the 1840s and 1850s by overpopulation, limited agricultural land, displacement of artisans by factory production, and the unsuccessful revolution in Germany in 1848. In contrast to the predominance of young, unmarried, and unskilled immigrants from Ireland, the German immigrant was more likely to be married, to arrive in a family group, and to possess skills as handworker or farmer.

The vast majority of the German immigrants—1,229,144 persons—lived in Northern states, with only 71,992 in future Confederate states. New York City had more German-speaking residents than any city except Berlin, Vienna, and perhaps Hamburg; there were 120,423 Germans in Manhattan plus 18,254 in Brooklyn. The second largest German settlement was in Philadelphia, which had 83,232 Germans. Germans were about a third of the population of three Midwestern cities—Cincinnati, St. Louis, and Milwaukee. There were also many Germans in Baltimore, Chicago, Buffalo, Louisville, Pittsburgh, Cleveland, and Newark.

A British journalist, Edward Dicey, described the German section of Cincinnati: "It was hard, strolling through the streets, to realize that you were not in some city of the old German vaterland. . . . Almost everybody you meet is speaking in the hard, guttural, German accents. The women, with their squat, stout figures, their dull blue eyes, and fair flaxen hair, sit knitting at their doors, dressed in the stuffed woolen petticoats of the German fashion. The men have still the woolen jackets, the blue worsted pantaloons, and the low-crowned hats one knows so well in Bavaria and the Tyrol. There are *Bier Gartens, Restaurations,* and *Tanz Saale* on every side. . . . There are German operas, German concerts, and a half a dozen German theaters. . . . At one of the small German theaters . . . the women had brought their babies and were knitting with them; the men had their long pipes, and both men and women sat drinking the lager beer, and eating the inevitable sausages and the 'butter-brot und schinken' sandwiches."[3] Despite the large numbers of Germans in many urban areas, nearly two-thirds of the German immigrants lived in small towns or on farms.

In 1860, 587,775 residents of the United States listed their birthplace as the British isles other than Ireland. They included 433,494 from England, 108,518 from Scotland, and 45,763 from Wales. In addition, 249,970 residents were born in "British America" (Canada); a high percentage of these residents were of French descent. Despite the sustained tensions between the British and American governments and the widespread distrust of "the British" in America, the individual British immigrant was usually cordially received in America. Immigrants from England and Scotland adjusted quickly to American ways and soon became indistinguishable from native-born Americans. Welsh immigrants, whose language and culture were distinct from those of both Britain and America, established distinctively Welsh communities in several states.

About 83 percent of the immigrants in America were born in British or German jurisdictions. Most of the rest were from western or northern Europe—109,870 from France, 53,327 Swiss, 28,281 from the Netherlands, 9,072 Belgians, 43,995 Norwegians, 18,625 Swedes, and 9,962 Danes. The era in which America would receive very large numbers of immigrants from eastern and southern Europe had not yet begun. The 45,763 "Austrians" included both German-speaking immigrants from the area of present-day Austria and many Hungarians, Czechs, Slovaks, and others from the Slavic dependencies of the Hapsburg empire. There were also 7,298 Poles, whose country was ruled by Russia, and 3,160 from Russia and the other eastern European areas under its control. Only 20,366 immigrants were from southern Europe; they included 11,677 from Italy, 4,244 from Spain, 4,116 from Portugal, and 328 from Greece.

Most of the immigrants—even most of those from Britain—had had no vote in their native countries and welcomed the opportunity to participate in the political process in America. In the 1850s immigrants could become citizens after five years' residence in the United States. In many cases immigrants moving into a new community were assumed to have become citizens and were allowed to vote without verification of their naturalization.

"As a rule," wrote a prominent German immigrant, Carl Schurz, "the foreign immigrants . . . drifted into the Democratic party, which presented itself to them as the protector of the political rights of the foreign-born population, while the Whigs were suspected of "nativistic" tendencies, hostile to the foreign born. Although these nativistic tendencies were in fact directed more against the Irish than against the Germans, the feeling that their rights were in danger was . . . much sharpened among the Germans . . . by the brutal excesses that were being committed in various places against the foreign born . . . and by the springing up of the 'Know-Nothing' organization, which was set on foot for the declared purpose of excluding the foreign born from participation in political power."[4]

In the years after the potato famine in Ireland and the abortive revolutionary movements in Europe in 1848, immigrants had arrived in America in unprecedented numbers. Many native-born Americans were fearful of the economic, political, and religious impact of this great influx of immigrants. Blue-collar workers thought employers were keeping wage levels low by hiring immigrants at low wages. Property owners feared that taxes would be raised to provide relief and services for the flood of poor immigrants. Conservative Americans were appalled by the radical ideas of some of the immigrants. Since almost all of the Irish immigrants, about half of the Germans, and many other immigrants were Catholics, Protestants feared the growth of Catholic influences—including Papal influence—in American education and politics.

The Know Nothings recognized that the country needed immigrants and did not propose limitations on immigration. Their primary goal was to limit the political influence of the immigrants. Tyler Anbinder wrote in a book on the Know Nothings that they "suggested that the newcomers wait twenty-one years before attaining the privilege of voting" and "urged voters to select only native-born citizens for office and to elect only those who would not appoint immigrants to patronage positions."[5]

Abraham Lincoln did not support the Know Nothings, but he did not publicly oppose them. His reaction to their ideas is documented in a personal letter he wrote in 1855: "How can any one who abhors the oppression of negroes, be in favor of degrading classes of white people. . . . As a nation, we began by declaring that *all men are created equal*. We now practically read it 'all men are created equal, *except negroes*.' When the Know-Nothings get control, it will read 'all men are created equal, except negroes, *and foreigners, and catholics*.' When it comes to this I should prefer emigrating to some other country where they make no pretense of loving liberty—to Russia, for instance, where despotism can be taken pure, and without the base alloy of hypocrisy."[6] But Lincoln biographer David Donald noted that Lincoln "had to recognize that Know-Nothings were a powerful political force. . . . He did not go out of his way to alienate his old political friends who had become nativists. . . . In public his position on nativism was circumspect."[7]

By 1856 the Know Nothing movement had ebbed, but many former Know Nothings had joined the new Republican party. It nominated for president the popular western explorer, John C. Fremont. Although he attracted considerable support among the Germans, the presence of many former Know Nothings in the Republican party limited immigrant support for the Republican ticket. Fremont was defeated by the Democratic candidate, James Buchanan of Pennsylvania, known as "a Northern man with Southern principles." "Buchanan . . . is not his own master," Carl Schurz wrote to a friend in Germany just after the election. "Because elected by a party that has its main strength in the South, he must follow Southern policies in order to preserve the party that is the only support of his Administration. . . . The Southern faction . . . is constantly trying to break the resistance of the Northern Democrats by threats of secession. The Northern faction . . . is accustomed to yield to the threats of secession and to the arrogance of the South."[8]

Lincoln attracted national attention in 1858 when he ran for the Senate against Democratic incumbent Stephen A. Douglas and debated Douglas in a series of Illinois communities. Henry Villard, a German-born journalist, described the first debate at Ottawa, Illinois: "The debate . . . attracted an immense concourse of people from all parts of the State. Douglas spoke first for an hour, followed by Lincoln for an hour and a half; upon which the forum closed in another half-hour. . . . There was on one side a skillful dialectician and debater arguing a wrong and weak cause, there was on the other a thoroughly earnest and truthful man, inspired by sound convictions in consonance with the true spirit of American institutions. There was nothing in all Douglas's powerful effort that appealed to the higher instincts of human nature, while . . . Lincoln's speech excited and sustained the enthusiasm of his audience to the end."[9] Another German immigrant, former Illinois Lieutenant Governor Gustave Koerner, described Lincoln's performance in the last debate at Alton: "Without any apparent effort he stated his propositions clearly and tersely, and his whole speech was weighted with noble and deep thoughts. There was no appeal to passion and prejudice."[10.]

Lincoln lost the Senate race but soon was thinking of a presidential bid in 1860. His interest in the German vote is indicated by his secret purchase in May 1859 of the German-language newspaper in Springfield, the *Illinois Staats-Anzeiger*. The editor, Theodore Canisius, continued to publish the paper in German with occasional articles in English. After the election, Lincoln sold the paper back to Canisius.

German support for Lincoln at the Republican National Convention in Chicago was assured by the adoption of an anti-nativist "Dutch Plank" drafted by a German member of the platform committee, Carl Schurz: "The Republican party is opposed to any change in our naturalization laws, or any state legislation by which the rights of citizens hitherto accorded to immigrants from foreign lands shall be abridged or impaired; and in favor of giving a full and efficient protection to the rights of all classes of citizens, whether native or naturalized, both at home or abroad.' "[11] Karl Bernays reported in the *Anzeiger des Westens* in St. Louis that at the convention "the German element was recognized as a vital part of the party of freedom and progress."[12]

Schurz was elected to the Republican National Committee with responsibility for efforts to reach German and other foreign-born voters. "I intend to get up a complete list of all the Germans, Norwegians, Hollanders, etc., . . . who can serve our cause," he wrote Lincoln, and "have them stump township after township. . . . I would, of course, go to all the principal points and do the heavy work myself."[13] Schurz traveled 21,000 miles during the campaign, speaking for Lincoln in German to German voters. He went "not only into the large cities, but into small country towns and villages, and sometimes into remote agricultural districts, where I found my audiences in schoolhouses and even in roomy barns or in the open air."[14]

Julian Kune, a Hungarian immigrant, was sent to southern Illinois where Republicans were "as scarce as hen's teeth." Later he saw Lincoln in Springfield and explained his frustration at the necessary concealment of Lincoln's opposition to slavery. Lincoln assured him that "no man has the right to keep his fellow man in bondage, be he black or white; and the time will come . . . when there will not be a single slave within the borders of this country." Kune didn't mention Lincoln's reply to anyone until after the election, fearing that "to have it publicly avowed that our standard bearer was an abolitionist would . . . insure his certain defeat."[15] But Ella Lonn wrote that many of the "Forty-Eighters" made "straight abolitionist speeches" in which "they espoused the antislavery cause with all the ardor and enthusiasm they had given the principles of the Revolution of 1848" in Germany.[16] Such speeches attracted some voters who opposed slavery, but undoubtedly lost Lincoln votes among conservative voters.

In later decades many German-Americans proclaimed that the German vote for Lincoln had been necessary for his election. This conclusion was eventually challenged by a historian, Joseph Shafer, who wrote that "Lincoln was elected through an upsurge of moral enthusiasm and determination on the part of the distinctly American folk. . . . The foreign-born contingents participated, but in no sense as determinative factors."[17] Most historians have agreed with Shafer's conclusions. "Republicans . . . achieved some success among German Protestants," wrote historian James M. McPherson, "though the lingering perceptions of Republican dalliance with nativism and temperance kept the Catholic vote overwhelmingly Democratic."[18] This conclusion is supported by studies of voting patterns in key states.

A Harvard historian, William E. Gienapp, has observed that "few if any groups . . . were as strongly anti-Republican as the Irish Catholics."[19] Although Lincoln attempted to conceal his support for abolition, his antislavery statements during the debates with Douglas in 1858 had been widely reported. In a study of immigrant politics, Shirley Blumenthal and Jerome Ozer wrote that "the Irish . . . feared freed blacks would compete for the jobs the Irish held at the bottom of the economic ladder. . . . The Irish, who were preoccupied with their own miserable condition, thought it hypocritical of Northerners to sympathize with blacks while ignoring the plight of the poor of the Northern cities."[20] A writer on Irish history, Lawrence W. Kohl, noted that there was "little sympathy for the slave among a people who saw black liberation as a threat to their own position in American society."[21] There were no abolitionists among prominent Irish-Americans. Influential Irish newspapers including the *Pilot* and *Irish America* were openly opposed to abolition.[22] James Hennessey, a Jesuit scholar, noted that "no Catholic bishop spoke for abolition in the prewar years. . . . No pope had ever condemned domestic slavery as it existed in the United States."[23]

In 1860 Lincoln received few Irish votes in the North, less than half the German votes in the North, and few immigrant votes in the South; a majority of the immigrant votes were cast for his opponents.

Henry Villard recalled the secession crisis in the four months between Lincoln's election in November and his inauguration as president on March 4, 1861: "The seven rebellious States . . . were striving with the utmost determination to solidify the structure of the Southern Confederacy they had erected during the winter, and to widen and strengthen it. . . . Such leading Republicans as Horace Greeley and Thurlow Weed came out openly in favor of peaceful separation rather than the use of force by the Federal government against the rebels. Other leaders were willing to go to great lengths in conciliating the South. . . . The bulk of the Republican party . . . were ready and anxious, however, for the utmost use of federal power for . . . the maintenance of the Union; but not a few of their principal guides, including Seward, still thought that the secession fever would . . . die out under proper treatment by Mr. Lincoln. The latter himself still held this belief."[24]

Villard recalled that "a great many of his visitors tried to draw him out as to his future policy as President. . . . But he could not be got to say what he would do in the face of Southern secession, except that as President he should be sworn to maintain the Constitution. . . . He was often embarrassed by efforts of radical antislavery men to get something out of him in encouragement of their hopes that the crisis would result in the abolition of slavery. He . . . made it clear that he did not desire to be considered an 'abolitionist' and that he still held the opinion that property in slaves was entitled to protection under the Constitution."[25]

Emil Frey, a future president of Switzerland, described Lincoln's inaugural address on March 4, 1861: "In vain did Mr. Lincoln assure the people of the South in his inaugural address that they had no cause of apprehension either as to their property or persons from the accession of a Republican administration. In vain he declared that he had no intention to interfere directly or indirectly with slavery in the States where it existed. In vain he declared that he held the Union to be perpetual. . . . In vain he added: "In your hands, my dissatisfied fellow-countrymen, not in mine, is the momentous issue of civil war. The Government will not assail you. You can have no conflict without being the aggressors.'"[26] Villard thought the address was "a heterogeneous compound of assertion . . . of the duty of the new federal executive to . . . enforce the laws and preserve the Union, and . . . of intimations and assurances that he would avoid action that might lead to a conflict."[27]

On March 29 the newly arrived correspondent of *The Times* of London, William Howard Russell, reported that many Republicans "regard the secession as a temporary aberration which a 'masterly inactivity'. . . will correct. 'In good time the violent men down South will come to their senses.' . . . But most impartial people, at least in New York, are of opinion that the South . . . will never enter the portals of the Union again."[28]

Several European immigrants and observers recorded the impact on the people in the North of the firing on Fort Sumter by the Confederates on April 12, 1861. "Until the first gun was fired," recalled Carl Schurz, "many patriotic people still entertained a lingering hope of saving the Union without a conflict of arms. Now civil war had suddenly become a certainty. A mighty shout arose that the Republic must be saved at any cost. It was one of these sublime moments of patriotic exaltation when everybody seems willing . . . to sacrifice everything for a common cause."[29] "The . . . striking down of the United States flag by rebel guns," Villard noted, "led to the bursting of the patriotic hurricane that swept away all dissensions, all partisan enmities, all fear, all apathy, and united the whole North in the determination to preserve the Union at all cost of blood and treasure."[30] "The Government and people . . . saw that the struggle was one of life and death," wrote Regis De Trobriand, a French immigrant.[31]

Edward Dicey, a British journalist, wrote that "when . . . the nation awoke to its danger at the attack on Fort Sumter, . . . the preservation of the Union was the overwhelming national instinct."[32] Later he continued: "Secession in Northern eyes is still an unaccountable and inexplicable act of madness. The Union appears so natural, so liberal, and so good a government, that it is impossible that anybody who has lived beneath its rule should leave it willingly."[33] Russell had been in the South when Fort Sumter was fired on. Returning to New York in early July, the correspondent of *The Times* was struck by the changed mood of the people: "I met men today who last March argued coolly and philosophically about the right of secession. They are now furious at the idea of such wickedness. . . . 'We must maintain our glorious Union! . . . We cannot allow two nations to grow up on this Continent!' "[34]

The Reverend George Fisch, a British pastor in Paris, wrote that the people in the North were "burning with love of country, and shedding tears of patriotic emotion at the insult offered at Charleston to their glorious flag."[35]

On April 16, 1861, the day after President Lincoln issued the call for 75,000 men, Villard received a summons to New York from James Gordon Bennett, the Scottish immigrant who was the editor of the *Herald:* "The sneaking sympathy of his paper for the rebellion and its vile abuse of the Republicans for their antislavery sentiments, made me share the general prejudice against him to such an extent that I had been thinking for some time of severing my connection with the *Herald*. . . . After dinner he disclosed his true purpose in sending for me. . . . He wanted me to carry a message from him to Mr. Lincoln that the *Herald* would hereafter be unconditionally for the radical suppression of the rebellion by force of arms. . . . The *Herald* was obliged to make this complete change in its attitude, there having been ominous signs for some days in New York of danger of mob violence to the paper."[36]

Although the majority of the immigrants had not voted for Lincoln in 1860, immigrants enlisted in the Union army in droves. The typical immigrant in the North enlisted for a combination of reasons that transcended his personal feelings about Abraham Lincoln or the abolition of slavery. He enlisted to maintain his own freedom and that of his friends and neighbors, to preserve the Constitution and the Union, to preserve and advance his own status in America by demonstrating his patriotism, and to support democracy and freedom in his native country and elsewhere around the world. For some immigrants, economic motives were also important. Most immigrants volunteered in the period in which Lincoln denied that abolition of slavery was a Union objective. There is very little evidence that immigrants—or indeed native-born enlistees—were thinking about the abolition of slavery when they enlisted.

A French observer, the Prince of Joinville, described the typical process by which a volunteer regiment was organized: "Persons present themselves offering to raise a regiment. Each sets forth his claims, his influence in the State or among a certain portion of the population, which will enable him to procure easily the necessary number of men, his devotion to the party in power, etc. From among the persons thus presented the Governor makes his choice. Generally the person upon whom the choice falls had laid it down as a condition . . . that he shall have the command of the regiment."[37] Another French visitor, Lieutenant Colonel Camile Ferri-Pisani, was intrigued by the "singular spectacle of an army organizing itself." He thought the process involved "the very spirit of all American enterprise—a free and boundless competition."[38]

During the first year or so of the war—the period of heaviest enlistments—volunteers were not asked for their birthplace. As a result, there are no statistics on the number of foreign-born men who joined the Union army. Estimates of the number of volunteers from each major immigrant group have been inflated by ethnic authors eager to prove that their group had made an important contribution to the ultimate Union victory. The percentage of foreigners in the Union army was greatly exaggerated by the Confederates and their friends to support their assertion that the Union was using European mercenaries to ravage the South. Charles Mackay reported to *The Times* in June 1862 that Irish and Germans were "at least two-fifths"—40 percent—of the fighting men in the federal Army.[39] The Confederate commissioner in Paris, John Slidell, told Napoleon III in July 1862 that "probably one-half" of the privates in the Union army were "foreigners, principally Germans and Irish."[40]

If the foreign-born residents in the North in 1860 had volunteered at the same rate as the Northern population as a whole (10.7 percent), there would have been about 418,000 of them in the Union army. If the European immigrants arriving during the war had enlisted at the same rate, the total foreign-born in blue would have been around 473,000 and they would have represented about 17 percent of the men in the army. Evidence presented in the following chapters indicates that the Germans volunteered at a somewhat higher rate than the general population, but that the Irish and British volunteered at somewhat lower rates. It therefore seems likely that the percentage of immigrants in the Union army was below 20 percent.

In 1905 a professor at Princeton, Woodrow Wilson, wrote that in the decades before the Civil War "the huge stream of immigrants . . . had its deep significance as a preparation for the war, . . . hastening that development and creating those resources which were to be the really decisive elements in the coming struggle between the slave section and the free section."[41] It is noteworthy that the historian and future president did not say that the immigrants had been a decisive element in the war itself but in the development of the superior resources that were crucial in the ultimate Union victory. The additional manpower provided by immigrants was an important Union asset, but the Union would still have had a vast superiority in manpower even without recent immigrants. The contributions to the Union war effort of men from many countries lent credibility to Lincoln's assertions that the Union fought for freedom and democracy for all men everywhere and that the outcome of the war would have a crucial impact on "the progress, civilization, and happiness of mankind."[42]

Chapter 2

SHOW YOURSELVES WORTHY OF FREEDOM

Germans *in the* North

Although the Germans were only the second largest immigrant group in the Union population, after the Irish, they were the largest foreign-born group in the Union army. The Germans volunteered to protect their newfound freedoms in America, to defend the Constitution and the Union, to promote the cause of democracy in Germany, to protect and advance their status in America by demonstrating their patriotism, and, in some cases, to solve their individual economic problems or to promote the abolition of slavery.

Many of the Germans had fled from oppression in Germany and they cherished the freedom and democracy they found in America. "The German spirit is the spirit of tolerance and freedom," presidential aspirant William H. Seward proclaimed in 1860; "it fights oppression everywhere."[1] The Germans saw secession in the South as a threat to their adopted country and to their own freedom. "Citizens, Your Land is in Danger! To Arms!" a recruiting poster in German proclaimed in New York.[2] "When the Union gives the call 'To Arms,'" Heinrich Boernstein wrote in the *Anzeiger des Westens* in St. Louis, "no German capable of bearing arms will fail to defend his hearth, his liberty, and his fatherland."[3] The *Staats-Zeitung* in St. Paul urged Germans to demonstrate that "we Germans . . . are prepared to defend our American home as the blessed place of freedom."[4]

Leonard Streiff exhorted fellow Germans in Kentucky to "show yourselves worthy of the freedom which this glorious country has hitherto bestowed upon you. . . . Our plain duty is . . . to stand by it in this hour of peril, and sustain it, if need be, with our fortunes and our lives."[5] A German in the California gold fields, Peter Klien, wrote his father in Germany that "the rebellion was started by slave-owners to overthrow the free constitution of the country and to set up a government by the nobility. These slaveowners are great lords who have a hundred or more black serfs and now want to enslave the free white workers."[6]

Most Germans agreed with Boernstein's statement that "defending freedom and defending the Union are one and the same thing."[7] "Our freedom . . . we owe to the Union," proclaimed the *Taegliche Metrople* in Washington. "With the Union breaks down the last asylum of the oppressed of the entire globe. And therefore must the Germans . . . stand for the united and undivided Union."[8] Constantine Grebner, who compiled the reminiscences of the veterans of the all-German 9th Ohio, wrote that they had fought "to save the Union and defend humanity and freedom."[9]

A German judge, John Bernhard Stallo, told a meeting of Germans in Cincinnati that they must "defend the Union and protect the Star-Spangled Banner. The Tree of Liberty wilts unless watered from time to time with blood."[10] At a meeting of Germans in Louisville, a German stated his belief that the "duty of every citizen is to fight to sustain the freest government in the world. . . . I had the intention . . . to marry, but . . . my fiancee said, 'First go and fight for your fatherland and then it will be time to think of family joy.' I have a good job, but I gave it up . . . to fight for the maintenance of our glorious Union."[11] German leaders feared that the secession of the Southern states would destroy the the American system of government. "If we admit secession," Gustave Koerner observed, "we destroy all stability in government."[12] Carl Schurz feared secession would destroy "that element of stability which consists in the absolute assurance that when the officers of the government are legally elected, their election is unconditionally accepted and submitted to by the minority."[13] A German leader in New York noted that the Germans "know too well, from experience in their dear fatherland, what it is to have a country torn asunder and divided into many small kingdoms and principalities."[14]

Many of the Germans in America, especially those who had fought in the abortive revolution in Germany in 1848, thought that the fight for the Union was inevitably linked with their hope for democracy in Germany. Franz Sigel, a "Forty-Eighter," proclaimed that "this great republic is the last refuge of liberty . . . for free men of Europe. When I saw that the same great principles to whose defense I had devoted my life were at stake here, I did not hesitate to embrace the cause of the Union with all the power of my soul."[15] "We all left our fatherland because we desired to rid our necks of the heel of the tyrant that trampled upon our rights," wrote Leonard Streiff. "The proud spirit of our race will never submit to the yoke of bondage which Jeff. Davis and his followers are striving to fasten upon us. . . . If this Government is destroyed, liberty will be again banished from the face of the earth."[16]

German language newspapers stressed the connection between maintaining democracy in America and establishing it in Germany. "The whole European world is on the brink of casting off its old chains," proclaimed the *Westliche Post* in St. Louis. "If this republic falls, there would be a great cry of despair . . . against us, for letting the holy banner of freedom fall to the earth. . . . If we win . . . the cry of jubilation . . . will echo across the ocean. . . . If we lose, . . . then the curse of all the oppressed peoples of the world . . . will be piled on our race."[17]

A French observer, the Marquis of Chambrun, noted the curious fact that many ex-revolutionaries from Germany were fighting to maintain the existing government in America: "Professed enemies of order and established institutions in Prussia or Austria, here they are . . . readily giving their intelligence, activity, and even their blood in the service of a new country."[18] Edward Dicey, a British correspondent, wrote that "the German settlers . . . are attached to the Union because it secures the prosperity and development of their new country, and because it has proved a good government to them, or rather, has allowed them the unwonted privilege of governing themselves."[19]

These German motives—protecting their own freedom, defending the Union, and enhancing the prospects for freedom in Germany—were intertwined with another strong motive—to protect and advance their own status in America by demonstrating their patriotism during the nation's hour of peril. Friedrick Kapp, a German leader in New York, proclaimed that the Germans in the Union army would "show the world that the German stands in the foremost ranks of fighters for freedom."[20] Peter Klein, the German miner in California, wrote his father in Germany proudly that "the Germans have shown themselves to be the keenest defenders of the Constitution, and provide entire regiments of the best and bravest soldiers and officers. . . . Now the Americans . . . know that we are the mainstay of their country and their freedom."[21]

Captain Frederick Otto Baron von Fritsch believed that "foreign-born soldiers, who believe in the institutions of this country, who have offered their services to save this glorious Union and to abolish slavery, who stand these tremendous hardships . . . and . . . fight and die for their adopted fatherland, are as much Americans as soldiers born in this country."[22] "We Germans are second to none in loyalty and patriotism," proclaimed a veteran of the 9th Ohio, George M. Schneider, "for we love this country as we love a mother; we are ready to offer our blood and our treasure for her free and matchless institutions."[23] A German historian, Michael Loeffler, wrote that "the German-Americans in the northern States fought . . . not only for the preservation of their beloved new homeland, but also for their position and equal rights in the American society."[24]

o

Most of the Germans volunteered for the Union army in 1861 and 1862, before the abolition of slavery was an avowed Union objective. The few Germans who cited emancipation of the slaves as a reason for enlistment were mostly "Forty-Eighters." Many of them thought the movement for the abolition of slavery in America was a kindred movement to their fight in 1848 for democracy in Germany. Heinrich Boernstein wrote that "their aversion to slavery grew to a fierce hate of this damnable institution and its friends."[25] Carl Schurz recalled that the Forty-Eighters had been convinced that "in our struggle against slavery we could not possibly be wrong. There was an imperative, indisputable necessity of fighting for our cause."[26] A French visitor, Auguste Laugel, noted in 1864 that "the most resolute enemies of slavery" were found among the Germans: "Having grasped from the beginning the character and object of the civil war, they have espoused the cause . . . of emancipation with an ardor and a passion."[27]

Most Forty-Eighters had been intellectuals or soldiers in Germany;[28] by 1861 many of them edited German-language newspapers in America. Their influence in mobilizing German support for the Union cause is well recognized. Some modern German writers, eager to enhance the unquestioned importance of the Forty-Eighters as nineteenth-century German freedom fighters, have exaggerated their influence on the Germans in America regarding the abolition of slavery. The few thousand Forty-Eighters were only a small faction in a predominantly conservative population of 1.3 million German immigrants.

Two historians have stressed the conflict between the liberal ideas of the Forty-Eighters and the conservative views of most German immigrants. Stephen D. Engle observed that the Forty-Eighters "were passionately committed to political concerns, . . . while the bulk of Germans were occupied primarily with making a living. Many advocated political idealism, social radicalism, and religious skepticism at a time when the members of the German community were generally conservative in their politics and orthodox in their religious beliefs."[29] About half of the Germans in America were Catholics, and most of the rest were conservative Lutherans. A. E. Zurcher noted that most of the Forty-Eighters were freethinkers: "They also believed in universal suffrage, abolition of the Sunday laws, taxation of church property, establishment of the eight hour day, government ownership of railroads, and a number of other equally precocious heresies."[30]

Some German immigrants volunteered for the Union army because they needed a job. The consul of Saxony in Baltimore reported that the army enlisted many German workers "who saw in the offer of $13 a month and rations the only chance to provide for themselves and their families."[31] When Marcus M. Spiegel volunteered for a Union regiment, he wrote his wife that it was the only way he could see "of getting enough money to keep us comfortable."[32]

If the percentage of Germans in the army had been the same as the percentage of the whole Union population that served in the army—10.7 percent—there would have been only about 130,000 Germans in blue. But all the estimates of the Germans in the Union army have been much higher. In 1869 A. B. Gould estimated that there had been 187,000 Germans in blue. Twenty years later William J. Fox used a slightly more conservative figure: 175,000. In a study of the Germans in the Civil War published in 1911, Wilhelm Kaufmann concluded that these estimates had been too low; he thought the figure should be 216,000. Later in the twentieth century several German-American authors used a round figure of 200,000 Germans in the Union army. Although this figure is probably too high, there is little doubt that the Germans provided more men for the Union army than did any other immigrant group.

In areas with large numbers of Germans, German volunteers usually joined regiments that consisted mainly of German immigrants and were commanded by German officers. A German immigrant who did not speak much English could function effectively in a regiment in which commands were given in German. In an era in which antiforeign attitudes were widespread among native-born Americans, Germans felt more comfortable in regiments with other Germans. The German regiments were also important symbols of German patriotism and the German contribution to the Union war effort. Captain William Vocke, 24th Illinois, wrote that the excellent record of several regiments that had been "drilled and commanded by their officers in undefiled High-Dutch" demonstrated that "one can be just as loyal an American citizen and just as brave an American soldier in Luther's German language as in the King's English."[33]

Other regiments consisted of a mixture of Germans, other immigrants, and native-born Americans. There is no precise definition of a "German" regiment and no agreement on the number of such regiments or the number of Germans who served in them. Scott Frank compiled a list of sixty "German" units in the Union Army using information from Ella Lonn's landmark study of foreigners in the Union army. The list includes forty-five infantry regiments, four cavalry regiments, and eleven artillery units. Most of them were from New York state (20 units), Ohio (15 units), Missouri (11 units), Pennsylvania (6 units), or Wisconsin (6 units), but there were also "German" units from Illinois, Indiana, and Kentucky.[34] In a study of German immigrants in New York state regiments, Tim Engelhart provided detailed information on ten predominantly German infantry regiments and five "mixed" infantry regiments, as well cavalry and artillery units with numerous Germans.[35]

Some of the German regiments were in brigades and divisions that were commanded by German officers and consisted of a mixture of predominantly German regiments and other regiments. About half of the regiments in the XI Corps were "German" units. The mostly German regiments accounted for 20 percent to 25 percent of the Germans in the Union army. The great majority of the Germans lived in small communities or rural areas in which there were too few Germans to form a regiment; they joined any regiment being formed in their area.

The men in the units made up mostly of Germans were frequently praised by their German officers. More impartial praise came from two officers born in other European countries. One company of Regis de Trobriand's regiment, the 55th New York, was made up of Germans; the French immigrant wrote that they were "good soldiers, prompt in obedience, animated with goodwill, and conspicuous for their fine bearing; they always did their duty well upon the field as in camp."[36] Brigadier General James Shields, an immigrant from Ireland, wrote that the Germans in General Blenker's division were like bulldogs: "They hang on the enemy without respite."[37] Ella Lonn concluded that "the Germans . . . gave to the army a conservative, stabilizing force. . . . The mass of German soldiers were patient, philosophical, plodding men. . . . They . . . were well disciplined, persevering, and inspired by some idealism. They were somewhat slow in response, but were stable and solid in battle."[38] German-American writers have frequently quoted words they attributed to General Lee: "Take the Dutch out of the Union army and we could whip the Yankees easily."[39] Wilhelm Kaufmann tried in vain to establish whether Lee ever made such a remark.[40]

But several historians have noted that the Germans were not well respected in the Union army. Bruce Levine wrote that "critics dismissed German troops as mechanical, plodding, and slow to take the initiative,"[41] although Irene M. Franck concluded that they were "unfairly considered to be thickheaded and slow, when actually they were just careful and sober."[42] The availability of beer in the German camps was another point of contention. Some thought no soldier should have alcohol and others could not see why the Germans should have the refreshing beverage when they did not. Some of the Germans claimed that German units were consistently given rough and/or dangerous assignments. Private Gottfried Rentschler, 6th Ohio, wrote that "if an entire company is required for rough service, . . . a German company will be ordered wherever possible. . . . The German has to wade through the mud, while the American walks on the dry road. . . . As a 'Dutchman' he is, if not despised, disrespected, and not regarded or treated as an equal."[43]

Two serious charges were repeatedly made against the Germans. The first was that they frequently engaged in looting and other depredations against civilians. Major General John E. Wool reported that a German regiment was "much complained of by the inhabitants for depredations and various outrages upon them."[44]

Brigadier General J. M. Schofield wrote of looting by a German cavalry battalion in Missouri: "If I trust them out of my sight for a moment, they will plunder and rob friends and foes alike."[45] Brigadier General E. A. Carr reported looting by Germans in a foraging party: "If these excesses are permitted, we cannot wonder at guerilla warfare."[46] "They pillage wherever they go," Charles Mackay wrote to *The Times* in 1862, "and are as instrumental in exasperating the already exasperated passions of the South as General Butler himself."[47] George Augustus Sala, correspondent for the *Daily Telegraph*, noted in 1864 that the Germans were known for "robbing, ravishing, and ravaging."[48]

One explanation for the frequency of such reports is that Confederate civilians were predisposed to believe the worst about the Germans in the Union army. They thought they were "mercenaries" and "the scum of Europe," and were quick to condemn any Union soldier with a German accent. Many of the reports of looting were made or forwarded by Union soldiers or civilians with strong prejudices against the Germans. Bruce Levine wrote that the Germans were often blamed for "problems common to the army as a whole."[49]

The second serious charge against the Germans was of cowardice, notably in the flight of the XI Corps when suddenly attacked by Stonewall Jackson's troops through the thick woods at Chancellorsville. Most historians have concluded that the rout of the XI Corps was primarily due to bad decisions by the army and corps commanders; evidence cited in Chapter 15 indicates that most of the German regiments in the corps resisted the Confederate attack as long as it was possible to do so. But the persistent stories of "the flying Dutchmen" severely damaged the reputation of the German troops. Sala reported in 1864 that the Germans in the Union army were known for "slinging down their arms, running away, or surrendering themselves to the enemy when there was the slightest danger."[50] Bernhard Domschke, captain in a XI Corps regiment, the 26th Wisconsin, recorded the anti-German sentiments of other Union prisoners in the Libby prison in Richmond: "We had to endure a hail of gibes, many of them about the notorious but false reports of German troops in the Battle of Chancellorsville."[51]

There were a great many German-born officers in the Union army. A biographic directory in Wilhelm Kaufmann's book contains information on about 500 "outstanding German Union officers," mostly with the rank of major or higher.[52] A German researcher, Tim Englehart, listed 248 German-born officers in New York regiments.[53] At least seventy German-born officers commanded Union regiments, about two-thirds of which were predominantly German regiments. An undoubtedly incomplete list of these German colonels is in Appendix I.

Ten officers born in Germany became Union generals. Except for Lincoln's friend Carl Schurz, all were initially colonels of regiments and later commanded brigades. Five Germans—Carl Schurz, Ludwig Blenker, Franz Sigel, Peter Osterhaus, and Adolph Von Steinwehr—were division commanders. Three of these—Schurz, Sigel, and Osterhaus—were ultimately corps commanders and reached the rank of major general, the top rank in the Union army until the rank of lieutenant general was recreated for Ulysses S. Grant in 1864. The careers of these officers are summarized in Appendix I.

The promotion of a number of German officers reflected Lincoln's awareness of both their abilities and the importance of recognizing the contributions of Germans to the Union army. In the fall of 1862, Lincoln's secretary of war presented him with a list of officers who might be appointed brigadier generals. Lincoln biographer Carl Sandburg described Lincoln's reaction when he saw Alexander Schimmelfenning's name on this list: "Lincoln said 'There has got to be something done that will be unquestionably in the interest of the Dutch, and to that end I want Schimmelfennig appointed.' 'Mr. President, perhaps this Schimmel-what's-his-name is not as highly recommended as some other German officers.' 'No matter about that. His name will make up for any difference there may be, and I'll take the risk of his coming out all right.' "[54]

Tim Englehart, a researcher in Germany, has estimated that between 150 and 200 German aristocrats served in the Union army.[55] These were typically young officers who did not share the conservative and antidemocratic attitudes of their elders in Germany. Most of them had come to America before the war, although some came to join the Union army without plans to remain in America. Lincoln did not think an aristocratic title should bar anyone from service according to his ability. When Frederick Otto Von Fritsch arrived in Washington in 1862, he obtained an interview with Lincoln and explained that he was a baron. "It will not hurt you to have a title," Lincoln replied, "but you'd better drop it, if you want to serve under our flag."[56]

In contrast to the large number of nonimmigrant British officers who joined the Confederate army, officers from Germany came mainly to the North. The imperial and economic factors that contributed to sympathy for the Confederacy among the British upper class did not influence the German officers. Although some German noblemen favored the more aristocratic system in the South, the Prussian king was known to support the Union; few Prussian officers thought of defying the powerful monarch.

Most of Prussia's 9,000 officers had had no combat experience. No German state had participated in the Crimean war—the only major war between European powers since the Napoleonic era—although a few German officers had joined the British forces in the Crimea. The war in America offered a unique opportunity for

German officers to acquire combat experience that they hoped would lead to promotion on their return home. The U.S. consul in Frankfurt reported in May 1861 that "several rather intelligent officers have expressed a desire to engage themselves, for a year, in the United States service . . . for the express purpose of studying their profession in America."[57] A German wrote to a New York paper in 1861 that the German officers "have come across from the same motives which brought Von Kalb and Steuben in the first revolution, an opportunity to find distinction and to serve the cause of the United States, which they regard as the right cause."[58] Some officers were seeking excitement and adventure; others came to escape problems in Germany, especially gambling debts or the aftermath of a scandal, duel, or a breach of discipline.[59]

Several of the nonimmigrant officers from Germany served as senior Union commanders. Baron Adolph Wilhem August Von Steinwehr was a division commander in four major battles. Baron George W. Von Schaack, a captain in the Prussian cavalry and son of a Prussian general, was colonel of the 7th New York. Edward Siber was colonel of the 37th Ohio and commanded a brigade in 1862. Valentine Bausenstein, formerly an adjutant with Garibaldi in Italy, was colonel of the 58th Ohio. Paul Von Radowitz, son of a Prussian minister of war, was a major on General McClellan's staff in 1862. Two Prussian barons, Hermann Von Haake and Otto Von Steuben, were killed at Spotsylvania while serving as lieutenants in the 52nd New York. Hubert Dilger, a former freedom fighter in Baden and captain of an artillery battery, won a Medal of Honor for his rearguard defensive actions at Chancellorsville.

German officers—immigrants and nonimmigrants—provided skills and experience badly needed by the Union army. These included experience with infantry drill and maneuvers, with artillery and cavalry operations, and as engineers, doctors, and mapmakers. There were many German doctors in the Union army, including the medical directors of several commands. German engineers held a number of important posts. Colonel Henry Flad, commander of the Missouri Regiment of Engineers, was one of the finest bridge builders in the Union army; after the war he played a major role in construction of the Eads Bridge across the Mississippi at St. Louis. Lieutenant Colonel William Hoelcke, an engineer in the Prussian army and in the Crimean war, was chief engineer for General Fremont in Missouri. Major Ernst F. Hoffman had been an engineer in the Prussian army, with the British in the Crimea, and with Garibaldi in Italy; in America he was chief engineer of the XI Corps and of General Thomas's army in Tennessee. Colonel Franz Hassendeubel designed the Union siege works at Vicksburg and died of wounds received there.

Some of the German line officers were not so well regarded in the army. Wilhelm Kauffmann observed that "Germany had not had a war for fifty years, and at West Point it was regarded as the country of parades and militaristic pedantry."[60] "Among the faults of the Germans," wrote Ella Lonn, "were a Prussian arrogance in the demeanor of some of the officers; an insistence on the Prussian severity in drill; . . . and an idolatry . . . of Prussian 'martinetism' and servility—all of which were obnoxious not only to Americans but to German-Americans."[61]

Negative comments about the Germans rarely found their way to Germany. There were no war correspondents in America representing newspapers in Germany; the press in Germany usually copied news of the American war from German-language newspapers in the North. The only German-born war correspondent was Henry Villard. He was born and educated in Bavaria before emigrating to Chicago. During the war he was correspondent first for the New York Herald and then for the New York Tribune. There is no record of any military or civilian observer from Germany with the Union army. Although Prussian authorities originally planned to send Captain Justus Scheibert to the Union army as a military observer, the Confederate sympathizer was somehow able to convince them to send him instead to the Confederate army.

Among the major immigrant groups in America, the Germans in the North were the most reliable and consistent supporters of the Union cause. The Germans shared neither the continuing allegiance to their mother country felt by many British residents nor the hopes of returning to fight for national liberation of many of the Irish nationalists. The early hopes of some of the "Forty-Eighters" to return someday to a democratic Germany had been abandoned during the 1850s. Beyond the general idea that supporting the Constitution and Union in America would support the cause of democracy in Germany, most Germans gave little thought to the old country. But they were still very concerned about their status as Germans in America.

In contrast to efforts by many Irish and Britons to avoid service in the Union army, the Germans usually accepted conscription without protest. They had found a new fatherland in America, and were ready to fight for it. But despite their nearly unanimous support for the defense of the Union, the Germans were sharply divided on other important political, religious, and social issues. Many Germans, especially the German Catholics, shared the strong antipathy of the Irish to Lincoln's policies on slavery and emancipation. The available evidence suggests that Lincoln did not win a substantial majority of the German votes in either 1860 or 1864. But supporters of Lincoln and his emancipation policies were nonetheless much more numerous among the Germans than among the Irish. The nearly unanimous Irish opposition to Lincoln and his policies is reviewed in the following chapter.

Chapter 3

PLANT THAT FLAG ON FORT AND CRAG

Irish *in the* North

The story of the reactions of the Irish in the North to the Civil War is a tale of strange contradictions. Almost all the Irish in the North were Democrats and most of them had voted against Lincoln in the 1860 election, yet around 150,000 Irish joined the Union army and fought valiantly for the Union. But by midwar many Irish were disenchanted with the war because of the Irish bloodbath at Fredericksburg at the end of 1862, Lincoln's emancipation policies, and the federal conscription act in the spring of 1863. Irishmen were the most active participants in four days of draft riots in New York in July 1863, and active Irish resistance to conscription continued in many areas until the end of the war. In 1864 most of the Irish apparently voted for Lincoln's opponent, General George B. McClellan. Yet thousands of Irishmen continued to serve gallantly in the Union army.

The Irish who enlisted in the Union army in 1861 and 1862 did so for a number of reasons that had little to do with Lincoln or the emancipation of the slaves. Their motives involved gratitude to the country that had given them refuge, patriotic support of their adopted country, defense of the freedom they had found in America, support for the Union as a form of government that protected their liberties, a chance to earn the respect and acceptance of native-born Americans, and—in some cases—a response to economic pressures and incentives or an opportunity to gain military experience that might be used in the liberation of Ireland from British rule.

Many Irish felt a strong obligation to defend the nation that had been a refuge for Irishmen from starvation and oppression. A large meeting of Irish in Boston in

April 1861 called on "every adopted citizen of Irish birth to stand true to the country which has become the home of so many millions of our race of the oppressed of the Old World."[1] Captain Michael Egan told fellow officers in western Virginia that spring that they must not abandon the flag "under whose folds the oppressed of all climes have found an abiding refuge and protection."[2] Brigadier General Francis Meagher, the first commander of the most famous Irish unit, the Irish Brigade, appealed to prospective recruits to support the "republic which . . . to hundreds of thousands of you has been a shelter, a home, a tower of impregnable security."[3] Sergeant Peter Welsh, an Irish immigrant in the 28th Massachusetts, wondered in 1863 "what would be the condition today of hundreds of thousands of the sons and daughters of poor oppressed old Erin if they had not a free land like this to emigrate to?" He thought every Irishman should "do all in his power to sustain . . . a government and a national asylum which is superior to any the world has yet known."[4]

This feeling of obligation was coupled with a strong wave of patriotism. An Irish priest in Auburn, New York, Father Creedon, observed that "this is the first country the Irishman ever had that he could call his own country. The Stars and Stripes is the only flag he can fight under and defend as his."[5] "Here Irishmen and their descendants have . . . a stake in the nation and an interest in its prosperity," Sergeant Welsh wrote to his wife.[6] The Irishmen meeting in Boston resolved that "every man who . . . enjoys the inestimable blessings and privileges of our free government" must "unite in support of the national administration and in defence of our common country, its flag, and its freedom."[7]

The Irish in the North believed that the protection of the refuge for Irishmen required them to support the Union. The Boston *Pilot* told its Irish readers that they must "stand by the Union; fight for the Union; die by the Union."[8] Charles P. Daly, an Irish-American judge in New York, noted that in America the Irish had "enjoyed an amount of political consequence and exercised a degree of political influence not found in the land of their nativity."[9] Captain Egan thought that "my first duty as a citizen is to the Government of the Union, and that my obligation to the State of Virginia is, and must be, secondary."[10]

"This is my country as much as the man that was born on the soil," wrote Sergeant Welsh. "I have as much interest in the maintenance of the government and laws and the integrity of the nation as any other man. . . . This is the first test of a modern free government in the act of sustaining itself against internal enemies. . . . All men who love free government and equal laws are watching this crisis to see if a republic can sustain itself in such a case. If it fails, then the hope of millions fails and . . . the old cry will be sent forth from the aristocrats of Europe that such is the common end of all republics."[11]

Irish volunteers viewed the war as a fight for freedom. St. Clair Mulholland, colonel of an Irish Brigade regiment, the 116th Pennsylvania, wrote that "our soldiers fought . . . to demonstrate that human freedom was not a myth and a dream, but a splendid reality."[12] The meeting in Boston proclaimed that Irishmen must not "permit the liberties for which Washington fought . . . to be trampled under foot by the slave oligarchy of the South."[13] But, like most others joining the Union army, the Irish were thinking of their own freedom, not that of the slaves.

The Irish also fought to win the respect and acceptance of native-born Americans. The *Pilot,* an Irish newspaper in Boston, announced its goal "to demonstrate that although the Celts might be hyphenated Americans in name, they were one hundred percent Americans in deed."[14] General Meagher remarked that the Irish soldier hoped to earn "a title . . . to the full equality and fraternity of an American citizen."[15] William Burton, who studied ethnic regiments, observed that the Irish and other ethnics fought "not to free the slaves, but to free themselves from prejudice."[16]

Some Irish leaders believed that the American war would give Irishmen military experience that would prove invaluable in a future fight for the liberation of Ireland. A recruiting poster for Corcoran's Irish Legion proclaimed, "Irishmen, you are now training to meet your English enemies!" But the liberation of Ireland was rarely cited by Irishmen as a reason for their enlistment in the U.S. army.

The decision of some Irishmen to enlist was mainly economic, driven by the enticement of enlistment bounties and army pay. "The dislocation of the economy caused by secession hit the working classes hardest," noted Lawrence Frederick Kohl, a writer on Irish history; "unemployed Irish laborers and domestic servants often found enlistment in the Union army to be the only alternative to starvation."[17]

The substantial literature on the Irish in the Union army contains some negative comments about their habits. Ella Lonn, author of the most comprehensive books about foreigners in the Union and Confederate armies, noted that intemperance was one of the Irish vices: "When they were intoxicated, there was constant brawling and fighting among themselves and with other groups." Brigadier General Regis de Trobriand, an immigrant from France, recalled that "when whiskey was introduced into the camp clandestinely, it was in the Irish quarter that the officer of the guard first found it. The most severe punishments availed nothing." Burton noted that "Irish regiments had a reputation for more rowdiness and disobedience of orders than most regiments." De Trobriand recalled that "on inspection, their uniforms were seldom without spots or their bearing without fault." Lonn also noted that "slovenliness was one of their unpleasant traits" and that "Irish soldiers were improvident, throwing away their knapsacks and blankets as they dashed to the scene of action."[18]

Even so, the performance of the Irish as combat soldiers has been strongly praised by their commanders, observers, and historians. An Irish journalist, D. P. Conyngham, summed up their reputation: "Whether storming the bloody heights of Fredericksburg, or checking the enemy's advance at Fair Oaks and Malvern Hill, or making that fearful dash at Antietam, or rescuing the abandoned cannon at Chancellorsville, or sweeping Early from the Shenandoah, or in planting the Stars and Stripes on the walls of Atlanta and Savannah, the Irish soldier has won a high reputation. . . . The greatest detractor of his race, . . . the London *Times* itself, has not dared to question his bravery as a soldier or his devotion to the flag under which he fought."[19] Even those who were critical of the habits of the Irish praised their performance in combat. Lonn wrote of the Irishman's zeal for combat, his watchfulness, poise and steadiness, and his loyalty and pride in his regiment, his brigade, and his race.[20] De Trobriand thought that when the Irish were under fire they were "fine fighters, . . . indefatigable, enthusiastic, and always ready for a joke or a fight."[21]

In areas with large Irish populations—notably urban areas in New York, Massachusetts, Pennsylvania, and Illinois—many Irishmen joined regiments consisting entirely or mainly of other Irishmen. There is no consensus on the number of these "Irish" regiments or the number of Irishmen that served in them. Burton provided information on twenty-one predominantly Irish regiments.[22] A researcher on the Irish in the Civil War, David O'Keefe, listed eighteen Irish-American regiments and three others that began service with many Irish-American soldiers.[23] Kevin Kenny, an Irish-American historian, wrote that "thirty-eight Union regiments had the word 'Irish' in their names."[24]

The best-known Irish regiments were those that served in the Irish Brigade. The record of this brigade and the regiments that served in it at various periods has been presented in at least ten books and numerous articles; the other Irish regiments have received much less attention from historians. The Irish regiments were the most visible symbols of Irish participation in the war, but they accounted for only a small fraction of the Irishmen who served in the Union army.

Although some Irish immigrants had previously served as enlisted men in the British army, very few of them had experience in Europe as officers. Several Irishmen who were senior commanders during the Civil War had previous military experience in America—in the war with Mexico (1846–48), in the Seminole war, or fighting Indians in the west. Ella Lonn noted that "the Irishman had traits which made for a good officer. He knew how to manage people. . . . A gift for oratory . . . gave him a hold over his men. . . . His nimble mind stood him in good stead on the battlefield."[25] Many Irishmen served as company and regimental commanders. At least ten men born in Ireland—Richard Busteed, Richard Byrnes, Michael Corcoran, Patrick Henry Jones, Patrick Kelly, James L. Kiernan, Michael K. Lawler, Stephen McGroarty, Thomas Francis Meager, and Robert Nugent—commanded Union brigades. Four officers from Ireland—Patrick Henry Jones, Robert Patterson, James Shields, and Thomas William Sweeny—were division commanders.

Despite the enthusiasm of the Irish volunteers in the first year of the war and the well-reported valor of many of them in various battles, Irish support for the war cooled dramatically during 1862. If the percentage of prewar Irish-born residents in the North and wartime Irish immigrants who served in the Union army had been the same as in the total Union population (10.7 percent), there would have been about 180,000 Irish-born men in blue not including second generation Irish-Americans. Although Conyngham asserted that there had been 175,000 "Irishmen" in the Union army,[26] other estimates of Irish participation were much lower. Dr. A. B. Gould estimated in 1869 that there had been about 144,000 Irish in the Union army.[27] In 1889 William J. Fox raised the estimate only slightly to 150,000.[28] Estimates by authors in the twentieth century ranged from 144,000 to 160,000 Irishmen; most or all of these estimates presumably included both immigrants from Ireland and second generation Irish-Americans. Princeton historian James M. McPherson gave no estimate but wrote that "the Irish were the most underrepresented group in proportion to population. . . . The under-representation of Catholic immigrants can be explained in part by the Democratic allegiance of these groups and their opposition to Republican war aims, especially emancipation. Some of them had not yet filed for citizenship—or claimed not to have done so—and were therefore exempt from the draft."[29] Kevin Kenny also wrote that "Irish immigrants were the most underrepresented group in the army compared to the population as a whole."[30]

Irish support for the war cooled dramatically after two events in the last months of 1862—Lincoln's announcement of his intention to issue an emancipation proclamation on January 1 and the great slaughter of Irishmen at Fredericksburg in December, which is reviewed in Chapter 15. In March 1863 the Congress passed a federal conscription act. In July, when officials in New York city attempted to implement the federal conscription program, the Irish disenchantment with the war, opposition to conscription, and hatred of blacks exploded during four days of rioting, arson, and murder.

Charles Mackay's first report to *The Times* on the riots began with a reminder of his previous reports that "the working classes were. . . . disgusted with the war and all relating to it; that they did not sympathize with or take any interest in the abolition of slavery, except to condemn it; that they looked upon the negroes with mistrust and dislike; that they felt the burden of the war in the enhancement of the price of food and clothing; . . . and that, above all, they were opposed to the principle of a conscription."[31] A British visitor that summer, the Reverend G. G. Lawrence, added that the working men were particularly unhappy about the provision of the conscription act that anyone might be exempted on paying $300.[32]

Mackay reported that the riot began with the publication in the Saturday evening papers of a list of those to be drafted: "By eleven o'clock on Sunday some thousands of persons had collected at the building in the Third Avenue where the formalities of the draught were to be resumed. . . . They rushed into the office, got hold of the enrollments and tore them to shreds. . . . In less than half an hour afterwards the whole edifice was in a blaze. . . . A detachment of the Provost Guard . . . fired a deadly volley into the crowd, and about 20 people fell mortally wounded. . . . Several soldiers and policemen . . . were killed. . . . The crowd . . . invaded an armoury . . . where a large store of arms and ammunition . . . was known to exist. . . . Although opposition to the draught was the main motive that impelled these people to lawless deeds, . . . hatred of the war and hatred of the negroes, whom they supposed to be the cause of it, were equally strong in their minds. No negro could venture into the crowd without insult or danger. One unfortunate man of colour, being hooted and pelted with brickbats, . . . drew a revolver from his breast and shot the foremost man dead. He was immediately pursued by a mob . . . and . . . hung, stark naked from a lamppost, and pelted with stones. . . . Several thousand persons . . . marched up to . . . an institution . . . devoted to the maintenance and education of orphan negro children. Giving the inmates an hour to escape, they . . . set fire to the building. . . . The sudden downfall of a drenching rainstorm . . . cleared the thoroughfares."[33]

Maria Lydig Daly, wife of Judge Charles P. Daly, described the first day of rioting in her diary: "There were dreadful scenes enacted in the city. . . . Many were killed, many houses were gutted and burned: the colored asylum was burned and all the furniture was carried off by women: Negroes were hung in the streets! . . . At last, in God's good mercy, the rain came down in torrents and scattered the crowds."[34]

Mackay reported that the next day "the riots were resumed at daybreak. . . . The house of the postmaster . . . was burned to the ground. The houses of scores of other persons who by their action in the war and their support of the Government had rendered themselves obnoxious to the working classes have shared a similar fate."[35]

"At last the riot is quelled," Mrs. Daly recorded on July 23, "but we had four days of great anxiety. Fighting went on constantly in the streets between the military and police and the mob, which was partially armed. The greatest atrocities have been perpetrated. . . . Three or four Negroes were hung or burned. . . . Leonard, the Superintendent of Police in our neighborhood, said the draft could not be enforced; the fireman are against it, as well as all the working classes. . . . I feel . . . much outraged at the cruelties inflicted. I hope it will give the Negroes a lesson, for since the war commenced, they have been so insolent as to be unbearable."[36]

Neither Mackay nor Mrs. Daly mentioned the prominent roles of Irishmen in the rioting mobs. Mackay probably thought that the pro-Confederate editors of *The Times* would be happier with a report of general unrest among the working classes than with one describing a riot led by Irishmen. *Harper's Weekly* asked its readers to remember "that in many wards of the city the Irish were . . . staunch friends of law and order; that Irishmen helped to rescue the colored orphans in the asylum from the hands of the rioters; that a large proportion of the police, which behaved throughout the riot with the most exemplary gallantry, are Irishmen; and . . . that the Roman Catholic priesthood to a man used their influence on the side of the law."[37]

But the dominant role of Irishmen in the rioting mobs was acknowledged by Irishmen and others, in 1863 and later. "I am very sorry that the Irish men of New York took so large a part in them disgraceful riots," Sergeant Peter Welsh, 28th Massachusetts, wrote his wife. "The Irish . . . are too easily led into such snares which give their enemies an opportunity to malign and abuse them."[38] When Colonel De Chenal, the French military observer, visited New York in 1864, he was told that the rioters had been "a mob recruited among the large foreign population of the city and aided by many Southern refugees."[39] Irish-American historians have written frankly of the Irish role: "For four days," wrote Kevin Kenny, "mobs of Irish workers, with longshoremen at the vanguard, roamed the waterfront in search of black workers, beating, lynching and driving them out."[40]

De Trobriand wrote that the "Peace Democrats," who opposed the continuation of the war, tried to exploit the riots to support their objectives: "The Governor, Horatio Seymour, whose attitude and conduct . . . had been of a nature to encourage the riot, . . . asked the President that the resumption of the drawing should be indefinitely adjourned. The object of this attempt . . . was to dry up the sources of reinforcements necessary to the armies."[41] But Lincoln refused to suspend the draft.

Opposition to the war, to Lincoln's emancipation policies, and especially to conscription remained strong among Irish civilians during the last two years of the war. The Official Records contain reports of actual or threatened violence by Irishmen in the Pennsylvania coalfields, in a marble quarry in Vermont, and in several cities and towns including Milwaukee; Columbus, Ohio; and even Lincoln's hometown of Springfield, Illinois.[42] Although there has been no thorough study of the Irish role in the election of 1864, the available evidence indicates that Irish civilians voted overwhelmingly for Lincoln's opponent, General McClellan, although support for Lincoln may have been somewhat stronger among Irish soldiers.

Late in the war a number of Irishmen from the North who were in Confederate prison camps were recruited as Confederate soldiers. Confederate General M. J. Wright reported in September 1864 that more than 1,000 Catholic Irish prisoners in Macon, Georgia, were willing to enlist in the Confederate service. Secretary of

War James A. Seddon sanctioned their enlistment.[43] In November Seddon informed General Lee that he had authorized several officers to raise battalions from among prisoners of war but had directed them "to prefer Irish and French." Another Confederate War Department letter stated that some Confederate officers "believe that by recruiting chiefly among Catholic Irish . . . and obtaining the influences of the Catholic priesthood, they may secure faithful soldiers."[44] The diary of Mary Chesnut, a prominent Richmond matron, contains several references to the "First Foreign Battalion," which drilled near her house from late October 1864 to early January 1865. She described the unit as "a regiment of foreign deserters" who had "taken the oath of allegiance to our government."[45] The battalion was sent to Charleston. On February 16, 1865, its commander, Lieutenant Colonel J. G. Tucker, was ordered to "recruit his command from the prisoners of war" but to "take only men of Irish and French nationality." The order said the men were to be used for "engineering services."[46] No information is available on the number of Irish or other foreign-born prisoners who took the Confederate oath.

Evidence of opposition to the war among Irish civilians and the desertion of many Irishmen from the Union army—both most significant in the second half of the war—does not obliterate the impressive record of valor and devotion to the Union cause of many thousands of Irish volunteers, especially in the first half of the war. Irish volunteers fought for their new country. Although many of them were technically still British subjects, few Irishmen attempted to avoid service on the ground of British nationality. As indicated in the next chapter, many other British residents in the North attempted to evade conscription by claiming that they were still loyal subjects of Queen Victoria.

Chapter 4

Putting Down This Awful Rebellion

Britons *in the* North

B ritons were the third largest foreign-born group in America, after the Irish and the Germans. The U.S. census of 1860 recorded 587,745 persons who were born in the British isles, not including Ireland. These included 433,494 from England, 108,518 from Scotland, and 45,763 from Wales. Only 24,559 of the Britons were in states that formed the Confederacy the following year. The largest concentrations of English and Scots were in states on the Northeast coast or on the border with British America (Canada). New York, both a coastal and a border state, had 106,011 residents born in England and 27,641 from Scotland. Other states with large numbers of Britons included Pennsylvania (46,546 English and 10,137 Scots), Ohio (32,700 + 6,535), Wisconsin (30,543 + 6,902), Michigan (25,743 + 5,705), and Massachusetts (23,848 + 6,855).

The English and Scots did not live in ethnic neighborhoods or form a distinctive element in the cultural or political life of their communities. They were not separated from native-born Americans by any important difference in language, culture, or religion. Most of them were, in Charlotte Erickson's phrase, "invisible immigrants."[1] Many British residents did not consider themselves immigrants. In the Victorian era, British imperial and business interests required that many Britons live abroad for years, but a great number of these overseas Britons retained their status as British subjects and intended eventually to return "home" to England or Scotland. The Welsh, on the other hand, had a language, culture, and religious heritage that was distinct from the mainstream cultures in both England and America. Welsh immigrants often formed distinctly Welsh communities or settled in already established Welsh communities in New York, Pennsylvania, Ohio, Minnesota, and Wisconsin.

Very little has been written about the roles of Britons in the American Civil War. After the war, the well assimilated British immigrants felt no need to enhance their postwar status by documenting their patriotism and loyalty during the war. The persistent resentment in the North of actions by Britons during the war— including upper-class support for Confederate independence, official recognition of Confederate belligerency, the construction in Britain of the Confederate raiders *Florida* and *Alabama,* and major British roles in the blockade-running system — undoubtedly discouraged British immigrants from calling attention to their country of origin. In the twentieth century, the descendants of British immigrants had no strong motive to publicize the role of Britons in the Civil War.

The very limited available evidence suggests that most of the British immigrants who enlisted in the Union army did so for reasons that were similar to those of the Irish and Germans. Immigrants who had accepted American citizenship— whether naturalized or not—enlisted to defend the freedom and opportunity they had found in America. John Pellet, an English immigrant from upstate New York, wrote to his father that he was sorry his father "was so much opposed to my going to do my duty towards putting down this awful rebellion," but "I . . . must fight for the rights and freedom of our adopted country."[2] "Liberty must and shall win is the cry of all the North," Titus Cranshaw, a British immigrant in the 3rd New Jersey, wrote his father in 1861. He explained that he had enlisted because "I thought the capital of Washington was in danger of falling into the hands of the rebels. . . . I was not forced to go, but I thought it my duty to do so."[3] Gwilyn ab Ioan and several other Welshmen in the 154th New York were from the town of Freedom, New York. "It is from Freedom that we have come," he wrote in 1863, "and it is for Freedom and Union that we are fighting."[4] In 1864 an English-born corporal in an Ohio regiment explained to his wife why he had decided to reenlist: "It will be not only for my country and my children but for liberty all over the world that I risked my life. If liberty should be crushed here, what hope would there be for the cause of human progress anywhere else?"[5]

The assimilated British immigrants were anxious to demonstrate that they were now patriotic Americans ready to fight for their new country. William E. Van Vugt, who studied the autobiographies of immigrants from Britain in the many county histories published in the 1880s, noted that "to show loyalty to his adopted country" and "to defend the honor of his adopted country" were frequently cited reasons for enlistment in the Union army.[6] Many of these immigrants also felt a sense of obligation to the country in which they had prospered. "I gloried in being of use to the land that had done so much for me," recalled Andrew Carnegie, a Scottish immigrant and future steel magnate.[7]

English or Scottish immigrants rarely cited the abolition of slavery as a reason for enlistment. In a recent study of British reactions to the Civil War, R. J. M. Blackett noted that by 1860 "the ravages of time had taken their toll on the British antislavery movement" and that visitors to Britain had noticed "a growing indifference to slavery."[8] On a riverboat in Louisiana in 1862, William Watson, a Scottish engineer, met two Scots who were in a Union rifle regiment: "They most emphatically repudiated the insinuation that they were fighting to abolish slavery. Were such a thing . . . embodied in the principles for which they were fighting, they would rebel and lay down their arms. . . . Then what were they fighting for? I asked. 'For the Union; to maintain the integrity of the Union, and for nothing else.' The question of slavery, they maintained, had nothing to do with the question for which they were fighting."[9]

In contrast, Welsh scholars have stressed that opposition to slavery was a strong motive for the enlistment of Welshmen in the Union army. Alan Conway wrote that to the Welsh soldier "the war was a moral battle between the forces of darkness and the forces of light, with the freedom of the Negro slave as the reward of Christian duty fully discharged."[10] T. G. Hunter, a scholar at the University of Wales at Cardiff, has assembled nearly a thousand letters and articles written in the Welsh language by Welshmen in America during the Civil War; they demonstrate that the Welsh were "very much in favor of abolition and . . . tended to see the war as a crusade to free the slaves, as well as save the Union."[11]

Some British immigrants were attracted by the enlistment bounty and the pay in the Union army. James Horrocks wrote his parents in 1863 of his plans to enlist in the 5th New Jersey Artillery: "I shall get when mustered in $200 from the state of New Jersey, 50 dollars from Hudson City (where I enlisted), and 25 dollars from the Government. This, together with a month's pay in advance, will make $288 cash down."[12]

Quite a few young Britons who had been swept up in the early wave of enlistments attempted later to obtain their release from the army on the ground of British citizenship. In October 1861, Secretary of War Simon Cameron acknowledged the receipt of seven letters from the British minister appealing for the discharge from the army of British subjects: "The numerous applications for discharges daily pouring, . . . which multiply with the encouragement given by every fresh discharge, have compelled me to deny all."[13]

By the summer of 1862 some states had passed conscription laws that required military service by foreign residents who had become "domiciled" by demonstrating their intent to become citizens. "It would be difficult to describe to you what a panic there is amongst British subjects all over the States with regard to this drafting," the acting head of the British legation reported in the summer of 1862. "I greatly fear from the present irritation against us that many may be forcibly impressed in some States, in spite of their British nationality."[14]

Ella Lonn described the reaction of many foreign-born to the Conscription Act passed by the U.S. Congress in the spring of 1863: "Thousands discovered immediately . . . that their original nationality was inexpressibly dear to their hearts. This brought a flood of applications to the various consular officers to secure the precious certificates of nationality to save them from the draft."[15] "I am beset with terrified British subjects who expect to be made soldiers of," reported the British minister, Lord Lyons. "In the case of those who have declared their intentions to become citizens, the terrors are not altogether without reason."[16] A few weeks later he wrote that "I have given myself a world of trouble to make the burthen of proving their claim to exemption as light as possible," but admitted that "British subjects . . . are far from being pleased" with his efforts.[17] "The number of British subjects who are serving in the U.S. army and navy is very considerable," Lyons reported in May 1864, "and complaints are constantly made to me of the practices by which the enlistment of many of them has been effected. . . . The most laborious and most painful and unsatisfactory part of the duties of this legation . . . is connected with these complaints. . . . In few cases, however, have our efforts produced any satisfactory results."[18]

The resistance by many Britons in the North to enlistment and conscription clearly limited the number of British-born in the Union army, although to a lesser degree than would have been the case had the Union authorities been more sympathetic to the appeals for exemption. If the ratio of British-born soldiers in blue to the total British-born in the North in 1860 had been the about the same as the ratio of the total Union army to the total Union population—10.7 percent—there would have been about 60,000 Britons in blue. But all the estimates of service by British immigrants in the Union army have been considerably lower. Dr. A. B. Gould estimated in 1869 that about 45,500 Englishmen and Scotsmen had served in the Union army.[19] William F. Fox wrote in 1889 that there had been about 50,000 "English" in the Union army.[20] In the twentieth century several authors have used Gould's figure, although Ella Lonn estimated that 54,000 English-born men wore Union blue.[21]

The only regiment with a high percentage of Britons was originally planned as an all-Scots regiment to be known as the New York "Highlanders." Recruiting was slow, in part because most Scottish immigrants in New York were Lowlanders. Eventually the unit, designated as the 79th New York, attracted a mixture of Scots, Irish, and Americans, but it was still called the "Highlanders." At first the officers wore kilts and the men wore pantaloons of the Cameron tartan; when active service began, the U.S. service uniform was substituted. The regiment's first commander was James Cameron, brother of the Secretary of war; he was killed at the first Bull Run. He was eventually succeeded by Colonel David Morrison, who had served in the famous Black Watch regiment in the Crimean war; Morrison later commanded the brigade that included the "Highlanders." William F. Fox thought the men of the 79th had "fought for the government of their adoption as gallantly as ever Scotchmen fought on native soil or on foreign fields."[22]

Two Illinois regiments were initially planned as Scottish regiments. The 12th Illinois, sometimes known as the "First Scotch" regiment, was initially commanded by a Scot, John McArthur. Another partially Scots regiment, the 65th Illinois, was organized in Chicago in early 1862 but was captured at Harpers Ferry in September and returned to Chicago under parole.[23] There were Welsh companies in two regiments— one from Scranton in the 77th Pennsylvania and one from Oneida County in the 97th New York. Large numbers of Welshmen served in the 117th and 146th New York, the 23rd Wisconsin, the 9th Minnesota, and the 50th, 76th, 115th, and 118th Ohio.

At least twelve men born in Britain commanded brigades in the Union army, typically after a period as a regimental commander. Nine were immigrants, including four from England (Edward D. Baker, John H. Fuller, Edward L. Molineux, and Thomas Stevens); three from Scotland (John Fraser, David Ireland, and John McArthur); and two from Wales (Joshua T. Owen and William H. Powell).

A few British officers crossed the Atlantic to join the Union Army after the war began, although the number of these nonimmigrant officers from Britain was much smaller than in the Confederate army. John Carwardine, member of a prominent family in Essex, was a major in the 6th New York Cavalry from 1861 to 1863. "What prompted him to become a soldier with the Union forces we shall never know," a London newspaper commented when his Civil War momentos were sold in 1998.[24] Since almost all of the British officers in the Confederate army remained in staff positions, some British officers may have joined the Union army to seek command experience they could not obtain in the South. Four of the nonimmigrant officers from Britain—Leonard Currie, John Fitzroy de Courcy, Robert Johnstone, and Percy Wyndham—were regimental and brigade commanders in the Union Army.

During the war, a number of British civilians and officers came to the North for some period to observe the American war. These British observers included correspondents for British newspapers and magazines, members of parliament, other civilians, army officers on leave, and, late in the war, official military observers sent by the British government.

The most influential British observers in America during the Civil War were the three correspondents of the most influential newspaper in Britain, *The Times* of London. The first of these was William Howard Russell. He had covered the Crimean war and is regarded as the first modern war correspondent. Russell arrived shortly after Lincoln's inauguration and met Lincoln on March 27: "Mr. Lincoln put out his hand in a very friendly manner and said, 'Mr. Russell, I am very glad to make your acquaintance. . . . The London *Times* is one of the greatest powers in the world. . . . I am glad to know you as its minister.' "[25] In the spring and early summer Russell traveled extensively through the South. He returned to Washington in time for the first battle of Bull Run, but his vivid and scornful report on the Union rout—which was widely reprinted in British and American newspapers—made him highly unpopular in the North. He remained in the North until the spring of 1862, when he applied for permission to accompany McClellan's army on the Peninsula campaign. Secretary of War Stanton refused, and Lincoln declined to interfere on the ground that "this fellow Russell's Bull Run letter was not so complimentary as to entitle him to much favor."[26] Russell immediately decided to abandon his assignment in America and return to England. There he discovered that despite his ill repute among Northerners, his outlook on the war was considered too pro-Union by the strongly pro-Confederate editors of *The Times*; he spent the rest of the war as editor of the *Army and Navy Gazette*. His letters to *The Times* in 1861 were published in book form in New York at the end of that year.[27] His reports from America in 1861 and 1862 were the basis for a book, *My Diary North and South*, published in London and Boston in 1863. As in the original reports, his skepticism about the Confederacy was well concealed, while his critique of the Union army and leadership in 1861–62 was unrestrained and devastating.

Russell was replaced by two correspondents—one in New York and one in Richmond. The editors apparently felt that, in light of the resentment of "Bull Run" Russell in Washington, another correspondent from *The Times* would not be welcome there. So the paper's Northern correspondent, Charles Mackay, was stationed in New York. Although Mackay had considerable experience on the *Morning Chronicle*, *Glasgow Argus*, *Illustrated London News*, and *London Review*, several authors have written very critical evaluations of his reporting from New York. A British scholar, Hugh Brogan, noted that he "had none of the instincts of a reporter" and told the editors of *The Times* what they wanted to hear from America.[28] James M. Perry wrote that Mackay rarely left New York, never witnessed a battle, and was "a complete bust as a war correspondent."[29] E. D. Adams commented that Mackay "invariably reported the situation from an extreme anti-Northern point of view."[30] Lord Leslie Stephen considered Mackay's reporting highly distorted: "Every patriotic action is explained to have really originated in corruption and selfishness. Scandal after scandal is raked together, and carefully exhibited as an average specimen of American affairs. . . . The whole political and social machinery is rotten at the core. . . . America is peopled by unprincipled mobs, sprinkled with charlatans and hypocrites, and governed by pettifogging attorneys."[31] The third correspondent for *The Times*, Francis Lawley, was stationed in Richmond; an introduction to his very pro-Confederate reporting is provided in Chapter 11.

In 1862 a young Briton, Edward Dicey, spent six months in the North as a special correspondent for two British periodicals, *The Spectator* and *Macmillan's Magazine*. On his return to England, he rewrote his articles for a book, *Six Months in the Federal States*, that contains the most perceptive and balanced reactions to the American Civil War presented by any British observer. Dicey's Northern sympathies conflicted with the opinions of upper-class readers in Britain, and his book received a cool reception. It was not published in America until 1971, when it appeared as *Spectator of America*. Herbert Mitgang, editor of the belated American edition, noted that Dicey "carried with him the powers of a magnifying camera-eye; he watched and listened with his mental shutter open almost all the way. Unlike many English travelers before him, he left his snobbery at home."[32]

From December 1863 to mid-September 1864, George Augustus Sala reported from the North for the *London Daily Telegraph*. His two-volume book, *My Diary in America in the Midst of War*, was published in London in 1865; it is full of very negative comments about America. The streets of New York were dirty, the trains were terrible, the government had become despotic, emancipation was the wrong policy, and much, much more. Sala's mother came from a long line of slaveholders in the British West Indies; he began his book with pages of intensely negative comments about blacks and a strong defense of the institution of slavery. George Alfred Lawrence, correspondent for the *Morning Post* of London, was another Confederate sympathizer. He arrived with letters of introduction from Confederate envoys Ambrose Dudley Mann and John Slidell, and planned to go South after a brief stop in Washington. "I utterly abominate and execrate the city, from turret to foundation-stone," he wrote after seven hours in the U.S. capital. He was arrested by Union troops while attempting to cross the Potomac in western Maryland, imprisoned for eight weeks in Washington, and eventually released with the understanding that he would leave the country as quickly as possible. His book, *Border and Bastille*, was published in London in 1863. It focused on his abortive effort to reach the Confederacy and his subsequent incarceration.

Three men born in Britain contributed to American newspapers during the war. Sylvanus Cadwallader, a Welsh immigrant, covered the western armies and later the Army of the Potomac for the New York *Herald*. He was at Grant's headquarters near Vicksburg in the spring of 1863 and became a friend of the Union general. In his memoirs, which were not published until 1955, he claimed that he had rescued Grant from his biggest drinking binge in the war.[33] William Swinton, an English immigrant reporting for the *New York Times*, was despised by both the army and his journalistic colleagues. Cadwallader thought he was "cold blooded, conceited, and prejudiced" and "heartily in sympathy with the Southern Confederacy."[34] After he was caught eavesdropping on a meeting between Generals Grant and Meade, was accused of bribing a telegraph operator to gain access to confidential documents, and was suspected of sending military information directly to the Richmond papers, Swinton was banished from the Union army by orders from General Grant.[35] Alfred R. Waud, an Englishman who retained his British passport, covered the Army of the Potomac for several years as an artist and reporter for *Harper's Weekly*.

Several young British aristocrats visited the North. The Marquis of Hartingdon, eldest son of the Duke of Devonshire, arrived in August 1862. Hartingdon did not think much of Lincoln and was highly critical of the Union army. After some time in the North, he went South. "I have certainly become much more Southern since I came here," he wrote his father from Richmond, after meeting Jefferson Davis.[36] Shortly after his return to England in February 1863, Hartingdon was appointed undersecretary in the British War Office.

A few British officers came down from Canada on leave to observe the American war. Lieutenant Colonel Henry Charles Fletcher of the Scots Fusilier Guards was at McClellan's headquarters during most of the Peninsula campaign in 1862 and later made a substantial visit to the Confederacy. He wrote an article for *Cornhill Magazine* in the spring of 1863 and a history of the American war, published in 1865.

There was no military or naval attaché at the British legation during the Civil War. Until 1864 there was no official British military observer with either the Union or the Confederate army. In the spring of 1864 the War Office sent two officers to the United States as official military observers. Colonel Thomas L. Gallwey had served with the Royal Engineers in the West Indies, Canada, and Gibraltar. Captain Henry James Alderson had been with British forces in the Crimean war.[37] That spring the British Admiralty sent a Royal Navy officer, Captain Goodenough, to study naval construction in the United States. His report convinced Lord Lyons that "the Americans are very seriously preparing for a foreign war,"[38] although the diary of Secretary of the Navy Gideon Welles demonstrates that he thought the United States had no need for warships capable of fighting European warships.[39]

The range of reactions to the Civil War was wider among Britons in the North than among any other major group of foreign-born individuals in the United States. These Britons included long-term British residents who nonetheless claimed exemption from military service because they had retained their British citizenship, British immigrants who proudly defended their new country, English and Scots who were lukewarm about abolition, Welshmen and some other Britons who passionately opposed slavery, British officers mainly interested in gaining combat experience in the Union army, British observers who were highly critical of Lincoln and his policies and doubtful that the Union could win the war, and many Britons who did not fit neatly into any of these categories.

After the three largest immigrant groups—the Irish, Germans, and British—the next largest immigrant group consisted of persons born in France. The rather limited available information, reviewed in the next chapter, suggests that French immigrants and visitors in the North supported the Union cause as consistently as the Germans and much more consistently than the Irish or British.

Chapter 5

A Fine Appearance
French *in the* North

I n 1860 there were 109,370 persons in the United States who had been born in France; 90,288 of them lived in states that would remain in the Union during the Civil War. The Northern states with the largest number of persons born in France were New York (21,826), Ohio (12,870), Illinois (9,493), Pennsylvania (8,302), California (8,462), Indiana (6,176), and Missouri (5,283). No author has estimated the number of French-born in the Union or Confederate armies. If the French in the North had volunteered in the same proportion as the Northern population as a whole, there would have been about 9,600 Frenchmen in the Union army.

A false impression of a larger number of Frenchmen in both the Union and Confederate armies was created by a number of regiments that were initially uniformed as "Zouaves." These units copied the uniforms of French soldiers in Algeria, who were considered some of the fiercest fighting units in the French army. They wore striped or red baggy trousers, bright waistcoats, short jackets with braided trim, fez-style caps, colorful sashes, and white gaiters.[1] In nearly all of these units, the design of the uniforms was of French origin, but the soldiers were not.

The first attempt to organize a regiment of French immigrants was a disaster. The 53rd New York was recruited as a Zouave regiment by a French immigrant, Lionel Jobert D'Epineuil, but Colonel D'Epineuil quarreled with his lieutenant colonel and attempted to kill him. A court-martial was scheduled, but New York authorities preferred to break up the regiment and pretend that the 53rd had never existed.[2]

The only Union combat regiment with an apparent majority of men born in France was the 55th New York. It was originally a militia unit, the Gardes Lafayette. French immigrants were a majority in six of the regiment's ten companies. The regiment's first wartime commander, Regis De Trobriand, wrote that the 55th was originally uniformed as Zoaves: "The state had furnished their red caps, their laced jackets, their close vests, their large red breeches, their leather shoes, and the regimental crest on their blue waistbands. When the clothing had to be renewed, the government very wisely sent us the regulation uniform."[3] De Trobriand wrote this characterization of the Frenchmen in the regiment: "Their merits and their defects were the same in America as in France. . . . National vanity . . . led them to exalt themselves and to underrate others. In reviews and in brigade drills . . . they made a fine appearance and maneuvered together with precision. Under fire, where nobody saw them, they did neither better nor worse than the others."[4] De Trobriand's memoir, *Four Years with the Army of the Potomac,* is one of the best accounts of the war by a European immigrant.

Another French immigrant, Charles Le Gendre, was colonel of the 51st New York. He lost part of his jaw at New Bern, North Carolina, in 1862 and the bridge of his nose and left eye in the Wilderness in 1864. After the war, Le Gendre was a U.S. consul in China and later an adviser to the Japanese and Korean governments.

The French government decreed in September 1861 that no French officer could observe or participate in the American war and retain his rank in the French army.[5] Napoleon III was preparing to embark on a bold adventure in Mexico and hoped to minimize friction with the Union and Confederate governments. Two French officers who had already left active service with the French army—Gustave Paul Cluseret and Alfred Napoleon Alexander Duffie—were brigadier generals in the Union army.

Two grandsons of former King Louis Philippe of France—the Count of Paris and the Duke of Chartres—were aides to General McClellan during the Peninsular campaign. G. P. Conyngham, an Irish journalist, wrote that the Duc de Chartres was "reared in sumptuous luxury, yet he cheerfully submitted to all the privations and hardships of the humblest officer of the staff."[6] In a letter to Queen Victoria, King Leopold of Belgium expressed horror that two grandsons of a French king were risking being shot "for Abraham Lincoln and the most rank radicalism."[7] The Comte de Paris's four-volume history of the American war was published in Paris in 1874; English translations appeared in Philadelphia between 1875 and 1888.[8] He was regarded by British historians as prejudiced in favor of the North, and aroused great anger in the South.

The young French aristocrats were accompanied to America in 1862 by their uncle, the Prince of Joinville. He was a former admiral in the French navy and a prominent writer on naval affairs. McClellan reported that the prince "constantly accompanied me through the trying campaign of the Peninsula and frequently rendered important services."[9] Joinville's account of the Peninsula campaign was published in Paris in October 1862 and was quickly translated and published in New York as *The Army of the Potomac: Its Organizations, Its Commander, and Its Campaign*.

The French government had no official military observer in America until the spring of 1864, when it sent a military mission to the Union army consisting of Colonel Francois De Chenal and Captain Pierre Guzman, both of the French Artillery Corps. They spent July, August, and September at General Meade's headquarters in Virginia, and then visited various other military establishments before returning to France in January 1865. De Chenal's book was published in Paris in 1872; an English translation, *The American Army in the War of Secession*, was published by the U.S. Army at Fort. Leavenworth in 1894.

Several French civilian observers wrote interesting accounts of their sojourns in America during the Civil War. The earliest of these was Salomon de Rothschild, a member of one of wealthiest and most conservative families in France. He came to America as a tourist in the fall of 1859 and remained until mid-1861. He was in New Orleans when the war began. Rothschild was very sympathetic to the Confederacy, and thought his influential family should support French recognition of Confederate independence. The French emperor, Napoleon III, would gladly have recognized the Confederacy if he could have done so in concert with the British. But he concluded that France could not recognize the Confederacy without risking a war with the United States.

Prince Jerome Bonaparte, a cousin of Napoleon III, visited the North in 1861. An accomplished artist, he painted many scenes of life in the Union army. A Civil War encyclopedia states that they "give an accurate and discriminating view of life in the Union army from the brush of a royal admirer." Upon his return to Europe, the prince consistently supported the Union cause. The letters of his aide in America, Lieutenant Colonel Camille Ferri-Pisani, were published in France; a translation appeared in America in 1972.

There were no French civilian observers in 1863 or early 1864, but three French writers came during the last year of the war. Auguste Laugel was a geographer, lecturer, and writer on political, economic, and scientific issues. He married a daughter of a prominent Boston family; her sister married Edward Dicey, correspondent in America for two British magazines in 1861–62. Laugel arrived in the North in September 1864 while the presidential election was in progress; he visited twelve Northern cities and the Army of the Potomac. He met Senator Sumner of Massachusetts while visiting his wife's family in Boston. Sumner introduced him to Lincoln; Laugel and Sumner accompanied Lincoln to Ford's Theater on January 13, 1865. His book, *The United States during the War*, was published in New York in 1866.

Marquis Adolphe de Chambrun, a lawyer and journalist, had published pamphlets that were highly critical of Napoleon III. He came to America in December 1864 to explore the possibility of immigrating with his family. Chambrun spent more time with Abraham Lincoln than any other foreign observer. He was with him during several historic events during the last days of Lincoln's life, including Lincoln's visit to Richmond after its capture. Chambrun's letters to his wife were discovered and translated in 1950 by his son, General Aldebert de Chambrun, and were published in New York in 1952.

Another French journalist, Ernest Duvergier De Hauranne, was in the North for several months in late 1864 and early 1865. A translation of his American diary was published in Chicago in 1975.

The reports of these French writers reflected the fact that French intellectuals were much more sympathetic to the Union cause than their counterparts in Britain. France had supported the American Revolution. Early French visitors to the United States—notably Alexis de Tocqueville—had written sympathetic accounts of the young American republic. Although the first two French republics had not survived, French intellectuals looked forward to the replacement of the regime of Napoleon III by a third republic. The Frenchmen who came to the North during the war expected to be favorably impressed, and they were.

Chapter 6

FOR *THE* SAKE OF RIGHT AND FREEDOM

Other Europeans *in the* North

AUSTRIANS

Although the 1860 census indicated that there were 25,061 persons in the United States in 1860 who were born in "Austria," it provided no breakdown between those born in German-speaking areas of the Hapsburg empire and those born in areas that became Czechoslovakia, Hungary, and Yugoslavia after World War I. The substantial participation by Hungarian immigrants in the Civil War is reviewed in a separate section below.

A number of German-speaking officers of the Union army were identified as former Austrian officers, and other German-speaking Austrians were undoubtedly mistaken as Germans. Herbert von Hammerstein, a former Austrian officer, was a major on McClellan's staff during the Peninsula campaign and later colonel of the 79th New York and the 102nd New York. A Colonel Wutschell commanded the 8th New York. Heinrich Boernstein was colonel of the 2nd Missouri. Colonel Von Pilsen commanded Fremont's artillery in the Shenandoah Valley. Adolf Von Luettwitz commanded the pioneers in General Schurz's division. Baron Wordier was an aide to the British commander of a Union cavalry brigade, Percy Wyndham.

BELGIANS

In 1860 there were 9,072 persons in the United States who were born in Belgium; 4,647 of them were in Wisconsin, and most of the rest were in other Northern states. If they had served in the Union army at the same rate (10.7 percent) as from the total Union population (10.7 percent), there would have been about 800 to 900 Belgians in the Union Army. A researcher in Belgium, Guy Gallez, has identified about 500 Belgian-born Union soldiers and estimates that the total may have been around 800. The most prominent Belgian in the Union army was Victor Vicquain, commander of the 97th Illinois, who won a Congressional Medal of Honor for his valor during the Mobile campaign in April 1865.

HUNGARIANS

Stephen Bezeidets, who has studied Hungarians in the American Civil War, estimates that about 4,000 Hungarians lived in the United States in 1860 and that 300 to 400 of them fought in the Union army. Many of these Hungarians were veterans of the abortive Hungarian revolution in 1848–49. Beszedits has noted that the Hungarian "Forty-Eighters," who had revolted against the Hapsburg rule in Hungary, "regarded the crowned heads of Europe as the main oppressors of citizens, constantly trying to thwart the development and establishment of egalitarian forms of government."[1] Nicholas Perczel later colonel of 10th Iowa, told citizens in Davenport, Iowa, in 1861 that dissolution of the Union would "threaten the very existence of the republican form of government since the aristocratically inclined citizens of the pro-secession states would soon seek to establish a monarchy. . . . Whether they would choose a ruler from amongst themselves or import one from one of Europe's dynasties, such an antagonistic neighboring government would pose a constant danger to the republic."[2] Emeric Szabad, a Hungarian who had fought with Garibaldi in Italy, was a captain on the staffs of General Fremont. When he was captured, he was asked by a Confederate officer "how a Hungarian could fight with the d—d Yankees against the Southern people, who were fighting for what the Hungarians had fought for in 1848. . . . I told him proudly that I came to America to fight for the Union, the destruction of which would cause joy to no one but tyrants and despots."[3]

Two of the Hungarian "Forty-Eighters"—Alexander Asboth and Julius Stahel—became Union generals. Eight or more Hungarians commanded Union regiments: Nicholas Perczel (10th Iowa), Frederick Kneffler (79th Indiana), Gabriel DeKorponay (28th Pennsylvania), Geza Mihalotzy (24th Illinois), Eugene A. Kozlay (54th New York), Frederick George D'Utassy (39th New York), Robert Rombauer (First Regiment of the U.S. Reserve Corps in Missouri), and Ladislas Zulavsky (82nd U.S. Colored Infantry).

Many Hungarians had settled in Missouri; quite a few of them joined the staff of General John C. Fremont in Missouri and later moved with him to his new command in western Virginia. Colonel Anselm Albert was on Fremont's staff in Missouri and was chief of his staff in western Virginia. Colonel Charles Zagonyi, a cavalry captain in the 1848, was Fremont's chief of cavalry. Colonel John Fiala was chief topographical engineer in both of Fremont's commands. Colonel Philip Figyelmessy was on the staffs of both General Fremont and General Stahel. "Because of the number of Hungarians serving on his staff and in various units attached the Western Department," Beszeidits wrote, "Fremont sent many of his communiqués . . . to his subordinate commanders in Hungarian [which] was simpler and safer than using some type of code. . . . There were very few Hungarian-speakers on the Confederate side."[4]

ITALIANS

The 1860 census showed 11,677 residents of the United States who were born in Italy, most of whom lived in the North. If the Italians had served in the same proportion as the rest of the Northern population, there would have been about 1,000 Italians in the Union army. Although the 39th New York was known as the "Garibaldi Guards" and has been called "a regiment of Italian-Americans," it was actually a polyglot mixture of men from fifty-two European countries and principalities. Three men born in Italy—Luigi Palma Di Cesnola, Eduadro Ferrero, and Francesco Spinola—were brigade commanders in the Union army. Enrico Fardella was a regimental commander.

In September 1861 a commission as a major general in the Union army was offered to Giuseppe Garibaldi, the hero of Italian liberation. The offer has been the subject of much misrepresentation. Reports in *The Times* of London and other British papers in February 2000 stated that the discovery of a postcard written by Garibaldi to King Victor Emmanuel II proved the previously "rumored" offer of a commission,[5] but the offer to Garibaldi was documented in diplomatic correspondence published in 1862. One Lincoln biographer wrote that the offer was made by a U.S. consul "quite on his own,"[6] but Secretary of State Seward wrote to the same consul that the offer had been made "by the President's direct authority."[7] Stories in *The Times* and *The Guardian* in Britain in 2000 stated that Lincoln had turned in desperation to the Italian hero for help at a time when his forces were being battered by the Confederates. In fact, the offer to Garibaldi was made in the fall of 1861 at a time of great hopes that the newly appointed commander of the Army of the Potomac, General McClellan, would be able to create and command an effective Union army. The article in *The Times* stated that Garibaldi was offered the command of the entire Union army. In fact, the offer of a commission was withdrawn after Garibaldi demanded that he be given both the supreme command of the Union army and power to free the slaves.

Lincoln's motives for offering a commission to Garibaldi remain obscure. In view of the small number of Italians in America at that time, a domestic political motive seems unlikely. The only apparent explanation is that Lincoln and Seward initially thought a Union command for the popular hero of Italian liberation and unification would increase support for the Union cause among liberals in Europe. They undoubtedly came to the view of James S. Pike, U.S. minister to the Netherlands, that Garibaldi was "a wolf whom it is not safe either to hold or to let go."[8]

NORWEGIANS

There were 43,995 Norwegians in the United States in 1860, almost all of whom were in the North. After Fort Sumter, Minnesota Governor Alexander W. Randall issued a proclamation in Norwegian: "The rebels . . . have struck the first blow. . . . The country's safety, preservation of our popular form of government, and the preservation of our civil and religious freedom . . . are at stake. . . . This is a war with traitors, a war for all that is good, right, and true, in America, a war for self defense."[9] "If this Union is divided," a Norwegian wrote to a Madison newspaper, "then is ended . . . all hope for freedom in Europe; then tyrants can . . . point to this ill-fated attempt at popular government as proof of the impossibility of creating a free republic."[10] If Norwegians had enlisted at the same rate as the Northern population as a whole, there would have been about 4,800 Norwegians in the Union Army. The most prominent Norwegian in the Civil War was Hans Christian Heg, commander of the 15th Wisconsin.

POLES

In 1860 there were 7,298 Poles living in the United States. Two men born in Poland—Wladimir Krzyzanowski and Albin Francisco Schoepf—became Union generals. Another Polish immigrant, Joseph Karge, commanded the 1st New Jersey Cavalry.

RUSSIANS

In 1860, there were 3,160 residents of the United States who were born in Russia. The only Russian of note in the Civil War was John Turchin, originally Ivan Vasilevitch Turchinoff, colonel of the 19th Illinois and later a brigade commander.

SWEDES

In 1860 there were 18,625 Swedes in the United States, almost all in the North. One Swedish immigrant, Hans Mattson, appealed to Scandinavians in Minnesota to place themselves "on the side of glory and our adopted country. . . . If death meets us in the strife, our parents, wives, children and friends will find comfort in having made sacrifices for the sake of right and freedom."[11] Hans Hokanson, a

Swedish-American author who looked for Swedish names in regimental records, concluded that there had been about 3,000 Swedes in blue.[12] If Swedes had enlisted at the same rate as the Union population as a whole, there would have been about 2,000 Swedes in the Union army. Estimates of the number of Swedes who were officers in the Union army have ranged from 75 to 118. The highest ranking Swedish immigrant was Charles Stohlbrand, who was a brigadier general and chief of artillery for the XV Corps in the Atlanta Campaign. About thirty-five to forty Swedish officers came to America during the war to join the Union army.[13] The highest ranking of these officers was Ernst Mattias Peter von Vegesack, a regimental and brigade commander and adjutant to General Meade at Gettysburg.

The Swedish immigrant who made the greatest contribution to the Union cause was a civilian, John Ericsson, designer of the *Monitor*. Several accounts by European immigrants and observers of the *Monitor*'s historic battle with the Confederate *Merrimac* are quoted in Chapter 18.

SWISS

In the 1860s Switzerland was the only sizable republic in Europe and the sole European country with a federal system of government; the Swiss system had been patterned after the only available federal model, that of the United States. Secretary of State William H. Seward instructed the U.S. minister in Bern to tell the Swiss "that with God's blessing we will preserve this model of federal republican government by which they have reformed their institutions. . . . Switzerland and the United States shall be honored . . . as the founders of the only true and beneficent system of human government—a system that harmonizes needful authority with the preservation of the natural rights of man."[14] The Swiss president replied that "Switzerland passed through a similar crisis fourteen years ago, which threatened to tear asunder the then loose connection of the twenty-two cantons. . . . May God grant . . . that the United States of America may also emerge renewed and strengthened out of this crisis."[15]

During the Civil War there were about 53,000 Swiss in the United States. More than 50,000 lived in the North, with only about 2,600 in the future Confederate states. The Swiss Consul General in Washington estimated that 6,000 Swiss served in the Union army.[16] If the ratio of Swiss service had been the same as in the population as a whole, there would have been about 5,000 Swiss in the Union army.

One Swiss volunteer, Emil Frey, recorded that he had been "inspired by the idea . . . of fighting for the preservation of the Union. The dismemberment of the Union would seriously injure the cause of liberty in the world."[17] Nearly a quarter century later, this Civil War veteran would serve a term as president of the Swiss union. Frey was born in Arlesheim in 1838, attended the University of Jena until a dueling incident required his departure, and arrived in America just before the Civil War. By 1862 he was commander of a company of Swiss sharpshooters in the 82nd Illinois; they fought with distinction at Chancellorsville, and Frey was promoted to major. He was captured by the Confederates at Gettysburg and nearly starved during eighteen months in the notorious Libby Prison in Richmond, but was exchanged in January 1865. After the war, he returned to Switzerland, edited a Basel newspaper, served for a decade in the lower house of the Swiss legislature, and was then the first Swiss ambassador to the United States. His later career included election to the Swiss Senate, a term as president of Switzerland in 1894, and many years as the director of the International Telegraph Union in Bern until his death in 1922 at the age of eighty-four.

Frey told a meeting of Swiss veterans of the Civil War in Lucerne in 1899 that they had fought for "the preservation of the Union and the abolition of slavery. For no better cause has any army taken to the field."[18] Another Swiss officer, Rudolf Aschmann, wrote that it had been "glorious to fight for an idea destined to bring freedom to all men . . . and to contribute to the success of a good cause." There were also more mundane motives for the Swiss enlistments. "Many of the immigrants were out of work," Aschmann noted. "A great many of them enlisted in order to escape dire need. Tempting bounty and good pay . . . were the enticements for joining the army. . . . Love of the military was an added factor; no Swiss can ever stand by idly when shots are fired and trumpets are sounding." Many Swiss thought that, like the Swiss civil war, the American conflict would last only a few months. "Had it been known at the onset of the war what superhuman efforts, what privations, what terrible bloodshed would have to be witnessed and participated in," Aschman observed, "many a European might have gladly let the Americans have the honor of fighting their own battles."[19]

Because of their proficiency with rifles, Swiss immigrants were often recruited for special units of sharpshooters. Lieutenant Aschmann, a Swiss immigrant, described the formation of the 1st U.S. Sharpshooters: "It was a Swiss, Captain Caspar Trepp of Spluegen, Canton of Grissons, who became the founder and organizer of a system of sharpshooters. . . . Our [Swiss] sharpshooter corps, consisting of the best marksmen, . . . was something completely unknown to the Americans. . . . In July 1861 he called attention to the establishment of such a corps, describing in some newspapers its usefulness and advantages. . . . An American by the name of Herman Berdan . . . soon obtained permission from the War Department to recruit in all loyalist states for a regiment of sharpshooters. . . . Appeals in the newspapers asking Swiss and Germans to join this cause did not fail to attract many, especially Swiss."[20] Later a second U.S. regiment of sharpshooters was formed, which also contained many Swiss.

The sharpshooters were frequently praised by Union generals. In his report on the Seven Days battle in 1862, General Winfield Scott Hancock stated that "a company of Berdan's Sharpshooters, under command of Major Gaspar Trepp, performed excellent service during the contest, driving back the enemy's skirmishers."[21] Trepp, by then a lieutenant colonel, was killed on November 30, 1863, during the Mine Run Campaign. Colonel Thomas W. Egan, commander of the brigade in which he served, called him "an officer of the highest merit, and one whose military knowledge and achievements have long been the admiration of all who knew him."[22]

Another regiment with a high percentage of Swiss was the 15th Missouri, known as the "Swiss Rifles." The historian of the regiment claimed that two-thirds of the men were Swiss. Its colonel was a trilingual Swiss immigrant, Francis J. Joliat. In the campaign for Chattanooga in 1863, the men of the 15th Missouri planted a Swiss flag at the top of Missionary Ridge.[23] Many other regiments had companies or smaller units consisting mainly of Swiss sharpshooters. At Gettysburg, a dozen Swiss sharpshooters, armed with the finest telescopic rifles, fired into narrow slits in the Gettysburg church tower to drive out a nest of Confederate sharpshooters.

Two Swiss immigrants—John Eugene Smith and Herman Lieb—became Union generals. Several other Swiss immigrants commanded regiments, including Joseph A. Moeschwas (83rd New York), John A. Kuhn (142nd Illinois), Arnold Suttermeister (11th Indiana), and Isaac Rutishauser (48th Illinois).

Switzerland was the first country to send an official military observer to report on the American war. Captain Ferdinand Lecomte studied the operations of the Union army in 1861 and early 1862. Lecomte's report to the Swiss Military Department was published in German in Switzerland in 1865; an English translation appeared in Bern and Frankfurt in 1972.[24] Colonel Augusto Fogliardi was the official Swiss military observer from March to November 1863.

Chapter 7

THE REPLENISHING STREAM

European Immigration *during the* Civil War

During the war, the Lincoln administration encouraged immigration as a means of filling civilian vacancies created by the enlistment or conscription of native-born Americans and as a source of additional volunteers for the army. But the administration resisted pressures from many U.S. envoys abroad to cover the transatlantic fares of immigrants, which would have been regarded as illegal recruiting in Britain and other countries with similar neutrality legislation.

From 1855 through 1860, immigration from Europe had averaged about 160,000 per year. In 1861 and 1862 the number of immigrants dropped sharply because of uncertainty in Europe about the effects of the war and stories reaching Europe about economic disruption and unemployment in America. Only 83,710 Europeans—about half the prewar average—arrived in 1861 and only 81,200 came in 1862. But in 1863 there were 163,733 European immigrants—about the same as the prewar average—and 185,233 came from Europe in 1864. The increased immigration in the last two years of the war was a result of conditions in Europe, increased opportunities in America, and U.S. legislative and executive actions that promoted immigration.

The Homestead Act, signed by Lincoln on May 29, 1862, was an important stimulus to immigration. It provided that any citizen or alien could acquire title to 160 acres of public land by residing on or cultivating the land for a period of five years. Secretary of State Seward knew that this legislation would provide a powerful incentive to land-hungry potential immigrants in Europe. He sent copies of the legislation to U.S. envoys with a memorandum calling the Homestead Act "one of the most important steps ever taken by any government toward a practical recognition of the universal brotherhood of nations."[1] In a subsequent circular Seward noted that no other country provided such opportunities "to active, industrious and intelligent men for the acquisition of abundant means of support and comfortable homesteads for themselves and their families."[2] From 1862 to 1865 about 2.5 million acres of land were taken up by homesteaders; the offer of free lands clearly contributed to the increased immigration during the last two years of the war.

Several other steps were taken in 1862 to promote immigration. In July Congress adopted a law giving citizenship to immigrants who had lived in the United States for one year and had served honorably in the army.[3] In August Seward sent a circular to all U.S. diplomats and consuls listing typical wages being paid to workers in America: "Nowhere else can the industrious laboring man and artisan expect so liberal a recompense for his services as in the United States. You are authorized and directed to make these truths known in any quarter and in any way which may lead to the migration of such persons to this country." But he noted that "the government has no legal authority to offer any pecuniary inducements to the advent of industrious foreigners."[4]

By late 1863 immigration had increased, but so had Union manpower needs. "Although this source of national wealth and strength is again flowing with greater freedom," Lincoln told Congress in December, "there is still a great deficiency of laborers in every field of industry, especially in agriculture and in our mines. . . . Tens of thousands of persons, destitute of remunerative occupation, are thronging our foreign consulates and offering to emigrate to the United States if essential, but very cheap, assistance can be afforded them."[5] Lincoln asked Congress for legislation encouraging immigration. The Congress eventually responded with the Emigrant Aid Act of 1864 which permitted private businesses to bring immigrants to the United States. This legislation was not popular with native-born workers, who felt the government was helping employers keep down wages by importing foreign workers.[6]

Lincoln also noted in his annual message in 1863 the large number of earlier immigrants who were attempting to avoid conscription or obtain release from the army by claiming that they were still citizens of other countries. "Such claims have been put forward . . . in behalf of foreigners who have lived in the United States the greater part of their lives. . . . Many persons born in foreign countries, who have declared their intention to become citizens or who have been fully naturalized, have evaded the military duty required of them by denying the fact. . . . The right of suffrage has often been assumed and exercised by aliens, under pretenses of naturalization, which they have disavowed when drafted into the military service." Lincoln proposed an amendment of the conscription law that would deny exemption of the ground of "alienage" to anyone who had voted in an American election.[7] The Congress responded in February 1864 with an amendment providing that no person of foreign birth could be exempted from conscription if he had voted or held office in any state or territory.

In June 1864 the Senate requested information regarding "the alleged enlistment in foreign countries of recruits for the military and naval service of the United States. "A few days later Lincoln sent the Senate reports by the secretaries of state, war, and navy. Seward stated that "the Government frankly avows that it encourages immigration from all countries, but only by open, lawful, and honorable agencies and means." Although a considerable number of Europeans were serving in U.S. forces, all had enlisted voluntarily after their arrival in the United States. "Exactly the same inducements to military service were open to them which by authority of law were offered . . . to citizens of the United States. . . . The Government of the United States has practiced the most scrupulous care in preventing and avoiding . . . any violation of international or municipal laws in regard to the enlistment of soldiers and seamen." Stanton attested that "no authority has been given by this Department to anyone, either in this country or elsewhere, to obtain recruits in Ireland or Canada for the Army of the United States." Welles made a similar statement.[8]

In his annual message in December 1864, Lincoln told Congress that he regarded the immigrants "as one of the principal replenishing streams which are appointed by Providence to repair the ravages of internal war," but he repeated earlier denials that the government was tricking or forcing immigrants to enlist in the army: "The government neither needs nor designs to impose involuntary military service upon those who come from other lands to cast their lot in our country."[9]

There is no basis for estimating the number of enlistments in the army from the 513,876 immigrants who arrived from Europe during the four war years (1861 through 1864). If these immigrants had enlisted at the same rate as the Union population as a whole (10.7 percent), there would have been about 55,000 of the wartime immigrants in blue uniforms. But the fact that two-thirds of the wartime immigrants arrived in the last two years of the war—when voluntary enlistments had declined and many civilian jobs were vacant—suggests a considerably smaller military contribution by these immigrants.

Most of the governments and people in the German states supported the North. August Belmont, a German-born banker, visited Germany in the fall of 1861. "The whole population," he wrote Secretary of State Seward, "is strongly for us and the warmest wishes are expressed for our success."[10] "When other European powers had only mockery, biting criticisms, and threats for us," a U.S. diplomat told a German Society meeting in New York in 1884, "only words and deeds of sympathy" came from Germany.[11] Carl Schurz recalled that "the German people . . . never lost its confidence in the ultimate victory of our good cause and the future of America. It loaned its savings by millions and millions to our hard-pressed republic, and gave it strength in the deadly struggle."[12] Almost all of the German press supported the Union cause.

Between 1855 and 1860, an average of about 62,000 German immigrants had come to America each year. Only about 30,000 Germans came during each of the first three years of the war; in 1864, the number jumped to 57,276, but this was still below the prewar average. Immigration from Germany could have been much larger if the U.S. government had been willing to pay for the transatlantic passage of the many Germans who were willing to enlist in the Union army.

"I am in the receipt of hundreds of letters and personal calls seeking positions in the American army and asking for means of conveyance to our shores," Joseph A. Wright reported from the U.S. legation in Berlin in May 1861. "So numerous . . . are the applications, that I had been compelled to place on the doors of the legation a notice . . . that 'this is the legation of the United States, and not a recruiting office.' "[13] The U.S. consul in Hamburg stated in May 1862 that he could send "10,000 soldiers for the Army and 1,000 sailors for the Navy" who were willing to enter U.S. service with only one condition—a free passage to America."[14] The legation in Berlin reported in August 1862 that it was receiving many applications for a free passage to the United States from Prussian soldiers whose term of active service was due to expire. If passage money were available, "thousands of valuable soldiers . . . could be added to our ranks."[15] In January 1863 the U.S. consul general in Frankfurt wrote that if passage money could be paid, he could send "20,000 to 30,000 experienced veteran soldiers who have seen service in the Italian and Crimean wars and who have been discharged by reason of a reduction by several German states of their military force."[16]

But Lincoln and Seward refused to pay the passage of any immigrant. Seward informed the legation in Berlin that "this government could not, without giving offense, offer to subjects of foreign powers inducements to enter the armies of the United States, much less could it properly make payments to them in order to enable them to reach our shores with a view to enlistment."[17] In the summer of 1862 a former Prussian officer, Otto Von Corwin, proposed to Lincoln a plan to bring 20,000 Germans to America to fight for the Union. Von Corwin recalled later that Lincoln had said, "We need people. Bring us some, and they will be very welcome." But he thought Corwin's recruitment plan would involve him "in difficult negotiations with other governments."[18]

About 165,000 Irishmen emigrated to the Union states during the war. This substantial emigration occurred despite the strong opposition by the Irish press and the Catholic priests in Ireland to the Union cause and to Irish emigration to America. The strong Confederate sympathies of a Dublin newspaper, *The Nation*, were evident in July 1861: "Those who profess to hold sacred the popular will, to reverence the desire for self-government, are proceeding to drown the popular will in blood and to answer the desire for self-government by butchery and slaughter! . . . This bloody war to force union on the southern people at the point of the sword—to saber them into brotherhood, and dragoon them into 'liberty'—is a blot upon humanity."[19] "America . . . should not expect our countrymen to be mercenaries in the present fratricidal struggle," the Belfast *Observer* stated in the spring of 1862. It implored Irishmen "not to be cajoled into a course fraught with danger and dishonor."[20] The *Examiner* in Cork proclaimed in 1863 that "three hundred thousand men are to be dragged from their homes to cut the throats of their Southern brethren" and that the draft riots in New York showed that the people were "beginning to show their disgust at the crimes of the government."[21]

Many of the Catholic priests in Ireland opposed Irish emigration to the North because they had accepted the pro-Confederate views of the Irish press. Confederate agent Edward De Leon believed that the priests opposed the emigration because they "live on voluntary contributions of their parishioners."[22] The U.S. consul in Dublin, William West, thought the priests feared that the Catholic faith of the emigrating Irishmen would be endangered by the freedom in America.[23]

In 1861 and 1862 the annual number of Irish immigrants coming to America was about 23,000, only half the prewar average of nearly 45,000 per year. But in 1863 the number of Irish immigrants—55,915—was well above the prewar level, and 65,523 Irish arrived in 1864. Kirby A. Miller, who studied Irish emigration, offered an economic explanation for this expanded emigration: "The early 1860s were especially bad years for rural Ireland; unusually wet weather ruined pastures, cash crops, potatoes, and turf. . . . The poor inhabitants of many midland and western countries endured near-famine conditions. . . . Male emigration from these 'wretchedly impoverished' districts increased markedly. . . . Probably the great majority were men . . . whose destitution at home contrasted so starkly with the lucrative bounties which the federal and northern state governments offered to prospective soldiers that they were willing to risk death to escape hopeless poverty."[24] An American consul in Galway reported that thousands of strong young Irishmen "would gladly embrace *any* opportunity of removal from the misery and starvation they are enduring."[25]

There were repeated charges by Confederates and Confederate sympathizers in 1863 and 1864 that U.S. agents in Ireland had paid the passage of some of the immigrants in return for their pledges to join the Union army on arrival. These charges were denied by Secretary of State Seward and the U.S. minister to Britain, Charles Francis Adams. Seward stated that "not one person has been enlisted, directly or indirectly, in Ireland, or in any foreign country, by any agent or under any authority or with any knowledge of this government."[26]

In 1863 and 1864 several Confederate agents were sent to Europe to attempt to stem the flow of immigrants from Ireland and Germany. James L. Capston went to Ireland in July 1863 with instructions to tell the Irish of the fate of the Irish Brigade and "explain to them that they will be called on to meet Irishmen in battle . . . in a quarrel which does not concern them."[27] The Reverend John Bannon, a Irish immigrant and former Confederate army chaplain, was sent back to Ireland to help the Irish priests discourage immigration.[28] Father Bannon circulated a handbill that pointed out the vulnerability to conscription of any immigrant who expressed, on arrival, the intention to become a citizen: "The unpretending emigrant . . . is persuaded by interested agents to declare his intention to come a citizen. . . . After his declaration being made, according to the late act of congress, he comes under the conscription law. . . . Let Irishmen remember the fate of Meagher's brigade on the bloody field of Fredericksburg."[29]

In November 1863 Confederate envoy Ambrose Dudley Mann was sent to Rome to deliver a letter from Jefferson Davis appealing to the Pope to discourage Catholic emigration to America. Mann told papal officials that "Christianity had cause to weep at such fiendish destruction of life as occurred from the beguiling of those people from their homes to take up arms against citizens who had never harmed or wronged them in the slightest degree."[30] The Pope's reply delighted Davis because it was addressed to "the Illustrious and Honorable Jefferson Davis, President of the Confederate States of America." That was the closest he ever came to European diplomatic recognition, but the letter contained no promise of papal action on the emigration issue.[31] In April 1864, the Right Reverend Patrick Lynch was appointed as a special Confederate commissioner to Rome. He had several audiences with the Pope, but was always received as the Catholic bishop of Richmond, not as a Confederate diplomat.[32]

The Marquis of Canricarde, a strong supporter of the Confederacy, charged in the British House of Lords in March 1864 that "recruiting for the federal States had been notoriously carried on in Ireland with very little check during the past two years." The foreign secretary, Lord Russell, replied that the U.S. minister had denied that there was any U.S. government recruitment in Europe and that the British government was unable to obtain sufficient evidence to warrant further action.[33] The attorney general asserted in the House of Commons in May that "agents for recruiting for the federal army . . . are in Ireland, and engage men upon the pretext of employing them on railways and public works, but really with the intention of enlisting them. . . . Representations have been made to the U.S. government respecting . . . persons who have been kidnapped into the service."[34] But Seward and Adams renewed earlier assurances that there had been no such recruiting or kidnapping in Europe by U.S. agents.

Between 1857 and 1860, the average number of immigrants arriving from Britain (not including Ireland) had been about 28,000 per year. Immigration from Britain decreased to 19,675 in 1861 and 24,639 in 1862, but the numbers in 1863 (66,882) and 1864 (53,428) were about twice the prewar average. This immigration continued and expanded during the war despite great hostility to the Union cause among the ruling classes in Britain, reviewed in Chapter 19. Most of the immigrants were from the working classes. They were attracted by the economic and political opportunities in the United States, opposed slavery, and did not care very much about the commercial and imperial advantages for Britain that contributed strongly to upper-class support for the Confederate independence.

Although the total number of immigrants from Britain from 1861 through 1864 (164,624) was only slightly smaller than the 166,587 who came from Ireland, there was very little discussion in Britain or America of this substantial British migration to America. The only apparent explanation is that British leaders, who preferred to avoid discussion of the political and economic complaints of the working classes, did not want to call attention to the substantial number of Britons who were seeking greener pastures in America even while it was engaged in a great civil war.

The U.S. minister to France, William Dayton, reported in September 1862 that the publication of Seward's circular on wages in the United States had produced a rush to his legation: "All seem to suppose that they are to have not only ample wages when they get to the United States, but their passage over . . . provided for by the government. They are of course greatly disappointed . . . to find the contrary." Dayton thought immigration from France would be greatly increased "if the government could induce shipowners to lower the price of passage for emigrants."[35] John Bigelow, the U.S. consul general in Paris, reported that "it would be easy to raise whole regiments here, if anyone had authority to pay the transportation."[36] The cost of transportation continued to inhibit emigration from western Europe; during the four war years there were only 17,021 immigrants from five western European countries—France, Switzerland, the Netherlands, Belgium, and Luxembourg.

During the five prewar years, immigration from four Scandinavian countries—Norway, Sweden, Denmark, and Iceland—had averaged about 1,700 per year. Although there were only 850 from these countries in 1861, the Scandinavian average rose to about 2,900 for the next three years. American consulates in Sweden were besieged by men seeking to emigrate, many of whom were interested in joining the Union army. As in Germany and France, consuls reported that they could have enlisted many soldiers if they had been able to pay their transportation to the United States. The war department informed the U.S. minister in Stockholm in October 1862 that while all foreigners reaching the United States "will be permitted to enlist . . . upon an equal footing with our citizens, the Government does not deem it expedient to procure enlistments in a foreign country."[37]

Chapter 8

THE SEEDS OF DISCORD HAD BEEN THICKLY SOWN

Europeans *in the* South: An Introduction

In 1860, 233,651 residents of future Confederate states were born abroad; 15,157 of these were in western Virginia counties that subsequently seceded from Virginia, leaving 218,494 foreign-born in the Confederacy. Although immigrants accounted for only about 4 percent of the population of the South, they were much more significant fractions of the populations of Louisiana and Texas and of six Southern port cities.

Over a third of the foreign born in the South—81,029 persons—were in Louisiana, mostly in or near New Orleans. In 1860 it had 174,791 people and was four times larger than the next-largest Southern city, Charleston. The 66,359 foreign-born in New Orleans were 38 percent of the city's residents. They included 24,385 Irish, 19,729 Germans, 10,525 persons born in France (who blended into the larger group of French-speaking Creoles born in Louisiana), 3,042 British, 1,390 Spanish, 896 Italians, 600 Swiss, 140 Swedes, 119 Poles, and 109 Portuguese, as well as 1,832 persons born in other counties in the Western Hemisphere.[1] Texas had more foreign-born residents than any Confederate state except Louisiana. The 43,422 foreign-born Texans included 20,553 Germans, many Mexicans who had remained in Texas after its independence from Mexico in 1836, and smaller numbers of immigrants from other countries.

Except in Texas, most of the Germans and Irish in the South were in or near cities and/or were employed on docks and steamboats on the Mississippi and other rivers. Memphis had a higher percentage of foreigners—30 percent—than any Southern city except New Orleans. About a fourth of Mobile's population were born abroad. Arriving in Mobile by steamboat, William Howard Russell of *The Times* of London noted "a fringe of tall warehouses and shops alongside, over which were names indicating Scotch, Irish, Spanish, German, Italian, and French owners."[2] The percentages of foreign-born were smaller but still significant in the Southern ports on the Atlantic. Over 20 percent of the population of Savannah, a major cotton-exporting port, were born abroad. More than 15 percent of Charleston's 40,578 residents were from other countries. The city's black population had declined in the 1850s, and about 60 percent of the working class in the city were immigrants, mainly Irish and Germans.[3] Richmond, an inland port, had the smallest percentage of foreign residents—13 percent—of any major Southern city. Among the 37,968 residents of the future Confederate capital there were 4,956 persons born abroad, including 2,244 Irish, 1,623 Germans, 556 British, and 144 French.[4]

Immigrants from Europe played a much more important role in the Southern economy than was acknowledged by Southern leaders. They provided many types of labor—as stevedores, draymen, waiters, boatmen, railroaders, construction workers, canal diggers, levee builders—for which neither slaves nor native-born whites were suitable or available. They did a number of dangerous and debilitating jobs for which slaveowners were unwilling to risk their valuable slaves. Some of the immigrants provided skilled services—as merchants, engineers, doctors, druggists, mapmakers, and engravers—that were badly needed in the South.

But many Southern leaders believed that the South did not need and should not encourage the immigration of white workers from Europe. La Vern J. Ripley noted the conviction of such leaders that "the economic system in the South did not require new blood and did not depend on an influx of low-paid, unskilled labor. Southerners *owned* their unskilled workers."[5] "We want no manufactures," a former U.S. Senator from Texas, Louis T. Wigfall, told Russell. "As long as we have our cotton, our rice, our sugar, our tobacco, we can command wealth to purchase all we want from those nations with which we are in amity. We desire no trading, no mechanical, or manufacturing classes."[6] This hostility to immigration was based primarily on fear that too many immigrants would endanger the crucial political and social consensus among Southern whites.

There has been very little analysis by historians of the response of immigrants in the South to secession and civil war. Several recent books have stressed the devotion of specific immigrant groups to the Confederate cause, but there has been no substantial effort to assemble the scattered but nonetheless substantial evidence of Unionist or other anti-Confederate attitudes among immigrants in the South. Evidence of the attitudes of immigrants about slavery is very limited because discussion of the South's "peculiar institution" was taboo in the South. Carl Schurz summarized the attitudes of the slaveowners in a speech in 1860: "We cannot be expected to tolerate opinions of persons among us that are opposed to the ruling order of things. . . . We cannot permit you to discuss the relation between master and servant, as it exists here in the slave states, for in doing so you would endanger our safety and undermine our social system."[7]

A British visitor, the Reverend George Fisch, noted that the Unionists in the South had been forced to yield "to the threats and cajolery of a small number of determined audacious men. . . . The authority of the great planters, the sinister influence of the secret societies, and terrorism . . . ended in triumphing over the whole Confederacy."[8] "The seeds of discord had been too thickly sown," recalled William Watson, a Scot living in Baton Rouge, "and the strife and enmity so effectually stirred up between North and South by the canting abolitionists of the North and bullying fire-eaters of the South that every word was distrusted."[9]

Watson wrote that Lincoln's inaugural address on March 4, 1861, was "disappointing and disheartening" to the moderates in the South: "He repudiated the abolition doctrine and distinctly avowed that he had neither the wish nor the intention to interfere with the institution of slavery in the States where it existed. . . . He advocated the preservation of the Union, and declared that the Constitution must be enforced at whatever cost. . . . In the Confederate journals it was treated in the most derisive way. . . . Confederate leaders . . . indulged in the most extravagant and insulting abuse of Mr. Lincoln and everything pertaining to the North."[10]

The immigrant from Scotland thought Lincoln's call for 75,000 volunteers, after the Confederates fired on Fort Sumter, eliminated the last chance of peaceful settlement of the crisis: "This proclamation was so sweeping and imperative and so menacing in its tone, that it caused the greatest excitement . . . throughout the whole of the Southern States. It seemed to outdo even the arrogance and pugnacity of Jefferson Davis and his cabinet. It left no opening for any peaceful settlement, and it entirely ignored the existence of any loyal or peaceful citizens within the Confederate States. . . . It gave them no alternative but unconditional surrender or the sword."[11]

"The North and South are going to hurl themselves upon each other like two locomotives driven at full steam and meeting on the same track," a French visitor in Louisiana, Salomon de Rothschild, wrote to his cousin.[12] Samuel Phillips Day, a British correspondent, recalled the response in the Confederacy to Jefferson Davis's call for volunteers: "The flower of the country had volunteered. . . . Young and middle-aged men were everywhere quitting their homes, parting from their families, and resigning their prospects in life to accept the doubtful chances of war. . . . Every man was . . . anxious to defend his native soil against the pollution of the invader."[13]

A great many European immigrants volunteered for the Confederate army, mostly in the first months of the war. The reasons that members of each of the major immigrant groups volunteered are examined in Chapters 9 through 12. They fall into four main categories. The first reason for enlistment was to support their friends and neighbors. Evidence of this motive is presented in several subsequent chapters. A second reason was to defend their homes, their country, and its institutions against attack from the North. Historian James M. McPherson observed that "in fighting for their home and their country, Southern soldiers took slavery for granted as the basis of the society and the country for which they fought. . . . Non-slaveholders also had a stake in slavery, for it was the basis of the South's social and economic organization and the instrument of white supremacy."[14]

A third reason for the enlistments was to protect and perhaps advance their own economic and social interests. Many poor immigrants thought that the maintenance of slavery was essential for the maintenance of their own fragile status. Edward Dicey, a British correspondent, noted that "the meanest and poorest of white citizens in a slave state belongs to the ruling caste. He is the recognized superior of the whole colored population, and the more wretched his own condition is, the more highly he values the one dignity belonging to him, as a white man, in a slave country."[15] Many middle-class immigrants often felt that they could not escape service in the Confederate army without severe damage to their business or professional interests.[16]

A fourth and often overriding motive for enlistment was to avoid the severe persecution that the immigrant feared would be his fate if he did not volunteer. Russell reported to *The Times* in May 1861 on the persecution of anyone in New Orleans suspected of being an abolitionist or even a pessimist about the Confederate cause: "Charges of 'abolitionism' appear in the reports of police cases in the papers every morning; and persons found guilty . . . of stating their belief that the Northerners will be successful are sent to prison for six months. The accused are generally foreigners, or belong to the lower orders, who have got no interest in the support of slavery. The moral persuasion of the lasso, of tarring and feathering, head-shaving, ducking, . . . deportation on rails, and similar ethical processes, are highly in favor."[17] Watson wrote that former Unionists had no choice but to support the Confederacy: "They were hopelessly in the power of the Confederate Government, which was strong, determined, and unscrupulous. They could not remain neutral; they would be coerced and pressed into service, . . . or they would be persecuted or banished, their goods and properties confiscated and their homes desolated."[18]

During the war the Confederate Congress and government sent confusing signals to the foreign-born in the Confederacy concerning their status and vulnerability to conscription. Confederate policies reflected public hostility to foreigners living in the South as well as the widespread belief that a third or more of the men in the Union army were European mercenaries who had been enlisted to conquer and ravage the South. The *Mercury* in Charleston proclaimed that "the Lincoln government . . . has . . . enlisted the refugees and adventurers of Europe for the invasion of the South."[19] A South Carolina planter told a Union officer that the North had sent "the off-scourings of Europe, . . . to invade our homes and firesides in an effort to overthrow constitutional right and rob us of our property."[20]

A British visitor in 1862, W. C. Corsan, noted the strong feeling in the South against naturalization of foreigners as citizens: "To the influx at the North of uneducated masses . . . Southern people attribute the steady deterioration in political virtue which, they say, has been going on at the North for years."[21] In the winter of 1861–62 the Congress enacted a bill that barred any foreign-born person from becoming a citizen of the Confederacy. Davis vetoed the bill on the grounds that it would impose "a legislative stigma" on aliens serving in the army and "on those of our fellow-citizens who are of foreign birth."[22]

The Confederate Conscription act, adopted on April 16, 1862, contained a provision that "foreigners who are not citizens of the Confederate States and who shall not have acquired domicile shall not be subject to military duty" and, if already enlisted, "shall be discharged at the expiration of their original term of enlistment."[23] The latter provision meant that aliens who had already volunteered must remain in the service for their original term of enlistment but would not be required, as would native-born enlistees, to remain beyond the expiration of the original term. The provision about "domicile," however, left many unanswered questions concerning the vulnerability for conscription of the numerous longtime residents who had not yet become citizens.

An attempt was made to clear up some of the confusion via General Orders 82 issued by the Adjutant-General's Office: "Foreigners not domiciled in the Confederate States are not liable to conscription. Domicile in the Confederate States consists of residence with intention permanently to remain in these States and to abandon domicile elsewhere. Long residence, of itself, does not constitute domicile. A person may acquire domicile in less than one year, and he may not acquire it in twenty years. If there be a determination to return to the native country and to retain the domicile there, no length of residence can confer domicile. The principal evidences of intention to remain are the declarations of the party, the exercise of rights of citizenship, marriage and the acquisition of real estate; but the intention may be gathered from other facts."[24] This ruling indicated that any foreign resident who had married, bought property, or voted in America could be considered a "domiciled" alien subject to conscription. In the first year of conscription, Confederate and state authorities usually accepted certifications of foreign nationality issued by foreign consuls, but such certificates were often ignored later in the war when Confederate manpower needs became more desperate.

In each major immigrant group in the South, reactions to the Civil War ranged from enthusiastic support of the Confederate cause to persistent efforts to avoid Confederate conscription and/or to escape from Confederate service. The pattern of reactions in each major group is reviewed in the following chapters.

Chapter 9

FRIENDS, BROTHERS, AND NEIGHBORS

Germans *in the* South

In 1860, 71,992 persons born in Germany were living in states that seceded from the Union the following spring. The largest numbers of Germans were in Louisiana (24,614), Texas (20,553), and Virginia (10,512); 16,313 Germans lived in the other eight future Confederate states.

Those Germans in the South who volunteered to fight for the Confederacy did so in spite of strong Southern prejudices against Germans that were evident in the many negative remarks by Southerners about German immigrants in the North and the Germans in the Union army. On the boat to America, William H. Russell of *The Times* met a major from Virginia who sneered at German immigrants as "the swine who are swept out of German gutters."[1] He reported later from Charleston that most Southerners thought the North attracted "hordes of ignorant Germans and Irish, and the scum of Europe, while the South repelled them."[2]

Erich W. Bright, who studied the Germans in Virginia, offered this explanation for the frequent references by Virginians to Union soldiers as "Northern Hessians," "filthy Dutch," "the foul German dragon," and "the scum of Europe": "The theme of German soldiers sent to the American South in order to repress and enslave the population . . . had taken root prior to the Civil War. . . . The longstanding hatred for the Hessian mercenaries who had fought for the British in the Revolution was given new life due to the fact that many Union soldiers were German-born and that bounties were offered to encourage Union enlistments."[3] Ella Lonn, author of the most comprehensive study of foreigners in the Confederacy, concluded that "the constant use of the words "hireling" and "mercenary" as applied . . . to the

Germans in the northern armies was a . . . reflection of race prejudice . . . in the Confederacy."[4]

Hostility to the Germans was especially strong in the Mississippi valley because of the decisive role played by the Germans in St. Louis in saving Missouri for the Union. Confederate Major General T. C. Hindman told his troops in Arkansas in 1862 that the enemy ranks were made up of "Dutch cutthroats" and other undesirable elements: "These bloody ruffians have invaded your country; stolen and destroyed your property; murdered your neighbors; outraged your women; driven your children from their homes; and defiled the graves of your kindred."[5]

Despite these prejudices against their race, many Germans in the South enlisted in the Confederate army to defend and support their new "fatherland" in America. Devotion to *Der Vaterland* was deeply imbedded in German culture. Many of the Germans had been driven out of their original fatherland by oppression, discrimination, and/or poverty, but they had found a new fatherland in the American South. In November 1860 the editor of the *Deutsche Zeitung* in Charleston began an editorial by citing the reasons why Germans had loved the Union as a "homeland for the oppressed." "But when . . . the North openly declares war on the South and its institutions, then the German . . . is true to the section which he voluntarily chose as his home [and] stands by those . . . who were friends, brothers, and neighbors to him."[6]

The attitudes of Germans in the South toward the most important Civil War issue—slavery—depended mainly on their economic situation. Many of the poorest and least skilled German immigrants shared the Irish fear that emancipated slaves would compete with them for jobs at the bottom of the economic ladder. A German-American scholar, Andreas Dorplalen, suggested that the attitudes of these Germans were not very different from those of most Irish immigrants: "Social outcasts themselves, the Germans still felt infinitely superior to the slaves. . . . Once the Negroes were no longer branded with the stigma of slavery, there was nothing that would distinguish them socially from the black man."[7]

Most of the middle-class Germans in the Southeast were very dependent on the goodwill of the planters and accepted slavery as an essential element of "the Southern way of life." A considerable number of these Germans were Jews. In a recent study of Jewish Confederates, Robert N. Rosen asserted that the enlistment of many Jews in the Confederate army primarily reflected their gratitude for the opportunity and acceptance they had found in America: "The Southern aristocrat's . . . quality of life was enhanced by the presence of Jewish teachers, musicians, innkeepers, lawyers, doctors, druggists, merchants, and men of learning. . . . Southern Jewry . . . had experienced a freedom unknown to Jews anywhere else in the world. They had been accepted by their fellow citizens of the Old South. . . . They repaid that freedom and respect . . . by loyalty to their homeland."[8] Many middle-class

Germans who were not Jews had similar reactions. Rosen also listed several other reasons why Germans enlisted, including "social and peer pressure."[9]

No Confederate regiment was made up mainly of Germans. Wilhelm Kaufmann wrote in 1911 that the Confederate authorities prohibited the formation of all-German regiments in the Confederacy: "Germans were distrusted due to events in Missouri, and for a while the authorities even hesitated to give them weapons."[10] A researcher in Germany, Jan Hochbruch, has asserted that the lack of all-German regiments was due to "lack of confidence in the German's dedication to the 'Cause.' Units with a large portion of German draftees tended to desertion and surrender in combat."[11] While there is considerable evidence of distrust of the Germans by Confederates, there is no documentary evidence that the government blocked the formation of an all-German regiment. The failure of the effort of a former Prussian consul to recruit the 20th Louisiana as an all-German regiment in New Orleans was probably a result of slow recruiting among the Germans; six of the regiment's companies consisted mainly of Germans, while four companies were mainly Irish. No other city in the South had enough Germans to fill a regiment.

There were German companies or batteries in regiments from Virginia, South Carolina, Alabama, Louisiana, and Texas. Germans commanded about fifty companies in the Confederate army.[12] Four Germans—Auguste Buchel, Gustav Hoffman, August Reichard, and Leon von Zinken—commanded Confederate regiments. No German was commissioned a general by the Confederate government, although a German immigrant, John A. Wagener, was a brigadier general in command of South Carolina state troops during the Union siege of Charleston in 1863–64.

Although many Germans were devoted supporters of the Confederacy, there is more evidence of opposition to secession, lukewarm support of the Confederate cause, and efforts to avoid or escape from military service among Germans in the South than in any other immigrant group in the Confederacy.

The most extensive and active opposition to the Confederate cause was among the German farmers in the Hill Country of west Texas, who were the great majority of the 20,553 Germans in Texas in 1860. They had established communities in which the German language, the Lutheran and Catholic religions, and German culture and music were fostered. Many of these Germans were liberals who had migrated to Texas after the unsuccessful democratic revolution in Germany in 1848. They farmed without slaves and were not economically dependent on slaveowners. When the question of secession was submitted to Texas voters in a referendum in the spring of 1861, a majority of the voters in eight predominantly German counties in west Texas voted against secession (as did voters in ten other Texas counties).[13]

Most of the Germans in west Texas attempted to avoid conscription into the Confederate army. Some of them fled to the Rio Grande and made their way via Mexico to New Orleans, which had been occupied by Union forces in April 1862. But many others were unwilling to abandon their farms and families. On July 4, 1862, 500 hundred Germans met in Gillespie County and organized three militia companies to protect young German men from seizure by Confederate conscription officers. The Confederate commander in west Texas, General Hamilton Bee, declared six German counties to be in rebellion against the Confederacy and sent in four companies of the tough 14th Texas Cavalry commanded by a Scot, Colonel James Duff. Martial law was declared in the Hill Country, and an epidemic of shootings, hanging, and other repressions ensued.

In a recent book on the Germans in Texas, Rodman L. Underwood described the dilemma faced by the Germans: "The members of the Union Loyal League felt it would be dishonorable to renounce their previous loyalty oath to the Union in favor of the Confederate oath. . . . They would not accept conscription into the CSA Army. This subjected them to possible death, their families to possible atrocities, and their property to confiscation or destruction. The situation had become untenable for them. They discussed fleeing to Mexico, but they did not have the means to take their families with them. They also discussed participating in guerrilla warfare, but were concerned about reprisals against their families. By July 25, 1862, . . . the decision was made that those who wished to flee to Mexico should do so."[14] On August 10, ninety-five of Colonel Duff's cavalrymen found sixty-five German Unionists camped on the Nueces River, en route to the Rio Grande. The Confederates attacked at dawn, killing sixteen Germans and wounding nine more. Three of these died of their wounds or were executed at the battle site. Nine survivors fled, but were subsequently captured and executed.

The massacre on the Nueces intensified the hostility toward the Confederacy of most of the Germans in west Texas. Many more fled to the Rio Grande; many of these joined a Union regiment known as the 1st Texas Cavalry, although there was a Confederate regiment with the same name. The new regiment consisted of 600 Germans, mostly from west Texas.[15] It served in the Union occupation of Brownsville in November 1863.

A British officer, Lieutenant Colonel James Arthur Fremantle, visited Colonel Duff in April 1863. He recorded that "in the neighborhood of San Antonio, one third of the population is German and many of them were at first by no means loyal to the Confederate cause. They objected much to the conscription, and some even resisted by force for arms. But these were soon settled by Duff's regiment, and it is said they are now reconciled to the new regime."[16] But the Germans were not reconciled. Most of them continued to resist conscription until the end of the war. The

Confederate authorities eventually relaxed the effort to conscript them into the Confederate army and allowed them to serve in militia units for local defense in west Texas.[17]

Not all the Germans in west Texas avoided Confederate service. Several companies were recruited in Comal County, which included the large German community of New Braunfels. One of these companies was initially commanded by Gustav Hoffman, the first mayor of New Braunfels, who later commanded the 7th Texas Cavalry.[18] There were a number of Germans from west Texas among the men of the 4th Texas Mounted Volunteers captured by Union forces during the battle of Glorietta Pass in New Mexico. They told their guards, who were Germans in the 1st Colorado, that they had been compelled to enlist or lose their farms.[19] Wilhelm Kaufmann wrote that 300 Confederates, "mostly Germans from Texas who had been compelled to serve in the Confederacy," surrendered at Arkansas Post in January 1863 and that most of them subsequently joined the Union army.[20]

Not all the Germans in Texas were Hill Country farmers. Some Germans had taken jobs in east Texas where they were closely associated with planters from the Deep South who were operating cotton plantations with slaves. A substantial German community in Galveston, the principal cotton-exporting port on the Texas Gulf Coast, furnished 140 infantrymen, two cavalry companies, and an artillery battery to the Confederate army.[21] Some of these Germans eventually became disenchanted with Confederate service. A German engineer, Captain Dietz, one of the designers of the fortifications at Galveston, deserted in 1864 and was later killed while serving as a Union officer in Virginia.[22] In March 1865 a Union ship picked up seven Germans who had deserted from the German artillery battery near Galveston; they had enlisted for one year, but been forced to serve for four. They gave Union officers a detailed report on the defenses of Galveston.[23]

There is also substantial evidence of Unionist sentiment and disaffection among the 24,614 Germans who were in Louisiana in 1860. Wilhelm Kaufmann, who contacted many Germans for his postwar study of the Germans in the Civil War, concluded that there had been "only isolated secessionists among the Germans of New Orleans. . . . Very many of them fled to the North at the start of the war."[24] William Watson, a Scot in Baton Rouge, recalled that the Germans had not "shown any marked zeal for the secession movement."[25] The slow recruiting for the 20th Louisiana, planned as an all-German regiment, and other evidence suggests that many Germans in New Orleans were reluctant to enlist in the Confederate army during the year that the Confederates controlled the city. Although there had been 19,729 Germans in New Orleans in 1860, the European Brigade organized in 1861 to contribute to the defense of the city reportedly included only 400 "Germans, Dutch, and Scandinavians."[26] The Confederate conscription act had not yet been implemented when the city was occupied by Union forces in April 1862. If the Germans in Louisiana had served in proportion to their numbers, there would have been about 3,200 of them in Confederate service; Kaufmann thought only about half that number had served.[27]

Ella Lonn asserted that the Confederate soldiers who mutinied and surrendered at Fort Jackson in 1862—when Union forces attacked the downriver fort protecting New Orleans—were mostly Germans.[28] In the Confederate court of inquiry on the Union capture of New Orleans, the mutineers at Fort Jackson were described only as "Europeans" but a Confederate officer testified that "a large portion of the German population was disloyal." When a civilian witness was asked about the determination of the population to resist the Union invasion, he replied that "the Germans took no active part."[29] A U.S. Navy officer reported that "the news of our squadron's approach to New Orleans caused some Union expressions on the part of some of the foreign population of New Orleans, and some 25 to 20 Germans were shot down on the levee, according to the account of one of our prisoners, who was present and saw it done."[30] The *Official Records* amply document General Butler's problems with the French and British residents of New Orleans, but they contain no indication of problems with the German residents. Ella Lonn wrote that "at Corinth, Mississippi, 400 Germans from a Louisiana regiment which had been sent out on outpost duty came into the federal lines in a body with white flags on their guns." She thought they were from the 20th Louisiana, the only Louisiana regiment with that many Germans.[31] There were undoubtedly many Germans among the 5,200 white men from Louisiana who joined the Union army, including many of the Germans who surrendered at Fort Jackson in 1862.

Historians have paid more attention to the considerable disaffection among the Germans in Virginia. Although the census showed 10,512 Germans in Virginia in 1860, only 1,623 of them were in Richmond and a sizable group of the Germans were far away at Wheeling on the Ohio River. One of the Virginia Germans, Hermann Schurich, wrote after the war that "not a single German Virginian, of American or German birth, was in favor of secession. . . . All recently immigrated Germans who joined the Confederacy did so with bleeding hearts and under compelling circumstances."[32] Erich W. Bright noted that "a substantial number of Richmond's German-Americans fled the Confederation during the war's first month."[33] In a book on the Germans in Virginia, Klaus Wust noted that "Germans who were not yet naturalized turned to the consul of Bremen, the only German state represented in Richmond, who obliged by issuing certificates showing nativity and citizenship. For a while, the enrollment officers respected such makeshift papers, but later they were of little avail."[34] The German rifle company from Richmond, a former militia unit that had seen action at the first battle of Bull Run as Company K of the 1st Virginia, was dissolved in May 1862 after its captain, Frederick W. Hagemeyer, and three others had been charged with desertion.[35] In January 1863 Confederate authorities arrested Frederick William Lohgman, a former lieutenant in the German rifle company, on the charge of running an "underground railroad" to the North for Germans.[36] A German scholar, Andrea Mehrlaender, discovered recently that between 1862 and 1864 a total of 384 Germans were arrested by the provost marshal in Richmond without stated charges; she attributed these arrests to the mistrust by the Confederate authorities of the loyalty of these Germans to the Confederate cause.[37] The numerous Germans at Wheeling did not have to flee from Confederate Virginia; after Virginia seceded from the Union, the western Virginia counties seceded from Virginia and formed a new Union state, West Virginia.

In 1860 there were 1,944 Germans in Charleston and about 1,000 more in several inland communities in South Carolina. There had been German militia units in Charleston since the 1830s. A German artillery unit from Charleston participated in the bombardment of Fort Sumter in April 1861 and fought valiantly but vainly in the defense of Hilton Head island against a massive Union attack in November 1861. The unit's German-born commander, John A. Wagener, told his men after the battle that he knew they would have died to a man rather than bring disgrace to the Germans in their "adopted Fatherland." "Let no man hereafter dare to asperse your patriotism!"[38] Wagener was later commander of South Carolina troops defending Charleston during the Union siege of 1863–64.

But many of the Germans in South Carolina tried to avoid or escape from service in the Confederate army. The Prussian consul in Charleston reported in December 1862 that 300 Germans had appealed for consular certification of foreign citizenship to avoid service in the army or militia.[39] George B. Shealy, a local historian in Walhalla—a farming community in upland South Carolina founded by Germans from Charleston—wrote that during the war the area "became a place of refuge for many Charlestonians and residents of the low country" and that "many deserters came to the area and hid out in tunnels, caves, and coves in the mountains to avoid service."[40] General Wagener commented that "many from the coast who did not want to participate in the war had found a way to bed themselves securely away [in Walhalla] from the Union cannons."[41] Most of those who chose a mainly German-speaking community as a refuge were probably German immigrants. In October 1864 the commander of a Union ship near Charleston reported that he had picked up eleven members of a German artillery battery who had deserted from their post on the South Carolina coast: "The deserters report great dissatisfaction among the troops, particularly the Germans, who, they say, would desert without an exception were they not so strictly guarded."[42]

The 1860 census showed 1,623 Germans in Savannah and 849 more in other Georgia communities. In the summer of 1864 the governor of Georgia proclaimed that foreign-born men living in Georgia must either volunteer for militia service or leave the state within ten days.[43] The Prussian consul in Charleston reported that several hundred Germans from Georgia had chosen the latter option and had arrived in Charleston, hoping to make their way to the North.[44]

Mobile, another important Southern port, had 1,276 German residents in 1860, and 1,325 Germans lived elsewhere in Alabama. The German Fusiliers of Mobile, a militia company that dated from the late 1840s, became Company H of the 8th Alabama. A German who escaped from Mobile in February 1864 told Union officers that many of the men defending Mobile, "particularly the Germans and the Irish, are tired of the war and will desert at the first opportunity."[45]

Before the war many Germans had been employed, as were many Irishmen, on the docks and steamboats on the Mississippi. Memphis had 1,412 Germans, a number that had tripled during the 1850s. There were several reports of disaffection by Germans who were in Confederate service along the Mississippi. Brigadier General Ulysses S. Grant reported in December 1861 that he had sent a German-speaking spy to the Confederate stronghold at Columbus, Kentucky; the agent learned that about 1,200 Germans and 600 Irish "intend to turn upon the garrison as soon as they feel there is any security in doing so when an attack is made."[46] In 1864 a cavalry company consisting of eighty Germans and twenty Frenchmen deserted from a Confederate camp in southern Missouri and made its way to a Union camp in St. Louis, where the Germans joined German regiments.[47]

The extent of a German's support for, or hostility toward, the Confederate cause was mainly influenced by his level of education or training and his economic situation and location in the South. The poorest and least educated German immigrants were mostly in the Deep South and were most likely to share the fears of their Irish counterparts that emancipated blacks would compete with them for jobs at the bottom of the economic ladder. Many of the middle-class Germans were in businesses or professions in the Deep South that were highly dependent on the goodwill and patronage of slaveowners. Both these groups thought their economic self-interests were best served by supporting their Confederate "friends, brothers, and neighbors."

On the other hand, many of the middle-class Germans (including many of the German farmers in Texas) were educated men who had fought in or sympathized with the abortive democratic revolution in Germany in 1848 and now found their political freedom and their economic status in America severely endangered. The German farmers in the Texas Hill Country were led by intellectuals determined to build free and liberal German communities in an area suitable for relatively small and self-sufficient farms operated without the use of slaves. They were not dependent on slave labor or—until the war—on the goodwill of slaveowners. Their friends and neighbors were not slaveowners. The Confederate conscription program threatened their liberty and their livelihood and attempted to force them to support a cause they abhorred. Many of them managed to stay on their farms, but many of the young men escaped across the Rio Grande and joined the Union army. Other Germans in the South—whose prewar livelihood had disappeared and who had no strong ties to the South—gladly took advantage of any opportunity to escape from the Confederacy.

Some authors have suggested that there were about 10,000 Germans in the Confederate army, but this estimate is greatly exaggerated. If the Germans in the South had provided the same percentage of soldiers as the total Confederate population (13.1 percent), there would have been about 9,000 Germans in gray. But the number of potential Germans in gray was greatly reduced by the subtraction of four sizable (if somewhat overlapping) groups: (a) those men of military age among the 19,729 Germans in New Orleans who had not enlisted prior to the Union occupation of the city in April 1862 and were thereafter beyond the reach of Confederate conscription; (b) those among the Germans in Texas who successfully resisted conscription; (c) those Germans throughout the Confederacy who were able to prove that they were "undomiciled" aliens and thus exempt from Confederate conscription; and (d) the sizable number of Germans who managed to leave the Confederacy during the war, including those who subsequently joined the Union army. A German scholar, Michael Loeffler, has estimated that about 2,000 Germans from the South joined Union regiments. Although there are no estimates of the size of the other groups listed above, it seems likely that the total number of Germans in gray was closer to 5,000 than to 10,000.

During the war only a handful of Germans came from Germany to observe or participate in the Confederate army. While U.S. minister to Spain in 1861, Carl Schurz heard from the Prussian minister that "a large portion of the Prussian aristocracy and many of the army officers sympathized with the rebellious Southern Confederacy. They hated democracy and thus hoped for the collapse of the U.S. republic."[48] But the powerful king of Prussia, soon to be the emperor of a united German empire, thought that Prussian and German geopolitical interests would be best served by a strong and united America. A considerable number of Prussian officers obtained leave to fight in the Union army, but only a very few Prussian officers came to the South during the war. There is no indication why any of these officers were allowed to come to the Confederacy.

The most prominent of the Prussian volunteer officers was Heros Von Borcke. Born into an aristocratic family in Prussian Pomerania, Von Borcke was on the staff of the Crown Prince of Prussia in 1861 but somehow obtained leave to come to America. He ran the blockade in May 1862 and soon joined the staff of the Confederate cavalry general, J.E.B. Stuart. Major Von Borcke's roles during a year on

Stuart's staff have been variously described as assistant adjutant, inspector general, or chief of staff, but he was also an active combatant. In June 1863 he was severely wounded at Middleburg, Virginia. A mini-ball lodged in his lung; his life was in danger for several months, but he gradually recovered. On January 30, 1864, the Confederate Congress gave Von Borcke a unique honor by adopting the following resolution: "Whereas Major Heros von Borcke of Prussia, . . . having left his own country to assist in securing the independence of ours, and by his personal gallantry in the field having won the admiration of his comrades. . . . Therefore, . . . the thanks of Congress are . . . hereby tendered, to Major von Borcke for his self-sacrificing devotion to our Confederacy and for his distinguished services in support of its cause."[49] Jefferson Davis sent him the resolution with the comment that it was "expressive of their admiration of the generous devotion you have shown to the welfare of a foreign people, and of their thanks for the gallant and efficient service you have rendered in the effort to secure their political independence."[50] General Lee wrote that "Major Von Borcke is an officer of singular worth and merit, of great zeal and gallantry."[51] Von Borcke was eventually promoted to colonel.

In the winter of 1864–65 Von Borcke was sent on a mission to London for the Confederate government; the possible objectives of this mission are reviewed in Chapter 23. He arrived in London only a few weeks before the Confederate surrender. A writer from Richmond, John R. Thompson, converted Von Borcke's diary in German into a polished narrative in English of his year with General Stuart. It appeared serially in the prestigious *Blackwood's Edinburgh Magazine* and was published as a two-volume book, *Memoirs of the Confederate War for Independence*, in London in 1866. A version in German was also published in Germany. The book contains no explanation of his reasons for joining the Confederate army; it ends with comments that he was glad the mission to England saved him from "the grief of being an eyewitness of the rapid collapse of the Confederacy and the downfall of a just and noble cause" and that "I shall ever rejoice that I drew my sword for the gallant people of the late Confederacy."[52]

Justus Scheibert, a captain in the Prussian engineer corps, probably contributed more to the Confederate cause than Von Borcke. He was ordered to America in January 1863 by the chief of his corps to observe the effects of artillery fire on fortifications and on armored ships. Under the original orders, he was to have been an official military observer with the Union army. But Scheibert, a strong Confederate sympathizer, somehow convinced the Prussian high command to send him instead to the Confederate army.[53] During the entire Gettysburg campaign, he was at Lee's or Stuart's headquarters. At first he acted only as a neutral observer. But at some point he decided to doff this status and become a combatant in the Confederate army. William S. Hoole wrote that Scheibert was "a sort of military handyman, making maps, helping build bridges, and otherwise making himself militarily useful."[54]

A few days after the battle at Gettysburg, General Lee sent Scheibert to the Potomac to assist a Confederate crew that was attempting to rebuild a pontoon bridge across the river. Evidence presented in Chapter 15 suggests that this Prussian engineer made a crucial contribution to the reconstruction of the bridge and to the escape to Virginia of Lee's army with its equipment as well as vast amounts of food and other supplies captured by the Confederates in Maryland and Pennsylvania. Scheibert's book on his experiences in America was published in Berlin in 1874. An English translation, *Seven Months in the Rebel States during the North American War, 1863*, was published in America in 1958.

Another Prussian engineer, Victor Von Scheliha, contributed significantly to the Confederate defense of Mobile. No information is available on his background in Germany or on the date or circumstances of his arrival in America. In the spring of 1863 Lieutenant Colonel Von Scheliha was chief of staff to General Simon Bolivar Buckner; that fall he was chief engineer at Mobile. An English officer, Captain Fitzgerald Ross, met him there in February 1864: "The Colonel is engaged in erecting a new line of forts round Mobile, which are perfect models of strength and judicious arrangements. They are built entirely of sand, with revetments of turf along. The turf on the embankments is fastened down to the sand by slips of the Cherokee rose, an exceedingly prickly shrub, which when grown will become a very disagreeable obstacle to a storming party. Mobile . . . will soon be one of the mostly strongly fortified places in the world."[55]

Although Von Borcke, Scheibert, Von Scheliha, and a few other nonimmigrant Germans made important contributions to the Confederate cause, German volunteers were much more numerous and made a more significant total contribution in the Union army. The reactions to the war of German immigrants in the South depended mainly on their economic status and their degree of dependence on the goodwill of slaveowners. Those Germans in areas that grew or exported cotton usually had a major (if frequently indirect) economic stake in the maintenance of the status quo in the South, while the German farmers in the Texas Hill Country were not economically dependent on slaves or slaveowners. In contrast the Irish in the South, discussed in the next chapter, were rarely independent of slaveowners and feared competition by emancipated slaves for low-paying jobs.

Chapter 10

They Caught *the* Spirit
of the Community
Irish *in the* South

I n 1860, 83,874 of the residents of future Confederate states had been born in
Ireland. A third of these—28,207 persons—were in Louisiana, mostly in or near
New Orleans. There were 16,512 Irish in Virginia, including some in the western Virginia counties that refused to secede from the United States and seceded
instead from Virginia; 12,498 were in Tennessee, mostly along the Mississippi; and
26,657 more were in the eight other Confederate states.

About half of the Irish immigrants (40,566 persons) lived in six Southern
cities. Ships bearing cotton from Southern ports to Liverpool, gateway to the cotton mills of Lancashire, offered low fares to immigrants on their return trips. In
addition to the large Irish settlement (24,398) in New Orleans, there were 4,159
Irish in Memphis, 3,263 in Charleston, 3,307 in Mobile, 3,145 in Savannah, and
2,294 in Richmond. Most of the rest of the Irish were in other Southern cities or
had been attracted to rural areas by jobs in land clearance or the construction of
canals, levees, or railroads. Very few Irish immigrants lived on plantations.

The Irish took the most menial, difficult, and/or dangerous jobs in the South.
They were construction workers, stevedores, hackmen, draymen, and riverboat men,
as well as waiters and servants. Many of these jobs had previously been filled by slaves
or free blacks, and the Irish felt they were in direct competition with the blacks for
these jobs. They were often hired for work that was considered too dangerous or
debilitating for valuable slaves. In her study of foreigners in the Confederacy, Ella
Lonn noted that "the labor of digging ditches and trenches, of clearing the waste
lands, of hewing down the forests on the plantations, and of repairing the levees was

generally done by the Irish laborers." The planters thought "it was much better to use the Irish, who cost nothing to the planter if they died, 'than to use up good field hands in such severe employment.'"[1] The overseer of a plantation near New Orleans, describing to William Howard Russell the intense labor of clearing swamp land, said "this work is death on negroes. Generally it is done . . . by Irishmen."[2]

Many Irishmen were employed in the loading and unloading of cotton on steamboats and oceangoing ships. Lonn noted that "Negroes were shielded from dangerous posts . . . in . . . the loading of a boat with cotton. Negro hands were sent to the top of the bank to roll the bales to the top of gangway, down which they slid with fearful velocity. Irishmen were at the foot of the gangway to move them into place. The callous reason given for this division of labor was that 'the niggers are worth too much to be risked here; if the Paddies are knocked overboard, or get their backs broke, nobody loses anything.'"[3] A riverboat pilot explained to a traveler that slaves were rarely used on older steamboats with dangerous boilers: "Every time a boiler bursts they would lose so many dollar's worth of slaves, where by getting Irishmen at a dollar a-day they pay for the article as they get it, and if it is blown up, they get another."[4]

Norman C. McLeod, who studied the Irish in antebellum Richmond, wrote that they "competed with Richmond's black laborers . . . for dirty, distasteful, backbreaking work that many southern white men refused."[5] Many of these jobs were in the iron industry. The Tredegar Iron Works in Richmond was the only sizable rolling mill in the South; it would play a crucial role as the Confederacy's only plant capable of producing heavy armaments and equipment and would provide exemption from conscription for many Irish workers.[6]

The Irish in the South supported the Confederacy more consistently and in larger numbers than any other immigrant group. Several interrelated reasons have been identified for the enlistment of Irishmen in the Confederate army. The first was a general feeling of solidarity with the people of the South. Just after the war John Francis Maguire, an Irish member of the British parliament, made a thorough study of Irish reactions to the war in both North and South. He wrote that in both regions the Irish "caught the spirit of the community of whom they formed part."[7] "I am with the South in life or in death, in victory or defeat," a future Confederate general, Patrick Cleburne, wrote his brother on the day Arkansas seceded from the Union. "These people have been my friends."[8] Merely by volunteering, the Irish gained status in the eyes of native-born Americans. "By donning a Confederate soldier's uniform," wrote James P. Gannon, author of a history of the 6th Louisiana, "they would take on the cloak of loyal sons of the South and show skeptical Southerners that they were not foreigners but new Americans."[9]

A second major motive for Irish enlistment was to maintain slavery in the South and prevent emancipated slaves from taking Irish jobs. Although they were near the bottom of the economic ladder, the Irish in the South had found a better life in America than they had had in Ireland. By enlisting to fight for "the Southern way of life," the Irish in the South were fighting to maintain their improved status in America and to prevent social and economic changes that threatened their status and livelihood. David T. Gleeson, the Irish-born author of a recent study of the Irish in the South in the mid-nineteenth century, wrote that "the Irish supported African slavery in the South. . . . Slavery . . . made them members of the 'ruling race.'. . . The oppressive slave society . . . provided more freedom and opportunity than they had ever attained in Ireland. . . . The Irish supported secession when it seemed the only option to prevent the destruction of the institution that had helped to give them their status in the South."[10]

Irish support for the Confederate cause was strongly bolstered by the Catholic priests in the South, most of whom were born in Ireland. Several Catholic bishops in the Southern cities were outspoken supporters of slavery and secession. Gleeson wrote that "advice from the hierarchy was very significant in influencing the Irish men's decision to join the Confederate army. . . . If Irish priests and bishops had opposed the Confederacy, it is likely that there would have been only a few Irish volunteers for the cause."[11] A number of Irish priests served as chaplains of Confederate units and did everything they could to sustain the Irish contribution to the Confederate cause.

Irishmen in the South also enlisted to protect their families and communities from a threatened invasion. "The North is about to wage a brutal and unholy war," Cleburne wrote his brother; "they are about to invade our peaceful homes, destroy our property, inaugurate a servile insurrection, murder our men, and dishonour our women."[12] Lieutenant Colonel Walter P. Lane of the Third Texas Cavalry, who was born in Cork, wrote that the "patriotic purpose" of each soldier in his command was "driving back the deluded bigots who had invaded our soil."[13]

Many Irishmen volunteered because they needed a job. A great many of them had supported themselves with a series of temporary jobs, especially the construction of railroads, canals, or levees or clearing swamps. When the war came, funds for such projects dried up and many Irishmen were unemployed. By early 1862, 3,788 Irish families in New Orleans were receiving support from the relief fund established by the city council.[14] Kelly J. O'Grady, who studied the Irish in Lee's army, wrote that many Irish volunteers "took army service as the best available work."[15] The author of a book on the Irish in New Orleans, Earl F. Niehaus, commented that the Irish laborer, who was "accustomed to signing on with construction gangs for work outside the city, regarded soldiering as an exciting variety of gang work."[16]

Estimates of the number of Irishmen in the Confederate army have been exaggerated by writers who were eager to inflate the Irish contribution to the Confederacy. John Mitchell, an Irish nationalist who edited a Richmond newspaper, wrote in

1863 that 40,000 Irishmen were serving in Confederate armies. Although one author has called this a "generally accepted number," Gleeson has suggested that a more plausible estimate would be around 20,000.[17] If the Irish-born men in the South had served in the same proportion as the Confederate population as a whole (13.1 percent), the number of Irish-born in the Confederate army would have been around 11,000. Although the large percentage of young single men among Irish immigrants and the high unemployment among Irishmen who had previously worked on railroad, canal, and levee projects tended to produce disproportionately high Irish enlistments, these factors were offset in a large degree by the claim of exemption from service by some Irish on the grounds of British citizenship and by the early Union occupation of the Confederate city with the largest Irish population—New Orleans—before Confederate conscription was implemented. It therefore seems likely that the number of Irish-born in gray was well below 20,000.

There was no predominantly Irish regiment in the Confederate army. In New Orleans—the only city with enough Irish to allow the recruitment of an all-Irish regiment—competition between recruiters was probably responsible for the division of the Irish volunteers among several regiments. There were three Irish companies in the 6th Louisiana and four Irish companies in the 20th Louisiana, which was originally planned as an all-German regiment. The 10th Tennessee, apparently drawn from the large Irish settlements in and around Memphis, was heavily Irish and is said to have been the only Confederate regiment that carried a green flag into battle. In most other areas, the numbers of Irishmen were only large enough to permit the recruitment of one or two Irish companies. O'Grady provided information on forty-five distinctly Irish infantry companies in Lee's Army of Northern Virginia. More than half—twenty-eight companies—were from Louisiana. There were also nine companies from Virginia, five from Georgia, two from South Carolina, and one each from Alabama and Mississippi. O'Grady estimated that these companies contained about 4,000 men.[18] There were also many Irish companies in the Confederate armies in the "west."

Some Irish companies were recruited from clusters of Irishmen engaged in similar work. The three Irish companies in the 6th Louisiana had many stevedores from the New Orleans wharves and numerous construction workers who had dug canals in New Orleans. Several companies were made up mainly of railroad workers, including companies from Lynchburg in the 11th Virginia, from Alexandria in the 17th Virginia, from the Shenandoah Valley in the 33rd Virginia, and from Nashville in the 10th Tennessee.

As in the North, the Irish companies flaunted their Irishness in various ways. Most of them were known by an Irish name such as "the Emerald Guards" or "Virginia Hibernians" or were named for an Irish dignitary. An Irish company from New Orleans was originally known as the "Meagher Rifles," but the indignant volunteers changed the name to "Mitchell Guards" after the first Irish namesake joined the Union army. A few of the companies had green uniforms or banners. The "Montgomery Guards" of the 1st Virginia began the war in green and gold uniforms. The "Emmett Guards" of the 17th Virginia were clad in green fatigue jackets and green trousers. The original flag of the Irish company in the 19th Georgia was green with a harp and shamrock.

In several battles, Irishmen in the Confederate army directly confronted Irishmen in the Union army. At the first Bull Run, the Irish company in the 1st Virginia met the Irishmen of the 69th New York, later a regiment of the Irish Brigade. At Freeman's Farm, the "Emerald Guards" of the 8th Alabama fought the Irish Brigade. At Corinth, the "Fighting Irish" company of the Confederate 5th Missouri, who were mostly from St. Louis, faced Unionist Irish from St. Louis in the 14th Missouri, a Union regiment. At Fredericksburg, the Confederate units that rose from the Sunken Road to meet the assault of the Irish Brigade included the Irish company in the 1st Virginia and two Irish companies in Cobb's brigade of Georgians. A British observer, Lieutenant Colonel James Arthur Fremantle, remarked that "Southern Irishmen . . . have no sort of scruple in killing as many of their Northern brethren as they possibly can."[19]

Several Confederate generals praised the contribution of the Irish to the Confederate war effort. General Beauregard wrote that the Irish "displayed the sturdy and manly courage of the English, combined with the impetuous and buoyant character of the French. They required, at times, only discipline . . . to be equal to the best soldiers of any country. They always exhibited on the field of battle great gallantry, and during the operations of a campaign showed much patience and fortitude."[20] General Simon Bolivar Buckner recorded that the Irishmen in Cleburne's command had "illustrated their high military virtues on many fields and displayed on so many occasions their fidelity to the cause they had espoused."[21] During the capture of Fort Henry, Brigadier General Lloyd Tilghman said of the mainly Irish 10th Tennessee: "I place them second to no regiment I have seen in the army."[22] At Shiloh, Major General B. F. Cheatham was impressed by the Irish and German troops in the 2nd Tennessee and 15th Tennessee: "Whether dashing forward in the charge or contesting ground inch by inch against overpowering numbers, their gallantry and steady courage in behalf of their adopted country equaled that of the native standing for his home."[23] Brigadier General Richard Taylor, son of President Zachary Taylor, thought the Irishmen in the 6th Louisiana "were stout, hardy fellows, turbulent in camp and requiring a strong hand, but responding to kindness and justice, and ready to follow their officers to the death."[24]

Although the Irish in the South supported the Confederate cause more consistently than the British or Germans, some of the Irish managed to avoid or escape from Confederate service. Many of those applying to British consuls for certificates of

British citizenship—as a means of avoiding conscription—were Irishmen. The Irish company in the 15th Virginia was disbanded in June 1862 because so many of the soldiers had claimed exemption from service as noncitizens. As the war went on, desertion rates, which were high in many Confederate units, were especially high in units with a large percentage of Irishmen. About one-third of the men in the 6th Louisiana's three Irish companies either deserted or took the Union oath of allegiance after capture.[25] Gleeson noted that a study of desertion rates in Louisiana regiments demonstrated that "Irish soldiers deserted more often than their native-born colleagues."[26]

Most Irish deserters merely took advantage of an opportunity to escape from the war. Married Irishmen often deserted after receiving pleas for their return from wives beset with horrendous problems at home. Gleeson asserted that the high desertion rate in Irish units is explained by the waning of support for the war among Irish Confederate civilians.[27] Many Irishmen deserted after serving for the period of their original enlistment. Seven Irishmen, who refused to continue to serve after completing a three-year enlistment in the South Carolina Artillery, were thrown in a Confederate prison but managed to escape.[28]

A significant number of Irish in gray decided—before or after capture by Union forces—to abandon the Confederacy and join the Union army. Most of these were presumably young single immigrants who did not have strong ties in the South. As indicated earlier, Union officers received a report late in 1861 that 600 Irish as well as 1,200 Germans of Colombus, Kentucky, "intended to turn upon the garrison" if the Confederate stronghold were attacked by the forces of Brigadier General Ulysses S. Grant.[29] There were apparently many Irishmen among the 250 "Europeans" who mutinied and surrendered in April 1862 at Fort Jackson, on the Mississippi below New Orleans, after a heavy bombardment by Union gunboats. Later that year the Irish 9th Connecticut recruited 350 Irishmen from surrendered Confederate troops in New Orleans, including those who had surrendered at Fort Jackson.[30] In September 1863 between 100 and 200 Irish prisoners at Camp Morton in Indiana were reported to be ready to volunteer for the Irish 35th Indiana.[31] Colonel James A. Mulligan's "Irish Brigade," the 23rd Illinois, gained forty new recruits who had formerly fought in the Confederate army.[32] There were many Irish prisoners from Texas among those at Camp Butler in Illinois who were reported to be ready "to take the oath of allegiance and fight for the Union."[33]

In the two major Confederate cities occupied by Union forces in 1862—New Orleans and Memphis—many Irish civilians cooperated with the Union authorities. General Sherman allowed the Irish-born mayor of Memphis, John Park, to remain in office and to hire Irishmen for the Memphis police.[34] The *New Orleans City Guide*, published in 1938, contains this account of the reactions of Irish-born Father James Mullon, pastor of St. Patrick's Church, to the occupation of the city by Union troops led by General Benjamin F. Butler: "It was a daily custom to have the congregation unite in prayer after mass for the success of the Confederate cause. Butler sent word that the public prayers must cease. Father Mullon complied, but requested his congregation to pray in silence thereafter. At another time General Butler sent for Father Mullon and accused him of having refused burial to a Union soldier, to which the good Father replied that he stood ready to bury the whole Union force, General Butler included, whenever the occasion offered."[35] But many Irishmen, including the Irish editors of the *True Delta*, recognized that the Union occupation offered opportunities to rebuild the city's economy and create jobs for many Irishmen in the city. In 1864 Irish leaders played important roles in the formulation of Louisiana's new constitution, which provided voting rights to every Irish immigrant but denied the suffrage to most former slaves and free blacks.[36]

Chapter 11

DUTY TO CAUSE
AND COUNTRY

Britons *in the* South

I n 1860 there were 24,559 persons in the future Confederate states who were
born in Britain, exclusive of Ireland. They included 17,110 English, 7,109 Scots,
and 950 Welsh.[1] The Confederate state with the largest number of Britons was
Louisiana, which had 3,989 English and 1,051 Scots. Although there were 4,104
English and 1,398 Scots in Virginia in 1860, many of them were in the western
counties that formed West Virginia and remained in the Union. The remaining
14,090 Britons in the Confederacy were widely distributed among the other nine
future Confederate states.

Unlike the Irish and Germans in the Southeast, who were strongly concentrated in cities, only about 20 percent of the Britons in the South—5,270 persons—
lived in the major port cities. About 60 percent of these—3,042 persons—were in
New Orleans, with small British groups in Charleston, Richmond, Savannah, and
Memphis. Many of these Britons in port cities were involved with the export of cotton to Britain. The census data on the large numbers of Britons in inland areas supports other evidence that many Britons in the South were involved, directly or indirectly, with the production of cotton or with businesses providing essential services
to the plantations or plantation owners.

Despite the strong upper-class support for the Confederate cause in Britain, evidence of resistance by Britons in the South to pressures to join the Confederate
army is much more abundant than evidence of their enthusiastic support for the
Confederate cause. In resisting military service, most of these Britons were attempting to serve their own personal interests rather than opposing the independence of

the Confederacy or the maintenance of slavery in the South. Milledge L. Bonham, who studied British consuls in the Confederacy, noted that many of the British residents in the South "had taken out naturalization papers for 'business reasons,' yet considered themselves British subjects in loyalty and feeling."[2] Others had married, voted, acquired property, and/or joined the militia without becoming citizens. When the war came, they strongly reasserted their status as British subjects, even though the Confederate government considered them "domiciled" aliens subject to conscription.

In the spring of 1861 William Howard Russell reported to *The Times* from New Orleans that many reluctant Britons were subjected to violent pressures to enlist: "British subjects . . . have been seized, knocked down, carried off from their labor at the wharf and workshop, and forced by violence to serve in the 'volunteer' ranks. These cases are not isolated. . . . These men have been dragged along like felons, protesting in vain that they were British subjects."[3] Another day he wrote that "the British consulate was thronged today by Irish, English, and Scotch, entreating to be sent North or to Europe. . . . For the third or fourth time, I heard cases of British subjects being forcibly carried off to fill the ranks of so-called volunteer companies and regiments. In some instances they have been knocked down, bound, and confined in barracks, till in despair they consented to serve."[4] The *New York Times* proclaimed in August that every strong able-bodied fellow in New Orleans not obtrusively attached to British allegiance is liable to a most unpleasant degree of persuasion to join some volunteer corps or other. He . . . is liable to be pounced upon, . . . and unless he should have a friend to go to the British consul and plead his foreign allegiance, be marched off to the seat of war."[5]

British consuls in the major Southern seaports were besieged by Britons seeking certification of British citizenship and/or a means of leaving the Confederacy. The consuls sent a series of protests of these forced enlistments to state and Confederate authorities. A Virginia official stated that Virginia law required military duty only by citizens, but he also noted that "it is a well-settled principle of national law that a subject of a foreign power may be enlisted in the defense of the country wherein he may be resident when that country is not at war with the nation to which he belongs."[6] But the British minister, Lord Lyons, insisted in a circular to the British consuls that "no state can justly frame laws to compel aliens resident within its territories to serve against their will in armies ranged against each other in civil war."[7] When Louisiana authorities attempted to enforce a law requiring all men in the state between eighteen and forty-five to perform militia duty, the British consul in New Orleans, George Coppell, told the governor that "the service imposed upon British subjects was contrary to the law of nations and placed them beyond that neutral position which had been enjoined upon them by their government."[8]

The enactment of the Confederate conscription law in April 1862 sparked a new round of British protests. In a circular to British diplomats and consuls, the Foreign Office in London condemned "the forcible enlistment of British subjects in the army of the so-called Confederate states." It argued that Britons could not be forcibly enlisted under an *ex post facto* law if no such law existed at the time they established domicile in America. The Foreign Office proclaimed that voluntary enlistments by British subjects were forbidden by the Queen's proclamation of neutrality and forced enlistments were forbidden by "the plainest notions of reason and justice." British consuls were instructed to make these points to the "*de facto* authorities" in the Confederacy.[9]

In a letter to a British consul, an assistant secretary of war in Richmond summarized Confederate policies regarding military service by foreigners in the South. Foreign-born volunteers who had not established "domicile" in America would be released from service at the expiration of their original term of enlistment. Foreign residents who had not established domicile would be exempt from conscription.[10] But the letter made it no easier to determine who had established domicile and who had not. Those who had accepted naturalization had little hope of avoiding conscription. A British officer, Lieutenant Colonel Fremantle, met an English mechanic in Texas who "deplored . . . that he had been such a fool as to naturalize himself, as he was in hourly dread of the conscription."[11]

The protests of the forcible enlistment or conscription of persons claiming to be British subjects created much bad blood between the consuls and Confederate authorities. In May 1863 the British consul in Richmond, George Moore, wrote a private letter in which he stated that "I have lived for thirty-two consecutive years in despotic countries, and . . . have met in those countries more official courtesy and consideration from the local authorities . . . than I met [here] on at the hands of my own blood and lineage."[12] The letter fell into the hands of the Confederate Secretary of State, Judah P. Benjamin, who notified Moore that he was banished from the Confederacy.

As Confederate manpower problems became more desperate during 1863, several states took steps to force unnaturalized aliens to join state militia units. The governor of Georgia, Joseph E. Brown, proclaimed that "any unnaturalized foreigner living under the protection of our Government and laws . . . is bound to defend his domicile and is liable to be drafted by the State and compelled to do so." Bonham summarized the governor's reply to a protest from Allan Fullarton, the British consul in Savannah: "It was impossible to retain amongst the Confederates a non-producing class of consumers who refused to bear arms. . . . The United States government was attempting to incite a servile insurrection, which would mean robbery, arson, butchering of women and children, and worse, to which British residents would be

as liable as anyone else. As many who claimed to be British subjects were slaveholders, they were as much interested in protecting their property and families as were
native Georgians." Fullarton replied that he felt compelled "to advise those drafted
to acquiesce in the duty until they are required to leave their immediate homes or to
meet United States forces in actual conflict; in that event, to throw down their arms
and refuse to render a service, the performance of which would run directly in the
teeth of Her Majesty's proclamation."[13] Fullarton's letter was the last straw. It convinced the Confederate government to terminate the consular status of all the
British consuls in the Confederacy.[14]

Even when the reluctant Britons in the Confederate armies were captured by
Union forces, they found no path to freedom. In July 1862 the war department
responded to a note from Lord Lyons regarding "British subjects, prisoners of war
in this country, who when captured by U.S. forces were serving against their will
in the ranks of the rebels." Lyons was informed that similar applications were
received almost daily, but "the Department has uniformly declined to inquire into
these cases."[15]

Some British civilians in the South were able to leave the Confederacy, either
by moving to the North or returning to Britain, but there is no estimate of the number who departed. Some British subjects had been denied passes through the Confederate lines but nonetheless managed to slip through.[16] The consul in Richmond
reported in 1863 that "there are numerous British workmen in the different government workshops who are very anxious to leave at their own expense, but are
refused passports."[17] A British warship, the *Cadmus*, visited Charleston when the
Union siege was imminent and took aboard the British consul and his family, but it
is not clear whether other British residents were allowed to depart with the ship.[18]

Despite the resistance of many Britons in the South to enlistment and conscription, many other Britons gracefully accepted service in the Confederate army.
There is very little direct evidence of the reasons that Britons enlisted. After the
war neither Britons still living in the South nor those who were back in Britain were
motivated to write about the reasons for their service on behalf of the Lost Cause in
the South. Nonetheless, several major reasons for enlistment can be established
from the available evidence.

A considerable number of the Britons fought to defend the "Southern way of
life" in which they had a strong personal interest. William Howard Russell reported
from the South in the spring of 1861 that many British in the South were strong
defenders of slavery: "Among . . . the most vehement friends of what are called

her 'domestic institutions' are the British residents . . . who have settled here for trading purposes and who are frequently slaveholders. These men . . . are convinced of the excellence of things as they are, or find it to their interest to be so."[19] "I meet many English people," he wrote in another report, "who are the most strenuous advocates of the slave system, although it is true that their perceptions may be quickened to recognize its beauties by their participation in the profits."[20] Henry Morton Stanley, who later who found Dr. Livingstone in Africa, recalled his reactions as a young British immigrant in Louisiana in 1861: "I was quite prepared to do all that was required, for I loved the South as I loved my Southern friends, and had absorbed their spirit in every pore."[21] William Watson, a Scot who had been in business in Baton Rouge, recalled he had been motivated to enlist in part by sympathy with the Confederate cause, although he had deplored secession and was highly critical of the Confederate leadership.[22]

One immigrant devoted to the Confederate cause was James Campbell, who was born in Scotland in 1835 and came to America in the early 1850s. He settled in Charleston; in 1862 he was a lieutenant in a company of Scots in the 1st South Carolina. Meanwhile, his brother Alexander, a stonecutter in New York, had joined the partly Scottish 79th New York "Highlanders." On June 16, 1862, both brothers fought in the battle of Secessionville; neither was aware that his brother was in the opposing army. A few days later a Confederate bearing a flag of truce brought a letter from to Alexander from James, who had learned that his brother had been in the battle: "I hope that you and I will never again meet face to face bitter enemies in the battlefield. But if such should be the case, you have but to discharge your duty to your cause, for I can assure you I will strive to discharge my duty to my country and my cause."[23]

Some Britons in the South were less certain about the Confederate cause, but were impelled to enlist by community pressure. William Watson, the Scot from Baton Rouge, wrote that "our firm would have . . . been regarded with suspicion had we . . . not contributed at least one man to the service. . . . I had been an active member of . . . the town volunteer company of riflemen. . . . To have . . . withdrawn from it in the hour of danger would not have been very creditable to myself and my countrymen [in] Scotland."[24] Watson also indicated very clearly that former Unionists in the South were forced to demonstrate their support of the Confederate cause in order to avoid severe persecution.

No author has estimated the number of Britons in the Confederate army. If the Britons in the South had served in the same proportion as the total population of the Confederacy, there would have been about 3,000 Britons in the Confederate army. But the evidence cited above of the efforts by Britons to evade enlistment and conscription, plus the early Union occupation of the city with the largest

British community in the South, strongly suggests that the number of Britons in the Confederate army was much smaller than 3,000. The only predominantly British military units in the Confederacy were small militia companies—in New Orleans, Mobile, and Richmond.

Four men born in Britain commanded Confederate regiments—James Duff (33rd Texas Cavalry), Collet Leventhorpe (11th North Carolina), Peter Alexander McGlashan (50th Georgia), and Robert Alexander Smith (10th Mississippi Rifles). Although Jefferson Davis nominated three British-born officers as brigadier generals in the last months of the war, no British-born officer served as a general in the Confederate army. Leventhorpe declined his appointment, McGlashan's commission never reached him, and the nomination of William M. Browne was rejected by the Confederate Senate.

Although there is no estimate of the number of British officers who crossed the Atlantic to fight for the Confederacy, the number was clearly much larger than the number of British officers who joined the Union army. Direct evidence of the motives of these officers is very limited. One motive was derived from the widespread conviction among the British upper classes that the Confederates were fighting for freedom from intolerable oppression. An unidentified "English combatant" wrote that he had been motivated to bear arms for the Southern cause by "that inherent love of liberty which animates every English heart" and by the "despotism which a blind and fanatical majority sought to thrust upon an unoffending and almost helpless minority."[25] A British observer, Captain Fitzgerald Ross, noted that "the foreigners who have taken service here have all been impelled to do so by their sympathy with the cause, which is in truth a very noble one."[26] Several English officers arriving at a Confederate proclaimed that "we come . . . like true knights errant to join as honorable volunteers the standard of the bravest lance in Christendom, that of the noble, peerless, Lee."[27] "Wherever and whenever a war of freedom is given," the *Examiner* in Richmond observed in 1863, "there Englishmen will be found, for glory only, for the natural bulldog love of fighting, and the inborn British love of the just cause and the weak side."[28]

Many of the officers crossed the Atlantic in the hope of acquiring experience and distinction that would help their future careers in the British army. Most of them served as staff officers for Confederate generals. They usually arrived with letters of introduction to Confederate leaders, who referred them to generals who needed competent staff officers. Generals selected their own staffs, but line officers were appointed by state governors or by the war department in Richmond. A staff position gave the British officer a good chance to observe large-scale operations and was less dangerous than service as a line officer. Any of these officers who had hoped to acquire experience as senior commanders were disappointed. No nonimmigrant Briton held a regimental or higher command in the Confederate army.

Some of the officers came to America to escape problems at home. Captain Ross noted that "in European armies numberless officers are obliged to quit their profession, mostly from having been extravagant; and to these 'soldiers of fortune' the American war has been a perfect godsend."[29]

Many of the nonimmigrant British officers were sons of British aristocrats. Charles Murray, later Lord Dunmore, was on Lee's staff. He was a descendent of Virginia's last Royal Governor. Lord Edward St. Maur, a member of the family of the Duke of Somerset, was on Longstreet's staff. Maurice Berkeley Portman, son of Viscount Portman, was an aide to General Wade Hampton. Henry Wemyss Fielden, son of a baronet, had been a British officer in Asia for seven years before joining Beauregard's staff. Major Hodges, son of an English lord, was also on Beauregard's staff. An officer who called himself Lord Charles Cavendish and claimed to be a cousin of the Duke of Devonshire and a former officer in the 18th Hussars was later discovered to have been only a sergeant or corporal in an English regiment.

There were also a number of British staff officers with no aristocratic pretensions. Colonel George A. Gordon was on the staffs of both General Stuart and General A. P. Hill, before being badly wounded in the Confederate charge at Gettysburg. Captain T. G. Peacock was assigned as an aide to General Pickett. Captain Francis W. Dawson, a university-educated Englishman, was an ordnance officer on Longstreet's staff. A former officer of a British infantry regiment, Captain Stephen Winthrop, was a conspicuously gallant member of Longstreet's staff. The son of an inspector of Cambridge police, Captain Davis, was on the staff of General Henry Heth, as was Captain Sidney Heth, probably an English relative of the general. Captain Edgar J. Franklin was General Drayton's staff. An English officer who lost a leg at Manassas, Captain Bryne, joined the staff of General Cleburne, a former enlisted man in the British army. Captain Llewellyn Sauderson was a staff officer for General Fitzhugh Lee. Captain John Cussons was an aide to General Law.

The strangest story of a British soldier of fortune in the Confederate army was that of Colonel George St. Leger Grenfel. He had previously served in French, British, Turkish, and Arab units in India, Turkey, Russia, and South America. Arriving in Charleston aboard a blockade runner in 1862, he served as adjutant general to General Morgan during Morgan's raid into Kentucky, as inspector of cavalry in Bragg's army in Tennessee, and as assistant inspector general of Stuart's cavalry corps in Virginia. Grenfel's association with Stuart was not a happy one, and Grenfel resigned shortly after a meeting with Jefferson Davis on April 11, 1864, about which nothing is known. He took a blockade runner to Nassau and a found a ship bound for New York. In Washington he convinced the secretary of war that he had deserted the Confederate cause; Stanton give him permission to travel freely in the

United States. Some weeks later Grenfel was arrested in Chicago on the charge that he had participated in a plot to liberate Confederate prisoners at Camp Douglas as the first phase of a revolt against the government by antiwar "copperheads" in the Midwest. Although he maintained that he was innocent, a military court found him guilty and sentenced him to death. In a book on Grenfel, Stephen Z. Starr stated that "facts which were not . . . known to the court, some of which did not come to light until many years later, prove his guilt beyond a doubt."[30]

The report of the judge advocate general to the president reflected the strong public feeling about the Grenfel case: "For the accused, . . . the subject of a foreign power at peace with our government . . . who . . . united himself with traitors and malefactors for the overthrow of our republic in the interests of slavery, . . . there can be neither sympathy nor respect. . . . It may be that the President will feel justified in sparing even so unworthy and dishonored a life as that of the accused. . . . If the death sentence is commuted, . . . the punishment substituted should be severe and infamous."[31] President Andrew Johnson set aside the death sentence, but Grenfel was sent to Dry Tortugas, a barren military post on an island off the Florida coast. In 1868 he escaped in a small boat, but it was swamped in a storm and no trace of Grenfel was ever found.[32]

Throughout the war, there were more British observers—correspondents, other civilian observers, and military observers—in the South than in the North. Many of them came with the intention to write an article or book on their experiences in the Confederacy, and most of them did so.

William Howard Russell, correspondent for the *The Times* of London, visited Charleston, Montgomery, Mobile, New Orleans, Jackson, and Memphis between mid-April and mid-June 1861. As the representative of the most influential newspaper in Britain at a time when Southerners had pinned great hopes on British recognition and support, Russell was warmly welcomed at the highest levels of the Confederate government and society. His letters to *The Times* were widely read in both North and South, were reprinted in New York as *Pictures of Southern Life, Political and Military* late in 1861 and recast as *My Diary North and South* after his return to England in 1862. Russell usually reported what he saw and heard, with few comments. Although he was considerably less sympathetic to the South than most of the British visitors, his opinions were usually concealed or muted to avoid offending his hosts in the South and his mainly pro-Confederate readers in Britain. In the end, however, Russell could not entirely conceal his opinions. Mary Chesnut, a leader of Richmond society, noted in her diary on August 16, 1861, that "Russell's letters are becoming utterly abominable."[33] He was the only correspondent who was strongly disliked in both North and South.

Francis Lawley, who represented *The Times* in the Confederacy from the summer of 1862 until the capture of Richmond in 1865, was never accused of opinions unsympathetic to the Confederacy. He was a son of Lord Wenlock, was educated at Oxford, and was briefly a Liberal MP and parliamentary private secretary to William Gladstone, but his political career had been terminated by gambling on horses. Lawley was based in Richmond for nearly three years, but frequently visited Confederate units and personally covered several major battles. A Prussian visitor, Captain Justus Scheibert, met him in 1863: "Lawley . . . was highly esteemed . . . as a gentleman and amiable man. . . . He excelled in tactful, restrained demeanor and in a calm view of things. . . . His reports were at that time the best that appeared in Europe concerning American affairs."[34] Yet William S. Hoole, author of a book on Lawley's coverage of the Confederacy, described him as "a very prejudiced reporter" and "a British propagandist for the Confederate states." "He believed the South unconquerable. . . . To Lawley the men of the Confederate high command . . . were all knights in shining armor. . . . In his boundless enthusiasm for the South, Lawley sometimes premised his communiqués more on hope than fact, more on wishful thinking than on reasoned logic."[35] The validity of Hoole's conclusions are amply demonstrated in the excerpts from Lawley's reports in later chapters of this book.

Samuel Phillips Day, correspondent for the London *Herald*, spent four months in the South from late May to late September 1861. His reports were compiled in a book, *Down South*, published in London in 1862. It reads like a manual for Confederate propagandists. He was totally negative toward the North, supported all Confederate viewpoints, and referred to Confederate forces as "our troops." A correspondent for the New York *Herald*, who was a fellow passenger on a boat to Baltimore, thought a reporter with such "secessh proclivities" should not be allowed to visit Union camps and fortifications. After the influential New York paper expressed the same view, Day was denied permission to visit Union camps. He decided to leave a country "where the liberty of the press is virtually ignored and free thought and free public opinion . . . are regarded as hostile to the interests of a nation which has vaunted so long and loudly for its free institutions."[36]

Frank Vizetelly covered the South in 1862 and 1863 as a reporter and artist for the *Illustrated London Times*. He had been a war correspondent in the Austrian-Sardinan war in 1859 and was with Garibaldi in Sicily in 1860. Vizetelly was initially in the North, covering the first battle of Bull Run and Burnside's expedition on the North Carolina coast. After problems about permission to accompany the Army of the Potomac, he came South in 1862. Another European recorded that Vizetelly enthralled the officers in General Stuart's headquarters with "his entertaining narratives, which may possibly have received a little embellishment in the telling."[37] A staff officer, G. Moxley Sorrel, recorded another example of embellishment by Vizetelly.

Sorrel showed him the site of a recent minor skirmish. Vizetelly returned several days later with an elaborate painting showing three lines of infantry, hundreds of guns, and soldiers surrounding a fallen leader. Sorrel responded that it was a splendid picture, but nothing like it had occurred. "No matter," Vizetelly replied, "it might have happened, and besides all battle pictures are drawn with such freedom."[38]

Several British businessmen visited the Confederacy during the war. W. C. Corsan, a manufacturer of cutlery and cutting tools in Sheffield, visited the South in October 1862 to seek customers and trading partners. His book, *Two Months in the Confederate States: An Englishman's Travels through the South,* was published in England during the war and republished in America in 1996. Lord John Brewerton spent two months in the South in the fall of 1863, apparently to assess the future availability of cotton. After a tour of cotton warehouses, Brewerton assured President Davis that the South would continue to receive the full support of all the upper classes in England."[39] Thomas Conolly was both a businessman and a member of the British Parliament. Already one of the wealthiest men in Ireland, he came to the South late in the war—too late, as it turned out—to explore the possibility of making more money in a blockade-running operation.

Other members of Parliament visited the Confederacy including the Marquis of Hartington (the future duke of Devonshire), Sir James Ferguson, Robert Bourke (later Lord Connemara), and Colonel William Leslie. Both Bourke and Edward Seymour (the future duke of Somerset) wrote articles on their experiences in America for *Blackwood's Edinburgh Magazine*.

Several British officers spent considerable periods with the Confederate army as unofficial military observers. Lieutenant Colonel Garnet Joseph Wolseley, was a twenty-nine-year-old officer who had served in major British campaigns in Burma, India, the Crimea, and China. He had been sent to Canada during the *Trent* crisis in 1861. In the fall of 1862 he obtained a month's leave in order "to get to the South and judge for myself as to the condition of its people, the strength of its government, and the organization of its armies."[40] After his trip he wrote an article for *Blackwood's Edinburgh Magazine* in which he praised the Confederate army and its leaders, described Lincoln as an insignificant country lawyer, and proclaimed that Confederate independence was clearly in the British national interest. Wolseley later wrote a laudatory article on Stonewall Jackson. In later years he held several important British commands and ended his career as a viscount, field marshal, and commander-in-chief of the British army.

Lieutenant Colonel Arthur J. Fremantle was a young officer in the Coldstream Guards who obtained leave to spend three months in the Confederacy in 1863. Extracts from his diary on the Gettysburg campaign appeared in *Blackwood's Edinburgh Magazine* in September 1863, and a full account of his American experiences, *Three Months in the Southern States: April–June, 1863,* soon appeared in London,

New York, and Mobile. In later years, as Sir Arthur Lyon-Fremantle, he commanded a British brigade in Egypt and was governor of Malta.

When the war began, Captain Fitzgerald Ross was a British cavalry officer of Scottish descent serving as captain in a regiment of Austrian Hussars. He obtained a year's leave, arrived in Richmond in June 1863, and remained in the Confederacy for a nearly a year. Ross's aristocratic instincts are indicated by his bringing with him his elaborate Hussars uniform which he wore in a Confederate parade. Ross's book, *A Visit to the Cities and Camps of the Confederate States*, was published in 1865.

Aside from William Howard Russell's well-masked skepticism about the Confederacy and its institutions in 1861, virtually all of the other British observers arrived and departed with attitudes that were highly favorable toward the Confederacy. Their articles and books reinforced a number of convictions of the British upper class—that the North fought only for "empire" over the South while the South fought only for freedom from intolerable oppression, that the South would be able to maintain its independence, and that British imperial and business interests were best served by Confederate independence. These and other views of the British observers are examined in later chapters.

Most of the members of the largest British colony in the South spent most of the war in a city—New Orleans—that was occupied by Union forces. In 1860 there had been 3,042 English-born residents and 736 Scots living in New Orleans; by April 1862, when Union forces occupied the city, some of these Britons had left the Confederacy and some had joined the Confederate army. The European Brigade organized in 1861 to defend the city included a "British Guard" of fifty or sixty Englishmen. On the night Union troops arrived, the members of the British Guard voted to send their arms and uniforms to General Beauregard. General Butler subsequently confined two officers of the British Guard to Fort Jackson; after the British minister, Lord Lyons, protested to Secretary of State Seward, they were released.[41] But most Britons in the city insisted—before and after the Union occupation—that they were still British subjects and must remain aloof from the internal conflict in America.

Two Britons, neither a resident of New Orleans, wrote highly critical accounts of General Benjamin Butler's rule in New Orleans. In a report to *The Times* from New York, Charles Mackay noted the determined opposition of the women of New Orleans to the Union occupation: "The women . . . not only wave Secession flags from their windows, and wear Secession ribbons in their bonnets, and teach their little children to revile the 'Yankees,' but when they pass a Federal soldier or officer in the streets they move out of his way with an expression of disgust in their faces. . . . General Butler would have done well to treat this display of feminine spite with indifference. . . . When he went so far as to say that women insulting the soldiers of the United States by word, or look, or gesture should be treated as 'harlots plying their vocation in the streets,' he outraged all decency and humanity."[42]

William Watson, the Scot from Baton Rouge, recalled his visit to New Orleans in 1862: "From a large richly furnished mansion . . . to the Custom House [Butler] was driven daily in a splendid carriage, surrounded by a numerous mounted bodyguard, . . . with more pomp and display than I have ever seen accorded to a European monarch. He then sat in imperial dignity in his judgment seat, and pronounced sentence according to his undisputed will. . . . To see such autocratic power vested in such a man . . . seemed to me to be strangely anomalous in a nation which had so long born the name of being the great seat and home of human liberties. . . . The brutal tyranny of Butler in New Orleans filled every heart in the South with indignation, . . . and roused them to a determination to fight to the bitter end."[43]

As among Britons in the North, the range of reactions to the Civil War was wider among Britons in the South than in any other major immigrant group. Many Britons—especially the those engaged in the cotton trade—had a direct economic stake in the maintenance of the status quo in the South. Their attitudes and those of British volunteers and British observers in the South also strongly reflected the pro-Confederate attitudes of the upper classes in Britain. Although inconsistent with the long antislavery tradition in Britain, this strong support for the Confederacy reflected the rarely acknowledged belief of the British upper classes that their economic and imperial interests were better served by the preservation of the status quo in the South than by the abolition of slavery. On the other hand, there is a more extensive public and diplomatic record of efforts by persons born in Britain to evade Confederate service than among any other major immigrant group.

There is little such conflicting evidence among the French in the South, the main subject of the next chapter. Immigrants from France fitted easily into the large community of French Creoles, the descendants of earlier French settlers in Louisiana. Most of the Creoles were slaveowners or other strong supporters of the Confederate cause.

Chapter 12

UNTIL *THE* LAND IS BLESSED *WITH* PEACE

French *and* Other Europeans *in the* South

FRENCH

Of the 109,370 persons in the United States in 1860 who were born in France, only 19,682 lived in future Confederate states; three-quarters of them lived in Louisiana. There were also 1,383 French-born residents in Texas, and 2,791 French-born were scattered among the other nine future Confederate states.

Although the 10,515 French-born residents of New Orleans were only half as numerous as the residents of the city born in Ireland or in Germany, they had joined a much larger number of French-speaking Creoles—the descendants of earlier French settlers in Louisiana. Most of the Creoles and French immigrants lived in the old "French Quarter," while other residents lived in newer sections upriver from Canal Street. A visitor from France, Salomon de Rothschild, noted in 1861 that "New Orleans is a very French city. . . . In all my travels thus far I have found nothing that is so much like Paris. . . . I asked what language I should speak in the city, and was told: 'French on the right of Canal Street, English on the left.'"[1] A few weeks later William Howard Russell reported that "there is an air thoroughly French about the people," who were speaking French in the street.[2]

As in the North, the popularity of Zouave uniforms in the South gave a misleading impression of the number of Frenchmen in the Confederate army. There were several Zouave units from Louisiana, all called the "Louisiana Zouaves." The 2nd Louisiana consisted of French Creoles, French immigrants, and men from a number of other countries. The 13th Louisiana was an even more cosmopolitan mix of Frenchmen, Spaniards, Mexicans, Italians, Germans, Chinese, Irishmen, and other foreign-born. A Zouave battalion assembled from detached Louisiana companies just before the first battle at Manassas consisted mainly of Irishmen.[3] There were several reports in the fall of 1863 of Union efforts to capture Major S. L. Dupeire and his mounted Zouaves—described as "500 French guerrillas"—who were attacking Union gunboats in Louisiana.[4] Several predominantly French companies and batteries were formed in other Confederate states; a battery of Frenchmen from Mobile in J. E. B. Stuart's "horse artillery" delayed the Union assault at Fredericksburg while singing the "Marseillaise."[5]

Three French immigrants—Xavier B. Debray, Victor Jean Baptiste Giradey, and Raleigh Edward Colston—commanded Confederate brigades. Three other French immigrants—Paul Francis de Gournay, Antoine-Jacques-Philippe de Mandeville de Marigny, and Aristide Gerard—commanded Confederate infantry or artillery units. The highest ranking Confederate officer born in France—Camille Armand Jules Marie, Prince de Polignac—was not an immigrant. Biographic information on all these officers is in Appendix II.

No author has estimated the number of men in the Confederate army who were born in France. If the percentage who served had been the same as in the whole Confederate population, there would have been about 2,600 French-born soldiers in gray uniforms, about 1,900 of whom would have been from Louisiana. But the large number of Frenchmen in a militia organization in New Orleans suggests that in 1861 and early 1862 many French Creoles and French immigrants had preferred to enlist in a militia committed only to local service rather than join the Confederate army. Before the Confederate conscription act could be implemented, New Orleans was occupied by Union forces.

The French Legion had been established in New Orleans in April 1861 "for defensive purposes within the city." Its charter began with the statement that "the dissolution of the American Union is a fait accompli." It prescribed an oath to be taken by the officers of the Legion "to maintain and defend the Constitution of the Confederate States."[6] The members of the Legion wore the uniform of the French army, including red pants and blue jackets. About 3,700 men were enrolled in the Legion's four regiments,[7] although some of them subsequently joined the Confederate army.

During 1861 most of the Confederate troops in New Orleans—not including the French Legion and other militia units—were sent north to General Beauregard. The French Creoles and French immigrants played prominent roles in the preparations to defend the city from a Union attack. In February 1862 the City Council appointed a Committee on Public Safety to make plans for the defense of the city; eighteen of the sixty-three committee members had French names.[8] The Council recommended the issue of $1,000,000 of city bonds to purchase arms and equipment for the defense of the city,[9] two French bankers, Rochereau and Quertier, were major purchasers of these bonds.[10] When martial law was declared on March 15, five of the six district provost marshals were men with French names—Freret, Dufour, Soule, Trepagnier, and Burthe.[11] A witness at the Confederate court of inquiry on the fall of New Orleans, Major W. H. Devereux, testified that about two-thirds of the assembled defense force of approximately 3,000 men "belonged to the French class of the population."[12] One of the commanders of the defense force was Brigadier General Benjamin Boisson, a sixty-eight-year-old French veteran of the Napoleonic wars.[13] But the senior Confederate commander decided that he had too few troops to defend the city, and withdrew his troops from the city. The French Legion never saw action.

Upon his arrival in New Orleans in April 1862, Union General Benjamin Butler at first accepted assurances that the several militia units of Europeans including the French Legion had been organized only to maintain order in the city. But Butler's attitude changed when he discovered that many of the officers of the Legion had taken an oath to support the Confederacy. He thought that for men claiming to be neutral French subjects, the oath had been "as gross a breach of neutrality as was ever committed." Butler had many problems with the French in New Orleans. Two of their leaders, Pierre Soule and M. Adolphe Mazureau, were arrested and charged with treason. They were sent to Fort Warren in Massachusetts but were eventually released.

On June 10 Butler issued an order declaring that many of the foreign residents had been "aiding rebellion by furnishing arms and munitions of war, running the blockade, giving information, concealing property, and abetting by other ways the so-called Confederate States, in violation of the laws of neutrality imposed upon them by their sovereigns as well as the laws of the United States." He proclaimed that "all foreigners claiming any of the privileges of American citizens or protection or favor from the Government of the United States" (except protection from personal violence) must take an oath that they would not give aid and comfort to the enemies of the United States.[14] But Secretary of State Seward doubted "the expediency of requiring oaths from those who do not owe a permanent allegiance to the Government" and the president directed that the oath requirement be discontinued.[15] Butler told the French consul in August that since so few French subjects had taken the oath, he had "no guarantee for the good faith of bad men."[16]

Butler's next move was to impose a tax on the persons who purchased the New Orleans defense bonds; the tax was 25 percent of the amount of the bonds purchased. He said the tax was to be used to provide for the relief of 10,490 destitute families, 90 percent of whom were born abroad.[17] In protesting this tax, French diplomats acknowledged that French residents had bought many of the New Orleans bonds. The French foreign minister in Paris claimed that the French subjects in New

Orleans had "lived so foreign to all the political events which were taking place around them that no kind of resentment should be evinced toward them."[18] The French legation in Washington tried to convince Seward that the French bankers in New Orleans had "become purchasers of the bonds in question without inquiring the use which the city might make of their proceeds."[19]

Although some of the French in New Orleans were refugees who had opposed Napoleon III's imperial regime in France, many in the French community hoped for help from France. In 1861, before the Union occupation of the city, two visitors had been told that the Louisianians would prefer French rule to Yankee oppression. William H. Russell reported to *The Times* of London that "the Louisianians . . . would far sooner seek a connection with the old country than to submit to the yoke of the Yankees."[20] Salomon de Rothschild wrote that "some very distinguished men . . . told me that they would prefer to live under the *liberal* government of Louis Napoleon rather than to endure the unbearable oppression of the North."[21]

In both 1862 and 1863, visits to New Orleans by French warships stirred dreams of French support. On May 16, 1862, the New Orleans City Council, noting the current visit of a French ship, recognized that "many ties of amity and good feeling . . . unite the people of this city with those of France" and resolved that the "freedom and hospitality of the city" should be extended to officers and men of visiting French ships. General Butler responded with a curt reminder that under the Union occupation, the Council was responsible only for public safety and public health and that the hospitality they could extend to the French sailors was thus limited to "an invitation to the calaboose or the hospital."[22] Butler's successor, General N. P. Banks, reported in 1863 that the visit of a French frigate had raised an expectation among the French residents of the city of "some assistance from the Government of France."[23] But hope for French support faded in Richmond and New Orleans during 1864, when it became apparent that Napoleon III was preoccupied with his effort to established a French-dominated empire in Mexico and had concluded that French support of the Confederacy would lead to an unwanted war between France and the United States.

In addition to the French in Louisiana, about 9,000 French-born residents and immigrants lived elsewhere in the Confederacy. A great many of these claimed that they were still citizens of France and thus exempt from conscription. A Confederate assistant secretary of war in Richmond wrote in 1863 that the French in the South were "seldom willing to forgo their relations with the empire, which is an object both of affection and pride."[24] In November 1864 the French foreign minister told John Slidell, the Confederate agent in Paris, that "frequent and grave complaints had been made of the forced service of French subjects" in the Confederate army. Slidell replied that "all demands of natives of France claiming to be exempted from military service were examined with impartiality and when well founded had been promptly accorded." But he also repeated earlier Confederate assertions that foreign residents could not expect "to remain passive spectators of a struggle in which the property, and even the lives, of all within our limits were at stake."[25]

The *Official Records* contain several indications that by mid-war some French Creoles and French immigrants were ready to abandon the Confederate cause. In June 1863 a Union Colonel reported from Trudeau's Landing, about twenty-five miles north of Baton Rouge, that "this parish is full of loyal Creoles and French. Large numbers have taken the [Union] oath."[26] In August 1864 the adjutant general of Indiana reported that 300 Confederate prisoners captured at Vicksburg hoped to be released upon taking the oath of allegiance to the Union: "They are nearly all French Creoles from New Orleans and its immediate vicinity and claim to have been either conscripted or forced into the rebel service."[27] When the governor of Georgia proclaimed in 1864 that foreigners must enroll in the militia or leave the state, many of them fled to Charleston. The French consul reported that "most of the French driven out of Georgia call aloud to get away from the Confederation."[28] The French legation in Washington asked Union authorities to approve the dispatch of a French warship to Charleston to pick up French subjects.[29] A communication from the legation stated that General Grant had approved the plan, but the *Official Records* contains no confirmation that the pickup actually occurred.

Very few Frenchmen visited the Confederacy during the war. Salomon de Rothschild, son of Baron James de Rothschild of Paris, spent several weeks in New Orleans in the spring of 1861. He was highly sympathetic to the Confederacy and urged that the substantial Rothschild influence in Paris be fully used to promote French recognition and support of the Confederacy.[30] In the summer of 1861 Prince Jerome Bonaparte and his aide, Lieutenant Colonel Camille Ferri-Pisani visited General Johnston in Virginia and General Beauregard in Charleston. But the prince, a cousin of Napoleon III, spent more time in the North, and upon his return to France was a strong supporter of the Union cause. Charles Frederick Girard, a Swiss-born journalist in France, had been commended in 1862 by Confederate agent Edwin De Leon for his pro-Confederate articles in the French press.[31] Girard wrote a book on his visit to the Confederacy in 1863 that included sweeping assertions of the unlimited public confidence in President Davis and the unrestricted freedom of speech and the press in the Confederacy.[32]

OTHER EUROPEANS

In addition to the Irish, Germans, Britons, and French, there were 30,595 other foreign-born in the South in 1860. About half of these—15,329 persons—were in Texas; the majority were born in Mexico, although there were also several sizable colonies in Texas of settlers from other European countries. About a fourth of the other foreign-born in the South—7,400 persons—were in Louisiana, with the remaining fourth scattered through the other nine future Confederate states.

In 1861 there was an effort to form a Polish Brigade for the Confederate army. There were too few Poles in the South for a brigade, but a considerable number of Poles were recruited for the 14th and 15th Louisiana. In February 1863 a Union officer at Camp Butler in Illinois reported that there were many Poles among Confederate prisoners from Texas who claimed they had been conscripted against their will and were willing to take the oath of allegiance to the Union and enlist in a Union regiment.[33]

Valery Sulakowski, a Pole who had been an officer in the Austrian army, was colonel of the 14th Louisiana in 1861. In 1863 he was chief engineer of the Department of Texas. That summer he proposed that he be sent to Europe to recruit some of the 12,000 to 15,000 Poles who were refugees in western Europe after an unsuccessful effort to throw off the Russian rule in Poland. By September 1864 Sulakowski had convinced Confederate Secretary of State Judah P. Benjamin that there were great opportunities to recruit Poles in Europe. Benjamin informed the secretary of war that Sulakowski's plan had been approved by Jefferson Davis, that the government would pay for the passage of the Polish recruits to Texas, and that they would be "allowed to organize themselves into companies, battalions, and regiments, and . . . into Polish brigades and divisions, if their numbers are sufficient."[34] Sulakowski reached Paris that fall, but nothing more was heard about Polish recruits for the Confederate army.

Two other Poles had senior positions in the Confederate army. Ignatius Szymanski had operated a plantation near New Orleans for two decades before the war. In 1862 he commanded the Chalmette Regiment in the forces assembled to defend New Orleans. He was captured by Union forces but was later exchanged. In 1863 and 1864 he was Confederate coordinator of prisoner paroles and exchanges in the Trans-Mississippi region. Another Polish immigrant, Hypolite Oladowski, a former ordnance sergeant in the U.S. Army, was Chief of Ordnance in the Army of the Tennessee in 1862–63. His dedication to the Confederate cause is indicated in a letter written in 1862: "My idea to prosecute this war is, never to rest, never to delay, from morning to night. . . . Far better to die from exhaustion in serving a just and right cause than to submit or to be overpowered. . . . I trust in God, but keep powder dry and plenty of it."[35]

Several Belgians commanded Confederate units. Henri Honore St. Paul was a captain in the 7th Louisiana and later lieutenant colonel in the 13th Louisiana. Two brothers, Gaston and Alfred de Coppens, were successive commanders of a battalion of Louisiana Zouaves; Gaston was killed at Antietam creek in 1862. Max van der Corput commanded a Georgia artillery battery at Vicksburg and Chattanooga and an artillery battalion in the Atlanta campaign.

In 1860 there were only about 1,100 Italians in the South, 900 of whom were in Louisiana. There was an Italian component of the European Brigade in New Orleans, an Italian militia company in Richmond, and Italians in several Confederate regiments. "I wish this war was over, for I am getting tired of soldiering," Italian immigrant John Garibaldi wrote his wife in September 1863 from Stonewall Jackson's brigade. "My time of enlistment will be out next spring, but I expect to soldier on until the land is blessed with peace."[36] In September 1864 a Union ship released an Italian named Antonzini, who was found in irons aboard a captured blockade runner. He had been condemned to death by the Confederates for treason, but the sentence had been commuted to deportation to Bermuda. Antonzini offered to provide information for the destruction of important bridges in Virginia.[37] The commander of a French warship, ordered in November 1864 to pick up Frenchmen in Charleston who wanted to leave the Confederacy, was also authorized to take a few Italians who were also eager to leave.[38]

Several Louisiana regiments contained volunteers born in a number of countries. The 10th Louisiana, which has been described as "Lee's Foreign Legion," included men from twenty foreign countries (Austria, Canada, Cuba, England, France, Germany, Gibralter, Greece, Ireland, Italy, Martinique, Mexico, Norway, Portugal, Russia, Sardinia, Scotland, Sicily, Spain, and Switzerland) as well as the United States and the Confederate States.[39] James P. Gannon identified the birthplaces of 980 of the 1,215 men in the 6th Louisiana, 664 of whom were born abroad. There were 468 from Ireland, 123 from Germany, 30 English, 13 French, 9 Scots, 9 Canadians, 2 Norwegians, 2 Swiss, and one each from Belgium, Cuba, Mexico, Sweden, Malta, Holland, Italy, and Wales.[40]

Chapter 13

TO OGLE *THE* PRESIDENT

Two Presidents

Some of the foreign observers who came to the North during the Civil War were able to spend a few minutes with Abraham Lincoln. Lincoln rarely discussed major issues with these visitors; their reports emphasized his appearance and manners and their opinions on his competence as president. In the first two years of the war most of the foreign observers were British. Their comments on Lincoln reflected the prevailing view in the British upper classes that this strange man from the frontier could not be qualified to lead a great nation. A French visitor noted later that it became "the fashion for European visitors to go to ogle the President, as they would go to stare at a strange animal, and make endless disparaging comments at his expense."[1]

The first of several accounts of Lincoln's uncouth appearance was by William Howard Russell of *The Times* of London: "Soon . . . there entered, with a shambling, loose, irregular, and almost unsteady gait, a tall, lank, lean man, considerably over six feet in height, with stooping shoulders, long pendulous arms, terminating in hands of extraordinary dimensions, which, however, were far exceeded in proportion by his feet. He dressed in an ill-fitting, wrinkled suit of black. . . . His turned-down shirt-collar disclosed a sinewy, muscular, yellow neck, and, above that, resting in the great black mass of hair . . . rose the strange, quaint face and head, covered with its thatch of wild republican hair, of President Lincoln."[2]

Edward Dicey of *The Spectator* wrote a similar account: "Fancy a man six-foot, and thin out of proportion, with long bony arms and legs; . . . large rugged hands; . . . a long scraggy neck, and a chest too narrow for the great arms hanging by its side; . . . a head . . . covered with rough, uncombed and uncombable lank dark hair, that stands out in every direction at once; a face furrowed, wrinkled, and indented; . . . a close-set, thin-lipped, stern mouth; . . . and a nose and ears which have been taken by mistake from a head of twice the size. Clothe this figure . . . in a long, tight, badly-fitting suit of black, creased, and soiled, . . . large, ill-fitting boots, . . . and a fluffy hat, . . . and then add to this an air of strength . . . and a strange look of dignity coupled with all this grotesqueness, and you will have the impression left on me by Abraham Lincoln."[3] After spending a few minutes with Lincoln in 1864, George Augustus Sala, correspondent for the *Daily Telegraph,* reported that his "dark face, strongly marked, tanned and crows-footed, and fringed with coarse and tangled hair, is so uncouth and so rugged that it narrowly escapes being either terrible or grotesque."[4]

Andrew Carnegie, an immigrant from Scotland and future steelmaker, saw Lincoln at the telegraph office in 1861: "He was certainly one of the most homely men I ever saw when his features were in repose; but when excited or telling a story, intellect shone through his eyes and illuminated his face to a degree which I have seldom or never seen in any other."[5] The Marquis of Chambrun, the last European observer to meet Lincoln, was the first of the observers to comment on the intelligence and ability reflected in Lincoln's face: "The face appeared equally strange and strong, revealing remarkable intelligence, great power of penetration, tenacity of will, and high-mindedness."[6]

Several visitors stressed Lincoln's democratic manners. "There is about him a complete absence of pretension," Dicey wrote, "and an evident desire to be courteous to everybody, which is the essence . . . of high breeding."[7] Carnegie noticed that "he had a kind word for everybody, . . . as deferential in talking to the messenger boy as to Secretary Seward. . . . He was the most perfect democrat, revealing in every word the equality of men."[8] Carl Schurz, the German immigrant who campaigned for Lincoln in 1860, wrote that "those who visited the White House . . . saw there a man . . . who . . . treated all men alike, much like old neighbors; whose speech had not seldom a rustic flavor about it; who always seemed to have time for a homely talk."[9] Chambrun noted that "he dominates everyone present and maintains his exalted position without the slightest effort."[10]

Two visitors thought Lincoln looked sad and careworn. Julian Kune, a Hungarian who had met Lincoln in 1860, visited him in 1861: "I was startled at the haggard appearance of the President. The cares of state seem to weigh heavily upon him. . . . I had never seen such a change within so short a time in the appearance of a man."[11] Ernest De Hauranne noted in 1865 that Lincoln "seemed sad and preoccupied, bent under the burden of his immense tasks."[12]

Lincoln's curious mixture of humor and melancholy was noticed by several Europeans. "He never was at a loss for a story or an anecdote to explain a meaning or enforce a point, the aptness of which was always perfect," wrote Henry Villard, a German-born journalist. "In spite of his frequent outbursts of low humor, his was really a very sober and serious nature, and even inclined to gloominess."[13] Dicey recorded that Lincoln "has a rich fund of dry, Yankee humor, not inconsistent . . . with a sort of habitual melancholy."[14] Chambrun observed Lincoln's frequent shifts from humor to melancholy: "After passing some time with Mr. Lincoln you were left with a profound impression of poignant sadness. He was, however, extremely humorous, with a trace of irony always to be found in his wit. His stories brought the point out clearly. He willingly laughed either at what was being said or what he himself was saying. Then, suddenly, he would retire into himself and close his eyes, while his face expressed a melancholy as indescribable as it was deep. After a while . . . his generous and open disposition again reasserted itself. I have counted, in one evening, more than twenty of such alternations of mood."[15]

All the British visitors who met Lincoln wrote negative or condescending comments about his capabilities. Upper-class Britons could not believe that a man of the people, with very limited previous experience in the national government, could be an effective president. Russell thought "this poor president is to be pitied." The correspondent of *The Times* wrote that Lincoln was "trying with all his might to understand strategy, naval warfare, big guns, the movement of troops, interior and exterior lines, and all the technical details of the arts of slaying."[16] Dicey wrote that Lincoln was "a shrewd, hardheaded, self-educated man, with sense enough to perceive his own deficiencies, but without the instinctive genius which supplies the place of learning. . . . He works hard, and does little; and unites a painful sense of responsibility to a still more painful sense, perhaps, that his work is too great for him to grapple with."[17] After meeting Lincoln in 1862, the Marquis of Hartington wrote his father that Lincoln "was a very well-meaning sort of man, but . . . about as fit for his position as a fire-shovel."[18] George Augustus Sala, a British correspondent, wrote that his impression of Lincoln was of "a thoughtful, weary, saddened, overworked being; of one who was desperately striving to do his best, but . . . who was continually regretting that he did not know more."[19]

In 1862, Colonel Garnet Joseph Wolseley thought Lincoln was only an "insignificant lawyer"; in 1887, however, General Wolseley wrote that he had been a "farseeing statesman of iron will, of unflinching determination."[20] The Vicar of Huddersfield, the Reverend G. G. Lawrence, commented in 1863 that it was "a terrible thing for a man of ordinary strength to be placed in a position where the strength of a giant is required."[21]

De Hauranne's ten minutes with Lincoln left "an impression of a man who is doubtless not very brilliant, not very polished, but worthy, honest, capable, and hardworking." The French journalist thought "his policy is to be like an intelligent weathervane, able to predict future winds, turning neither too late nor too soon in their direction and remaining always in accord with them."[22] Chambrun was the only European visitor to comment very favorably on Lincoln's abilities: "No one who heard him express personal ideas . . . could fail to admire his accuracy of judgment. . . . I have heard him give opinions on statesmen and argue political problems with astounding precision. . . . His short, clear sentences captivate and his remarks become proverbs."[23]

There were very few comments by European observers on Lincoln's roles as commander-in-chief, chief diplomat, or emancipator of the slaves, and most of these were negative or condescending. The rare comments on his role as commander-in-chief were mainly limited to strong criticisms—cited in Chapter 14—of his "ill treatment" of General McClellan and of his strategic errors during the period when he had no general he could trust. Almost all European observers assumed that U.S. foreign policy was determined solely by the secretary of state. The primarily negative reactions of European observers to his Emancipation Proclamation are reviewed in Chapter 20.

The European immigrant who knew Lincoln best was Carl Shurz, the German who mobilized immigrant votes for him in 1860 and 1864. Schurz wrote to a friend in Germany in 1864 that Lincoln was "a man of profound feeling, correct and firm principles, and incorruptible honesty. His motives are unquestionable, and he possesses to a remarkable degree the characteristic, God-given trait of this people, sound common sense. . . . I have seen him . . . work his way through many a desperate situation with strength born of loyalty to conviction. I have criticized him often and severely, and later found that he was right. I also know his failings; they are those of a good man."[24] Regis de Trobriand, the highest-ranking French immigrant in the Union army, recalled that Lincoln had been "animated by the most sincere patriotism, enlightened by a certain political sagacity, guided in his views and in his ambitions by an irreproachable honesty, sustained by the people. . . . He followed the straight path, regulating his steps by the march of events."[25]

All of the Europeans who met Jefferson Davis were strong supporters of the Confederacy, and most of them were also great admirers of its president. Four British visitors commented on his appearance and manners. Russell of *The Times* met Davis in Montgomery in 1861: "He has a very haggard, careworn, and pain-drawn look, though no trace of anything but the utmost confidence and great decision can be detected in his conversation."[26] Samuel Philips Day, correspondent for the London *Herald*, also met Davis in 1861: "In appearance he is tall, slim, prim, and smooth—rather precise, but gentlemanly in manner, and exhibits a stiff military carriage, which to a stranger savours of austerity. . . . However, his temper is genial, and he quickly wins upon those with whom he comes in contact."[27] Lieutenant Colonel Arthur Fremantle of the Coldstream Guards visited Davis in 1863: "He is only fifty-six, but his face is emaciated and much wrinkled. He is nearly six feet high, but is extremely thin and stoops a little. . . . He looked what he evidently is, a well-bred gentlemen. Nothing can exceed the charm of his manner, which is simple, easy, and most fascinating."[28] Francis Lawley, Richmond correspondent for *The Times*, found Davis "one of those calm, firm, undemonstrative men, inclined to reticence. . . . Each word is slow, weighty, and luminous, the countenance and voice agreeable and convincing."[29]

The Prince of Joinville, a former French admiral, thought Davis "had all the requisite conditions to perform his tasks well. He applied to it his rare capacity."[30] Colonel Fremantle noted that that, unlike Lincoln, Davis was thoroughly familiar with the men who were now Union and Confederate generals: "His post of Secretary of War under the old government brought officers of all ranks under his immediate personal knowledge and supervision. No man could have formed a more accurate estimate of their respective merits."[31]

British visitors in 1861 noted Davis's popularity. "Every Southern man I have as yet met," Russell wrote, "expresses undoubted confidence in Mr. Jefferson Davis."[32] Samuel Phillips Day thought "there is no individual 'down South' more universally popular than the President of the Confederates States."[33] But in 1863 Colonel Fremantle wrote that "it is a great mistake to suppose that the press is gagged in the South, as I constantly see the most violent attacks upon the President."[34]

A few European visitors detected a stubborn streak in Davis's character. Captain Justus Scheibert, a Prussian engineer, was impressed by his "firmness."[35] Thomas Conolly, a member of the British Parliament, thought "his quiet manner and ready easy conversation . . . mask a man of extraordinary determination."[36] Colonel Fremantle observed that "having formed his opinion with regard to appointing an officer, Mr. Davis is almost always most determined to carry out his intention in spite of every obstacle."[37]

Several British observers thought Davis's determination and stubbornness was a mixed blessing. Colonel Wolseley acknowledged that "he sincerely believed in the justice of the cause he espoused and brought to the service of his country an honesty of purpose, a fervid patriotism, ability of no mean order, a zeal, and a persistent determination." But Wolseley thought he was "a third-rate man and a most unfortunate selection for the office of President."[38] Francis Lawley reported early in 1864 that "President Davis, by his well-intentioned though ill-judging obstinacy in adhering to his friend General Bragg, has done more to shake the stability of his hold upon the affection and confidence of the Confederate people than any other act."[39] William Watson, a British engineer in Louisiana when the war began, thought Davis was "a man of considerable talent, unbending will, and great ambition; but . . . he prolonged the war long after he saw the cause was utterly hopeless, when he might have made terms which would have saved tens of thousands of lives and saved hundreds of thousands from untold misery."[40]

Chapter 14

A HEAD CAPABLE
OF MANAGING
GREAT ARMIES

The War *in the* East: 1861–1862

Whe the Civil War began, the general-in-chief of the United States Army was Major General Winfield Scott. He had been a major general since the war of 1812; in 1847 he led an American army to victory in Mexico. But in 1861 Scott was seventy-five years old and too frail to command an army in the field. Henry Villard, the German-born reporter for the New York *Herald*, recalled Scott's condition: "His physical infirmities were such that he could scarcely leave his invalid-chair. His mind, too, clearly showed the effect of old age. He formed plans for the coming offensive movements of the troops, but he vacillated much with respect to them, and discussed them with indiscreet garrulousness. . . . The makeshift was finally resorted to of leaving him nominally in supreme command, but giving the command in the field to others practically independent of him."[1]

The new field commander in Virginia, Brigadier General Irwin McDowell, was described by Regis De Trobriand, a Frenchman who was colonel of the 55th New York in 1861: "His military education had been begun in France, and completed at West Point. He had been through the Mexican war. . . . and had been a professor at the military academy. He was a well informed and experienced officer, who knew . . . the risks of an attack made with recruits hardly organized, against a numerous enemy fortified in a strong position."[2]

William Howard Russell, correspondent for *The Times* of London, had breakfast with McDowell on July 6: "He did not hesitate to speak with great openness of the difficulties he had to contend with, and the imperfection of all the arrangements of the army. As an officer of the regular army, he has a thorough contempt for what he calls "political generals." . . . Nor is General McDowell enamoured of volunteers, for he served in Mexico and . . . formed an unfavorable opinion of their capabilities in the field."[3] Russell, who had covered the Crimean war, noted the many deficiencies of the Union infantry, artillery, and cavalry during an all-day ride through Union camps on July 13: "I doubt if any of these regiments have ever performed a brigade evolution together. . . . And it is with this rabblement that the North propose not only to subdue the South but, according to some of their papers, to humiliate Great Britain and conquer Canada afterwards."[4]

On July 21, 1861, McDowell's ill-prepared Union army met Beauregard's Confederate army at Bull Run Creek near Manassas, Virginia. "The Confederates had every advantage," De Trobriand recalled. "Strongly established in a good position, protected by complete lines of works, they had only to defend themselves with vigor, which they did. . . . The Union attack was badly executed . . . because . . . it was impossible for our troops to act together or to move with any precision. . . . The officers were nearly all incompetent. A regiment which had had any practice in firing was an exception, as was a colonel knowing how to command. . . . Some regiments fought well, others fought very little, others did not fight at all. With troops without discipline and without experience, an unsuccessful attack is easily changed into a rout."[5]

Lieutenant Rudolf Aschmann, a Swiss immigrant in the 1st U.S. Sharpshooters, observed the Union rout: "The first brigade had advanced barely fifty steps outside of the wood when it was greeted by terrible fire from the front and the right flank which created frightful devastation in its ranks and forced it to fall back. A second line was sent after it, but . . . it was soon broken up by the fleeing men of the first line and rushed back to the wood in disarray. . . . Suddenly panic seemed to have overcome the army and everything turned into a complete rout. . . . The fleeing hordes, pursued by fierce artillery fire, could not be brought under control by anyone. Everyone fled for his life. Even regiments of cavalry, ordered to stop the frantic troops, were broken through. . . . On the road . . . to Centreville, . . . cannons, wagons, ambulances, parts of regiments, fleeing and wounded men, all were rushing in wild disorder toward the only bridge across the Bull Run."[6]

The report by the correspondent of *The Times* on the flight of the Union troops, which was widely reprinted in Europe and America, convinced Europeans that the Union could not win the war, gladdened Southern hearts, and enraged public opinion in the North. In a later dispatch, Russell described the panic in Washington after the fiasco at Bull Run: "The miserable fragments of a beaten, washed out, demoralized army were flooding in disorder and dismay through the streets of the capital. . . . All the editors and journalists in the States . . . poured out invective, abuse, and obloquy on their defeated general and their broken hosts. The

President and his ministers, stunned by the tremendous calamity, sat listening in fear and trembling for the sound of the enemy's cannon. . . . At any moment the Confederate columns might be expected in Pennsylvania Avenue."[7] "Never was a victory so triumphant, never a defeat so disgraceful," wrote another British correspondent, Samuel Philipps Day. "The 'Grand Army of the North' . . . have been . . . put to ignominious flight, and by an antagonist far inferior . . . in everything but valour."[8]

Lincoln appointed Major General George B. McClellan as the new commander of the Union army in the east. He had finished second in his class at West Point, won three brevets during the war with Mexico, and spent a year observing European armies. The American press hailed McClellan as the savior of the country, but Russell suspected as early as September that he was not "a man who intends to act as speedily as the crisis demands."[9] Carl Schurz recalled that "McClellan . . . shrank from taking any risk with an army that, in his opinion, was not quite perfectly appointed. . . . That [Lincoln] did not during the long period of hesitancy on the part of McClellan . . . remove that general from command, is one of the most debatable points in Mr. Lincoln's conduct of the war. Perhaps he had no more promising officer to put in McClellan's place. . . . The Democratic party had taken up his defense, and it was thought desirable to avoid occasions for political jealousies and splits. . . . McClellan persistently asserted that his force was lamentably inadequate to an attack on the enemy in his front, and pressed upon the President the transfer of his army to the lower Chesapeake, and an operation thence upon Richmond, a plan which Mr. Lincoln finally accepted."[10]

"The program laid down by McClellan," wrote David P. Conyngham, an Irish journalist, "was to transport his army to the Peninsula, between the York and James rivers, . . . and operating directly on Richmond itself. This movement would oblige the enemy to abandon his entrenched position around Manassas and Centreville, in order to cover Richmond and Norfolk." According to the original plan, McDowell's 40,000-man corps, which had been watching the Confederates at Manassas, was also to march upon Richmond. Conyngham wrote that if McClellan had had McDowell's corps, he would have captured Richmond and "spared the country the horrors of wading through near three years more of blood and misery."[11] The Count of Paris, aide to McClellan during the Peninsular campaign, believed that McDowell's "junction with McClellan would have proved the decisive blow of the campaign."[12] But Lincoln and Secretary of War Stanton, worried about Stonewall Jackson's movements in the Shenandoah valley, diverted McDowell's corps to the valley. McClellan complained bitterly about the diversion and used it as an excuse for his failures on the Peninsula.

De Trobriand wrote that "the disastrous result of the Seven Days will forever bear testimony against the military incapacity, the political blindness, and the delinquencies of every kind of General McClellan. . . . In his timorous brain . . . our advantages were transformed into adverse chances. His troubled look never saw the enemy but with fantastic exaggerations, nor his own army but in extravagantly diminished proportions."[13] Lincoln appointed Major General Henry Halleck as general-in-chief of the Union army, and Major General John Pope was given the command of a new Army of Virginia composed of the Union forces in northern Virginia.

The Count of Paris blamed Lincoln, Stanton, and Halleck for the failure of the Peninsula campaign: "Mr. Lincoln was beset by those who . . . were urging him to consolidate the two armies of Virginia and the Potomac by bringing the latter back to the line of the Rappahannock. The President resisted a long time . . . but, conscious of his own incompetency, submitted to this new authority." He claimed that McClellan was "knocking at the gates of Richmond" when he received "the fatal order" to abandon the campaign on the Peninsula.[14]

McClellan and most of his army were languishing in Alexandria when the Confederates met Pope's army at the second battle of Bull Run on August 30, 1862. Major Heros Von Borcke, a Prussian cavalryman, was with the Confederates: "About three o'clock in the afternoon the close columns of the Yankees emerged suddenly out of the dark green of the opposite forest at a double-quick, in five extended lines, at intervals of sixty yards, comprising at the least 15,000 men. . . . Forty pieces of artillery poured a withering shower of shells into the very midst of the advancing host, while . . . their first line was received with a perfect sheet of fire from our triple infantry line concealed in the dense undergrowth of the forest. . . . With the utmost energy and courage the Federal officers brought their men forward for three . . . assaults, and three times were they hurled back. . . . At last . . . the whole force fled in disorderly rout, . . . leaving behind them many thousands of dead, wounded, and prisoners."[15]

Von Borcke described Lee's decision, after the second Confederate victory at Bull Run, to carry the war into Maryland: "He would be able there to subsist his army, relieved from the necessity of protecting his lines of communication for supplies. The confident belief was also entertained that the army would be increased by 20,000 to 25,000 recruits, who were supposed to be only waiting for the opportunity of taking up arms against the federal Government. Being so reinforced, our commander-in-chief doubted not that he might easily strike a blow against Baltimore, or even Washington."[16]

Lincoln was appalled by the news that Lee was invading Maryland. "Great . . . was the astonishment and indignation of the loyal public," recalled Villard, "when the President again put McClellan at the head of the remnants of the armies of the Potomac and of Virginia."[17] A British officer, Lieutenant Colonel Garnet Josef Wolseley, thought Lincoln had responded to pressure from Union soldiers: "Incapable as they were of defending their frontier from hostile invasion, they were powerful enough to have crossed into Washington, and, overturning the vile faction which sits there in the name of a government, to have proclaimed McClellan dictator. Such a line of conduct was openly talked of, and many of the best informed men now believe that it would have actually been carried into execution, had not Lincoln called back the favorite to command the Union armies in defense of the empire's capital." General Lee told Wolseley that fall that he had been amazed by the rapidity with which McClellan had reassembled "the disorganized mob under General Pope's command, whom Lee had lately seen flying before his own victorious troops more like scared sheep than soldiers."[18]

"Poorly clothed, poorly shod, poorly fed," De Trobriand wrote, "the Confederates had . . . entered the promised land of Maryland, which, they were told, awaited them as liberators. . . . But Maryland did not respond to that appeal. . . . It was a cruel disappointment."[19] Von Borcke recorded that the Confederate force "had been greatly reduced by the continuous fighting, . . . by the long and wearisome marches, . . . and the cruel hardships. . . . A great multitude of stragglers were left behind on the Virginia side of the Potomac. . . . Lee commenced this tremendous struggle with no more than 30,000 men. . . . The Federal army . . . amounted to not less than 90,000."[20] Lee told Wolseley that nearly half of the Confederates who had crossed the Potomac did not arrive at Antietam in time for the battle because of "sore feet occasioned by want of shoes or boots."[21]

De Trobriand described the battle at Antietam Creek on August 17, 1862: "At daylight, Hooker attacked the Confederates so vigorously that he threw them into disorder. But the First Corps had attacked all alone. After terrible losses, it was soon stopped by new troops sent against it, and forced to fall back in confusion, while Hooker, severely wounded, was carried off the field of battle. . . . The enemy was . . . driven back a second time. . . . Again reinforced, he had retaken the position twice lost, when he found Sumner with his Second Corps in front of him. . . . The Confederate troops were rapidly, for the third time, driven back upon their shaken centre."[22]

Sergeant Francis Galwey of the 8th Ohio, an Irish immigrant, was in the thick of the battle: "Forward we go over fences and through an apple orchard. . . . The air is alive with the concussion of all sorts of explosions. . . . Bullets are falling thickly round us. . . . Our men are falling by the hundreds. . . . I contemplate the prospect of sudden death without flinching. . . . Fixing our bayonets, we raise a cheer and go forward. But it is no use. The pelting rain of missiles is redoubled. Unfixing our bayonets we retire . . . to our old position. . . . I heard later that there were six hundred bodies . . . in less than four hundred yards of line. . . . We see two fresh, whole lines of Confederates advancing toward us. We have but three rounds left to the man. . . . The order is to retire slowly. . . . Our company went into action with thirty-two men; twenty-eight have been hit."[23]

Von Borcke wrote that McClellan "concentrated the whole weight of his attack upon Jackson's centre, which for a time gave way, and was driven through a large patch of forest. . . . But the grim Stonewall soon rallied his men, and having been reinforced, drove back the Yankees in his turn for several miles with great slaughter. . . . Longstreet, hard pressed by the superior numbers of enemy, had been giving way slowly, but defending the ground like a wounded lion, foot by foot, until, receiving reinforcements at the outskirts of Sharpsburg, he recovered the lost ground after a severe and sanguinary combat."[24]

That night, De Trobriand recalled, everyone in the Union army was "convinced that the next day's sun would witness the destruction of Lee's army by a united attack and that what remained would be driven into the Potomac, captured, or dispersed. The generals took their measures accordingly. . . . McClellan had only to say the word. But that word he did not say. It was still the McClellan of the Peninsula, faint-hearted and irresolute, not daring to follow up a success."[25] "The perfect quietude of the morning," Von Borcke wrote, "was interrupted only by a flag of truce sent in by the Yankees asking permission to bury their dead. . . . The work occupied them until the afternoon, when it became evident that the battle would not be renewed."[26]

The Prussian major outlined the reasons the Confederates believed that the battle at Antietam Creek should be considered a Confederate victory: "Every inch of the ground lost by Longstreet at noon had been recovered. Our centre had greatly gained ground. On our left, the enemy had been pushed back for nearly two miles. And we remained masters of the entire field covered with the enemy's dead and wounded. . . . Our loss . . . had indeed been heavy, amounting to not less than 2,000 killed and 6,000 wounded. . . . The Federals having been the assailants, their loss was yet more severe, reaching the terrible aggregate of 12,000 dead or disabled men."[27] After his visit to Lee that fall, Colonel Wolseley wrote that the expedition into Maryland had been "highly favorable" for the Southern cause: "fourteen thousand men made prisoners—over fifty guns and an immense quantity of ammunition and stores captured—together with the fact of having fought with thirty-five thousand men a decidedly drawn battle, without loss in guns or prisoners, against a force of ninety thousand men."[28]

For the next seven weeks, McClellan did little to follow up on his "victory" at Antietam. "The passiveness into which McClellan relapsed," wrote Villard, "rekindled the general impatience and distrust of him. Again the President exercised altogether too much forbearance."[29] But Lincoln's patience eventually ran out. On November 5 he relieved McClellan and appointed General Ambrose Burnside as the new commander of the Army of the Potomac.

Two Irish immigrants—Private William McCarter of the 116th Pennsylvania (Irish Brigade) and Sergeant Francis Galwey of the 8th Ohio—recorded the reactions of the troops to the dismissal of McClellan. McCarter considered it "a sad and heavy blow for McClellan's brave soldiers, by whom he was loved, honored and almost idolized. . . . The Army of the Potomac lost its best commander. . . . The common soldier . . . lost his best and most faithful army friend."[30] Galwey described McClellan's last review of the troops: "When he appears, a half-shout and a half-sob is heard throughout the lines. The very roughest and apparently most unfeeling men are red about the eyes. . . . There are oaths, only partly repressed, ejaculations of affection, and wild yells as of defiance at the loyal stay-at-homes and the Washington politicians."[31] McCarter wrote a similar account of the review and added that the march back to camp "bore more resemblance to the 'Dead March' of a soldier's funeral than the movement of live and active men. All appeared dejected, lonely, and lost. Hundreds wept bitterly."[32] "Upon our return to camp," Galwey noted, "a very mutinous feeling is apparent everywhere."[33]

European observers were rarely critical of McClellan, and several of them wrote that his dismissal resulted from "evil influences" or "intrigues" by politicians and officials. George Augustus Sala, correspondent for the *Daily Telegraph*, believed that McClellan had been "forced into retirement owing to the basest of intrigues" and that he was a "decidedly ill-used chieftain."[34] Colonel Wolseley wrote in 1862 that McClellan's recall had resulted from "the well-known jealousy of Stanton, Seward, and Halleck on account of the army's attachment to him."[35] The Count of Paris thought the cause for McClellan's dismissal was "the hostility of General Halleck and the Secretary of War and . . . that of the Republican party." He believed the deciding factor was Democratic successes in the 1862 elections: "Mr. Lincoln was made to believe that this result was the beginning of a political movement of which General McClellan would be the leader. . . . They may have placed before him the danger of a military revolution. . . . Mr. Lincoln . . . could no longer resist the evil influences by which he was beset."[36] The idea that McClellan had been a victim of political intrigue persisted in Britain well into the twentieth century. Before he was prime minister, Winston Churchill wrote that "ill treatment was meted out to General McClellan by the Washington politicians and Cabinet. . . . For this Lincoln cannot escape blame. . . . His instinct had been to stand by his chosen General. Instead he had to yield to political outcry."[37]

Several factors may have contributed to the persistent British belief in a plot against McClellan. In the British governmental system, most major decisions are made by a group of ministers around a cabinet table, rather than by a single executive acting alone. British leaders couldn't believe that the "country lawyer" from Illinois was capable of making major decisions on his own. In the Victorian era, the concept of civilian control of the military was much less well established in Britain than in the United States. Colonel Wolseley commented in 1862 that in prodding McClellan to take the offensive, Lincoln was only "giving expression to the decrees of an entirely ignorant public opinion."[38] In 1903 the recently retired commander-in-chief of the British army, Field Marshall Viscount Wolseley, wrote that "to allow civilians to interfere in the selection of officers for command or promotion is injurious to efficiency. During war to allow them, no matter how high their political capacity, to dictate to commanders in the field any line of conduct . . . is simply to ensure disaster."[39]

Although McClellan was praised by many immigrants in the army, several high-ranking immigrants were highly critical of the general. One of the highest ranking German generals, Carl Schurz, thought Lincoln had been too patient with McClellan.[40] General De Trobriand, the highest ranking Union officer born in France, wrote that "McClellan had not the burning ardor which was necessary to put an end to the rebellion. . . . He appeared . . . to be always afraid of hurting the rebels too much."[41] Colonel Nicholas Perczel, the Hungarian-born commander of the 10th Iowa, put it more bluntly: "His spirit was not with our cause. . . . That is why he vacillated for so long."[42]

General Burnside had not sought or welcomed the command of the Army of the Potomac. "He had at first declined the promotion," Villard wrote, "on the ground that he was not qualified for the highest command. . . . To force the gravest responsibilities upon a reluctant man was almost to invite the further disaster that came. . . . He inspired confidence in his honesty of purpose and ardent loyalty . . . but there was nothing . . . in his conversation that indicated intellectual eminence or executive ability of a high order."[43] But there was no doubt about his commitment to the Union cause. Private McCarter of the Irish Brigade wrote that Burnside's "loyalty, honesty, sobriety, good intentions and earnest effort to crush the Rebellion was well known. It entitled him to the esteem and respect not only of the army but of all good Union men."[44]

The next major battle was at Fredericksburg. "All along Marye's Heights," wrote Major Von Borcke, "runs a sunken road, fenced in with a stone wall on either side, which in itself constituted a most formidable defensive work for our [Confederate] troops. A little higher up the hill there was a regular defensive line of entrenchments, the defenders of which might fire over the heads of those below them, and the crest was occupied by the numerous pieces of the famous Washington Artillery, so that the assailants were received with a triple sheet of fire which swept them away by the hundreds."[45]

Three men in the Irish Brigade described the deadly Confederate fire. Private William McClelland (88th New York): "Up hill and forward over an open plain a quarter of a mile wide we rushed, the enemy firing with their rifles deadly volleys. . . . When we were within thirty or forty yards of the rifle pits, . . . we met dreadful showers of bullets from three lines of the enemy, besides their enfilading fire. Our men were mowed down like grass before the scythe of the reaper."[46] Lieutenant John Donovan (69th New York): "We gain the second fence, within sixty yards of the enemy's batteries, and are met by a most disastrous fusillade and direct fire from the rebel artillery and infantry. . . . The ranks are already horribly thinned, and still 'leaden rain and iron hail' is streaming upon them. . . . The Irish Brigade was left to be sacrificed between the fire of the enemy from the front and the flank and the fire of our own troops, afraid to advance from the rear."[47] Private William McCarter (116th Pennsylvania): "When . . . we were within 50 paces of the stone wall, Cobb's solid brigade of Rebel infantry, said to have been then about 2,400 strong, suddenly sprang up from behind it. . . . The Rebs poured volley after volley into our faces, at once stopping our further progress. . . . Other Rebel infantry, in long lines behind earthworks and in rifle pits on Marye's Heights, were blazing away at us at the same time. It was simply madness to advance as far as we did and an utter impossibility to go further. . . . We had lost nearly all of our officers. . . . In this assault, lasting probably not over 20 minutes, . . . our division lost in killed and wounded over 2,000 men, . . . nearly 35 percent of the entire number. . . . I distinctly heard the order . . . 'Fall back, men, and every man for himself'. . . . The men turned their backs to the foe and fled in the greatest confusion."[48]

The Welsh-born commander of the mostly Irish 69th Pennsylvania, Colonel Joshua T. Owen, was also in the thick of the fight: "A most terrific fire opened upon us from behind a stone wall at the base of the steep declivity, from rifle pits on the face of the hill, from two batteries on either side of a large brick house at the top of a hill, from traverses on the right and left flanks of my line, and from a line of infantry drawn up on the top of the hill. . . . About 3 P.M. a heavy column . . . marched gallantly toward the enemy's lines. . . . But . . . this new line staggered, reeled, and fell back in confusion under the awful fire which was poured in upon it. . . . Each time the [the Union line] was reformed it advanced a little beyond where the other advance had been made, but each time the line was broken and finally fell back to the town."[49]

Lieutenant Donovan had been pinned down by the deadly Confederate fire: "I considered it certain death . . . to endeavor to get out of what remained of the regiment; I gave the order to all the men to lie flat till the firing in our rear would somewhat cease. . . . At dusk, the fire having slackened, I gave the order to fall back; about a dozen men rose from amongst the dead and followed. . . . I got through the first fence, and . . . shed tears of gratitude for my own deliverance from instant death."[50] Private McCarter was wounded, and was left behind by his fleeing comrades: "To my right and to my left . . . solid rows of Union soldiers were advancing up the slope to attack the enemy. Brigade after brigade and division after division were hurled against him time and again, but like my own, were blown back as if by the breath of hell's door suddenly open. Shattered, disordered, they ran pell-mell back down the declivities."[51]

Three Europeans who were with the Confederate army attested to the bravery of the Irish. Major Von Borcke thought "the federals certainly behaved with the utmost gallantry. Line after line move forward to the assault, only to recoil again and again from the murderous tempest of shot, shell, and bullets and to strew yet more thickly with dead and wounded the crimsoned field."[52] A British officer, Captain Fitzgerald Ross, recorded that "Meagher's Irish Brigade attacked Marye's Hill with a gallantry which was the admiration of all who beheld it."[53] Francis Lawley reported to *The Times* that "the bodies which lie in dense masses . . . are the best evidence what manner of men they were who pressed on to death with the dauntlessness of a race which has gained glory on a thousand battlefields."[54]

Not all the reactions by European observers were so gracious. *Punch* printed a particularly nasty dispatch by an unidentified Reuters correspondent: "A Good Riddance—'Tis an ill wind that blows nobody good.' . . . They have perished in warring as mercenary soldiers . . . to subjugate men who are fighting for their country. So may the foes of England fall! But now, having used up all their Irish, had not our Yankee friends better conclude peace with the South . . . rather than . . . begin to spend really valuable lives in a hopeless struggle?"[55]

Officers and men of the Irish Brigade blamed Burnside for the slaughter. Lieutenant Donovan wrote that "the many thousands of brave young fellows and comrades who fell that day were victims of a grand blunder."[56] Private McCarter blamed Burnside for "rushing his men into the jaws of death."[57] "We are slaughtered like sheep," Captain William J. Nagle, 88th New York, wrote his father, "and no results but defeat."[58] Two Europeans with the Confederate army agreed. Von Borcke thought "the folly of the federal commander in sending his men to certain death and destruction is utterly incomprehensible."[59] Lawley did not believe that "any mortal men could have carried the position before which they were wantonly sacrificed, defended as it was."[60]

Henry Villard brought news of the battle to Lincoln at the White House: "He followed up my account with one question after another for over half an hour. . . . I made bold to say as earnestly as I could . . . . : 'It is not only my conviction but that of every general officer I saw during and after the fighting, that success is impossible and the worst disaster yet suffered by our forces will befall the Army of the Potomac . . . unless the army is withdrawn at once to the north side.' . . . The President . . . remarked, 'I hope it not so bad as all that.'"[61]

As Charles Mackay reported to *The Times*, the battle of Fredericksburg ended Burnside's short career as commander of the Army of the Potomac: "General Burnside resolved to lead his dispirited and insubordinate army to the attack but at the council of war called to consider the matter, . . . found none to agree with him. . . . He resigned himself to his fate, countermanded the movement, . . . and proceeded to Washington, determined to resign his command. The President did not wish to accept the resignation, but General Burnside . . . would listen to no advice or persuasion. . . . On Saturday morning he ceased to be commander of the Army of the Potomac, and . . . General Hooker . . . was appointed to his place."[62]

Many immigrants in the army were very frustrated by the failure of another Union commander. "All our efforts are coming to a deadlock," an English immigrant in the 14th Connecticut, Sergeant Ben Hirst, wrote his wife, "for want of a head capable of managing great armies like ours."[63] Some immigrants still blamed Washington officials and politicians for the removal of McClellan in November. Sergeant Galwey, 8th Ohio, wrote that "the Army of the Potomac has felt that injury has been premeditated against it for low party reasons. Upon Secretary of War Stanton, chiefly, they lay the blame."[64]

During the same period that European observers in the North were reporting on the failures of Union generals in the North, European observers in the South were writing highly complimentary reports about Confederate generals. Such reports continued throughout the war. Every foreign visitor who met Robert E. Lee was effusively enthusiastic about his appearance and personality. As Richmond correspondent for *The Times*, Francis Lawley had many opportunities to study the Confederate commander. "General Lee . . . strikes you as the incarnation of health and endurance," he wrote in 1862. "His manner is calm and stately, his presence impressive and imposing. . . . The most entire and trusting confidence is placed in General Lee by his subordinate officers."[65] In 1865 Lawley wrote that "it is difficult for one who . . . has watched the career of Robert E. Lee, has been cognizant of his stately simplicity, his unostentatious self-abnegation, his ceaseless and ever active unselfishness, his lofty courage, his uncomplaining persistency, to speak of him otherwise than in the language of extravagant enthusiasm." Lawley added more effusive comments about Lee in an article a few weeks after Appomattox: "He has the thoughtfulness about others, the unobtrusiveness and renunciation of self, the truthfulness, purity, modesty, charity, guilelessness, which cannot long be unnoticed by those around him."[66]

Colonel Wolseley, who had a long talk with Lee in the fall of 1862, thought Lee "a splendid specimen of an English gentleman, with one of the most rarely handsome faces I ever saw. . . . His whole face is kindly and benevolent in the highest degree."[67] Colonel Fremantle, who met Lee in 1863, also thought he was "the handsomest man of his age I ever saw. He is . . . a thorough soldier in appearance; and his manners are most courteous and full of dignity. . . . Throughout the South, all agree in pronouncing him to be as near perfection as a man can be."[68] Captain Scheibert, another visitor in 1863, was very impressed by "the tall, handsome sexagenarian with snow-white hair and with dark, beneficent eyes, which had a look of kindness for every human being."[69]

The Count of Paris, who never met Lee, studied the general's operations while an aide to McClellan and as a postwar historian: "He was always a patient, persevering, and prudent calculator, yet ready to risk much at the opportune moment; handling a large army with great dexterity in the midst of the thickest forest; understanding men, selecting them carefully, and securing their attachment by his equity; worshipped by his soldiers, obtaining from them what no other chief could have thought of asking them; respected and obeyed by all his lieutenants; humane, of a conciliatory disposition, one whose only fault as a general was an excess of deference to the opinion of his subordinates."[70]

Few European immigrants met Lee. William Watson, a Scot, wrote rather sardonically that "the noble character, the able management, and skillful generalship of General Lee and his brilliant successes inspired Southerners with renewed confidence and hope, and prolonged the struggle for nearly three years."[71]

After Lee, the Confederate most admired by Europeans was General Thomas "Stonewall" Jackson. Francis Lawley met him in 1862: "We had been taught to expect a morose, reserved, distant reception; we found the most genial, courteous, and forthcoming of companions."[72] Major Von Borcke thought "his conversation was lively and fascinating. . . . For General Lee his admiration and affection were alike unbounded. . . . He would often say, 'All the credit of my successes belongs to General Lee. . . . I only executed his orders.'"[73]

Jackson was admired by Europeans for his adroit harassment of the Union forces in the Shenandoah valley: "It has been the practice of General Jackson," Lawley wrote in 1862, "to throw himself, disregarding his own inferiority of numbers, upon large bodies of his enemy, and the day is ordinarily half-won by the suddenness and desperation of the attack. . . . His usual policy then is to retire. . . . In a few days, however, . . . he pounces upon them again. . . . The upshot . . . is that no permanent foothold has been gained by the Federals in the Valley."[74] Private McCarter recorded that "General Jackson was . . . distinguished for the great and wonderful ability which he possessed of moving or marching large bodies of troops from one point to another in the shortest possible space of time, far outstripping our Union generals. . . . In the morning we would find him in our rear, harassing and perplexing us. And in the evening he would be at our front, provoking an engagement or an advance."[75]

Lawley reported that General James Longstreet was "one of the most valuable officers of the Confederacy. . . . As brave and imperturbable under fire as in his tent, remarkable for his promptitude in thinking correctly when in the greatest danger, his value to the Confederacy can hardly be overestimated."[76] Fremantle recorded that "Lee . . . relies very much upon his judgment. By the soldiers he is invariably spoken of as 'the best fighter in the whole army.'"[77] Von Borcke thought Longstreet's "steady courage . . . and serene indifference to the extremest peril, . . . his constant energy in the campaign and obstinacy in the fight, and his strict obedience to orders, made him one of the most useful . . . officers in the Confederate service."[78] A more balanced view of the corps commander was provided by Francis W. Dawson, an English officer on Longstreet's staff: "When in action there was no lack of energy or of quickness of perception, but he was somewhat sluggish by nature. A better officer to execute a prescribed movement, and make such variation in it as the exigencies of battle required, would be hard to find, but he needed always a superior mind to plan the campaign and fix the order of battle. . . . Whenever he had an independent command, he was unsuccessful."[79]

British observers were not so impressed with Beauregard, perhaps because of traditional British attitudes toward the French. An unidentified "English Combatant" wrote that "Beauregard is a small man with a sallow complexion, a heavy black mustache, and closely cut hair. With the left hand in his trousers pocket, a cigar in his mouth, a buttoned-up coat, and a small cap, he is the exact type of a French engineer. . . . He is jaunty in his gait, dashing in manner."[80] William H. Russell met the general in October 1861: "Beauregard has something of pretension in his manner, . . . a folding-armed, meditative sort of air, which seems to say, 'Don't disturb me; I'm thinking of military movements.' . . . He is . . . subtle, crafty, and astute, . . . a thorough soldier."[81] William Watson noted that "General Beauregard . . . had a thorough military education. . . . He is brave, skillful, and cautious, and possesses the universal esteem and confidence of the troops."[82]

During 1861 and 1862 the reports of European observers in America bolstered the persistent belief of most of the leaders and people in Europe that the Union could not win the war and that the Confederacy would maintain its independence. These early European assumptions were now rooted in the failure of Lincoln to find an effective general, the failure of the Union army to win any decisive victory in the east in the first two years of the war, and the impression of highly effective political and military leadership in the Confederacy. Although the first doubts about the validity of these convictions would emerge during 1863, they would nonetheless remain the dominant European beliefs about the American war until late in 1864.

Chapter 15

THE VALLEY
OF THE SHADOW
OF DEATH

Chancellorsville *and* Gettysburg: 1863

E ach year of the war, the winter weather and muddy spring roads delayed the
opening of the spring campaign until late April or early May. The winter
interval in 1863 gave General Hooker a chance to reorganize the Army of the
Potomac. Henry Villard, the German-born correspondent of the New York *Herald*,
was not too impressed with the new commander: "He was fully six feet high, finely
proportioned, with a soldierly, erect carriage, handsome and noble features; . . . he
looked, indeed, like the ideal soldier and captain."[1] But Villard wondered whether
this latest commander would be any more effective than his predecessors.

Sergeant Thomas Francis Galwey, an Irishman in the 8th Ohio, was among the
60,000 men reviewed by Lincoln and Hooker on April 8: "President Lincoln,
accompanied by part of his cabinet, was at the colors. . . . I have never before seen
the army in such good physical condition. The men are all fat, healthy, well uniformed, thoroughly equipped; the horses are prancing; the guns shining; and everything indicates an army in splendid fighting order. . . . But there was little of the old
enthusiasm."[2]

The first big battle of 1863 was at Chancellorsville, in central Virginia not far
from Fredericksburg, in the first days of May. Stonewall Jackson marched around the
perimeter of Hooker's army and attacked the unprepared and badly positioned
XI Corps. A Prussian officer, Captain Justus Scheibert, was with the Confederates:
"The noise that now arose in the thick, echoing woods really defies description. . . .
No longer were single salvos heard, nor sporadic cannon shots, but a howling of
firearms in deep bass and high voice which surged and subsided like a somber

melody, while shot and shrapnel whizzed though the air, causing leaves and twigs to rain down. . . . Suddenly, there arose on all sides a loud outcry, the so-called rebel yell, which the Northerners fear so much. The firing diminished, and the Confederates now fell like lions upon the confused enemy."[3]

Major General Carl Schurz commanded the Third Division of the XI Corps: "A short time after the first attack a good many men of Colonel Von Gilsa's and General McLean's wrecked regiments came in disorder out of the woods. A heavy rebel force followed them closely with triumphant yells and a rapid fire. The 58th New York and the 26th Wisconsin received them firmly. . . . The 26th Wisconsin . . . maintained the hopeless contest for a considerable time with splendid gallantry. It did not fall back until I ordered it to do so, . . . which it did in perfect order, facing about and firing several times as it retired."[4]

The recollections of Brigadier General Regis De Trobriand were similar to Schurz's: "The enemy, emerging from the woods in deep masses with the rebel yell, threw himself upon the few regiments which were opposing him. The latter endeavored to resist, but they were quickly swept away and beaten down. The remainder of the division, taken in flank, melted away, was broken, and rolled upon the next division, which it carried with it. . . . In vain, a few superior officers endeavored to stop the flight. . . . It was not an engagement, it was a rout. . . . Two brigade commanders, Schimmelfenning of Schurz's division, and Buschbeck of Steinwehr's division, . . . fought until, overwhelmed and carried away by numbers, they were compelled to fall back on the Twelfth Corps. All the rest went on in the greatest confusion toward Chancellorsville."[5]

Because the XI Corps had previously been commanded by a German, Franz Sigel, and contained a number of predominantly German regiments, it was regarded as the "German" or "Dutch" corps. Many officers and men in Hooker's army blamed the Germans in the XI Corps for the Union defeat at Chancellorsville. "We certainly would have gained a great victory were it not for the cowardice of the 11th Corps," Colonel Patrick Guiney, commander of the Irish 9th Massachusetts, wrote to his wife. "The Dutch Corps ran. The rest of the Army fought well. Hooker . . . was beaten by two things—want of numbers and the disgraceful flight of the flying Dutchmen."[6] The story of the "Flying Dutchmen" appealed to the widespread anti-German prejudices in the army and among civilians. Stephen W. Sears, author of a book on Chancellorsville, wrote that these prejudices "ranged from one man's irritation that the Germans 'were allowed lager beer & ale when no other part of the army could get any,' through intolerance for the numerous abolitionists and freethinkers in their ranks, up to unthinking outright contempt for anyone foreign, an outgrowth of the anti-immigrant Know-Nothing politics of the 1850s."[7] Another author suggested that the Germans were blamed because the Northern press was looking for a scapegoat for Hooker's defeat.[8]

Less than half of the men in the "Dutch Corps" were Germans. The order of battle of the XI Corps at Chancellorsville in the *Official Records* includes 27 regiments, only eleven of which are on a comprehensive list of "German" regiments in the Union army.[9] Most of the regiments that Schurz and De Trobriand said had resisted the attack as long as possible were German units. These included two regiments in Krzyanowski's brigade—the 58th New York and 26th Wisconsin—and five of the nine regiments in Schimmelfennig's and Bushbeck's brigades—the 29th New York, the 68th New York, the 27th Pennsylvania, the 74th Pennsylvania, and the 82nd Illinois.

Two Gemans in the 26th Wisconsin wrote letters to Wisconsin newspapers defending Schurz and his troops. The first was by Major Frederick C. Winkler: "Some northern papers tried to hold General Schurz responsible for our defeat. . . . Our troops were in a wrong position, but that was not General Schurz's fault; he protested against it without avail. . . . That his command gave way, fled, is true. . . . They stood, received and returned the murderous fire of the enemy . . . as long as it could be done. . . . General Schurz, personally in the midst of danger, made all reasonable efforts to rally the fleeing troops."[10] A second letter was by Sergeant Carl Wickesberg: "The *Christliche Beobachter* writes that Schurz's division and the whole 11th Corps . . . ran away in wild flight even before the enemy had fired one shot. That is not true. Our regiment was in front and was attacked first. We stood firm, and first receded after we saw the superior force of the enemy and were ordered to recede. We fired about 8 or 10 shots. . . . They say we ran away out of our trenches. I would have liked to see some trenches. We were standing in front of a bush."[11]

Schurz wrote a letter to the *New York Times* demanding a congressional investigation of the role of the XI Corps at Chancellorsville, but there was none and a cloud hung over the XI Corps until it was somewhat dissipated by the performance of the corps at Gettysburg in July.[12] Lieutenant Colonel William F. Fox wrote in 1889 that "the men of the Eleventh Corps were good soldiers—for the most part tried and veteran troops, and were in no way responsible for the disaster which befell them at Chancellorsville. Their commander in that battle allowed himself to be surprised and . . . had made a very faulty disposition of the troops. . . . Anything beyond a brief resistance was impossible."[13] Most historians in the twentieth century agreed with Fox's conclusions.

Many officers and men who were born in Europe took part in the great battles in Gettysburg on July 1, 2, and 3, 1863. Brigadier General Adolph Von Steinwehr, a former Prussian officer who commanded the Second Division, XI Corps, described the battlefield on July 1: "At about 2 o'clock I arrived with my division near

Gettysburg and was ordered to occupy Cemetery Hill, . . . the commanding point of the whole position. . . . Toward the east and south, low ranges connect with it, while toward the north and west a belt of open fields from 1 to 2 miles in width extends along the whole length of these hills. . . . Our position . . . was quite strong, the infantry being placed partly behind stone fences, and forming with our batteries a front fully able to resist an attack of even greatly superior forces.[14] General Schurz, commanding the Third Division, reported that "at about 3 o'clock the enemy appeared in our front with heavy masses of infantry. . . . The Third Division had to sustain a furious attack, . . . which was almost a hand-to-hand struggle, . . . Second Brigade . . . lost all its regimental commanders; several regiments nearly half their number in killed and wounded."[15]

The beginning of the battle on the second day, July 2, was described by Lieutenant Rudolf Aschmann, a Swiss immigrant in the 1st U.S. Sharpshooters: "Each opponent seemed determined to await the act of the other, since the positions of both were very favorable for a defense. . . . At 2 o'clock the enemy infantry line began advancing. . . . With well-aimed shots our line of riflemen brought them to a halt right in front of us, but when a second column appeared . . . we hastily retired behind the main force. . . . The Confederates charged with death-defying vehemence. . . . Our extreme left was backed against a cone-shaped hill . . . called Sugarloaf Mountain, which the Rebels tried to storm . . . but . . . did not succeed."[16]

Colonel Fremantle of the Coldstream Guards was with Lee's army: "Longstreet suddenly commenced a heavy cannonade on the right. Ewell immediately took it up on the left. The enemy replied with at least equal fury, and in a few moments the firing along the whole line was as heavy as it is possible to conceive. A dense smoke arose for six miles."[17] "The tremendous shelling continued until half past six," recorded Captain Otto Baron von Fritsch, a Prussian staff officer in Colonel Von Gilsa's brigade. "Then . . . we saw large columns approaching us. . . . They charged Colonel von Gilsa's Brigade, screaming, 'We are the Louisiana Tigers!' "[18] The Tigers were the 6th Louisiana, a polyglot regiment of Irishmen, Germans, and men born in other foreign countries.[19] "On came the enemy, . . . climbing the wall and forcing the Brigade up the hill behind the batteries. Now our batteries began to fire grape and canister, but some brave fellows came up to one of the batteries and demanded surrender; the battery men, assisted by General Ames, two officers, and myself, cut them down. With handspikes and rammers the cannoneers struck at their heads, and my good sword behaved well again. . . . General Schurz had sent a brigade to reinforce us."[20]

"Some rebel infantry had scaled the breastworks and were taking possession of the guns," Schurz recalled. "But the cannoneers defended themselves desperately. With rammers and fence rails, hand spikes and stones, they knocked down the intruders. In Widerich's battery, manned by Germans from Buffalo, a rebel officer, brandishing his sword, cried out: "This battery is ours!" Whereupon a sturdy German artilleryman responded: "No, dis battery ist *unser!*" and felled him to the ground with a sponge-staff. Our infantry made a vigorous rush upon the invaders and, after a short but very spirited hand-to-hand scuffle, tumbled them down the embankment."[21]

"In the evening," Lieutenant Aschmann recalled, "the Confederates retreated to the position which they had held in the morning, leaving most of their dead behind. Night fell on a battlefield which in many places was completely hidden beneath a cover of dead, dying, and gravely wounded men."[22] The performance of the Germans in the XI Corps at Gettysburg improved their reputation in the army. General David Hunter wrote that "the Dutchmen showed that they were in no way inferior to their Yankee comrades, who had been taunting them since Chancellorsville."[23]

Three Europeans commented on Lee's direction of Confederate operations on the second day at Gettysburg. Colonel Fremantle and Captain Scheibert, a Prussian officer, observed the battle from the branches of a tall tree. "As soon as the firing began," Fremantle wrote, "General Lee joined [General] Hill just below our tree, and he remained there nearly all the time, looking through his field-glass. . . . During the whole time the firing continued, he only sent one message, and he only received one report. It is evidently his system to arrange the plan thoroughly with the three corps commanders, and then leave to them the duty of modifying and carrying it out to the best of their abilities."[24] Scheibert wrote in 1877 that Lee said, "I do everything in my power to make my plans as perfect as possible. . . . The rest must be done by my generals and their troops, trusting to Providence for the victory." But Scheibert had different recollections of Lee's behaviour at Gettysburg. He thought that Lee had not manifested "the quiet self-possessed calmness" that he had shown at Chancellorsville: "Lee was not at his ease, but was riding to and fro, . . . making anxious inquiries here and there, and looking careworn. . . . Want of confidence, misapprehensions, and mistakes were the consequences . . . of the absence of Jackson, whose place up to this time had not been filled. After this, it was filled by Lee himself."[25] The Count of Paris, who was not at Gettysburg but studied the battle after the war, wrote that "the way in which the fights of 2nd of July were directed does not show the same coordination which ensured the success of the Southern arms at Gaines' Mill and Chancellorsville."[26]

Two Britons wrote vivid accounts of the artillery barrage at midday on the third day at Gettysburg, July 3. "In all upon the Confederate side alone there must have been a concert of about 200 guns," Francis Lawley reported to *The Times*. "Their thunder was echoed back from a similar number of pieces on the federal side. . . . Far back into the mountains the reverberations rolling from hillside to hillside started strange and unmusical echoes."[27] To Sergeant Benjamin Hirst, an English immigrant in the 14th Connecticut, "it seemed as if all the demons in Hell were let loose, and were howling through the air. . . . You dared not move either hand or foot, to do so was Death."[28]

Pickett's famous charge on July 3 was described by several Europeans. Francis Lawley (*The Times*): "Across the Valley of the Shadow of Death the Confederate advance [was] swept by the concentrated fire of the countless Federal guns and exposed when nearing those guns to hailstorms of musketry bullets. . . . General Pickett . . . seemed . . . to lead his men into the first jaws of death."[29] Lieutenant Thomas Francis Galwey (8th Ohio): "From time to time the smoke of bursting shells would envelop them for a few seconds, but when the smoke lifted, the gray mass was still coming on, still compact, still orderly, ever and anon raising one of those piercing yelps which had been so terrifying for our new troops to hear. . . . With the fresh ammunition which a short time ago was issued us, we play havoc with them. Still brave and cheering, they ascend the stone wall. . . . The enemy has taken Griffin's battery and are beginning to train its guns on our own line. Then in the nick of time Major Rorty of Hancock's staff, rallying a portion of the 29th New York, charges them and recovers the battery."[30]

Captain Justus Scheibert (Prussian observer): "The victory lasted only a few anxiously tense moments. . . . The attack began to waver, and the unanchored wing was outflanked by a clever, enfilading maneuver of the enemy. . . . The defenders . . . brought a three-fold superiority in firearms to bear in the fight. . . . The brave men were laid low by the thousands. The failure of the left flank completely staggered the strength of the attack, and the bloody remnants of the Confederates now reluctantly fell back to take refuge from the terrible fire in the woods at the bottom of the hill."[31] Lieutenant Galwey: "The retreat is, almost at once, turned into a flight! . . . As far as the eye could reach, the ground was covered with flying Confederates."[32] Sergeant Hirst: "A great number of rebels threw up their hands in token of surrender. . . . Then . . . the whole rebel force gave way in utter confusion. . . . Where but a short time before had stood the flower of the rebel army . . . was now covered with dead in every conceivable posture."[33] Lawley: "Out of a division of 4,300 men, Pickett brought out . . . about 1,500, though I believe that another 1,000 men straggled in the next day. His three brigadier generals lay dead or desperately wounded upon the field."[34]

Colonel Fremantle, who had been observing another part of the battle, returned to Longstreet's headquarters just as Pickett was returning from his unsuccessful charge: "The general told me that Pickett's division had succeeded in carrying the enemy's position and capturing his guns, but after remaining there twenty minutes, it had been forced to retire. . . . No person could have been more calm or self-possessed than General Longstreet under these trying circumstances." Fremantle added that the face of General Lee "which is always placid and cheerful, did not show signs of the slightest disappointment, care, or annoyance."[35]

Brigadier General Wladimir Krzyzanowski, a Polish immigrant, wrote that Lee "twice attacked the heights at Gettysburg on which stood our center. He attacked in the face of a hellish cannon fire. Our center did not budge."[36] Lieutenant Francis W. Dawson, the English officer on Longstreet's staff, thought the Federals "had a right to claim Gettysburg as a decisive victory, for we had failed utterly in what we had undertaken."[37]

"We owe our success," Sergeant Hirst wrote, "to the grit and courage of the rank and file of the grand old Army of the Potomac, stripped for the fight as it never was before, and still smarting under the useless sacrifice at Fredericksburg and our humiliating defeat at Chancellorsville. . . . The long and dreary marches under a burning sun by day and the drenching storms by night . . . culled out the sick and those who were physically incapable of standing the strain and gave those who had no heart in the cause or were cowards by nature ample opportunities of sneaking away. . . . The man . . . who reached Gettysburg in time to do his duty in the hour of need is entitled to as much credit for the victory as the grandest general on the field."[38]

Lawley reported the grim scene at Gettysburg on July 4: "A steady downpour of rain from a low brooding leaden sky. . . . In every grove . . . burying parties, sometimes with tears of convulsive and agonized grief, rendered the last sad offices to the fallen."[39] Lieutenant Aschmann recorded that his Swiss regimental commander, Lieutenant Colonel Trepp, commanded one of the grave-digging detachments: "He came back at night feeling unwell from the grisly nauseous sights he had seen. He had supervised the burial of 1,200 bodies, most of which had lain on the battlefield already for three days."[40] General Schurz toured the battlefield: "There can be no more hideous sight than that of the corpses on a battlefield, . . . some lying singly or in rows, others in heaps, having fallen over one another, some in attitudes of peaceful repose, others with arms raised, others in a sitting posture, others on their knees, others clawing the earth, many horribly distorted by what must have been a frightful death-struggle. . . . Around me were the dead bodies of men who, but three days ago, had cheered me when I rode along their front. . . . Only a few paces away, some Confederate dead . . . now looking just like our men, and having in all probability died with the same belief in the justice of THEIR cause."[41]

Meanwhile, the Confederate retreat had begun. "All day long," Lawley reported, "General Ewell's enormous train . . . was filing off behind the Confederate centre and right, and pushing into a pass of the South Mountains . . . which leads obliquely to Hagerstown. Towards evening the wagon train of A. P. Hill's corps . . . followed Ewell; and it was not till long after midnight the train of Longstreet's corps got under way. . . . On the morning of the 5th the rain stopped . . . but . . . in the afternoon the pertinacious downpour was resumed. Another wretched night, passed half on the march, half in a saturated wheat field, another long day's march, and on the night of the 6th we reached the little town of Hagerstown, distant about five miles from the Potomac."[42]

Two English officers recorded very different views of the morale of the Confederate troops as they withdrew from Gettysburg. "The army is in good spirits in spite of our own retreat and the bad news from Vicksburg," wrote Captain Fitzgerald Ross. "As for despondency, or being weary of resistance and of the war, . . . there are certainly no symptoms of it in this army. 'We will fight them, sir, till hell freezes, and then, sir, we'll fight them on the ice,' said an energetic officer to me; and the same sentiment seems to animate everyone."[43] But Lieutenant Dawson wrote that "the march back to the Potomac was dreary and miserable indeed. The rain fell in torrents. The clothing of the men was worn and tattered, and too many of them were without shoes. . . . It was a heart-breaking business, and gloom settled down upon the army. . . . We received the news of the fall of Vicksburg. It needed only this to intensify the feeling that the star of the Confederacy was setting."[44]

For ten crucial days after the battle of Gettysburg, Lee's army was trapped in Maryland by high water in the Potomac that prevented fording and by the lack of pontoons to replace those at Falling Waters that had been destroyed by Union cavalry. "When crossing the Potomac into Maryland, I had calculated upon the river remaining fordable during the summer, so as to enable me to recross at my pleasure," Lee wrote President Davis on July 7, "but a series of storms commencing the day after our entrance into Maryland had placed the river beyond fording stage and the present storms will keep it so for at least a week. I shall therefore have to accept battle if the enemy offers it, whether I wish to or not, and . . . the result is in the hands of the Sovereign Ruler of the universe."[45]

A Prussian engineer, Captain Justus Scheibert, played a crucial role in rebuilding the pontoon bridge at Falling Waters that allowed Lee to return to Virginia with his artillery and ammunition and a vast train of horses, food, and other booty obtained in Maryland and Pennsylvania. Ella Lonn wrote that "an important engineering service was . . . rendered by the Prussian visitor, Scheibert. . . . During the retreat from Gettysburg, at the request of General Lee, he rode ahead of the retreating army to the Potomac where the army engineers and pioneers were to replace the bridges which had been destroyed by the Unionists. He helped under the greatest difficulties to direct the building of a pontoon bridge in sixty-eight hours. This bridge greatly facilitated the crossing of the Potomac by Lee's army, and by means of it and the ford, which became passable as the water fell, the entire army made its escape."[46]

In a book published in 1874, Scheibert described the rebuilding of the bridge: "I rode at the General's request to the Potomac, where the engineers . . . were to rebuild . . . the urgently needed bridge. . . . The trees standing by the river were mostly oaks, which are not suitable for floats. . . . A section of bridge about 300 feet in length was entirely gone. Thus the decision was made to build new pontoons with slanting front and rear, 30 feet long on top and 18 feet on the bottom, 7 feet wide on top and 6 feet on the bottom. . . . Several sawmills were discovered, which provided a sufficient supply of boards and crossbeams. . . . All of the material for the bridge about 800 feet long was floated downstream five and three-fourths miles . . . and assembled in 68 hours. . . . Altogether, 15 new pontoons were built, 7 old ones were repaired, the bridge floor for the 300 feet was built, the pontoons were caulked with oakum picked from old rope and tarred at the seams, and stone anchors and wooden crossbeams were made."[47]

Scheibert's account does not specify his own role in the process, probably because the king of Prussia—who preferred a united America—would not have approved of an important contribution to the Confederate cause by a Prussian officer who was supposed to be only an observer. Scheibert's account is generally consistent with other evidence on the rebuilding of the bridge at Falling Waters. Two authors—Shelby Foote[48] and John W. Schildt[49]—wrote that Stonewall Jackson's former quartermaster, Major John Harman, was in charge of the bridge project. There is no evidence that Harman, a prewar wagon-builder, had any experience with bridge construction; he probably welcomed the help of an experienced Prussian engineer. A memoir by John A. Casler, a private in the Stonewall brigade, contains an account of the bridge project that is consistent with Scheibert's account except for several minor details.[50] Casler did not mention the name of any officer involved with the project.

Major General George G. Meade, who had been given the command of the Army of the Potomac just before the battle at Gettysburg, thought his battered army was in no shape to undertake an immediate pursuit of Lee's army. A week after the battle, two Irish officers in the Union army recorded their anger that Meade was allowing Lee to escape. On July 11 Captain Michael Egan, 15th West Virginia, learned from two deserters that Lee was about to cross the river. "There were a great number of large trees overhanging the banks of the then turbulent stream . . . which, if cut down and allowed to fall into the rapid current after a portion of the enemy had crossed, would undoubtedly crush and sweep away his pontoon bridges and effectually separate his army. This accomplished, we could safely engage the first portion of his command with at least equal chances of success. I tendered to the general the services of my company for this work, . . . the majority of them being practical wood-choppers, . . . but the orders never came. . . . There was never a grander opportunity for a brilliant coup de grace than was lost to the Union cause on this occasion."[51] "Today was an opportunity such as we have never had before," Lieutenant Galwey of the 8th Ohio wrote on July 12. "But it has been thrown away by Meade's indecision. . . . Here is Lee's defeated army, with a large part of its wagon train and all of its artillery still on this side of the river. . . . Here we are, a victorious army, full of spirit and eager to attack. From hour to hour . . . come rumors of an advance, but no advance is ordered."[52]

Two German officers were relieved to learn that there would be no attack on Lee's army. Major Winkler of the 26th Wisconsin feared that "an attack by our very much weakened army, where the regiments average perhaps only two hundred men, upon a strong defensive position of the enemy would be of doubtful success."[53] Captain Von Fritsch recorded that "after sending out a reconnoitering party, we found that the enemy had crossed on a bridge at Falling Waters and forded the Potomac. . . . So we were safe."[54]

By July 13 the level of the Potomac had dropped sufficiently to allow many units to ford the river. Lieutenant Hermann Schurich, a German in the 14th Virginia Cavalry, was one of the last to ford at Williamsport: "At 3 o'clock in the morning on July 14, Captain Moorman instructed me to call in our outposts at about 5 o'clock, but to keep up the camp fires and quietly withdraw to Williamsport, where I was to ford the Potomac. . . . Federal cavalry and artillery appeared on the Maryland side after I had safely crossed the river."[55]

Although the extent of Scheibert's contribution cannot be determined, the successful rebuilding of the bridge at Falling Waters allowed Lee to return to Virginia with all of his artillery, supplies, and equipment as well as an immense hoard of supplies and livestock captured by the Confederates in Maryland and Pennsylvania. Colonel Fremantle had noted on July 4 that "wagons, horses, mules, and cattle captured in Pennsylvania, the solid advantages of this campaign, have been passing slowly along this road . . . all day" and that it was "highly desirable" to get these "spoils of Pennsylvania . . . safely over the Potomac."[56] Captain Ross wrote later that "enormous supplies have been obtained, which will maintain the army for several months to come. Wagons and horses . . . have also been secured in incalculable numbers. Fifteen thousand cattle have been driven to the rear for the use of the army. The men, whose meat ration for several months past has been a quarter of a pound of bacon, now get a pound and a half of beef."[57]

The previously cited accounts by German, Irish, English, French, Swiss, and Polish officers and soldiers demonstrate the varied roles in both armies at Chancellorsville and Gettysburg of men born in Europe. Accounts by three English observers and a Prussian observer, all with Lee's army, contributed to misjudgments in Europe of the significance of the Confederate defeat at Gettysburg and to the persistence of the belief in Europe that the Union could not win the war.

Disparaging comments published by British visitors about U.S. president Abraham Lincoln confirmed the prevailing view in the British upper classes that the former frontier lawyer was not competent to lead a great nation. (*National Archives*)

U.S. secretary of state William H. Seward directed U.S. diplomats in Europe to promote immigration, but he and Lincoln vetoed proposals that the government pay transatlantic fares for immigrants who were willing to enlist in the Union army. (*National Archives*)

Irish priests encouraged Irish enlistments in both North and South and served as chaplains in both armies. In this photograph, a priest conducts mass for the Irish 69th New York. But Catholic leaders in the North opposed Lincoln's emancipation and conscription policies, and Irish support for the war waned after the Emancipation Proclamation. (*National Archives*)

Carl Schurz, a German immigrant shown here as a postwar senator, campaigned for Lincoln in 1860 and 1864, but Lincoln did not win a majority of the immigrant votes in either election. Between elections, Schurz was U.S. minister to Spain and then a major general in the Union army. (*Library of Congress*)

William Howard Russell, the first war correspondent in America for *The Times* of London, was condemned in the North for his vivid account of the Union rout at Bull Run in 1861. After he was refused permission to cover McClellan's peninsular campaign in 1862, he returned to England. His successors in Richmond and New York were strongly pro-Confederate. (*Contemporary engraving from William Howard Russell's* My Diary North and South)

GEN! MEAGHER AT THE BATTLE OF FAIR OAKS V!, JUNE 1ST 1862.

Thomas F. Meagher, a prominent Irish immigrant, was organizer and first commander of the most famous immigrant unit, the Irish Brigade. In this Currier and Ives print, he leads the brigade at Fair Oaks during McClellan's peninsular campaign in 1862. (*Library of Congress*)

Franz Sigel, a German immigrant, commanded Union units at Wilson's Creek, Pea Ridge, and the second battle of Bull Run. The slogan "I fights mit Sigel" encouraged German enlistments. German regiments in the XI Corps, previously commanded by Sigel, were unfairly labeled as "the flying Dutchmen" after Stonewall Jackson's surprise attack at Chancellorsville. (*Library of Congress*)

Confederate president Jefferson Davis yearned for European recognition but was not very sympathetic to Europeans in the South. Although nearly all Europeans who met him were enthusiastic supporters of the Confederacy, several of them were critical of Davis's stubbornness. (*Library of Congress*)

Confederate secretary of state Judah P. Benjamin thought the British government's recognition of Confederate independence would end the war, but he resented the efforts of British consuls to prevent the conscription of British residents and in 1863 prohibited further official functions by these consuls. (*Library of Congress*)

In 1862 a number of British officers came down from Canada to inspect the Union and Confederate armies. In this photograph, two officers of the Scots Fusilier Guards and other foreign officers meet the Union cavalry leader, Maj. Gen. George Stoneman (center, standing). Several British visitors wrote articles or books sustaining the upper-class British opinion that the Union could not win the war. *(National Archives)*

Visitors from France were more sympathetic to the Union cause than visitors from Britain. The Count of Paris and the Duke of Chartres, grandsons of a former French king, were volunteer aides to General McClellan in 1862. The Count of Paris wrote a comprehensive history of the war. *(Library of Congress)*

Maj. Gen. Patrick R. Cleburne, the highest-ranking Irish immigrant in the Confederate army, proposed that slaves be emancipated and enlisted as soldiers to meet manpower needs and promote British recognition of Confederate independence. Jefferson Davis suppressed the proposal. Cleburne was killed in November 1864 while commanding a division at Franklin, Tennessee. (*Library of Congress*)

Twelve men born in Britain commanded Union brigades or divisions; Joshua T. Owen, a Welsh immigrant, commanded a division at Cold Harbor. Four immigrants from Britain commanded Confederate brigades, and many British volunteers were staff officers for Confederate generals. (*Library of Congress*)

British artist and correspondent Frank Vizetelly portrayed Confederate valor in rough sketches that were converted to elegant engravings in the *Illustrated London News*. This engraving shows the Union bombardment of Fort Fisher, which protected blockade runners entering the Confederate port of Wilmington, North Carolina. *(North Carolina Office of Archives and History)*

Heros Von Borcke, a Prussian cavalryman, was a volunteer with Gen. J.E.B. Stuart's Confederate cavalry. After Von Borcke was severely wounded in 1863, the Confederate Congress commended his distinguished service to the Confederate cause. *(Library of Congress)*

Chapter 16

VICKSBURG HAS FALLEN!

The War *in the* West: 1861–1863

Most of the European visitors during the Civil War limited their direct observations to the war in the east, which was confined to Virginia, Maryland, and Pennsylvania. But there were many European immigrants in the war in the "west." In the first two years of the war, the western battles were mainly in Missouri, Arkansas, Tennessee, and Mississippi.

German volunteers played a crucial but controversial role in Missouri in the spring of 1861. Although Missouri was a slave state, most of the 50,000 Germans in St. Louis were strongly Unionist and antislavery. When pro-Confederate militia threatened the important U.S. arsenal in St. Louis, four hastily enlisted regiments of German volunteers and two companies of regulars surrounded their camp and disarmed the militia. Later, when a mob of Southern sympathizers threw brickbats at the Germans, they fired on the crowd and killed twenty-eight civilians. But the Germans had saved Missouri for the Union. Lieutenant Colonel Camille Ferri Pisani, a French visitor to St. Louis in September, wrote "without . . . the energetic appeal of the German population, the whole of Missouri would have been lost to the Union."[1]

"The taking of Camp Jackson had a good and a bad effect," Ulysses S. Grant wrote in his memoirs. "Many Union Democrats were offended by it, seeing it as a violation of state's rights. . . . The fact that the Germans had been used to coerce . . . free Americans, who stood in their own camp ordered by the governor of that state, gave offense. But . . . the taking of the camp saved St. Louis for us, spared us a long and dreadful siege of the city, and was one of the greatest successes of the entire war."[2] President Theodore Roosevelt stated in 1903 that "it would have been out of the question to have kept Missouri loyal had it not been for the German element."[3]

In 1861 and early 1862 the one of the most prominent Union generals in the west was a German immigrant, Franz Sigel. He had fought in the German revolution of 1848; by 1860 he was superintendent of schools in St. Louis. Sigel was appointed a brigadier general in May 1861 and commanded Union divisions at the two most important battles west of the Mississippi—Wilson's Creek in southwest Missouri in September 1861 and Pea Ridge (Elkhorn Tavern) in northern Arkansas in March 1862. Although not a particularly adept general, Sigel was valued by Lincoln because of his popularity with the Germans. "I fights mit Sigel" became a rallying cry in the German community.

By the spring of 1862 Ulysses S. Grant had emerged as the dominant figure in the war in the west. There is no evidence that any European observer talked with Grant, before or after his elevation in 1864 to the command of the entire Union army, but two European immigrants recorded early contacts with Grant. Major Julian Kune, a Hungarian in the 24th Illinois, met Colonel Grant in 1861: "He appeared more like a prosperous farmer . . . than a Colonel of a regiment. There was no sword dangling from his side; all the adornment about his plain blue army blouse was the colonel's 'insignia.' "[4] "There was certainly nothing in his outward appearance or in his personal ways or conversation to indicate the great military qualities he possessed," wrote Henry Villard, a German-born war correspondent who talked with Grant in 1862. "Firmness seemed to me about the only characteristic expressed in his features. Otherwise, he was a very plain, unpretentious, unimposing person, easily approached, reticent as a rule, and yet showing at times a fondness for a chat about all sorts of things."[5]

Several European immigrants wrote descriptions of the battle of Shiloh (Pittsburg Landing) in Tennessee in April 1862. An English immigrant, Henry M. Stanley—who later found Dr. Livingstone in Africa—was in the 6th Alabama: "The battlefield consisted of low ridges separated by broad depressions, which sunk occasionally into ravines of respectable depth. . . . The enemy resolutely maintained their ground. . . . We lay down, and availed ourselves of trees, logs, and hollows, and annoyed their upstanding ranks. Battery pounded battery, and we hugged our resting-places closely. Of a sudden, we rose and raced toward the position and took it by sheer weight and impetuosity. . . . We were continually pressing them toward the river Tennessee. . . . As it drew near four o'clock, . . . the long-continued excitement, the successive tautening and relaxing of the nerves, the quenchless thirst, made more intense by the fumes of sulphurous powder and the caking grime on the lips caused by tearing the paper cartridges, and a ravening hunger, all combined had reduced me to a walking automaton."[6]

Captain Bernhard Hund was in the mainly German 6th Kentucky: "The day before, General Grant had a hot fight with the Rebels and was beaten back. If General Buell had not come at the right time with his army to help, the Rebels would have driven Grant and his army into the Tennessee River. . . . Around 10 AM our regiment made a bayonet charge on the Rebels, which they could not withstand; two of their regiments fled; however, they came back again reinforced, so we had to retreat. . . . Our regiment . . . stood like a wall; . . . if they had fallen back in disorder, probably all would have been killed. . . . On the second day of the battle was won back all that was lost on the first day, and, with it, much more."[7]

William Watson, a Scottish engineer, read accounts of the battle in Memphis newspapers: "They all seem to have been carefully prepared . . . under the most approved Government inspection. . . . The Confederates had gained a great victory and had driven the enemy back into the Cumberland River and taken many of their guns, but by some means they had been obliged to fall back again to Corinth. . . . Here the Memphis and Charleston railway crossed the Mobile and Ohio railway and from a place called Meridian, some distance south of Corinth, lines branched off to Jackson, Vicksburg, New Orleans, and Mobile. If Corinth should fall into the hands of the federals, Memphis would be cut off from inland communication and be of comparatively little value."[8]

Benjamin Thomas, a Welsh immigrant in the 7th Iowa, described the battle of Corinth: "They were at least forty thousand in number whilst we were half their strength. It was a very bloody battle for some hours. I was never so tired in all my life. It was an unbelievably hot day so that with the smoke, the firing and the sound of cannons, I was almost on the point of collapse. . . . Hundreds of men fell at my side. The enemy was completely victorious. . . . When the sun set the battle ended for the day . . . About three o'clock in the morning . . . a general attack was launched and the awful fighting went on until ten o'clock at night. The enemy made a most determined assault upon our lines. . . . Now our turn came to attack and . . . we slaughtered them like sheep. About 2000 were taken prisoner, 1000 killed, and 2000 wounded. . . . The loss of Corinth was a bitter blow the enemy, for they lost a valuable line of communication."[9]

Watson recorded two other great Confederate losses in the spring of 1862: "A great disaster . . . had befallen the Confederacy, . . . the fall of New Orleans. . . . The news came like a thunderclap upon the men. . . . A number of troops were now sent off to occupy and fortify Vicksburg. . . . About the middle of May, we were apprised of the destruction of the Confederate gunboats . . . on the Mississippi at Memphis and the capture of that city. . . . This was another serious . . . blow to the Confederacy, as it left the Mississippi open to the Federals down to New Orleans . . . unless the fortifications at Vicksburg could be got into such a forward state as to prevent it."[10]

Lieutenant Colonel Henry Fletcher of the Scots Fusilier Guards was apparently the only British observer to get a firsthand look at the war in the west; he visited Vicksburg in the fall of 1862: "At a short distance above the town the river makes one of those sharp bends so common in the Mississippi, leaving a narrow peninsula of low land in front of the town. The town stands on rather high bluffs. . . . Batteries have been placed above the town in order to command the upper reach of the river, others below the town to prevent the advance of vessels from the lower Mississippi and also to command the low point of land through which the Federals endeavored last summer to cut a canal. . . . The town was attacked, toward the end of the summer, by two fleets from the Upper and Lower Mississippi. . . . Little damage was done to the town during the six week's bombardment. . . . Only fifteen lives were lost, most of the inhabitants having left the town previous to the bombardment."[11]

As long as the Confederates held Vicksburg, they prevented Union ships from navigating the Mississippi and maintained their line of communication with Confederate forces in the trans-Mississippi region. "Never will the day dawn," Lawley wrote to *The Times* in April, "when the words, 'Vicksburg has fallen' will fill the Northern heart with exultation and delight."[12] The persistent Union efforts to take Vicksburg were described by General De Trobriand: "Vicksburg . . . was generally regarded as impregnable. . . . As the place was unapproachable from the front, . . . Sherman was sent to take it in reverse by way of the Yazoo River, and he failed. Grant undertook to cut a canal, which would connect two bends of the Mississippi, in order to send through them the gunboats out of reach of the enemy's guns." The canal route was flooded by the rising Mississippi. "Grant resolved to send his gunboats down the river, past the Vicksburg batteries. Admiral Porter . . . succeeded in a dark night, without any loss except that of one steamer and injuries . . . to a few others. . . . On May 14 General Johnston is beaten and the city of Jackson . . . falls into Grant's hands . . . On 18th Pemberton retired to Vicksburg, which is then immediately invested."[13]

"This campaign . . . stamps General Grant as a man of uncommon military ability," Sylvanus Cadwallader, a war correspondent born in Wales, wrote to his wife on May 21. "The result has been five hard fought battles in two weeks; a march of two hundred miles; the capture of over six thousand prisoners; the taking of sixty pieces of field artillery and nine heavy siege guns; besides destroying small arms, ammunition, and Confederate state property beyond computation; and finally the close investment of Vicksburg from every quarter. . . . All his plans have worked to a charm."[14]

Lieutenant Colonel Victor Vifquain, a Belgian immigrant commanding the 97th Illinois, described the Union siege of Vicksburg: "No less than 40 forts ringed the town, and each of these was joined to its neighbor by trenches for the infantry.

On May 19, 20, 21, and 22 we charged their works. Each time we were almost successful but . . . the ditches were so deep and the parapets so high that climbing them was impossible. . . . Therefore we began to mine, and one mine was placed beneath each fort. The work would have been completed if the enemy had resisted 24 hours more."[15]

"The cannons are sounding loudly tonite," a Welsh immigrant in the 23rd Wisconsin, John G. Jones, wrote home on June 9. "I do not think that the Rebs have slept very much for three weeks, as we are shelling them from every direction. . . . They say the shells have killed General Pemberton's wife. Our pickets are within 150 yards of their fort. The pickets talk to each other every night. The Rebs say, 'We have a new General commanding us.' 'What is his name?' 'General Starvation.' "[16]

Colonel Vifquain described the surrender of Vicksburg on July 4: "After a terrible 42-day siege, the enemy surrendered on July 4, the anniversary of the independence of this country. We took 32,000 prisoners, 250 siege cannon, 70,000 guns, a hundred or so flags, and ammunition enough to continue the siege for ten years. It was a great victory."[17]

The Confederate surrender at Vicksburg, on the same day General Lee began to withdraw after his unsuccessful attacks at Gettysburg, led some Europeans in America to reconsider their previous conviction that the Union could not win the war. William Watson, the Scot in Louisiana, thought that "the enemy getting control of the Mississippi rendered the cause hopeless and that further fighting was only to gratify a vindictive spirit or vain ambition."[18] But nearly two more years of bitter fighting lay ahead.

Chapter 17

THE ZEAL AND BRAVERY OF CITIZEN SOLDIERS
Union *and* Confederate Armies

In the first year or two of the war, most British observers in both North and South were highly critical of the Union army. The favorite theme of the observers in the South was that it consisted mainly of Irish and German "mercenaries" who were the "scum of Europe" and did not understand or care about the Union cause. "The foreigners, attracted by an enormous bounty, . . . can be but mercenaries," noted George Alfred Lawrence of the London *Morning Post;* "in history, the Swiss almost monopolize the glory of mercenary fidelity."[1] A British officer, Colonel Garnet Joseph Wolseley, thought Stonewall Jackson's ragged but committed veterans could never be defeated by "mobs of Irish and German mercenaries, hired . . . to fight in a cause they know little and care less about."[2]

British observers in the North, on the other hand, thought that the chief weakness of the Union army was that it consisted mainly of untrained volunteers. The British, who were accustomed to a standing army, doubted that volunteer units would ever acquire the necessary discipline. The Marquis of Hartington, who was appointed undersecretary at the British War Office soon after his visit to America in 1862, reported to Parliament that the Union army was poorly disciplined, had poor morale, and was inefficient in aggressive warfare.[3] Lawrence wrote that "the volunteer carries with him into the ranks an ostentatious spirit of self-assertion and independence. . . . He goes into action fully prepared to criticize the orders of his superiors, and even to ignore them if they clash too strongly with his private judgment."[4]

141

Lieutenant Colonel Henry Charles Fletcher, Scots Fusilier Guards, thought that attempts to enforce discipline in the volunteer regiments would limit their combat effectiveness: "It is difficult to carry out discipline without injuring the very feeling that ensures them victory. . . . Latitude in discipline must be allowed, in order to keep them as good volunteers."[5] Captain Ferdinand Lecomte, Swiss military observer in 1862, thought the volunteer regiments were "too numerous and too weak in effective force. . . . When reinforcements are needed, new regiments are ordinarily raised. . . . How much more advantageous would it not be in all respects to introduce . . . the new recruits into . . . the regiments which have already had experience."[6]

During the first two years of the war, most European observers were very critical of the regimental officers in the Union army. William H. Russell reported to *The Times* in London that "with the exception of the foreign officers and some of the staff, . . . very few of the colonels, majors, captains, or lieutenants . . . know anything of their business."[7] Lord Hartington inspected a New York regiment in 1862; "it seems a great pity," he commented, "that such fine material should be thrown away . . . by having utterly incompetent officers."[8] Captain Lecomte thought "the mode of recruiting furnished a great number of bad officers. . . . It is often difficult . . . to ascertain whether . . . an officer is a pretender, an adroit actor, or a man of merit."[9] British novelist Anthony Trollope remarked that "political influence or the power of raising recruits had been the standard by which military rank was distributed. . . . Generals, colonels, majors, captains, and lieutenants had been all appointed . . . without reference to age or qualification."[10]

Several Europeans blamed the inexperienced officers for poor discipline in the volunteer regiments. Edward Dicey, a British journalist, remarked that "the officers . . . have not the military air, the self-possession which long habit of command alone can give."[11] A French officer, Lieutenant Colonel Camille Ferri-Pisani, observed that "American armies lose much of their value by discarding, in obedience to democratic prejudice, all the natural requirements of military hierarchy."[12] Captain Lecomte thought the orders from these inexperienced officers lacked "the precision and authority which they ought to have" and "might be taken for diplomatic notes" rather than orders.[13] "There is no superiority of knowledge on the part of the officer over the soldier and no superiority of social position in a country where no such superiority is recognized," wrote the Prince of Joinville, a former French admiral. "All these causes bring about the want of authority with officers, and the want of respect among soldiers."[14]

The inefficiency of the staff officers and the lack of a general staff were also apparent when Russell visited General McDowell's headquarters shortly before the first battle of Bull Run: "I look around me for a staff, and look in vain. . . . The worst-served English general has always a young fellow or two about him who can fly across country, draw a rough sketch map, ride like a foxhunter and find something out about the enemy and their position, understand and convey orders, and obey them."[15] The Prince of Joinville regretted that "there is no special branch of the service whose duty it is to regulate, centralize, and direct the movements of the army,"[16] and several other French and German officers also remarked on the lack of a general staff.

Beginning in 1862, however, there were more favorable comments by foreign observers, although they were still accompanied in most cases by negative assessments of the discipline in the Union army. "Both officers and men are wonderfully well equipped," Edward Dicey reported early in 1862. "Their clothing is substantial and easy-fitting; their arms are good; and their accruements are as perfect as money can purchase."[17] A year later he thought "American volunteers looked . . . more businesslike than our own. . . . The general impression left upon me by my observations of the Army of the Potomac was a very favorable one."[18] Captain Lecomte reported that after the first defeat of Bull Run the Union had "created an army of six hundred thousand men in from three to four months. In the last actions it has shown military capacities equal to those of the best troops in the world." The Swiss officer thought "their patience and their sangfroid under disappointments, their force of will, and their persistence against obstacles, are truly remarkable," but that "discipline, the respect for authority . . . fall short of what is desirable."[19] But Major Heros Von Borcke, a Prussian officer serving with the Confederate cavalry, was impressed by the evidence of good discipline in a Union camp he visited while on a "flag of truce" mission in the fall 1862: "The soldiers were well dressed, and had the look of being well fed; their arms were in excellent condition. . . . Their cantonments spoke of a high degree of military discipline, the absence of which I had so often regretted in our own bivouacs."[20]

Two Europeans attributed the improvement in the army to the combat experience of the volunteers during the previous year. Brigadier General Alexander Schimmelfenning, a former Prussian officer, commented in the spring of 1862 that Union officers had learned more about military affairs in the previous year than "an officer after ten year's service in the old country."[21] The Prince of Joinville thought the Peninsula campaign in 1862 had been a tremendous learning experience for the Union troops: "Men do not . . . go through such experience as they had endured, without coming out more or less formed to war. If their primitive organization had been better, the survivors of this rude campaign . . . might be regarded as the equals of the best soldiers in the world."[22]

British observers persisted in a very qualified assessment of the Union army. Lieutenant Colonel T. L. Gallway and Captain H. J. Alderson, official British observers in 1864, conceded that "the soldiers are well-behaved, and their bravery is indisputable" and that if "properly disciplined and well commanded," the federal army would be second to no army in the world. "But as presently constituted, with so many deficiencies, it must as a whole be considered greatly inferior to European armies."[23] On the other hand, Colonel Francois De Chenal, official French military observer in 1864, concluded that earlier observers had exaggerated discipline problems in the Union army: "The very fact that these immense levies have either elected their officers or obtained them by appointments made by the local authorities, has transferred the social hierarchy to the army. . . . In all that is essential, the discipline of the American army is as good as, if not better than, that of European armies."[24] Ernest de Haurrane, a French journalist, thought the Union army was as good as a professional army and that its officers were more effective than "our garrison veterans who become generals without ever having been under fire."[25]

Foreign observers in the South were unanimously enthusiastic about the Confederate army. "If I had at any time entertained misgiving as to the ability of the Southerners to defend their country and liberties against Northern invasion," wrote Colonel Wolseley, "they were at once and forever displaced when I examined for myself the material of which the Confederate armies are composed."[26] Francis Lawley reported to *The Times* that fall that "there is only one opinion with regard to the discipline of the Southern troops, and that is that it is perfect. . . . There is about them the calmness and self-assured confidence which springs from enthusiastic belief in their general, and from successful experience of their own prowess."[27] His comments were echoed in 1863 by Lieutenant Colonel James Arthur Fremantle of the Coldstream Guards: "Their obedience and forbearing in success, their discipline under disaster, their patience under suffering, under hardships or when wounded, and their boundless devotion to their country . . . are beyond all praise."[28] Captain Justus Scheibert, a Prussian observer that year, thought that "the Southern soldier's religious character . . . made him braver and more dutiful. . . . A moral code of rectitude, together with a vital Christianity, made the Confederate army a match for the enemy three times its size."[29]

How can the difference between the reactions of foreign observers to the Union and Confederate armies be explained? For imperial, political, and economic reasons, the European observers who visited the South wanted the Confederacy to maintain its independence and therefore wanted to believe that the ragged Confederate armies were capable of preventing a Union victory. They were bombarded with statements of Confederate determination to sustain their new country, and they thought that would be enough to ensure Confederate independence. The European observers in the North, on the other hand, came to America with the persistent European belief that the Federals could not win the war and that the Union could not be restored. In the period before Gettysburg and Vicksburg, they saw nothing that changed their minds.

Some Europeans thought slave owners were uniquely qualified for army commands. Lieutenant Colonel Charles Fletcher wrote that "the rich planter possessing many slaves entirely dependent on him in regard to food, clothing, medicine, and discipline, acquired habits of command and organization highly useful to the officers of an army."[30] The Prince of Joinville believed that slave owners, "living by the labor of their inferiors and accustomed to command them, . . . possess to a certain extent, the qualities of aristocrats. In their hands the discipline of the army could not suffer."[31] Captain Scheibert expressed similar views. But Russell of *The Times* thought inexperienced officers in the South were just as ineffective in maintaining discipline as in the North: "The officers are . . . energetic, determined men, but utterly ignorant . . . of military science. . . . The privates are quite well aware they know as much of soldiering as the great majority of their officers."[32]

"Among volunteer regiments," wrote another British correspondent, Samuel Phillipps Day, "the election of officers is fraught with abuse and is likely to prove disastrous. . . . Mere bravery in an officer, without experience, is . . . more to be avoided than desired. . . . Gallant officers have been cut down for want of exercising ordinary discretion."[33] In some units, officers were periodically reelected, providing a degree of rotation in office. William Watson, a Scot in the Confederate army, thoroughly disapproved of this practice "on the ground that it kept always inexperienced men in office, because the incumbents were turned out just as they were becoming acquainted with the duties of their offices."[34]

On the whole, however, Watson thought the volunteer system had been essential for mobilizing "in an incredibly short time a large and effective army and the zeal and general bravery displayed by the citizen soldiers. . . . Volunteers . . . might not attain that clockwork precision which looks so well on parade but which is quite unnecessary in actual warfare, but they could be made thoroughly efficient for every practical purpose. . . . Their intelligence gives them a sense of duty, and they know that strict obedience is indispensable."[35] But he was shocked by the Conscription Act passed by the Confederate Congress in April 1862. It provided that "all troops enlisted or mustered into the service for short periods should be continued in the service. This was a great disappointment to the men of our regiment, . . . who had volunteered for one year only . . . and were now looking forward to getting home." The new law provided that every male citizen between 18 and 35 was subject to military duty. Watson wrote that "the volunteers . . . considered that men forced compulsorily into service were of little value."[36]

Two German immigrants in the Union army wrote of their encounters with some of the Confederate conscripts. General Carl Schurz recalled his talk with Confederate prisoners late in 1863: "The knowledge of the world of the "Southern poor white" had been confined to . . . the immediate surroundings of his wretched log-cabin. . . . They had but a very dim conception . . . of what all this fighting and bloodshed was all about . . . and could hardly be expected to be sentimentally loyal to the 'Southern cause.' Many of them saw, therefore, nothing dishonorable or criminal in desertion or voluntary surrender. . . . But while . . . in the ranks, they proved in many respects excellent soldiers. They suffered hunger and all sorts of privations with heroic endurance. They executed marches of almost incredible length and difficulty, and bore all kinds of fatigue without much complaint. And they were good, steady fighters . . . and many of them good marksmen, having been 'handy' with the rifle or shotgun from their childhood up."[37] Captain Bernhard Domschcke, 26th Wisconsin, was less charitable in his description of the men who guarded him in the Libby Prison in Richmond in 1864: "The guards were from Georgia, . . . in gray rags, unwashed, unkempt. . . . They were of the last conscription, reserves, companies of boys and old men with gray hair. . . . They belonged to the South's population of poor whites [and] stood lower than Negroes in the eyes of the slaveholding aristocracy. . . . Born impoverished on tiny plots of land or to [other] low stations, these people . . . grow up ignorant and illiterate, they know nothing but a few practical skills of everyday living."[38]

European observers in the South often commented on the shortages of uniforms, shoes, supplies, and food in the Confederate army. The most frequent comments were on clothing. "Never, perhaps, were soldiers uniformed . . . with such utter disregard to outward appearances," wrote Samuel Phillips Day. "I seldom found two articles of dress to harmonize, either in texture or colour, upon the same person."[39] Colonel Ferri-Pisani noted that "the question of uniform, not very well solved in the North, was not solved at all in the South."[40] Lawley often commented on Confederate supply problems, but always accompanied them with remarks about the effectiveness of the Confederate troops despite the shortages. "Although I saw much suffering, great want of shoes, frequently very inadequate clothing," he wrote after a visit to Jackson's army in the Shenandoah valley, "I was astonished to observe how confident was the spirit pervading the entire body. . . . Any battle into which these men enter is half won when the first shot is fired."[41] "It is a never failing source of wonder and admiration," he wrote in another dispatch, "to see these men, . . . so sparsely fed, so destitute of blankets, and yet so cheerful and lighthearted under every privation, so resolute and indomitable in suffering, and . . . so irresistible in the field."[42]

Captain Scheibert described the food at Confederate headquarters: "The courses were simple, the same in the morning as in the evenings: cornbread and wheat bread lay on the table. . . . There was also coffee mixed with parched wheat or corn, and some tea, . . . meat, and molasses. Butter was a rare delicacy, as were eggs. . . . On many days there was . . . nothing but bacon and crackers, which was drunk with the splendid spring water that gushes forth . . . every thousand steps in Virginia."[43] Lawley quoted a wry comment by Lee late in the war on the food at his table: "Occasionally we have only beef, occasionally only bread; but if we have both together, and salt is added to them, we think ourselves Sybarites."[44] Private Henry Morton Stanley, a British immigrant, described the rudimentary arrangements for feeding the men in the 6th Arkansas: "The 'Dixie Greys' . . . consisted mostly of young men and lads who were . . . ignorant of the art of converting their ration of raw beef and salt pork, field beans, and flour into digestible food. . . . They learned how to cook in time, but meanwhile they made sorry messes of it, and suffered accordingly. . . . I do not remember ever to have seen an officer who examined the state of our messes."[45]

Several observers mentioned the Confederate dependence on arms and supplies captured from the Union army. "Into whatever camp you go," wrote Colonel Wolseley, "you are sure to see tents, carts, horses, and guns all marked with the 'U.S.' Whole regiments go into action with smoothbore muskets and without greatcoats, and . . . in the evening are well provided with everything, having changed their old muskets for rifles!" Wolseley was amused to find General Lee's tent "stamped as belonging to a colonel of a New Jersey regiment."[46]

European observers frequently commented on infantry tactics in America that differed substantially from practices in Europe, especially specific targeting by infantrymen, the utilization of units consisting of skilled sharpshooters, and the extensive use of entrenchments. These developments had resulted from the improvements in infantry weapons and from the fact that most of the Civil War was fought in rugged, tree-covered terrain or fenced farmland rather than the open plains on which most European battles were fought.

At the beginning of the war, many of the Confederate troops were armed with old muskets. Private Stanley described the use of these weapons at Shiloh: "Our weapons were the obsolete flintlocks, and the ammunition was rolled in cartridge-paper which contained powder, a round ball, and three buckshot. When we loaded we had to tear the paper with our teeth, empty a little powder into the pan, lock it, empty the rest of the powder into the barrel, press paper and ball into the muzzle, and ram home." These weapons were rarely aimed at specific targets. At one stage of the battle "twenty thousand muskets were being fired. . . . Though accuracy of aim was impossible, . . . many bullets found their destined billets on both sides." After the battle, many of the Confederates were able to replace the old flintlocks with rifles found on the battlefield.[47]

Observers in the South were frequently told that Southerners were much more skilled with rifles than the Yankees. "Almost every individual Southerner," wrote an English officer, Captain Fitzgerald Ross, "has been accustomed to use the rifle from his earliest youth and has thus acquired a skill in handling the weapon which no amount of drilling can supply and which the Irish, Dutch, and city Yankees, who form the mass of the Federal army, can never hope to attain."[48] But this Southern view underestimated the number of Yankees who had lived on the frontier and the number of the "city Yankees" who were immigrants from Germany, Switzerland, and other countries in which rifle clubs and expert marksmanship were taken very seriously.

In contrast to the European practice of massed firing by infantry in the general direction of the enemy, American riflemen did not fire until a specific target was in range. Colonel De Chenal, the French military observer, was surprised to discover in 1864 that "the American infantry have acquired the habit of reserving their fire and of aiming.[49] General De Trobriand, the highest ranking Frenchman in the Union army, described the two U.S. regiments of sharpshooters "composed exclusively of the best marksmen. . . . Their arms were Sharps breech-loading rifles. Fighting always as sharpshooters, they had a firmness of hand and correctness of aim which rendered them particularly dangerous. At a distance which the rifled Springfields could not reach, their deadly balls struck the mark almost with certainty."[50] Colonel De Chenal was very impressed with the American sharpshooters: "They fire very accurately, so that in both armies, the percentage of officers and general officers killed is considerable. At the battle of Spotsylvania, General Sedgwick, one of the best of the Union generals, was killed by a Confederate soldier who was perched in a tree, more than 700 metres distant."[51]

Lieutenant Rudolf Aschmann, a Swiss immigrant in one of the U.S. sharpshooter regiments, described a battle between sharpshooters during the siege of Yorktown: "In two consecutive nights we dug a trench, reinforced it with fascines and gabions and equipped it with well-placed loopholes. It was a task not for the fainthearted; working in pitch-dark night without lights of any kind, silent and avoiding all noise as much as possible, at less than 250 steps from the enemy. The slightest noise betraying us to the enemy would have attracted the fire of eight cannons. . . . Because of the short distance from the enemy marksmen, . . . the detachments . . . had to enter the shelter before daybreak and remain all day long until darkness of night enabled them to withdraw. From this ditch, about six feet deep, we closely watched the enemy cannoneers and marksmen and very soon made it impossible for the former to serve their guns. But our opponent, too, had his watchful eye on us. It was dangerous to show one's head above the breastwork for even an instant, and more than one man paid for this carelessness with his life."[52]

General De Trobriand recalled his use of sharpshooters at Kelly's Ford: "During the cannonade I had thrown forward the sharpshooters, commanded by Colonel Trepp, to the edge of the river. . . . They kept up so deadly a fire on the opposite entrenchments that the enemy did not dare to show himself, except occasionally for a chance shot. . . . Profiting from this advantage, the rest of the battalion entered resolutely into the water. . . . Before I had reached the opposite bank, my skirmishers, led by Lieutenants Aschmann and Garrison, had carried the first line of rifle-pits."[53]

The use of sharpshooters and other skilled riflemen on both sides required infantry, artillery, and even cavalry units to dig entrenchments to protect themselves from the deadly enemy fire. "At the beginning of hostilities," Colonel De Chenal noted, "it was with great difficulty that the soldier could be made to use the pick and shovel, . . . but he soon saw the necessity for it. . . . Hardly has the army halted, with its bivouac not yet complete, before it is entrenched." The French observer was impressed by the use in field fortifications "of timber revetments, of thick abatis in front of the lines, and of wire entanglements, made by fastening iron wire to stumps of trees cut off two and one-half feet from the ground. In front of Petersburg, a trench ten kilometers in length was, in two days, so well covered with field-works as to be proof against attack."[54]

Early in the war, European observers were not impressed with American artillery. After riding through the Union camps just before the first battle of Bull Run, Russell wrote that "their artillery is miserably deficient; they have not . . . more than five . . . or six batteries . . . and these are . . . badly horsed, miserably equipped, and provided with the worst set of gunners and drivers which, I, who have seen the Turkish field guns, ever beheld."[55] But the Union had both the industrial capacity and the skilled manpower necessary for the rapid development of an effective artillery force. A considerable number of Union artillerymen were German immigrants who had previously served in artillery units in Prussia or other German states.

There were many descriptions by European observers and immigrants of artillery barrages from both sides, some of which are quoted in other chapters. The Reverend J. D. Jones, the Welsh chaplain of the 117th New York, described Grant's bombardment of Petersburg in September 1864: "From where we stood on a little hill, we could see the shells from our rear defences landing in the middle of one of the enemy's fortifications. As they landed, trees and earth if not bodies were thrown in the air in all directions. The sight of the 300 pound shell from the big mortar 'Dictator' which is on the railroad near us, as it spun in its trajectory toward the centre of Petersburg, was really amazing."[56]

The development of an effective artillery arm was more difficult in the South. When an Englishman, Francis W. Dawson, applied for a commission as ordnance officer in the Confederate army, he told Colonel Gorgas, Confederate Chief of Ordnance, that "I knew nothing whatever of the duties of an Ordnance officer and hardly knew the difference between a Napoleon gun and a Belgian rifle. Colonel Gorgas . . . said very quietly . . . 'I reckon you know as much about it as many other officers who have been assigned to the same duty."[57] The only large works in the Confederacy capable of casting cannon was the Tredegar Iron Works in Richmond. Captain Scheibert described the many problems encountered in producing cannon and other arms at the Tredegar works: "Some of the machine tools first had to be brought through the blockade, others had to be manufactured, and the technicians for the most part had to be trained. . . . The ore for the cannons had to be procured and then transported to Richmond. . . . Nevertheless, it was possible as early as the fall of 1862 to procure in Richmond weapons of all types and munitions even in adequate quantities and to cast cannons of all calibers."[58]

Colonel Fremantle claimed in 1863 that "the Tredegar Works at Richmond and other foundries cast more cannon than is wanted." But he noted that many cannon used by the Confederate army had been captured from the Yankees: "The Federal generals have always hitherto proved themselves the most indefatigable purveyors of artillery to the Confederate government. Even in those actions which they claim as drawn battles or victories, . . . they have never failed to make over cannon to the Southerners without exacting any in return."[59]

European observers and participants on both sides agreed that during the first half of the war Confederate cavalry was superior in quality and numbers to the Union cavalry. "The rich young men of the South . . . brought to the army excellent horses, which they already knew how to manage," recalled General De Trobriand. "These detachments, well mounted and equipped, . . . were very useful to the Confederate army. They acted as advance parties and scouts, and gathered exact information as to our movements. They protected their convoys, and carried off our wagons. They covered their own lines, and captured our pickets, appearing where they were least expected, disappearing before their retreat could be cut off, seldom returning without booty or without prisoners."[60]

Lawley reported from Richmond that "there is but one opinion as to the superior horsemanship of their cavalry soldiers and the excellence of their horses."[61] The reputation and effectiveness of the Confederate cavalry was widely credited to its commander, General J. E. B. Stuart. Major Von Borcke, who served with Stuart in 1862 and early 1863, thought Stuart was "the model of a dashing cavalry leader . . . and one of most fearless and dexterous horsemen in America. . . . His jaunty uniform . . . consisted of a small gray jacket, trousers of the same stuff, and over them high military boots, a yellow silk sash, and a gray slouch hat surmounted by a sweeping black ostrich plume."[62] Another Prussian, Captain Scheibert, wrote that Stuart "impressed his men with his courage, cold-bloodedness, tenacity, and resourcefulness. . . . His looks and presence also won loyalty and fired up his men."[63] When Stuart was killed in 1864, Lawley wrote a eulogy: "Fearless to a fault, singularly enduring of fatigue, never sick, never absent from duty, never daunted nor dispirited, he died as he had lived, . . . the most cheerful victim to a cause for which he would have given a thousand lives. His loss is bewailed by General Lee as that of a son."[64]

In contrast, in the first two years of the war Europeans had few good things to say about the Union cavalry. "On the outbreak of the war," wrote George Alfred Lawrence, correspondent for the London *Morning Post,* "a conscript who could keep his saddle through an entire day . . . was considered by his fellows as a credit to the regiment."[65] Before the first battle of Bull Run, Russell wrote that "they have no cavalry, only a few scarecrow-men who would dissolve partnership with their steeds at the first serious combined movement, mounted in high saddles, on wretched mouthless screws, and some few regulars from the frontiers."[66] In 1862 Captain Edward Hewett, a British observer, thought "their horses were poor and ill kept, their equipment ragged, and their discipline bad." But he noted that the Union cavalry was "well armed with swords, revolvers, and breech loading carbines, which . . . fire seven rounds without reloading and may with ease be discharged by one hand."[67]

European officers made significant contributions to the training and operations of the Union cavalry. Lieutenant Thomas Francis Galwey, an Irish immigrant in the 8th Ohio, wrote that "good cavalry requires more training than is necessary to make good infantry; our cavalry lacked this training owing to the hurried manner in which our armies have been assembled and the scarcity of competent officers. . . . A few experienced foreign officers, Irish, English, French, German, Italian, Hungarian, and others, have done wonders in training our mounted troops."[68] General De Trobriand described the role of his fellow Frenchman, Alfred Duffie, colonel of the 1st Rhode Island Cavalry: "He had found it in a truly pitiful condition. A few months had sufficed to transform his command into one of the best regiments. . . . The horses were in good condition, the men appeared finely, and the equipments were irreproachable. . . . The ignorant or incapable officers had given place to others, better instructed and more skillful. The cavalry men, novices at the beginning of the war, had better learned their trade."[69] De Trobriand noted that "the initial superiority of Confederate cavalry lasted for nearly two years, . . . until the day when our horsemen, inured to war and better commanded, were able to . . . defeat everywhere the adversaries against whom, as novices, they had not been able to hold their ground."[70]

Europeans frequently noted that the use of cavalry in the American armies differed sharply from European practices. Observers with both armies were impressed by the effective use of cavalry for raids and reconnaissance. "To make a reconnaissance or an adventurous raid," Captain Lecomte noted in 1862, the Union cavalry "would not yield in any thing to the best Cossacks of the Russian army. . . . Expeditions . . . over frightful roads or across woods, rivers, and marshes, by day or by night, constitute the ordinary service of a good number of the regiments."[71] Captain Scheibert and Major Von Borcke were very impressed with Stuart's raid into Maryland and Pennsylvania in the fall of 1862. "Stuart . . . succeeded not only in spreading fear and confusion in the rear of the hostile army," Scheibert recorded, "but also outfitted his entire cavalry division with the booty and augmented it with 600 horses."[72]

But Scheibert also recorded Lee's regret on July 2, 1863, that Stuart's second raid into Pennsylvania had prevented his participation in the initial phases of the battle of Gettysburg: "General Lee was very much concerned and restless about General Stuart, of whom he had heard and seen nothing for several days. . . . News finally arrived . . . that this bold general had marched across the Potomac at Seneca, between Washington and the enemy army, from which he took 200 wagons, and was now at York, from whence he was ordered up, and he rode ninety miles with 3,000 men without dismounting or feeding. Lee would have preferred to have him present on July 1, *without* this daring venture, in order better to harvest the fruits of the victory of the first day, and he would also have preferred to have him fresh and able to fight, while the cavalry naturally required twenty-four hours of rest in order to be ready again for effective service after the long march."[73] Nevertheless, cavalry raids continued to be an important Confederate military tactic and an important source of supplies for the Confederate army. Lawley reported in July 1864 that General Early's raid, which reached the Washington suburbs, had yielded an "unprecedented haul of horses which will furnish fresh teams for General Early's ninety guns, will remount his cavalry, and admit of large supplies being hauled into Virginia."[74]

At first several European observers did not fully understand or approve of the way cavalry was used in battle in America. In a study of the military legacy of the

Civil War, Jay Luvaas wrote that "in 1861 European cavalry still relied upon the lance and saber and fought primarily by what were known as shock tactics. Massed into dense formations, cavalry was literally hurled at the enemy in an effort to crush his forces by the sheer impact of the mounted charges. In the melee that followed, the sword and saber . . . were effective weapons, far handier than firearms at closer range."[75] Although European shock tactics were taught at West Point, they were ignored by graduates when they encountered the realities of service on the American frontier.[76] Luvaas noted that during the Civil War "the new tactics stemmed from an increase in firepower. . . . Cavalry was forced to dismount and rely upon firearms in order to survive or be effective on a modern battlefield."[77]

Captain Ross was with a Confederate brigade when it met a Union cavalry troop: "The Yankees got to their horses, mounted, and I fully expected would charge and ride down the Confederate brigade. . . . But nothing of the kind occurred. . . . Mounted cavalry never attacked infantry." Ross perceived several reasons for the reluctance of the Confederates to fight while mounted. "Every man's horse is his own property. . . . If a man loses his horse, and cannot get another, he has forthwith to join the infantry. . . . With the use of the rifle they have been familiar from their earliest youth. To handle a rifle efficiently . . . a man must dismount." He also recognized that "the country is so wooded and broken up with high fences that opportunities for a regular cavalry charge on a large scale seldom occur."[78] Major Von Borcke came to similar conclusions: "The nature of the ground in Virginia did not favour the operations of cavalry and . . . the great improvement in firearms in our day had necessitated a very material change in cavalry tactics."[79] Although Captain Scheibert insisted that the Confederates thought the main role of cavalry was "warfare by shock," he acknowledged that "forested thickets, cut through by fences and ravines, together with skill in firearms, tempted the mounted to dismount."[80]

Colonel Fremantle described the widespread use of cavalry as dismounted infantry in both armies: "Their system is to dismount and leave their horses in some secure place. One man is placed in charge of his own and three other horses, whilst the remainder act as infantry skirmishers. . . . The horses . . . were never far from the men, who could mount and be off to . . . another position or act as cavalry as the case might require."[81]

The European cavalrymen were also disappointed by the rarity of conventional battles between cavalry units. Colonel Fremantle thought the few cavalry clashes were "miserable affairs." "Neither party has any idea of serious charging with the saber. They approach one another with considerable boldness, until they get to within about 40 yards, and then, at the very moment when a dash is necessary, and the sword alone should be used, they hesitate, halt, and commence a desultory fire with carbines and revolvers."[82] "When two cavalry parties meet," Captain Ross commented scornfully, "they do not fight themselves, but set their artillery to work."[83]

Neither Fremantle nor Ross was at the battle between large Union and Confederate cavalry forces at Brandy Station on June 6, 1863, which Von Borcke called "the greatest cavalry battle ever fought on the American continent." Edwin B. Coddington described the Europeans' view of the battle: "Much of the fighting conformed to classical concepts of cavalry engagements dear to the heart of the European traditionalists, but . . . the Americans could not get over their bad habits. . . . Both sides dismounted a very large proportion of their troops and fought them as infantry. Every Confederate cavalry brigade had squadrons of sharpshooters armed with rifles, which in action were always placed behind stone walls, if there were any, to protect the flanks of the horsemen. These tactics were much in evidence at Brandy Station. General Buford too dismounted practically all of his First Division of about 2,100 troopers. . . . Pleasonton committed the further unforgivable sin of using infantrymen in what was supposed to be a bonafide cavalry fight." But Coddington noted that, "in so doing, he equalized his smaller cavalry force and Stuart's larger one, and thus did not need to have as many of his cavalry troopers fight dismounted as did Stuart. The presence of eight infantry regiments . . . helps to explain why Pleasonton had no trouble in withdrawing his force across the river in the face of a formidable foe."[84]

Most of the European observers were ill-equipped to report objectively on the effectiveness of the Union or Confederate armies. There had not been a large-scale land battle in Europe since Waterloo, and most of the Europeans had never been in combat. Used to standing professional armies, the Europeans were scornful of volunteer armies with untrained officers and men. The heavily wooded or fenced American terrain was very different from the open plains on which most European battles had been fought. The observers only gradually realized the extent to which improvements in weapons since Waterloo required new tactics for infantry, cavalry, and artillery. Most important, their judgments of both armies were colored by their preconceptions and their sympathies. Most of the observers in both North and South wanted to believe that the Union army could not defeat the Confederate army, and their reports on both armies reflected their wishful thinking.

Chapter 18

A BOLD AND DARING ENTERPRISE

Naval Dimensions *of the* Civil War

D uring the Civil War, seamen born in Europe filled large percentages of the berths in three types of ships: Union warships, including both those engaged in offensive operations at Confederate coastal and river ports and those in the squadrons blockading Confederate ports; Confederate warships, including those defending Confederate ports and those raiding Union commerce on the high seas; and merchant ships running the Union blockade of Confederate ports.

The U.S. Navy, which had only about 7,500 men at the beginning of the war, grew to about 51,500 men by war's end.[1] Throughout the war the navy was in competition with the army for men. Until 1864 the navy was not authorized to offer enlistment bounties.[2] The great majority of Americans lived in inland areas and had no knowledge of the sea, but large numbers of British, Irish, and Scandinavian immigrants and some of the German immigrants were from coastal areas in Europe and had at least some familiarity with naval service. These immigrants were prime targets for naval recruiters. The passage of the Conscription Act in the spring of 1863 encouraged many European immigrants to enlist in the navy to avoid conscription into the army. The system for sharing prize money provided a major incentive for enlistment in the squadrons blockading Confederate ports. Half the proceeds of the sale at auction of a captured blockade runner was retained by the government, but the other half was divided among the officers and men of the ships that had participated in the capture.

Ella Lonn estimated that between one-fourth and one-half of the enlisted seamen in the Union navy were born abroad.[3] Men born in England and Ireland were the most numerous, but there were seamen from many other countries. One study noted that men from 29 nations and principalities were on the *Colorado*, 26 nationalities were on the *Minnesota*, and 25 were on the *Hartford*.[4]

Although the Confederacy had an abundant supply of officers who had previously served in the U.S. Navy, there were few native-born sailors in the South and the Confederacy's small navy relied heavily on foreign-born men. Some Confederate officers praised the European sailors. Lieutenant William H. Parker recorded that he had never sailed with a better crew than the Englishmen, Danes, and Swedes who manned the *Beaufort*. The crew included two gunners who had been trained at a Royal Navy gunnery school and had won medals in the Crimean war. "I used to wonder," he wrote, "at their eagerness to go into battle considering the fact that they knew nothing at all about the cause of the war."[5]

Other Confederate officers doubted the loyalty to the Confederate cause of the foreign-born sailors. An officer assigned to the *Morgan* at Mobile was shocked to discover that "out of a hundred and fifty, not one is even American, much less a Southerner. We have Irish, Dutch, Norwegians, Danes, French, Spanish, Italians, Mexicans, . . . and Indians." He thought they were "a set of desperate cutthroats" and that their loyalty was doubtful."[6] Flag Officer William W. Hunter reported from Savannah early in 1864 that "no reliance whatever can be placed on the men of foreign birth . . . in this squadron. . . . All of the men who have been and are being tried by the naval court-martial here for mutinous conduct are Irish and English." He thought that the foreign-born sailors would prove to be "very detrimental and dangerous to our cause."[7]

Although most of the officers of the *Alabama* and the other Confederate commerce raiders were Confederate citizens, virtually all of the sailors on these Confederate warships were Europeans. Captain Raphael Semmes of the *Alabama* wrote in his memoirs that his crew had consisted of "110 of the most reckless sailors from the groggeries and brothels of Liverpool."[8] Researchers in Liverpool have developed a list of eighty-five men from the Liverpool area who served on the *Alabama*, including two Welshman, two Irishmen, one Scot, and one German. Fifty-seven of these men remained with the ship until it was sunk by the U.S.S. *Kearsarge* at Cherbourg in 1864; eleven of them died at Cherbourg.[9]

Some of the original crew members deserted during port visits, and replacements were recruited from among the crews of captured vessels. Arthur Sinclair, a lieutenant on the *Alabama*, wrote that "Semmes would never ship from the captured vessels any seamen of North American nativity."[10] The substantial literature on the Confederate commerce raiders contains almost nothing on the reasons the British and other European sailors served on the *Alabama* and its sister raiders. Charles G. Summersell noted that the apparent incentives were "the prospect of prize money and relatively high wages, about double prewar wages."[11] But the hope of prize money soon proved illusory. No foreign government allowed the Confederate raiders to bring captured ships into its ports. Most of the captured ships were burned, after the removal of their crews and of any cargo of use to the raiders. A few ships were released after they took aboard the crews of other captured ships and their captains had signed bonds pledging payments by the shipowners after the war.

Most of the original crew of the *Alabama* had served on British merchant ships, but at least four men in the crew were members of the Royal Naval Reserve, who had previously served in the Royal Navy. When the secretary of the navy sent a congratulatory letter to the captain of the *Kearsarge* following the sinking of the *Alabama*, he stated that many of the crewmen of the raider had "received superior training on board Her Majesty's gunnery ship, the *Excellent*."[12] The H.M.S. *Excellent* was the hulk of a warship moored at Portsmouth, which housed a Royal Navy gunnery school. Welles was presumably referring to gunnery training that some of crew members had received during previous service in the Royal Navy, since the *Alabama* never returned to England after its escape from Liverpool in 1862.

Several Britons served as officers on the raiders. John Low, first officer on the *Alabama*, was born in Aberdeen and had served on British merchant ships before immigrating to Savannah. Low was the only watch officer on the *Alabama* who had not previously served in the U.S. Navy.[13] When Captain Semmes decided to convert a captured clipper into a Confederate cruiser, the *Tuscaloosa*, Lieutenant Low was assigned to command her. By then there were few merchant ships flying the U.S. flag, and Low made no captures.

George Townley Fullam, masters's mate on the *Alabama*, was born at Kingston-upon-Hull. Fullham was usually the boarding officer sent to a ship whose registry was uncertain. Until the registry was determined, the *Alabama* flew the British flag. If the ship proved to be a true neutral, Fullam's Yorkshire accent supported his assertion that the *Alabama* was a British warship and prevented the captain of the merchant ship from spreading the word that he had been boarded by a Confederate commerce raider.[14] Fullam kept a journal, but it contains no hint of his motives for serving on the *Alabama*.

Two British officers were drowned when the *Alabama* was sunk by the U.S.S. *Kearsarge* near Cherbourg on June 19, 1864. Dr. David Herbert Llewwellyn, the ship's surgeon, was the son of an English clergyman; he was educated at Marlborough College and studied medicine at Charing Cross Hospital in London. William Robertson, assistant engineer, had left an English vessel at Cape Town and joined the *Alabama*. The chief engineer, Miles J. Freeman, was a Welsh immigrant in New Orleans and had served with Semmes on the *Sumter* as well as on the *Alabama*. He was rescued by the *Kearsarge* and spent the rest of the war as a prisoner in Fort Warren near Boston.

At Cape Town two officers of the Prussian navy, Baron Maximilian von Meul-nier and Julius Schroeder, joined the *Alabama*'s crew. They were on a leave of absence and were making a world tour but had been shipwrecked near Table Bay. Semmes recruited the two Prussians despite the prohibition in the Foreign Enlist-ment Act against recruiting by belligerents in British dominions. Von Meulnier spoke several languages and was used as boarding officer when the *Alabama* met a ship flying a German or other European flag.[15]

Two Englishmen wrote accounts of the capture of Union merchant ships by Confederate raiders. The first was by Francis S. Dawson, who was on the C.S.S. *Nashville* in January 1862 en route to join the Confederate army: "A fine schooner was running under full sail within half a mile of us. . . . The American flag was flying at our peak. . . . A boat crew was called away, and I jumped in. We found her to be the *Robert Gilfillan*, from Boston to Hayti with an assorted cargo. . . . Lieutenant Ingraham, who was in command of the boat, very quietly said: 'That vessel is the Confederate States steamer *Nashville*, and you are my pris-oner.' . . . Resistance was useless, and he did as he was ordered. . . . The bells, chronometer, glasses and nautical instruments, some provisions, brooms and a lot of 'notions,' were taken aboard the *Nashville*. The schooner was then set on fire, and in a few hours had burned to the waters edge. . . . The master and crew were given as comfortable quarters as we had, and all possible care was taken of them."[16]

Master's Mate Fullam described a capture by the *Alabama*: "Pulling under his stern, I saw it was the whaling ship *Benjamin Tucker* from New Bedford. . . . I told the captain that he was a prize to the C.S.S. *Alabama*, ordered him to put his clothes in one trunk, allow the mates and men one bag each, all navigation books and instruments being left behind. At daylight sent the Captain and crew with the ship's papers and their luggage to the *Alabama*. I then examined the ship, and finding some cases of stores, they were transferred to our ship. The preparations to fire her were soon made, so that after seeing her well fired we pushed off and regained our vessel."[17] Fullam recorded feelings of regret about the destruction of only one ship, which carried a cargo of grain and flour: "It seemed a fearful thing to burn such a cargo as the *Brilliant* had, when I thought how the operatives in the cotton districts would have danced with joy had they shared it amongst them. I never saw a vessel burn with such brilliancy, the flames completely enveloping the masts, hull and rig-ging in a few minutes, making a sight as grand as it was appalling."[18]

Reports of the depredations of the *Alabama* and its sister raiders were greeted with icy fury in the North. Most of the fury was directed at the British for allowing the ships to be built in Britain for the Confederacy. The issues surrounding the Con-federate raiders embittered U.S.–British relations during the war and for a decade thereafter. John Francis Macguire, an Irish member of the British Parliament, observed that "that terrible *Alabama* caused many a man in the North to grind his teeth with rage and fiercely pray for the opportunity for retaliation."[19] The Count of Paris thought the career of the *Alabama* was "a perpetual violation" of international law. "As soon as she had received her armament, this vessel, constructed in England, carrying English guns, with a crew composed almost entirely of Englishmen, started on her cruise without being registered at a Confederate port. Consequently, the Americans did not greatly exaggerate . . . in calling her an English pirate and had a perfect right to call upon the British government to seize her as soon as she should appear in an English port. No attention was paid to this request." The French count also noted that the depredations of the *Alabama* and its sister raiders had led to a "flight from the flag," that is, the transfer of many ships from American to British registry: "The English . . . profited by the damage done to the United States by a vessel fitted out in one of their ports, and which it was their duty to have stopped."[20]

When the *Alabama* was sunk by a U.S. warship, Secretary of the Navy Gideon Welles recorded in his diary that "this success . . . is universally and justly conceded a triumph over England as well as over the Rebels." He thought the "perfidy" of the British was as infamous as the treason of the rebels and that "both were whipped by the *Kearsarge*, a Yankee ship with a Yankee commander and a Yankee crew."[21] But the crew was not 100 percent Yankee. James Haley, born in 1824 in Ireland, was awarded a Congressional Medal of Honor for his service as a captain of the forecastle and gun captain on the *Kearsarge* during the battle with the *Alabama*.[22] No information is available on the number of foreign-born sailors on the *Kearsarge* when it sank the Confederate raider.

The extensive literature on the ships that evaded the Union blockade of Confederate ports includes only brief references to the fact that most of the blockade-runners were British built and British owned, carried British cargoes, were commanded by British officers, and manned by British crews. Several British observers pointed with pride to the British roles in the blockade-running system. Colonel Fremantle thought blockade-running was "an extraordinary instance of British energy and enterprise."[23] W. C. Corsan, a British businessman visiting the Confederacy, wrote that "blockade-running was looked upon as a legitimate and patriotic pursuit."[24] William Watson, a Scot who turned to blockade-running after a stint in the Confederate army, noted that it "was not regarded as either unlawful or dishonorable, but rather a bold and daring enterprise."[25]

Two British colonial ports played crucial roles in the system. Most of the arms and supplies bound for the Confederacy came from England in deepwater ships to the British port of Nassau in the Bahamas or to Bermuda. There the cargoes were transferred to shallow draft blockade-runners that could navigate the shallow side channels of the Confederate ports. The Count of Paris wrote that Nassau became "the mart where all merchandise intended for the South was concentrated, and where blockade-runners came to load before venturing on their perilous voyages. . . . Most of the vessels belonged to shipowners in Liverpool and sailed under the British flag."[26] Frank Vizetelly wrote to the *Illustrated London News* that "Nassau is the point when most of the blockade-runners start with the cargoes destined for the Southern Confederacy, and it is here that they return with their bales of . . . cotton which they have obtained in exchange for rifles, blankets, and shoes so much needed by the southern soldier. . . . The enterprise of British merchants has lined its quays with long light-coloured, rakish looking steamers, discharging their rich freights of cotton that have run the gauntlet through the Federal cruisers off Wilmington."[27]

Some of the men on the blockade-runners were officers or sailors from the Royal Navy ships. The officers usually had been given leave; the sailors were often deserters. One blockade-runner, the *Don*, was commanded by Captain Augustus Charles Hobart-Hampden, a younger son of the Earl of Buckingham. He had commanded Queen Victoria's yacht and won the Victoria Cross in the Crimean war. Hobart-Hampden wrote that "our crew consisted of a captain, three officers, three engineers, and twenty-eight men. . . . They were all Englishmen; and as they received very high wages, we managed to have picked men. . . . The British men of war on the West-India station found it a difficult matter to prevent their crews from deserting, so great was the temptation offered by the blockade-runners."[28]

At first British observers echoed the Confederate view that the Union could never mount an effective blockade of the long Confederate coast. Samuel Phillips Day reported early in 1862 that "the blockade . . . is, for the most part, a *paper* blockade, and consequently ineffective and *illegal*. To effectually blockade the whole Southern seaboard, is more than the North can possibly accomplish."[29] In the fall of 1863, however, Francis Lawley reported to *The Times* that the Union was "investing the ports of Secessia with a *cordon* of vessels so numerous as . . . to make access to the Confederate coast really dangerous and difficult."[30]

"Every ruse was resorted to, to enable the vessel to evade the vigilance of the American cruisers," recalled Captain Hobart-Hampden. "We prepared the vessel for the work . . . by reducing her spars to a light pair of lower masts . . . with only a small crow's nest on the foremast. . . . The hull, which showed about eight feet above water, was painted a dull gray colour, to render her as nearly as possible invisible in the night. . . . Coal was taken on board of a nature that never smoked (anthracite). The funnel could be lowered close down to the deck. In order that no noise might be made, steam was blown off . . . under water. . . . Among the fowls, no cocks were allowed, for fear of their proclaiming the whereabouts of the blockade-runner."[31]

An unidentified correspondent of *The Times* of London reported on his arrival in Charleston: "We saw . . . the low, dark hull of one of the blockading ships. . . . Great was our relief when we found we had not been observed. . . . As we approached, two more ships were seen lying right in the narrow channel over the bar, through which it was necessary to pass. The captain hesitated about proceeding further and . . . ran her out to sea again. She was followed by a howling pack of cruisers, but speed, good luck, and the darkness favoured us. . . . The same programme was gone through the next night, and then we had to return to Nassau for coals. Under another captain we returned on the 29th of January to try our fortune again. . . . In one hour we ran through the north channel and arrived safe and sound under the guns of Fort Beauregard."[32] Captain Ross described his departure from Wilmington on a blockade-runner: "The moon having set at midnight, we slipped out of the Cape Fear river, and dashed at full speed through the blockading fleet. It was pitch dark, and not even a cigar was allowed to be alight on deck. For nearly an hour we kept peering through the night to discover whether any Yankee ship lay in our way, but we passed unobserved."[33]

Tom Taylor, a British blockade-runner, recalled the anger among other blockade-runners when Union ships began stopping at sea British ships suspected of carrying arms and supplies intended for the Confederacy: "The Northerners . . . were extending the doctrine of the operations permissible to belligerents. . . . If we were building a whole fleet of steamers for the express purpose of defying their cruisers, they were . . . justified in trying to intercept them at any point they chose. . . . Still, the methods were none the less galling to the susceptibilities of British merchants . . . and every day those engaged . . . became more pronounced in their Southern sympathies and louder in their denunciation of the Northerners' high-handed ways."[34] Ella Lonn recorded a favorite toast of the blockade-runners: "To the Confederates that produce the cotton; the Yankees that maintain the blockade and keep up the price of cotton; the Britishers that buy the cotton and pay the high price for it. . . . Here is to all three . . . and a long continuance of the war."[35]

The roles of the various Confederate ports in the blockade-running system depended on the fortunes of war. New Orleans was captured by Union forces in April 1862, before the system was fully in operation. When W. C. Corsan visited Charleston in the fall of 1862, he noted that "the business caused by these sales of blockade-goods formed almost the whole business of the city."[36] But a year later its role as a port for blockade-runners was virtually eliminated by the Union siege of Charleston. Francis Lawley wrote that its role was rapidly being taken by Mobile.[37] When Corsan visited Mobile in the fall of 1862, he wrote that "the people of Mobile seem to drive a thriving trade with Havana by running the blockade—their swift, well-handled steamers going in and out just when they please. . . . The newspapers announced daily sales of clothing, boots and shoes, hats and caps, hardware, hosiery, etc, etc, all of which had run the blockade, and everything was snapped up at ridiculous prices."[38] Captain Ross was in the Cuban capital in November 1863; he recorded that "Havana is a great place for blockade-runners, which make their trips from thence to Mobile, Galveston, and many other points on the Texas and Florida coast."[39] Mobile's role in the blockade-running system declined sharply in the fall of 1864, when Admiral Farragut approached Mobile bay.

Wilmington, North Carolina, was the closest Confederate port to Lee's army in Virginia. Colonel Fremantle was there in June 1863: "The river was quite full of blockade-runners. I counted eight large steamers, all handsome leaden-coloured vessels, which ply their trade with the greatest regularity."[40] When Captain Ross was there in November, he found "about a dozen blockade-running steamers lying at the wharves, loading cotton and unloading all manners of stores brought from Bermuda and Nassau. . . . Wilmington is at present the most important port of entry in the South."[41] Lawley visited Wilmington a year later, in November 1864: "It is doubtful whether any other town in Secessia . . . has exercised such an influence over the fortunes of this war as the insignificant little port of Wilmington . . . from which . . . cotton bales have flowed out uninterruptedly to England for three years, while a vast amount of war material and of supplies of all kinds has been sucked through this same gate."[42] For a while Savannah and Wilmington were the last links in the lifeline of the Confederacy. Savannah was captured after Sherman reached the sea in December 1864; Wilmington remained open to blockade runners until nearby Fort Fisher was captured by Union forces on January 15, 1865.

A Swedish immigrant, John Ericsson, designed the U.S.S. *Monitor*, which had a profound effect on the history of the Civil War and revolutionized the design of warships. Ericsson's background and momentous contribution to the war was described by President Calvin Coolidge at the dedication of a statue of Ericsson in Washington in 1926: "Born in the province of Vermland in 1803, . . . at 23 he went to England . . . and entered an engineering firm. . . . Within a year his fertile mind had begun improvements of far-reaching extent upon boilers and engines. . . . He soon designed the fire engine and developed the screw propeller for marine use. . . . This new invention brought him to America in 1839. . . . He was soon building . . . the *Princeton*, . . . the first man-of-war equipped with a screw propeller. . . . This great mechanical genius wrote to President Lincoln offering to 'construct a vessel for the destruction of the hostile fleet. . . . 'Attachment to the Union alone impels me to offer my services in this frightful crisis.' . . . This offer was accepted, and as a result a strange new craft . . . steamed into Hampton Roads . . . on March 8, 1862."[43]

It arrived just in the nick of time. That morning a Confederate ironclad, reconstructed from the *Merrimac*—but called the *Virginia* by the Confederates—attacked the federal fleet. The Confederate ship was described by the Prince of Joinville, a former French admiral: "The *Merrimac* . . . was an old and very large screw steam frigate . . . covered with an iron roof, inclined just far enough to throw off any ball which might strike her. In this roof portholes were made for 100-pounder Armstrong guns, and for other pieces of very heavy calibre. The bows were armed with an iron spur, resembling that of the ancient galleys. . . . The *Merrimac*, escorted by several ironclad gunboats, leaves the Elizabeth river and steers straight for the mouth of the James, where lay anchored the two old-fashioned sailing frigates, the *Cumberland* and *Congress*. Both open with full broadsides . . . but . . . the balls ricochet from the iron roof. . . . The *Merrimac* . . . strikes her spur into the side of the *Cumberland*. . . . She was seen to career and go down majestically, carrying with her two hundred men. . . . . The *Congress* . . . ran ashore, hauled down her flag, and burst into flames."[44]

President Coolidge described the initial reactions to this surprising Confederate success: "The result was consternation among the federal authorities. A Cabinet member is said to have claimed that a shell from this new engine of destruction might be expected to fly into the White House at any time. In the South expectations were entertained of a complete destruction of the northern ships, the raising of the blockades, the capture of Washington and other cities, recognition of the Confederacy by Europe, and ultimate victory."[45]

Colonel Ernst Von Vegesack, a Swedish officer, was on the shore when the *Merrimac* went out the next morning, March 9, to finish its work of destruction: "This *Merrimac*, . . . black and gloomy, slowly kept advancing, . . . proud in her consciousness of spreading death and devastation. . . . As a rescuing angel, . . . Ericsson's iron battery *Monitor* appeared."[46]

The Prince of Joinville wrote that, from a distance, only the *Monitor's* revolving turret was visible. "The iron tower was pieced with two openings, through which peer the muzzles of two enormous cannons. This tower is made to turn upon its axis by a very ingenious contrivance, in such a fashion as to direct its fire on any point of the horizon." The turret rested on "a kind of lid of iron set on at the water level upon the hull which contains the engine, the storage for provisions and for the crew. . . . The *Merrimac* . . . ran boldly down to meet this unexpected adversary. . . . The balls ricocheted and struck without appearing to leave a trace but the very slightest bruises. . . . The *Monitor*, short, agile, easily handled . . . escaped her blows with a speed which the *Merrimac*, from her excessive length, could not attain. . . . The two adversaries turned one about the other, the little *Monitor* describing the inner circle. . . . The conflict went on with no visible results for several hours."[47]

Hans Anderson was one of two Swedish gunners on the *Monitor:* "I said to Peterson, 'Let us put in two cannon balls so as to get results.' Peterson agreed and the resulting shots made holes in the *Merrimac* through which one could drive a horse and wagon. The *Merrimac* was unable to continue and withdrew to the protection of the shore batteries.[48]

Francis W. Dawson, an Englishman in the Confederate army, described an elaborate but abortive Confederate attempt the following day to capture the *Monitor:* "When the *Monitor* came out to meet us, the *Patrick Henry*, the *Jamestown*, the *Beaufort*, and the *Raleigh*, at a signal from the *Virginia*, were to run down upon the enemy, endeavoring to strike her on the bows and quarter. The *Monitor* was to be mobbed by the gunboats while *Virginia* engaged her attention. . . . Picked men from the infantry regiments stationed at Norfolk were placed on each of the vessels. . . . Boarding parties . . . numbered one in each vessel were provided with hammers and wedges, and were to endeavor to chock the turret of the *Monitor* so as to prevent it from revolving. . . . Those numbered two were supplied with balls of tow, steeped in turpentine, which were to be ignited and thrown down the ventilators, which were then to be covered. Those numbered three were to throw a wet sail over the pilothouse so as to blind the helmsman. Meanwhile other boarders, armed with pistols and cutlasses, were to guard against any attempt on the part of enemy's crew to escape from the confinement which was prepared for them. I had the command of the boarders on the *Beaufort*." As indicated earlier, the crew of the *Beaufort* consisted of Englishmen, Danes, and Swedes. "The *Monitor* and her consorts skulked under the guns of the forts. . . . We did not get the fight we sought. It was a terrible disappointment. Had we succeeded in disabling her, the whole coast would have been at the mercy of the *Virginia*."[49]

Ericsson's timely invention, the *Monitor*, removed a serious threat to the Union navy and probably had a greater impact on the outcome of the Civil War than the single contribution of any other European immigrant. It also had an enormous impact on naval design and construction. Colonel Von Vegesack wrote that "the fight that day . . . inspired a complete conviction that . . . wooden vessels forever have lost their value as Men-of-War. . . . Our compatriot, Captain Ericsson, has made himself immortal."[50] President Coolidge described the battle's impact on naval warfare: "The London *Times* stated that the day before this momentous battle England had 149 first-class warships. The day after she had but two, and they were iron-plated only amidships. Naval warfare had been revolutionized. The great genius of Ericsson had brought about a new era in naval construction."[51]

Chapter 19

WILL EUROPE EVER RECOGNIZE *THE* CONFEDERACY?

Union *and* Confederate Relations
with Britain: 1861–1863

T he four years of civil war in America were a period of great tension between the United States and Great Britain. Long-standing resentments on both sides of the Atlantic were inflamed by events and reactions during the war. There was also much misunderstanding and misjudgment by governments and peoples in America and Europe.

The Civil War began only forty-six years after the end of the War of 1812. The memories of older Americans of that war with Britain were just as vivid in 1861 as those of older Americans of World War II in 1991. Americans had not forgotten that the British occupied Washington, burned the Capitol and White House, and attempted to capture New Orleans. William Howard Russell of *The Times* of London encountered the legacy of that war while on a boat near Washington: "The old pilot had the most wholesome hatred of the Britishers, and . . . favored me with some very remarkable views respecting their general mischievousness and inutility. As soon as he found out my secret, he . . . explained to me that . . . all he had in the world, as pretty a schooner as ever floated and a fine cargo, had been taken and burnt by the English when they sailed up the Potomac to Washington."[1]

The hostility toward the British of the Irish in America, the most numerous and vocal of the immigrant groups, broadened the range of American resentment of Britain. An Irishman in the 28th Massachusetts, Sergeant Peter Welsh, thought "England hates this country . . . for its republican liberty and she hates it because Irishmen have a home and a government here and a voice in the counsels of the nation."[2] "Twisting the tail of the British lion," a common feature of American political oratory, appealed to both Irish and native-born voters. The British minister in Washington, Lord Lyons, suspected that Secretary of State William Henry Seward hoped "to set himself at the head of a new party . . . which should rally to itself the important Irish vote by hostility to England."[3] The Fenians—Irish nationalists—initially welcomed the enlistment of Irishmen in the Union army because they would gain military experience that could be invaluable in a future revolution against British rule in Ireland. A favorite song of the Irish Brigade included these words: "We swear it now, and forever, To free green Erin, land of slaves, And banish tyrants from her shore."[4]

In 1861 and 1862 a primary cause of U.S.–British tensions was the persistent fear in the North—and hope in the South—that the British government would extend diplomatic recognition of the independence of the Confederate states and provide other important support and assistance to the Confederacy. The correspondent of *The Times* arrived in Washington in late March 1861 just as the new Lincoln administration was making clear its hostility to any form of European recognition of the Confederate rebels. Russell dined with Seward, who told him that "the Southern Commissioners who had been sent abroad could not be received by the Government of any foreign power, officially or otherwise, . . . without incurring the risk of breaking off relations with the Government of the United States." The next day he dined at the White House: "They seemed to think that England was bound by her anti-slavery antecedents to discourage to the utmost any attempts of the South to establish its independence on a basis of slavery." Russell saw Seward again on April 4: "Mr. Seward fears that . . . Great Britain may recognize the Government established at Montgomery, and he is ready, if needs be, to threaten Great Britain with war as the consequence of such recognition."[5] Anthony Trollope, a visiting British novelist, wrote that Northerners "regarded . . . the action of the South as a rebellion and said . . . that so . . . conservative a nation as Great Britain would surely countenance them in quelling rebels. If . . . Great Britain did not respond to her friend as she was expected to respond, then it would appear that Cotton was king, as least in British eyes."[6]

U.S.–British tensions were soon increased by Lincoln's proclamation of a blockade of Southern ports. British industry and trade was highly dependent on large supply of Southern cotton, which was sharply curtailed as the blockade was implemented. A Scot in the South, William Watson, wrote that the blockade "was calculated to have a very paralyzing effect on the South. . . . It was, however, to some extent gratifying to the Confederate leaders, . . . as it would bring the Federal Government into conflict with foreign powers."[7] During a trip through the South in the spring of 1861, Russell reported that the Confederates were confident of British recognition and hopeful that the British would send the Royal Navy to break the blockade. A Charleston merchant told him that "if those miserable Yankees try to blockade us and keep you from our cotton, you"ll send their ships to the bottom and acknowledge us." Edmund Rhett, whom Russell described as "one of the most ultra and violent speakers against the Yankees I have heard," insisted that "you must recognize us, sir, before the end of October."[8] In Montgomery, Russell met Judah P. Benjamin, a member of the Confederate cabinet: "At present, he says, their paper blockade does no harm; the season for shipping cotton is over. But in October, when . . . all the wharves are full, it is inevitable that the Yankees must come to trouble with this attempt to coerce us."

In Mobile, Russell noted Confederate hopes "that Mr. Gregory, who was traveling through the States some time ago, will have a strong party to support his forthcoming motion for a recognition of the South." William Gregory was a leader of the Confederate "lobby" in Parliament. In Jackson, Russell was told by the governor of Mississippi that "England is no doubt a great country and . . . may have a good deal to do in Eu-*rope*; but the sovereign State of Mississippi can do a great deal better without England than England can do without her." From New Orleans, Russell summed up Confederate expectations: "Through the present gloom come the rays of a glorious future, which shall see a grand slave confederacy . . . with a . . . monopoly of the great staples on which so much of the manufacture and commerce of England and France depend. . . . Cotton is king—not alone king, but czar."[9]

In 1861 and early 1862, many Confederates believed that the way to hasten European recognition and support was to embargo cotton exports temporarily and thus accelerate the arrival of a "cotton famine" in Europe. The unofficial cotton embargo launched in the summer of 1861 was described by Robert Bourke, a British aristocrat who spent a month in the Confederacy that summer: "Self-consituted authorities have . . . made it impossible for ships to load. . . . The popular feeling . . . is caused . . . by the impression that in laying on a general embargo they would incline European governments to recognize the Confederacy. . . . The prevalent conviction throughout the South is that England cannot do without the 'king.' . . . In vain we would tell them . . . that our Government was making great exertions to procure cotton from India and Africa . . . and that it was our interest to foster our own colonies. . . . But they were ineradicably impressed with the conviction that . . . the distance from England at which its rivals are placed must always give the Confederacy a great advantage."[10] The unofficial Confederate embargo on cotton exports persisted until mid-1862, when Confederate leaders began to realize that the export of cotton through the blockade was the only way to pay for desperately needed arms and supplies from Europe.

Confederate confidence in ultimate European recognition had been boosted in May 1861 by a royal proclamation in which the British government recognized both the Union and Confederate governments as "belligerents" under international law. Anthony Trollope described the bitter reaction in the North: "This declaration . . . has been taken as indicating British sympathy with the cause of the seceders." The British novelist added that Northerners believed that "because the South was in rebellion, England should have consented to allow the North to assume all the rights of a belligerent, and should have denied all those rights to the South."[11]

"The recognition of the Confederates as belligerents," wrote British correspondent Edward Dicey, "is believed . . . to have inflicted incalculable injury on the North by raising the hopes of the insurgents in foreign intervention and thus giving the rebellion a tenacity of life which it could not otherwise have acquired. . . . The unfortunate precipitation with which our proclamation of neutrality was issued, four-and-twenty hours previous to Mr. Adams's expected arrival, created . . . a good deal of annoyance. It is a pity that an act which . . . could not fail to be offensive to a nation preparing to fight for its existence, should have been done in such a form to give unnecessary offense."[12] Charles Francis Adams, the new U.S. minister to Britain, read the British proclamation in a newspaper while on a train from Liverpool to London.

Both Dicey and Trollope acknowledged that Americans in the North had good reasons for resenting British reactions to the conflict in America. Dicey recorded a typical American reaction: "Not only did your Government recognize . . . the South as belligerents with unwonted promptitude, but the people of England repudiated at once all fellowship with our cause. Every disaster of ours was magnified by your press, every success was derided. . . . Your statesmen, and writers, and politicians . . . rejoiced in the prospect of our dismemberment. In your society sympathy was with the South from the beginning."[13] Trollope admitted that "some of us never tire in abusing the Americans . . . for having allowed themselves to be driven into this civil war. We speak . . . as though there had been some plain course by which the war might have been avoided. . . . We . . . speak of them as a steady father of a family is wont to speak of some unthrifty prodigal who is throwing away his estate and hurrying from one ruinous debauchery to another. . . . In these days of their trouble, . . . we might have borne with them more tenderly."[14]

But most upper-class Britons were insensitive to these American resentments. The Reverend G. G. Lawrence noted American complaints "about the hostility of the English press, about the recognition of the South as belligerents, about the *Alabama* being allowed to leave an English port, and that so many troops have been sent over to Canada," but the English vicar dismissed these complaints as "utterly ridiculous and only showing what a thin-skinned, sensitive being an American is."[15]

The British consistently misjudged Lincoln and Seward and their foreign policy. They thought Lincoln was only a country lawyer who could not be expected to know anything or care very much about foreign relations. They assumed that the foreign policy of the United States was determined entirely by Seward. British visitors were impressed by Seward's abilities, but distrusted his intentions. Russell described him as "a subtle, quick man, . . . bursting with the importance of state mysteries and with the dignity of directing the foreign policy of the greatest country—as all Americans think—in the world."[16] Dicey was impressed by Seward's informality, conviviality, ability, knowledge, and wide perspective: "He was . . . dressed in black, with his waistcoat half-unbuttoned, one leg over the side of his armchair, and a cigar stuck between his lips. . . . Mr. Seward is good company. A good cigar, a good glass of wine, and a good story, even if it is a little risqué, are pleasures which he obviously enjoys keenly. . . . He is a man of remarkable ability."[17] George Augustus Sala, correspondent for the London *Daily Telegraph*, noted that "Seward talks like a book, and like a very clever book, too. . . . I retired from the secretary's presence much edified by his eloquence, his affability, and his indomitable cheerfulness."[18] But these visits did little to dispel the illogical but widely held British view that Seward was eager for a war with Britain. "My first reflection . . . on meeting Mr. Seward," Dicey recalled, "was one of wonder that so small a man should have been near creating a war between two nations."[19]

The British also misjudged the objectives of the Lincoln administration at home. Lincoln's early denials that the abolition of slavery was a Union objective led to a statement by the British prime minister—and a widely held conviction in Britain—that the North fought only for "empire" over the South. "The Federal Government . . . cautiously avoided the mentioning of the slavery question as the cause and origin of the conflict," Carl Schurz noted in September 1861, while U.S minister to Spain. "The ultimate extinction of an institution so hateful to the European mind was most emphatically denied to be one of the objects of the war. . . . It was exceedingly difficult to make Europeans understand, not only why the free and prosperous North should fight merely for the privilege of being reassociated with the imperious and troublesome slave States, but also why the . . . right to have a government and institutions of its own choice, should be repudiated in America."[20]

Since they had no experience with a federal form of government, the British had no basis for judging the conflicting claims of the North and South concerning the previous operation of the American federal system. Although the concept of "state's rights" was totally unknown in the unitary system of government in Britain, the British were ready to believe that the rights of the Southern states had been violated by the North. British visitors to the Confederacy generally accepted the

Confederate view that they were fighting for freedom from intolerable oppression. A British visitor, Lieutenant Colonel Garnet Josef Wolseley, ended an article on his visit to the Confederacy in 1862 with the statement that the United States had become "a military despotism of a portion of the states striving under the dictatorship of an insignificant lawyer to crush out the freedom of the rest."[21] The Reverend Lawrence concluded during his visit to America in 1863 that the key issue in the war was whether Southerners "should be allowed to govern themselves or not."[22] This view was widely accepted by upper-class Britons. "The South have shown themselves a great nation," a woman in Manchester wrote her immigrant brother in Michigan; "the whole sympathies of England are with them in their great struggle for liberty."[23]

Until the last few months of the war, most upper-class Britons believed that the Confederates would be able to maintain their independence. This persistent conviction was based primarily on a stream of reports from British observers. Russell's reports to *The Times* from North and South in 1861 described a country torn apart by irreconcilable differences.[24] "Let there be no mistake whatever," he wrote from the temporary Confederate capital, "as to the unanimity which exists at present in the South to fight for . . . its independence."[25] "Neither a reunion of states nor of people can ever be effected," Samuel Phillips Day reported to the *Herald* in London; "the bitter feeling on either side is as strong as death—the enmity as lasting as eternity."[26] Such reports continued in 1862. Frank Vizetelly wrote to the *Illustrated London News* that Confederates were "resolved to fight for their independence till the last man has been called from his home and the last plantation laid waste. . . . There is not a mother with two sons, having lost one by a Northern bullet, who will not freely offer up the other on the altar of her country."[27] Colonel Wolseley proclaimed in a leading British journal that "there is no personal sacrifice that the people of the South are not prepared to make. . . . There are no terms upon which they would reenter the Union."[28] "I have traveled far and wide through Virginia," Francis Lawley reported to *The Times*, "but never . . . heard a word of regret by reason of the war, a timid note sounded in regard to its issue, a sigh breathed over the departed Union, or a ghost of a desire expressed in favour of compromise or reconstruction."[29]

These statements reflected several levels of wishful thinking. The Confederates wanted to believe that they would be able to maintain their independence; they also wanted the British to believe they would do so, because they thought Britain would be more likely to recognize and support a Confederacy that seemed strong and determined enough to sustain its independence without outside help, if necessary. The British upper classes wanted to believe that the Confederacy would sustain its independence because they welcomed the division of the American giant for imperial, political, and commercial reasons and because, in their hearts, they strongly preferred the continuation of the existing system for producing cotton in the American South to the chaos they thought would follow the abolition of slavery. The inescapable conflict between the British antislavery tradition and the British need for American cotton is reviewed in the following chapter.

Public statements of British preference for a divided America were rare. One was Colonel Wolseley's statement in a prestigious magazine that "it is in the interest of all nations, but especially of England, to have more than one great republic upon the American continent, as the United States were fast becoming such a nuisance in the republic of nations. . . . If . . . they should succeed in their war of subjugation, their insolence and arrogance would be more intolerable than ever."[30] An officer of a Cunard steamer, mistaking an Irish-American passenger for an Englishman, remarked that "we shall all feel glad to see the Yankee nation go to pieces."[31]

The perception that the British hoped for a Confederate victory was especially strong among Irish and German immigrants. Sergeant Peter Welsh, an Irishman in the 28th Massachusetts, wrote that England's objective "is and has been for years to divide this country for two reasons: First, for her liberal government and laws and, second, because America was out rivaling her both in . . . commerce and manufacture."[32] Carl Schurz made a similar comment in his memoirs: "A large part of the ruling class in Great Britain, which befriended and encouraged the Southern Confederacy, did not do so because it sympathized with slavery as such, but because it disliked and feared the American Republic as a democracy and a rival power which it would have been glad to see stripped of its strength and prestige."[33]

For a few weeks at the end of 1861 all other aspects of U.S.–British relations were overshadowed by the removal of two Confederate envoys and their secretaries from a British mail packet while on their way to represent the Confederacy in Europe. Russell heard the news at the British legation in Washington on November 16: "Captain Wilkes of the U.S. steamer *San Jacinto* had forcibly boarded the *Trent*, British mail steamer, off the Bahamas, and had taken Messrs. Mason, Slidell, Eustis, and McClernand from on board by armed force, in defiance of the protests of the captain and the naval officer in charge of the mails."[34] Trollope described the reaction of the American public: "Captain Wilkes . . . was recognized as a hero. He was invited to banquets and feted. Speeches were made to him as speeches are commonly made to high officers who come home . . . victorious from the wars. His health was drunk with great applause, and thanks were voted to him by one of the Houses of Congress."[35]

Several Britons wrote of the reactions in Britain to the "*Trent* affair." "The people are frantic with rage," Charles Mackay, soon to become the New York correspondent of *The Times* of London, wrote to Seward from London. "Were the country polled, I fear that 999 men out of 1,000 would declare for immediate war. Lord Palmerston cannot resist the impulse if he would. If he submits to the insult to the flag, his ministry is doomed. . . . Englishmen would rather fight with any power in the world than with America, but I do assure you their blood is up and they mean mischief in this business. . . . The Southern men in London . . . already see the South recognized by England and France in unison and cannot conceal their exultation."[36] The Reverend Lawrence recalled that "large and enthusiastic meetings of British seamen were held in nearly all the principal British ports and . . . unanimous resolutions were passed, that the flag of England had been insulted and that they were ready, . . . at the peril of their lives, to wipe out the insult."[37] Thomas E. Taylor, a British blockade-runner, recalled that "the English nation was prepared to make any sacrifice to resent this outrage."[38] "Every Englishman feels himself insulted," a woman in Manchester wrote to her brother in Michigan. "Unless the American government returns . . . Slidell & Mason and make us an ample apology, we shall go to war. . . . We shall teach America . . . that England is not be trifled with."[39]

The government in London instructed the British minister in Washington, Lord Lyons, to demand an apology and the release of the Confederate envoys and, if the United States did not comply within seven days, to break diplomatic relations. British observers praised Lincoln's decision at the end of December to release the envoys. Trollope thought "the American government behaved well in its mode of giving the men up. . . . The illegality of the arrest was at once acknowledged."[40] Sala commented later that "the good sense of the American people . . . led them to see that . . . by refusing the rendition of Mason and Slidell a most perilous and ominous precedent would be set."[41] "Let us be thankful," Russell wrote to *The Times*, "that we are spared the war which would have been forced on us in vindication of our honor."[42]

But the *Trent* affair left a bitter legacy in both countries. Carl Schurz, who was a U.S. diplomat in Europe at the time of the crisis, recalled that "a feeling was left behind . . . of sore disappointment among many people in England that the 'impudence' of an American ship in overhauling a British mail-steamer went 'unpunished.'"[43] Taylor, the blockade runner, regretted that "the 'spoiled child of diplomacy' was not made to apologize. She barely expressed regret, and her omission of this international courtesy, combined with the extravagances of her press, confirmed in many Englishmen their inchoate partisanship for the South."[44]

Other British observers stressed that the surrender of the envoys had been a "humiliation" of the United States. Dicey wrote that "the Americans are too sharp a people to be able to delude themselves . . . that they had won a great diplomatic victory. . . . The Secretary of State suffered, perhaps unjustly, as the scapegoat for the national humiliation."[45] Lieutenant Colonel James Arthur Fremantle of the Coldstream Guards also referred to the *Trent* affair as the "great national humiliation of the United States."[46] Russell thought "such a dish of humble pie cannot be taken into stomachs without a great deal of nausea."[47]

Many Americans agreed that the surrender of the envoys had been humiliating. Russell had guessed in mid-December that the Americans would release the envoys and then "solace themselves by a vow of eternal hostility to Great Britain and the promise . . . of future revenge upon her in some moment of weakness or difficulty."[48] "It is owned, though reluctantly," Dicey wrote later, "that England was in the right, even if she exacted her full right to the extreme letter. It is not for what we did, but for the manner in which we did it, that we are condemned."[49] Schurz recalled that there had been "a feeling of bitter resentment among many people in this country because England had brutally 'bullied' us in the hour of our distress and we were obliged to submit to her 'insolence.' "[50]

Two immigrant groups reacted angrily to the surrender of the envoys. The German-language press thought the release of the envoys was a national humiliation and a capitulation to British arrogance.[51] The Fenians—Irish nationalists— welcomed trouble between the United States and Great Britain that might lead to U.S. support for Irish independence and were sorely disappointed when the *Trent* affair was peacefully settled."[52] Congressman Owen Lovejoy of Illinois, son of an Irish immigrant and a friend of Lincoln, proclaimed that "the time is not far distant when we shall have suppressed this rebellion and be prepared to avenge and wipe out this insult that we have received."[53]

Most people in the North were glad that the immediate danger of war with Britain had been removed but continued to worry about the possibility that Britain would recognize and support the Confederacy. Schurz recalled the influences that seemed to be pressing the British government toward recognition in 1862: "the anti-democratic element, naturally sympathizing with anything that promised to demonstrate the failure of the great democratic experiment in the new world; business interests both in France and England depending upon the regular supply of raw cotton; . . . the displeasure created by our new tariff on imports, . . . while the Confederate Government was profuse in its free-trade professions; and finally the widespread belief that the breaking up of the Union was an established and irreversible fact, that . . . to subjugate so large an extent of country . . . was a hopeless undertaking, . . . and that it would be rendering a service to humanity to stop such a war."[54]

The leading Confederate propaganda agent in Europe was a Swiss immigrant to America, Henry Hotze. He had been sent to London with orders "to impress upon the public mind abroad the ability of the Confederate states to maintain their independence . . . and to publish whatever information you possess calculated to convey a just idea of their ample resources and vast military strength and to raise their character and Government in general estimation."[55] His first effort was to get editorials favorable to the Confederacy in major newspapers. In May 1862 he founded a weekly newspaper, *The Index*, which was the Confederate propaganda organ in Europe for the rest of the war. Although *The Index* and other Confederate propaganda efforts in Europe did not win many new converts to the Confederate cause and there was never a majority for recognition of the Confederacy in the British cabinet or Parliament, these facts were not evident in America for some time. Anxiety in the North about the prospect for and consequences of British recognition persisted during 1862 and most of 1863. "Once let the Southern Confederacy be recognized by European powers," a Welshman in the Union army wrote to a Welsh newspaper, "and . . . our task is ten times a more difficult one."[56]

Meanwhile, Confederate leaders had become very frustrated by the delay in the expected European recognition and support. In June 1862, G. W. Clarke, an Englishman representing the New York *Herald*, was in a Union camp in the Shenandoah valley when it was captured by Confederates. Clarke asked Stonewall Jackson for the return of his horse, but Jackson replied that it was "contraband of war." "I stand as a neutral," Clarke protested, "and you know it to be the law of nations that a neutral flag covers neutral goods." "Yes," Jackson replied, "but the Southern Confederacy is not recognized by neutral nations and, consequently, cannot be bound by neutral laws." Clarke was released, but the Confederates kept the horse.[57]

That fall W. C. Corsan, a British businessman visiting Richmond, noted the conviction of many Southern leaders that British businessmen were anxious to prolong the war: "We believe the people of England [are] with us; but . . . your capitalists, who hold United States and Northern stocks; your Manchester men, who are making money out of their stocks of manufactured and raw cotton; your Sheffield men, who are selling steel to the Northern Government; your Birmingham men, who are selling rifles, swords, and bayonets; your Huddersfield, Leeds, etc. men, who are selling shoddy clothes; and your shipowners, into whose hands our *Alabamas* . . . are throwing all the carrying-trade of the world—are against us and want the war to go on."[58] In fact, most British businessmen hoped for an ultimate Confederate victory, but those selling arms and equipment to the North or South clearly had a vested interest in a prolonged war.

"The first question always asked me," Colonel Wolseley wrote in *Blackwood's Edinburgh Magazine*, "was why England had not recognized their independence. . . . Had they not done sufficient to prove their determination to be an independent people, and had they not sufficiently shown already their ability to maintain themselves as a separate nation? . . . In the cause of humanity, would not England interfere to put an end to the fratricidal war? . . . There is a general impression . . . that the English people sympathize with the Southerners, and would gladly help them if they were permitted to do so, but that Lord Palmerston's Government is opposed to Southern independence. . . . Our policy is generally attributed to . . . a fear that . . . [the United States] would carry out their threat of making a declaration of war."[59] The last thing Lincoln and Seward wanted was a war with Britain, but they had convinced British leaders that diplomatic recognition of the Confederacy would lead to war between Britain and America during or after the internal conflict in America.

The British government's reasons for withholding recognition were not understood by Confederate leaders or by most of the British observers in the Confederacy, who were strong supporters of the Confederate cause. "How long will England and France . . . delay," Frank Vizetelly asked in an article in late 1862 for the *Illustrated London News*, "before putting an end to 'the butchery which disgraces the century we live in?' "[60] "Will Europe ever recognize the Confederacy?" Francis Lawley asked in a letter to *The Times* in March 1863. "Will not England and France rush in to bring an end to this slaughter? If they could only witness the misery which is . . . crying aloud to Heaven, . . . they would risk some chance of failure rather than permit humanity to be outraged by a continuance of such excess of anguish."[61]

In June 1863, Colonel Fremantle met General Beauregard in Charleston. The Confederate general told the Coldstream Guards officer that an eventual war between Britain and the United States was an "inevitable necessity." "He remarked that if England would join the South at once, the Southern armies, relieved of the present blockade and enormous Yankee pressure, would be able to march right into the Northern States, and, by occupying their principal cities, would give the Yankees so much employment that they would be unable to spare many men for [an attack on] Canada." But in Richmond the following week Fremantle met Confederate Secretary of State Judah P. Benjamin, who was eager to discredit the idea that British recognition of the Confederacy would lead to war between Britain and the United States. Benjamin "denied that the Yankees really would dare to go to war with Great Britain. . . . The certainty of an entire blockade of their ports, the total destruction of their trade, and an invasion on a large scale by Southern troops, in reality prevents the possibility of their declaring war upon England." Later that day Fremantle met Jefferson Davis, who "agreed with Benjamin that the Yankees did not really intend to go to war with England if she recognized the South."[62]

Several former European observers in America, who had returned to Europe, opposed European recognition of Confederate independence. "I could not wish the distress in Lancashire," Edward Dicey wrote in March 1863, "to be removed at the price of a great national sin, . . . the interference of England to establish a slave power in order to procure cotton. . . . England would be virtually dependent on the South, entangled in her alliances, involved in her wars, and liable for her embarrassments."[63] Russell noted in June that "some people in England . . . imagine that by recognition we would give life to the South . . . and bring this war to an end." But he believed that "recognition would not aid the South one whit, and it would add immensely to the unity and the fury of the North."[64] The Count of Paris commented after the war that European recognition of Confederate independence "would have made no change in their military condition, . . . but it would have caused much irritation in the North and perhaps finally involved it in a war with some of the powers of the Old World."[65]

Except during the *Trent* affair, Dicey was the only British observer who commented substantially on the chances of a war between Britain and the United States. "The wonder to me," he wrote early in 1862, "is that the American nation are not more intoxicated with the consciousness of their new-born strength . . . That when the . . . rebellion is suppressed this people will lay down their arms, . . . is a thing more to be hoped for than expected."[66] A year later he had concluded that "the danger of war between England and America . . . is far greater in the event of the failure of the North than in the event of its success. If the North should subjugate the South . . . the necessity of keeping down insurrection in the South would render impossible [foreign] aggression in the North. But take the other alternative . . . The necessity of cementing together what remains of the Union will render a foreign war politically desirable. No war will be so satisfying to the national pride as a war with England. . . . Those who wish for peace . . . must desire the success of the North."[67]

When Dicey returned to England in 1863, he was amazed by the contrast between his observations in America and opinions in Britain about America: "I saw a country rich, prosperous, and powerful, and am told I have returned from a ruined, bankrupt, and wretched land. I saw a people eager for war, full of resolution, and confident of success, and learn that this selfsame people has no heart in the struggle and longs for foreign interference to secure a humiliating peace at any price."[68] Dicey was about the only British observer who was sympathetic to the Union cause. His book, *Six Months in the Federal States*, was not well received by upper-class readers in Britain.

By late 1863 nearly all of the British observers quoted in this chapter had returned to Britain and were producing a flood of articles and books on their impressions of the war in America. There were few new observers from Britain during the second half of the war. The only important representative of the British press in the North in this later period was the very pro-Confederate correspondent in New York for an emphatically pro-Confederate London paper, *The Times*. British opinions about the conflict in America, which had been firmly established during 1861–63, persisted with little change in 1863–65.

Chapter 20

THIS ABOMINABLE INSTITUTION

Slavery *and* Emancipation

M ost European immigrants and observers in North and South opposed the abolition of slavery—both before and after Lincoln's Emancipation Proclamation.

Europeans in the South usually accepted Southern viewpoints on the causes of the war. Major General Patrick Cleburne, an Irish immigrant, wrote that the slavery issue was merely a pretense used by the North "to establish sectional superiority and a more centralized form of government and to deprive us of our rights and liberties."[1] Major General Camille Jules Armand Marie, Prince de Polignac, a French volunteer, noted that Northern leaders "advocated the supremacy of the Federal government over the states. The Southern statesmen . . . adhered to the doctrine of States Rights as the only means of preserving an equitable balance of power throughout the Union. With these two conflicting political tendencies . . . the social question of domestic slavery had nothing whatever to do."[2]

Salomon de Rothschild, a French visitor in the South in 1861, thought "the true reason which impelled the Southern states to secede is the question of tariffs. The South . . . could supply itself with all necessary items in Europe, at prices from twenty-five to forty percent lower than what they have been paying up to now. . . . Since a Republican President was elected, the South felt that its cause was lost. . . . It therefore preferred to fight at once rather than be paralyzed by the measures of the President."[3] Lieutenant Colonel Camile Ferri-Pisani, a French officer who visited General Beauregard's headquarters in 1861, recorded that Beauregard and his officers "dismissed as secondary problems . . . questions concerning

179

slavery, tariffs, territories, Lincoln's election, even the constitutionality of secession. . . . They are waging an implacable war because the North invaded by force their territory, their native land. . . . They will defend their homes, their honor, and their liberty against the invaders."[4]

After ten days in Richmond in mid-1862, Edward A. Seymour (later Duke of Somerset) wrote that although "the Southern States seceded mainly for the better security of their slave property," they were now fighting for their soil. "Slaveholder and non-slaveholder are standing shoulder to shoulder in the ranks to struggle against what they feel to be an intolerable oppression."[5] Another future English duke, the Marquis of Hartington, wrote in 1862 that the Northerners "mix up . . . the slavery question, which they say makes theirs the just cause, with the Union question, which is really what they are fighting for."[6]

But most European observers in the North acknowledged that slavery was the basic cause of the war. The Swiss military observer, Captain Ferdinand Lecomte, reported in 1862 that "it is pretended in Europe . . . that slavery is not at stake in this war. Nothing equals the falsity of this assertion. . . . It is for the defence . . . of this abominable institution . . . that the South has put herself at war with her brethren."[7] Anthony Trollope, the British novelist, wrote in 1862 that "it is vain to say that slavery has not caused secession and that slavery has not caused the war. That and that only has been the cause of this conflict."[8]

"The one *casus belli* has been, throughout, the question of the extension of slavery," wrote British journalist Edward Dicey. "The North is fighting against, the South is fighting for, the power of extending slavery across the American continent. . . . The Southern leaders . . . seceded from the Union, solely and avowedly, because slavery was in danger . . . If . . . the extension of slavery was prohibited, . . . slavery was doomed. The system of cotton production under slave labor exhausts the soil so rapidly, that slavery would be starved out without a constant supply of fresh ground to occupy." Dicey recorded that when the Count of Paris arrived in England late in 1862, he was surprised to be told that slavery had nothing to do with the American war. "From the day I set foot in America to the day I left it," the count told a British friend, "I never heard of anything except the question of slavery."[9] French journalist Ernest De Hauranne observed in 1864 that "the true causes of the war are slavery, the mutual hostility of the two rival societies and, above all, the ambition of the Southerners . . . who raised the flag of revolt as soon as the presidency slipped out of their hands."[10]

Several European observers in the South wrote very positive accounts of the condition of the slaves. Salomon de Rothschild visited a Louisiana plantation: "I cannot deny that the negroes are punished when they do not behave well, but at the same time the great care is taken of their health and even of their well-being. Each settlement has its hospital and its doctor. The negroes do not work on Sundays, and often they are taken, as a reward, in carts to the neighboring city, where they can dance and have as much fun as they want. Consequently, a negro prefers to receive twenty-five lashes than to be kept in on Sunday."[11] A British correspondent, Samuel Phillips Day, described the slaves he saw on a Sunday drive in Louisville: "They were dressed so showily and so finely, and appeared so happy and contented, that I was voluntarily forced to exclaim several times—'Surely these people are not *slaves?*' The response was 'Certainly they are.' . . . Some of the women wore lace shawls and gold watches. . . . The men, too, were well attired— most of them in light clothes, and immaculate shirts and collars, ornamented with gold studs. . . . In the evening I went to the African Church. . . . The congregation were all well dressed. . . . When I considered that these people had been removed from a state of barbarism in Africa and had become semi-civilized, . . . the thought flashed across my mind that there was nothing so very wicked in slavery after all—that it possessed a *bright* as well as a *dark* side."[12]

Robert Bourke (later Lord Connemara) wrote of slaves he saw in Alabama: "They were all well dressed, and seemed happy and cheerful. . . . They are well fed, chiefly upon pork, corn, potatoes, and rice, carefully attended to when sick, and on Sundays dress better than their masters. Many of them had six or seven hundred dollars of their own."[13] An English officer, Captain Fitzgerald Ross, visited a South Carolina plantation: "The 'hands' . . . have each and all a cottage allotted to them, with a 'patch' to raise corn and vegetables and poultry. . . . They are well fed and well clothed. . . . The family physician attends them when sick, and in their old age and imbecility they are well protected. . . . In South Carolina negroes are as well protected by the laws as white men. . . . In criminal cases . . . a negro is tried before a court of three judges, the jury being composed of five white men, who must themselves be owners of negroes, and he can only be convinced by a unanimous verdict of this jury."[14]

Several of the visiting Europeans concluded that the slaves in the South were no worse off than the working classes in Europe. Rothschild thought they were "better fed and in better health and happier than many of our countrymen" in France.[15] After visiting a plantation near Richmond, the Marquis of Hartington wrote his father that "the negroes . . . are not dirtier or more uncomfortable looking than Irish labourers."[16]

In 1861 and most of 1862, when emancipation of the slaves was not yet an avowed Union goal, most European observers in both North and South cited various reasons for opposing the immediate emancipation of the slaves. Those who visited the South heard Southern arguments similar to those recorded by Ferencz

Pulsky, a Hungarian who visited the United States in 1851–52: "They often enlarged on the difficulties of universal emancipation in respect of the negroes themselves. 'What would they do,' they say, 'if they were free! They have not learned to care for themselves; they cannot do anything else than plant cotton and sugar. To give them political rights would be a most dangerous thing, for . . . they would become the tools of demagogues.' . . . 'After the abolition of slavery,' an American explained to me, . . . "anarchy will begin. Slavery alone maintains order, society, and family in the [Southern] United States against Communism, Socialism, and all the *isms* of Europe.'"[17]

In a report to *The Times*, William Howard Russell summarized the economic arguments for the maintenance of slavery that he heard in South Carolina in 1861: "We hold that slavery is essential to our existence as producer of what Europe requires. . . . England and France . . . require our products. In order to meet their wants, we must cultivate our soil. . . . The white man cannot . . . work in the manner required by the crops. He must, therefore, employ a race suited to the labour, and that is a race which will only work when it is obliged to do so." General Braxton Bragg assured Russell that "if a Northern population were settled in Louisiana tomorrow, they would discover that they must till the land by the labor of the black race, and the only mode of making the black race work was to hold them in a condition of involuntary servitude."[18]

Two British observers cited the aftermath of the abolition of slavery in 1838 in the British colony of Jamaica as grounds for skepticism about abolition in the American South. Lieutenant Colonel Garnet Joseph Wolseley thought "abolition, . . . as carried out in our West Indian possessions, . . . has been a failure in every respect."[19] Lieutenant Colonel James Arthur Fremantle wrote that "Southerners believe it to be impracticable to cultivate cotton on a large scale in the South without forced black labour, as the British have found it to produce sugar in Jamaica. . . . They say that that magnificent colony, formerly so wealthy and prosperous, is now nearly valueless—the land going out of cultivation—the whites ruined—the blacks idle, slothful, and . . . relapsing into their primitive barbarism."[20]

Anthony Trollope recalled "the vehement abolition enthusiasm" of a German colonel and lieutenant colonel he met in Illinois: "They regard slavery as an evil . . . and argued that . . . it should therefore be abolished at once. . . . When you asked them what they would propose to do with 4,000,000 of enfranchised slaves and their ruined masters, . . . they again ask you . . . whether anything acknowledged to be bad should be allowed to remain." Trollope thought "the preaching of abolition during the war is . . . either the deadliest of sins or the vainest of follies. . . . If they could emancipate those four million slaves, in which way would they then treat them? . . . Everything must be done for them. They expect food and clothes and instruction as to every simple act of life, as do children."[21] Several other foreign observers argued that emancipation would not really benefit the slaves. "Freedom! It is but a name to them," wrote Samuel Phillips Day. "What do beings of that class care for freedom, which would only have the effect of destroying their present happiness by bringing their labour into competition with that of the white man?"[22] Colonel Wolseley talked to General Lee about emancipation: "Lee hated slavery, but . . . he thought it wicked to give freedom suddenly to some millions of people who were incapable of using it with profit to themselves or the state."[23]

British observers rarely admitted their concern that emancipation of the slaves in the South would seriously threaten the supply of Southern cotton that was crucial to Britain's manufacturing and trade system. Robert Bourke attempted to reconcile the inescapable conflict between the long-standing British opposition to slavery and British commercial interests: "We all pray for universal emancipation. We have made enormous sacrifices in the cause ourselves; but we cannot help sympathizing with tens of millions of people struggling for independence. . . . If European intercourse be established with the Confederacy and she be admitted into the family of nations, commerce, always favourable to freedom, will then gradually but surely effect far more humane results than those which the most sincere Abolitionists can ever attain."[24] His assertion that commerce is "always favorable to freedom" is contradicted by the previously cited statements by Southerners that slavery was necessary to supply the cotton Britain needed.

Two other British observers in the North challenged the assertion by James Spence, a Confederate propagandist in Britain, that the Confederates would eventually free the slaves. Henry Yates Thompson wrote his father that he had read Spence's book, which was much praised by *The Times*: "He seems to be under the supreme error of believing that the South would of itself abolish slavery, whereas its leading politicians have all declared the contrary."[25] "I have never seen any address or proclamation of the Southern leaders in which the possibility of emancipation was even hinted at," wrote Edward Dicey. "Those who wish the South to succeed, wish slavery to be extended and strengthened. There is no avoiding this conclusion."[26]

Most of the European observers in America reacted negatively to Lincoln's Emancipation Proclamation. Some observers thought the Proclamation was only an inept and inadequate political maneuver. Lord Hartington wrote his father that the preliminary proclamation was "only a little political business to keep the 'infernal radicals' . . . quiet."[27] Charles Mackay reported to *The Times* that "it has the fatal demerit of being insufficient to please the ultra-abolitionists and of being more than enough to offend the Southern slaveowners, the Northern Pro-slavery party, the advocates of State rights, and all that large class of persons, American as well as Irish, who have a social, political, and economic objection to the negro."[28]

The most frequently stated objection by Europeans was that the proclamation didn't really free any slaves. "The proclamation . . . only declares slaves to be free," Mackay wrote, "in states where the President has no more power either to make them free or white than the Imaum of Muscat has, while it retains them in bondage in every place in which his armies could give effect to his words."[29] Dicey was about the only foreign observer who understood the constitutional reasons for the restriction of the proclamation to areas controlled by the Confederates: "By virtue of the war power, the Government has, or believes it has, authority to emancipate the slaves in the insurgent states, since it has power to perform any other act necessary for the preservation of the Union. But, by the Constitution, it has no more power to interfere with slavery in any loyal state, than England has to interfere with serfdom in Russia."[30] Captain Lecomte, the Swiss observer, thought "the friends of Christian equality ought to hail with pleasure the acts of Mr. Lincoln, even though they have been brought about incidentally and qualified as measures of war rather than acts of justice. . . . The fact and the right of the emancipation proclaimed will remain for those whom it has been able to reach."[31]

Another view, widely held in the South and in England, was that the proclamation was a cruel plan by Lincoln to foment a "servile insurrection," the British expression for a bloody slave revolt. Charles Mackay, the correspondent of *The Times* in New York, thought the proclamation was "a direct and palpable incentive to a servile war—of which no *imagination* . . . can exaggerate the horrors. . . . Mr. Lincoln deliberately counsels the negroes to defend by force the liberty which his proclamation but not his arms has bestowed upon them. . . . Should a war of races and a repetition of the atrocities of St. Domingo be the result, every drop of blood that may be shed in the struggle . . . will lie upon Mr. Lincoln's head."[32] But his colleague Francis Lawley, based in Richmond, took the Southern view that slaveowners had nothing to fear from their slaves: "Not one of those prophecies . . . has found a tittle of realization. Women and children without one adult white male have constantly lived in . . . the South surrounded by negroes; in no instance known to me has anything but the greatest loyalty and affection been evinced."[33] Yet there were signs of a hidden anxiety about a possible slave revolt. William Howard Russell noted in 1861 that "there is something suspicious in the constant never-ending statement that 'we are not afraid of our slaves.' "[34]

A few foreign observers recognized that Lincoln was using the Emancipation Proclamation as a weapon against the Confederacy. Edward Dicey noted that in the North "the abolitionists were unpopular at the commencement of the war because it was believed their policy retarded the restoration of the Union by embittering the South. As it has grown apparent that there is no chance of conciliating the South, the policy of abolition has become popular, as the one best adapted for preserving the Union."[35] "As long as the fight was merely to preserve the Union," observed the Marquis of Chambrun, "the Southern adversary was never attacked at his most vulnerable point. . . . Having found the chink in the adversary's armor, it was against that vulnerable spot that all Lincoln's energies were directed."[36] Another French journalist, Auguste Laguel, thought Lincoln "meant to show the South that the North was determined to yield to her in nothing. He was punishing an arrogant oligarchy that had given the signal for a fratricidal war."[37]

But no European observer recognized the Proclamation as a watershed event in the history of human freedom, or saw Abraham Lincoln as the Great Emancipator. With only a few exceptions, the observers were men of the upper classes who paid little attention to the welfare of the lower classes in their own countries or in European colonies in Africa and Asia. Most of the observers were Britons who supported Confederate independence for many imperial, political, and commercial reasons. They believed that slavery was both an essential element of Confederate society and a prerequisite for the production of the Southern cotton that was an essential requirement of Britain's manufacturing and commercial system. Those who visited the South accepted the Southern description of well-fed and contented slaves and the Southern arguments for the maintenance of slavery because these ideas fit with their strong desire for the maintenance of the established order around the world.

Only a small percentage of the European immigrants who enlisted in the Union army in 1861 or 1862 did so to fight for the freedom of the slaves. One of these was Lieutenant William Esbjorn, a Swedish immigrant in the 1st Illinois Cavalry. "I came to the conclusion lately to do something for my country and for the poor African race," he wrote his father just after Lincoln's call for volunteers. "Should I meet my death on the battlefield, [it would be] to die in a glorious cause."[38]

A Welsh scholar, T. G. Hunter, has assembled extensive evidence of the strong antislavery sentiments among Welshmen in America. Articles and editorials about slavery in Welsh-language publications contained many condemning phrases such as "the slavery curse," "the barbarism of the slave system," and "the oppressive plantation owner." One editor proclaimed that slavery was "one of the worst sinful evils which exists in this sinful world." "We will cast slavery out of our midst," proclaimed one Welsh soldier, Llanc Egryn; "let 'Freedom for Slaves' be our battlecry." Another soldier, Thomas R. Griffiths, wrote of the "heroic and determined spirit of the Union's soldiers . . . to spill the last drop of blood for the freedom of humanity and the defeat of slavery, violence, and oppression."[39] Alan Conway, who studied the letters of Welshmen in the Union army, wrote that they considered the war "a moral battle between the forces of darkness and the forces of light, with the freedom of the Negro slaves as the reward for Christian duty fully discharged."[40]

Some of the immigrant soldiers became more interested in abolition after seeing slaves on plantations in the South. Captain Mons Grinager, a Norwegian in the 15th Wisconsin, wrote home that "they are shabbily dressed, as they are seldom given more than one cheap outfit each year. They speak broken English and are generally very ignorant. . . . The owners sell them as we sell our animals, no attention being paid to family relationships. Not infrequently it happens that plantation owners sell children whom they themselves have begotten with female slaves. . . . The overseer always goes armed with a large blacksnake whip, which is frequently used when the slaves fail to exert themselves to the utmost. . . . The abhorrence I have always felt toward slavery is considerably stronger now than ever before because of these firsthand observations."[41] Stephen O. Himroe, a Norwegian surgeon in the 15th Wisconsin, concluded that "the only way to put down this rebellion is to hurt the instigators and the abettors of it. Slavery must be cleaned out."[42]

But the great majority of Union soldiers—including most of the immigrants—were lukewarm or hostile toward emancipation. Archbishop Hughes of New York wrote in 1861 that "the Catholics . . . are willing to fight to the death for the support of the Constitution, the Government, and the laws of the country. But if it should be understood that . . . they are to fight for the abolition of slavery, . . . they will turn away in disgust from the discharge of what would otherwise be a patriotic duty."[43] Colonel Marcus W. Spiegel of the 20th Illinois was in Washington in June 1862: "In the House I heard Mr. Sedgwick of New York say that he 'hoped and trusted that the war would not end until the sun would no longer shine on a single slave in America.' If it is the object of Congress to prolong the war until this is accomplished, I wish they would be honest enough to say so at once, and give us who are engaged in this war for a different purpose a chance to go home."[44] "I don't want to fire another shot for the negroes," wrote Valentin Bechler, a German immigrant in the 8th New Jersey.[45]

The hostility of most immigrant soldiers to emancipation was derived mainly from their prejudices and their perceptions of their own self-interest. Their attitudes toward blacks were essentially those of most native-born soldiers. Bell Irvin Wiley, author of a study of the common soldier in the Union army, noted that "one who reads letters and diaries of Union soldiers encounters an enormous amount of antipathy toward Negroes. Expression of unfriendliness range from blunt statements bespeaking intense hatred to belittling remarks concerning dress and demeanor."[46]

Many Union soldiers objected to the enlistment of black soldiers in the army. William Todd described the reactions of his fellow soldiers in the predominantly Scottish 79th New York: "The Highlanders, with possibly a few exceptions, were bitterly opposed to raising the Negro to the military level of the Union soldiers. When we saw the Negroes, uniformed and equipped like ourselves, . . . it was more than some of our hotheaded pro-slavery comrades could witness in silence. For a while the air was filled with vile epithets hurled at the poor darkies, and overt acts against their persons were only prevented by the interference of our officers."[47]

Other immigrants shared the view of most British observers that emancipation would not improve the lot of the slaves. "We are hailed by darkies in the most cheering spirit and great manifestation of joy," Colonel Spiegel wrote his wife from a Mississippi riverboat late in 1862. "The poor devils frequently . . . ask to be taken out of bondage. . . . It seems hard to deny a privilege to *be free*. Yet when . . . you see thousands of the contrabands pulled away . . . from their masters, in a miserable and starving and filthy condition, . . . you will say better be in slavery than such freedom as I can give you."[48]

A number of editors of German language newspapers were disappointed that the Proclamation did not free slaves in the three slaves states—Maryland, Kentucky, and Missouri—that had remained in the Union. Lincoln biographer Carl Sandburg quoted an account by Dr. Emile Pretorius, editor of the *Wesliche Post* in St. Louis, of his meeting with Lincoln in September 1863: "We Germans had not felt so kindly toward Mr. Lincoln since he had set aside Fremont's proclamation of emancipation. . . . Now that he himself had issued an emancipation proclamation, we felt wronged because it applied only to the States in rebellion and not to our own state. . . . "We need the Border States," said he. "We must patiently educate them up to the right opinion." . . . The attitude of the Border States was of the very highest importance. I could realize that the more fully as Lincoln argued the case."[49] Nonetheless, in the summer of 1864 Pretorius advocated that the Cincinnati convention of dissident Republicans reject Lincoln and nominate Fremont for president. Other Germans thought the administration was on the right track. Carl Schurz wrote a friend in Germany late in 1863 that "slavery is being driven out of its last citadel. . . . The people of the new world are taking an immeasurable step forward in its cleaning and ennobling."[50]

But the majority of the German immigrants had very mixed feelings about emancipation. "I . . . do not . . . want to fight for Lincoln's Negro proclamation one day longer than I can help," Colonel Spiegel wrote his wife in January 1863.

"The whole Army is discouraged and very much dissatisfied in consequence of Lincoln's proclamation, which fell like a thunderbolt among the troops."[51] When some of the Germans in his regiment said they would not fight in a war for abolition, he told the regiment that they must "stand by the government, right or wrong." "If there is one man in the regiment who would refuse to shoot at a rebel in an engagement, let him step three paces to the front in order that he can be *marked as a coward* and *receive the reward of a traitor*."[52] But a month later he wrote his wife that the administration had made two great errors: "1st, the removal of McClellan; 2nd, the Emancipation Proclamation. The first weakened us, the second strengthened the enemy."[53]

During a year in the South, however, Colonel Spiegel's attitude toward slavery changed radically. "Since I am here I have learned and seen more of what the horrors of slavery were than I ever knew before," he wrote his wife in January 1864. "I am now in favor of doing away with the institution of Slavery. . . . This is no hasty conclusion but a deep conviction, . . . as a good citizen doing duty to my God, my family, my Country, and myself."[54] A month later he wrote that "slavery . . . has been an awful institution. I will send you the 'black code' of Louisiana. . . . It will make you shudder. I am a strong abolitionist . . . for the best interest of the white man in the South and the black man anywhere."[55] Colonel Spiegel was killed during the Red River campaign in Louisiana in the spring of 1864.

There was much less division and evolution of opinion on emancipation within the Irish community. Support for the Emancipation Proclamation was extremely rare among Irish immigrants. Maria Lydig Daly, wife of an Irish-American judge in New York, thought Lincoln was becoming a dictator: "The Cabinet were not consulted. He told them it was there for them to criticize verbally, not to argue upon. What supreme impertinence in the railsplitter of Illinois! . . . There is no law but the despotic will of poor Abe Lincoln!"[56] Irish opposition to Lincoln's emancipation policy was a major cause of Irish resistance to conscription and of the draft riots in New York in 1863, previously reviewed in Chapter 3.

Perhaps the most vehement condemnation of the Proclamation was by the son of an Irish immigrant, Confederate Senator James Phelan of Mississippi: "Our brutal foes . . . seek to light in our land the baneful fires of servile war, by emancipation among us of four million of negro slaves, with the design of effecting an indiscriminate slaughter of all ages, sexes, and conditions of our people. A scheme so atrocious and infernal is unparalleled in the blackest and bloodiest page of savage strife."[57]

The range of attitudes toward slavery and emancipation among immigrants in the North was not fundamentally different from the attitudes of other Americans, except that more of the newcomers were in low-paying jobs and feared competition for those jobs from emancipated slaves. The hostile attitudes toward blacks of many immigrants in the Union army were not very different from the attitudes of the majority of men in the army. In the South, most immigrants felt that their relative freedom and prosperity were dependent on the maintenance of the Southern way of life including slavery.

The failure of most European observers to perceive the Emancipation Proclamation as a landmark event in the history of human liberty is attributable to their generally negative view of Lincoln and their unacknowledged but apparent preference for the continuation of the existing system of cotton production in the American South.

Chapter 21

WITH *THE* SUBLIMITY OF GENIUS, OR OF MADNESS

Gettysburg *to* Atlanta: 1863–1864

I n the weeks after the Confederate defeats at Gettysburg and Vicksburg, two Europeans in the South thought that two years of fighting had produced only a stalemate. "It is almost an impossibility that an influential and decisive victory should . . . be ever gained by either party," Francis Lawley reported to *The Times* in July. "If no other solution of this quarrel can be found than that which is attained by fighting, the child just born will be mature before the dispute is settled."[1] "I don"t look for any peace during the Lincoln administration," Private John Garibaldi, an Italian immigrant in the Stonewall Brigade, wrote home in August. "If at the end of this term another president is elected belonging to the same party or Lincoln is reelected, we may look for another four years of war."[2]

Auguste Laugel, a French observer, traced events in the west after the fall of Vicksburg: "The Federals advanced into Tennessee, and Bragg was obliged to retire to the frontiers of Georgia. Rosecranz seized Chattanooga, and pursued his enemy. Bragg, reinforced by Longstreet and Hood, turns round suddenly and gives battle to Rosecranz on the banks of the Chickamauga. On September 19, the federal division under Thomas resists all assaults. The next day the Confederates, unable to break Thomas's line to the left, throw themselves on the right, overwhelm it, and finally put the center to rout."[3] Colonel Leon Von Zinken, a German immigrant commanding the combined 13th and 20th Louisiana regiments, described the Confederate attack: "We advanced steadily to about 60 yards from the enemy's line, when they opened a most terrific fire upon us. For a moment our line seemed to waver, but, cheered on by the officers, the men rushed forward . . . and carried the enemy's position, which . . . had been barricaded by logs piled up from 3 to 4 feet high. . . . The enemy was completely routed and fled in great confusion."[4]

"The enemy came up and endeavored to carry the position by storm, but . . . we drove them back with great slaughter," wrote a Norwegian in the 15th Wisconsin, Lieutenant Colonel Ole C. Johnson. "They soon rallied, . . . but were driven back as before. After the second repulse, I . . . saw the regiment on our left was already some distance to the rear and the rebels getting over the breast works. . . . The regiment to the right of us had also given way, and . . . we were almost entirely surrounded. . . . The next moment I was without much ceremony requested to march to the rebel rear."[5]

Dr. Konrad Soelheim, a German physician, was in charge of a Union field hospital with six physicians and fifteen orderlies: "All day countless ambulances arrived loaded with wounded. . . . The scene was indescribable. . . . We could not start amputating until the morning of the 20th, . . . after we had done what was critical to minimal care for the many injured. But by 9:30 . . . fresh fighting raged near us. . . . We were soon under artillery bombardment. Then an order arrived from the chief physician. I was to take all the severely wounded with me in ambulances to Rossville, about ten miles off. The rest of the wounded, those not badly hurt, were to walk there. Too late! The battle already threatened the hospital. Refugees, the wounded and the dying crowded around us, enemy infantry stormed at us. . . . Ghastly chaos! Then came new wounded." Dr. Soelheim described the high fatality rate among the wounded on both sides. "In Rebel hands, very many of our officers and men, lacking care and proper treatment, had died of wounds. With us, too, far more of the injured perished than should have perished, for lack of nourishing food and much else."[6]

After Chickamauga, "Thomas . . . retires slowly, still defying the enemy," Laugel wrote. "Bragg takes up his post on Lookout Mountain and Missionary Ridge, in front of Chattanooga, where the Federals are entrenched. Grant takes command; Hooker is sent to his assistance with one of the corps that gained the victory at Gettysburg."[7] "Our army is terribly broken by vastly overwhelming numbers," Brigade Surgeon Stephen O. Himoe, 15th Wisconsin, wrote to his wife. But the Norwegian immigrant assured her that "we will never surrender Chattanooga to the enemy while a single battalion remains to die in its defence. The country must and shall be saved."[8]

Captain Frederick Otto Von Fritsch, a Prussian officer, was with a mainly German brigade at Brown's Ferry: "The charge of Colonel Smith's brigade of Steinwehr's division of the Eleventh Corps up an almost inaccessible mountain in face of a firing enemy (known as the battle in the clouds) was, without doubt, the most heroic during the entire war. With their bayonets only, they drove Longstreet's brave veterans out of their entrenchments on the top of a hill which tourists now

can hardly climb assisted by alpine sticks." The German baron wrote that this battle "proved the material the Eleventh Corps was made of."[9]

"It was not at first intended," Carl Schurz recalled, "to attempt the actual
storming of Missionary Ridge—a fortified position which seemed well-nigh impregnable by a front attack—but rather to make a threatening demonstration calculated
to induce Bragg to withdraw forces from his right to his center. . . . But the brave
men of our Army of the Cumberland, once launched, could not be held back. With
irresistible impetuosity, . . . they rushed forward, hurled the enemy's advanced
lines out of their defenses on the slope, scaled the steep acclivity like wildcats, suddenly appeared on the crest of the ridge, where the rebel host, amazed at this wholly
unlooked-for audacity, fled in wild confusion, leaving their entrenched artillery and
thousands of prisoners behind them."[10]

"I was ordered . . . to advance and take the rifle pits of the rebels in our
front," reported Colonel Frederick Kneffler, a Hungarian immigrant who commanded the 79th Indiana. "Upon our approach, the rebels abandoned their rifle-
pits. . . . Crossing the open space beyond the works, we met a terrible
fire. . . . The line advanced firmly . . . under a most furious fire of artillery and
small arms, . . . but the ground was held and contested with the utmost determination. . . . We remained in our position, . . . keeping up a heavy fire, until support came on the right and left, advancing up the mountain. . . . Orders were
given to fix bayonets and to charge them; once the effort failed, but advancing
again succeeded, and gained the enemy's works, which were covered with dead
and wounded. . . . As my men swarmed upon the crest, the rebels made another stand, . . . but they were quickly broken and fled in the greatest
confusion. . . . The command bivouacked upon the crest of Missionary Ridge."[11]
The Scotsman who commanded the 137th New York, Colonel David Ireland, wrote
a similar report.[12]

"When General Grant noticed this brilliant charge," Captain Von Fritsch
recorded, "he asked . . . 'Who ordered those troops to charge Missionary
Ridge?' . . . General Thomas . . . replied 'General Grant, it seems to me that
they started on their own free will.' General Grant watched them for some time,
then . . . lit a fresh cigar and said: 'If this turns out well, all right; if not, someone
will have to suffer for it.' It turned out well."[13]

Laugel sketched the beginning of the "overland" campaign in Virginia in the
spring of 1864 after Grant had been promoted to lieutenant general: "Grant . . .
goes direct to the Rapidan, while Butler ascends the James River toward Richmond. Lee and Grant begin to fight on the 6th of May, in a valley called the

Wilderness. . . . Two immense armies look for each other all day in the woods, and are decimated without seeing each other."[14] "General Jenkins, who commanded a South Carolina brigade, . . . fell mortally wounded from his saddle," wrote Captain Francis W. Dawson, an Englishman on Longstreet's staff. "Longstreet . . . reeled as the blood poured down his breast, and was evidently badly hurt. . . . Longstreet had been wounded and Jenkins had been killed, as Jackson was, by the fire of our own men. . . . I mounted my horse and rode in desperate haste to the nearest field hospital. Giving the sad news to the first surgeon I could find, I made him jump on my horse, and bade him, for Heaven's sake, ride as rapidly as he could to the front where Longstreet was. I followed afoot. The flow of blood was speedily staunched."[15]

The battle in the Wilderness continued for six days. "Grant never retreats an inch," Laugel wrote; "he advances . . . as far as the Chickahominy. There he makes a circuit, quietly crosses the river, reaches the James, and rejoins Butler's army, established in front of Petersburg and Richmond."[16] "He sees no obstacles, and goes blindly and ruthlessly on," Charles Mackay wrote to *The Times*. "The lives of his men are of no value. . . . With the sublimity of genius, or of madness (the fortune of war must determine which), he has declared . . . "that he will go to Richmond by that line, if it takes him all summer to do it." . . . The people . . . think Grant is the greatest as well as the most daring General that the world ever saw, and are content to wait a little longer for the results before they change their opinion."[17]

Several letters written by an English officer with the Confederate army, Captain Fitzgerald Ross, reflect Confederate and British wishful thinking about Grant and his army. "There are symptoms of great discontent, both amongst officers and men, at the way in which they have been handled by Grant," he wrote on May 17. "His army, the finest and best equipped that the Yankees ever put in the field, is now pretty nearly destroyed." A week later Ross wrote that "Grant's soldiers are getting tired of him and call him a butcher, and won't fight."[18] Lawley reassured his British readers that "Grant with the shattered residuum of his once mighty host is impotently held in check at Petersburg by an army which is more than a match for his own, and by a general who is markedly his superior."[19]

During the summer, public attention in North and South shifted to Sherman's campaign to capture Atlanta. "The genius of strategy is spontaneously and fully developed in this ardent soldier," wrote Auguste Laugel. "He first forces Johnston, who is sent against him, to retreat from Tunnel Hill to Dalton, and from there to Resaca. Rome is the first reward of his efforts; he . . . turns his adversary and makes him retreat to Marietta, forces him to abandon Kennesaw Mountain, and at last to cross the Chattahoochee."[20] Lawley reported that Richmond was stunned by

Sherman's progress in Georgia: "Great and increasing anxiety is here felt as telegram follows telegram announcing that General Johnston has again and again fallen back until . . . his bold antagonist, General Sherman, is seen to be within three leagues of Atlanta."[21] Mackay soon reported from New York that "General Johnston . . . has been superseded in his command . . . because the Southern people and his own subordinates were of the opinion that a stand ought to be made for Atlanta, at any risk and any cost. General Hood, appointed to succeed him, . . . attacked the Federals in their entrenchments between the city and the Chattahoochee. The contest was a stubborn one, . . . but without the desired results."[22]

"We are so near Atlanta we can see the city from some of the hills," wrote Sergeant John O. Wrolsted, a Norwegian in the 15th Wiscosin, on July 25. "It is still five miles to the city and along these five miles there are nothing but forts and entrenchments and hundreds of cannon and all that Hell itself can think of."[23] Sherman's bombardment of Atlanta was described by Private Thomas H. Tucker, an English immigrant in the 22nd Michigan: "This morning at 5 AM, signal guns were fired . . . and then every battery of ours . . . commenced firing on Atlanta. It lasted over 2 hours. . . . The ground fairly trembled. . . . I pity the poor people that stayed in the city and was under fire."[24]

"The fortifications around Atlanta were . . . very extensive," noted Lieutenant Colonel Frederick C. Winkler, a German in the 26th Wisconsin; "to surround them completely, would have taken an immense army. The way to get them out was . . . to move upon their communications."[25] "Our whole brigade have been tearing up the railroad track all day," Private Tucker wrote home on August 27. "We have destroyed several miles of the track. . . . Our whole regiment would line up close together and then we would take ahold of one side of the track and tip the whole thing right over. Then with heavy sledges and crowbars, we would get the ties loose and put a lot of them in a pile, set them on fire, then lay a lot of the iron rails across the burning ties and when the iron rails got red hot in the centers of the rail, 8 or 10 of us would carry the iron rail and wrap it around a tree or a telegraph pole. It was awful hard work, but great fun."[26]

Colonel Winkler commented that the destruction of the railroad "left two courses open to Hood, to retreat at once towards Augusta or to meet General Sherman and stake the fate of the city and perhaps his army on the result of a battle. He followed his pugnacious instincts and was badly beaten. . . . Hood has fought four battles, one north, one east, and one west, and finally one south of the city, and raided on our railroad. He [held] the city long enough to see a great portion of it devastated, and then left it, his army broken, reduced and demoralized, and valuable stores of munitions of war left a prey to the flames."[27]

"The rebs tried to get out of the city with the ammunition train, but could not," Private Tucker recorded. "So the rebs blew up the whole thing, trains, engines and everything." Sherman occupied Atlanta on September 2. "We marched clean through the city of Atlanta and when we got to where the depot is, my what a sight. Engines, cars, trucks, exploded shells, and other wreckage all in heaps every where."[28]

A month later Hood turned the tables on Sherman, and cut his supply line. "On the 4th of October," wrote the French military observer, Colonel De Chenal, "Hood moved around Sherman's army and destroyed the railroad, first at Big Shanty and afterwards to the north of Resaca; tearing up thirty-five miles of railway."[29] Tucker recorded that "Old Hood . . . has torn up the railroad and destroyed the bridges . . . between here and Chattanooga. We can't get the food supplies through. . . . A strong detail from our regiment goes out 6 or 7 miles in the country to get supplies of provisions."[30] De Chenal was impressed by the rapid reconstruction of the railroad by the Union troops: "Before retiring, Hood destroyed all the supplies of railway material, so that it was necessary to cut the ties and place them further apart than usual. . . . The rails needed to relay the southern part of the breach had to be brought from the railways south of Atlanta and those for the northern part were brought from Nashville. . . . Notwithstanding all these difficulties, this gap of thirty-five miles was completely repaired . . . in seven and a half days."[31]

Meanwhile, Union General Philip Sheridan had been busy in the Shenandoah Valley, the "breadbasket of the Confederacy." "On September 19 Sheridan attacked the enemy near Winchester, and, after a desperate battle, carried the position . . . with two thousand five hundred prisoners, five guns, and nine colors," recalled General De Trobriand. "General Early, beaten at Winchester, retreated thirty miles up the valley, and took position at Fisher's Hill, where Sheridan quickly followed him. On the 22nd, the position, although very strong, was carried by assault. . . . Sheridan pursued with great vigor beyond Harrisonburg and Staunton to the passes of the Blue Ridge. . . . He returned to take position behind Cedar Creek, after having completely destroyed the provisions and forage in that part of the valley. . . . The destruction embraced more than two thousand barns full of grain and forage, and more than seventy mills full of wheat and flour. Four thousand head of cattle were driven off by the troops, and three thousand sheep were issued as rations."[32]

The Second Cavalry Division of Sheridan's army was commanded by Brigadier General William H. Powell, a Welsh immigrant: "On the first of October I moved the division . . . from Harrisonburg down the Page Valley to Luray, driving off all stock of every description, destroying all grain, burning mills, blast furnaces, distilleries, tanners, and all forage. . . . The country . . . has been left in such a condition as to barely leave subsistence for the inhabitants."[33] Captain Dawson, a British volunteer, described the devastation: "Columns of smoke were rising in every direction from burning houses and burning barns. . . . The brutal Sheridan . . . was soon in position to boast . . . that 'if a crow wants now to fly over the Valley of Virginia, he must carry his rations with him.' "[34]

Despite Sherman's capture of Atlanta and Sheridan's campaign in the Shenandoah Valley, the Confederate press continued to insist that the Confederacy would sustain its independence. Captain Bernhard Domschcke of 26th Wisconsin, a former newspaper editor, read the Richmond papers while a prisoner in the Libby prison in Richmond: "From every angle and with recklessness, Rebel papers splashed sophistry and distortion in their papers. . . . Southern papers . . . represented the rebellion as . . . a justifiable revolt of a great and glorious people against the tyranny of a malignant and brutal usurper. . . . The press . . . agitated the public's worst impulses with articles so rabid that they seemed written with daggers dipped in poison. . . . Regularly it boasted of . . . the certainty of Confederate triumph."[35]

A Royal Navy captain and blockade runner, C. Augustus Hobart-Hampden, visited Richmond in 1864: "The people had that wonderful blind confidence in the Southern cause which had supported them through all difficulties. . . . Though a line of earthworks . . . at Petersburg was nearly all that kept Grant's well-organized army from entering the capital; though the necessities of war, and of life, were growing alarmingly short; though the soldiers were badly fed, and only half clothed, . . . everyone seemed satisfied that the South would somehow or other gain the day and become an independent nation. . . . The talented correspondent of *The Times* . . . never seemed to despair. . . . All of us . . . should have seen the end coming, months before we were obliged to open our eyes."[36]

By November even Francis Lawley's optimism was sagging: "From the 4th of May until the present hour, Lee's army has been continuously in the trenches. . . . The uninterrupted pressure for more than five months [has] told fearfully on the poor Confederates, exposed to one of the fiercest summers ever known in Virginia, scantily fed upon . . . mostly salt meat and bread, without vegetables, with only occasional coffee, with no other stimulant, and threatened ceaselessly by overwhelming numbers. . . . Officers and privates . . . are half worn out. . . . Though the spirit is the same as ever, they urgently need rest."[37]

Chapter 22

THIS TURBULENT DEMOCRACY

The Presidential Election *of* 1864

A uguste Laugel, a French observer, described the National Convention of the Union (Republican) party which opened on June 7, 1864: "The Baltimore convention . . . declared itself for an amendment of the Constitution prohibiting slavery forever . . . in all the states of the republic. The language of the platform was simple and categoric: the war must be continued until the entire submission of the rebel states. . . . Mr. Lincoln was nominated unanimously and no other name was offered for discussion."[1]

Despite the convention's endorsement, the summer of 1864 was a very difficult time for Abraham Lincoln. The war was not going well, and many people were dissatisfied with Lincoln's conduct of the war. "I think the country might afford us an abler and a stronger Chief Magistrate," observed a German immigrant, Lieutenant Colonel Frederick Winkler of the 26th Wisconsin. "But it is hard to say . . . who the proper man in the present crisis would be."[2] Ernest Duvergier De Hauranne wrote that "never has an outgoing administration had more sources of weakness than at this moment, when the need for strength is most keenly felt." But the French journalist acknowledged that "Mr. Lincoln represents better than anyone the policy of winning the war and saving the Union."[3]

Charles Mackay, New York correspondent of *The Times* of London, wrote that "as a President he is the worst failure that America has ever produced. . . . It is a pity that he . . . does not earn the respect of his true friends and the forbearance of his foes by retiring into private life."[4] Carl Schurz visited Lincoln in late July:" 'They urge me with almost violent language,' he said, 'to withdraw from the

199

contest, although I have been unanimously nominated, in order to make room for a better man. I wish I could. Perhaps some other man might do this business better than I. . . . But I am here, and that better man is not here.' "[5]

In 1864 a German immigrant, August Belmont, was the chairman of the Democratic National Committee. Born in the Rhenish Palatinate in 1813, he learned the banking business in the Rochschild bank in Frankfurt before coming to America in 1837 at age twenty-four. He became the Rothschild agent in America, served as U.S. consul general in Vienna for a while in the 1840s, and was later U.S. minister to the Netherlands. By the 1860s he was a prominent international banker and a leader of New York society. In the opening speech at the Democratic convention on August 29, 1864, Belmont proclaimed that "four years of misrule by a sectional, fanatical and corrupt party" had "brought our country on the very edge of ruin" and that the reelection of Lincoln would lead to "the utter disintegration of our whole political and social system amid bloodshed and anarchy."[6]

The Democrats were divided into two factions, described by Laugel: "The *war Democrats* . . . were ready to maintain the Union by force of arms, if the rebel States could not be brought back of a political compromise. . . . The *peace Democrats* were the least numerous, and public opinion had branded them with the name *copperheads,* but they were skillful, active, and logical."[7] The position of the Peace Democrats was summarized by the French military observer, Colonel Francois De Chenal: "The only results of all the bloody campaign were that Grant had lost 100,000 men and was no nearer success than McClellan had been in 1862, and that Sherman's army was lost. They claimed that the rebels were soon going to regain the West; that Mobile, Savannah, Wilmington and Charleston were always open for assistance from Europe; that there were 100,000 deserters; that the people were everywhere resisting the recruiting officers; that the widows and orphans were everywhere to be seen; and that the country was unwilling to continue the war."[8]

"The Democrats . . . declared in their platform," Schurz recalled, "that the war against the rebellion was a failure and that immediate efforts must be made for a cessation of hostilities with a view to an ultimate convention of all the states for a peaceable settlement on the basis of reunion. Considering the fact that the leaders of the rebellion . . . defiantly insisted on the independence of the Southern Confederacy as a condition *sine qua non* of any settlement, this proposition looked like a complete surrender."[9] Mackay noted that "the platform very judiciously refuses to prescribe . . . what the party will do should the Southern people make conditions of armistice that the North could not accept without humiliation."[10]

Many Union soldiers were appalled by the Democratic platform. Brigadier General Regis De Trobriand, a French immigrant, recalled that "the Republicans wished the war to continue until the extinction of the rebellion and the reestab-

lishment of a Union consummated by victory and ennobled by the immediate abolition of slavery. . . . The Democrats . . . demanded the suspension of the war
by a compromise with the rebellion and the conditional restoration of a Union subject to the pretended rights of the South, implying . . . the maintenance of slavery."[11] Captain Charles Alexandre Lucas, a Belgian immigrant in the 24th Illinois,
thought the Democratic convention had offered an "abominable" program: "For the
benefit of the enemy they wish to sacrifice the cause and the honor for which the
Union has already sacrificed so much during these past four years."[12]

The Democrats nominated the former commander of the Army of the
Potomac, General George B. McClellan, as their candidate for president. The country waited to see whether McClellan would run on the party's platform. "After some
hesitation," Laugel recorded, "the General accepted the nomination; but he did it
in terms which were an indirect disavowal of the platform of the party. He took the
bride, but refused the dowry. 'I could not,' he says, 'face my brave comrades of the
army and navy who have survived so many bloody battles, and tell them that their
toil, and the sacrifice of our brothers had been in vain, that we have abandoned the
Union, for which we have risked our lives so often.' Elsewhere he says again, 'The
Union must be maintained at all hazards.' He separated himself thus from the *peace
Democrats,* and became the faithful organ of the sentiments of the *war Democrats.*"[13]

McClellan's letter made him acceptable to many Democrats who had supported
the war but were reluctant to vote for another term for Abraham Lincoln. Maria
Lydig Daly, wife of an Irish-American judge in New York, recorded that "McClellan's letter made a great commotion, frightening the Republicans, dissatisfying the
peace men, but contenting the moderate people."[14] Colonel Winkler thought there
was "no doubt as to his loyalty to the United States and hostility to the Rebellion,"[15]
but many other immigrants were not convinced of his loyalty to the Union cause.

There were also dissidents among the Republicans. "A small fraction . . . of
the Republican party had openly broken with Mr. Lincoln," Laugel wrote; "it had
held its convention at Cleveland, and had chosen for its candidate General Fremont. . . . It declared that . . . the presidency of Mr. Lincoln had been only a
series of faults and errors."[16] Many of the "Forty-Eighters"—men who had fought in
the revolution in Germany in 1848—supported Fremont. They were disenchanted
with Lincoln because he was moving too cautiously on emancipation. Carl Wittke,
editor of a book on the Forty-Eighters, wrote that many of them "wanted the South
reduced to a conquered territory, the rebels severely punished, their property confiscated, and a new order created based on unconditional surrender and the enfran-
chisement of the Negro."[17]

Caspar Butz, a Forty-Eighter, called Lincoln "the weakest and worst man that
ever filled the Presidential chair."[18] Fritz Anneke, formerly McClellan's chief of

artillery, wrote that many Germans opposed the reelection of "the weak-headed, unprincipled log-splitter."[19] Colonel De Chenal noted that "radical German journals . . . spoke of Lincoln as a dictator, a tyrant."[20] But the Fremont movement fizzled out. Laugel recorded that "Mr. Fremont . . . kept still a remnant of influence among the German populations of the West, but little by little his popularity declined. . . . When he found himself abandoned, Mr. Fremont retired from his candidature."[21] After Fremont's withdrawal, the radical Germans had no option but to give their votes to Lincoln.

The most important spokesman for each of the candidates was a German immigrant. August Belmont, chairman of the Democrats, repeatedly demanded the election of McClellan and the restoration of "the Union as it was,"—the Democratic phrase for the continuation of slavery—insisting that the "fatal policy of confiscation and forcible emancipation" would force the South to "fight to the last extremity."[22] Carl Schurz, who had resigned his commission as major general in order to campaign for Lincoln, insisted that restoration of "the Union as it was" was totally unrealistic: "Not even in the wildest flights of your imagination," he told an audience in Brooklyn, "can you conceive the possibility that the relations between a dominant and an enslaved race can be placed upon the ancient footing, when two hundred thousand men of the enslaved race have been in arms against their masters. . . . Slavery is dying fast. Its life is ebbing out of a thousand mortal wounds."[23]

In the end, many Germans and others voted against McClellan, rather than for Lincoln. They were unwilling to vote for a man who was increasingly seen in the South as the salvation of the Confederacy. "There is great hope that McClellan will be elected," a German in Texas wrote his son in the Confederate army; "that . . . would mean, to be sure, only an approach to peace and not peace itself. But . . . I am full of hope."[24] Wittke concluded that "the majority of the German radical press finally supported Lincoln for reelection, and although some Germans may have stayed away from the polls, the majority probably voted for the President, if for no other reason than to avert the disaster of a Democratic victory."[25]

The Irish disenchantment with the war, their hatred of conscription, and their strong opposition to Lincoln's emancipation policy—and the similar views of many other New Yorkers—had led to the draft riots in New York City in June 1863. Irish attitudes had not changed by November 1864. The crucial factor was the Irish fear that emancipated negroes would take the jobs of Irishmen. William F. Zornow, who studied the election of 1864, wrote that "the Irish were traditionally Democratic, and in 1864 they showed no tendency to depart from their normal pattern. "They voted against us almost to a man," said one Union leader."[26]

De Haurane was impressed by the "profound calm" on the day the voters went to the polls: "Election Day was a truce, and all parties laid down their arms with astonishing unanimity. . . . The people sensed the solemnity of the occasion and voted quietly. This turbulent democracy . . . spontaneously felt the need to impose self-discipline and to invest the new government with gravity and order." The French observer thought the orderly voting "does the greatest honor to the good sense and patriotism of America."[27]

Of the 4,015,902 votes cast, Lincoln received 55 percent (2,212,665 votes) and McClellan 45 percent (1,802,237 votes). Lincoln won 212 of the 233 electoral votes. McClellan carried only three states—New Jersey, Delaware, and Kentucky.[28] Historian James M. McPherson noted that "a striking majority of all Union soldiers—78 percent, compared with 53 percent of the civilian vote—went for Lincoln. This was all the more remarkable because some 40 to 45% of soldiers had been Democrats or came from Democratic families in 1860."[29] Even Charles Mackay conceded that Lincoln's leadership had been endorsed by a clear majority of the people: "Unfair votes may have been cast for Mr. Lincoln and undue means may have been employed on his behalf in the army and in districts under military control, but the results prove that he needed neither to be successful and that it was the firm determination of a decisive though not very large majority of the Northern people to intrust him for a second term with the destinies of the Republic."[30]

The *New York Times* reported that Lincoln's strength had been greatest among farmers and among skilled workers and professional men in the cities, while McClellan's votes had come mainly from unskilled laborers and foreign-born voters.[31] Despite the strong vote for McClellan among civilian immigrants, the very large soldier vote for Lincoln indicates strong support for him by immigrant soldiers. Private John P. Jones, a Welshman in the 23rd Wisconsin, had written home in September that "nearly all the soldiers are in favor of Lincoln. . . . The people have decided that he will be elected."[32] In Wisconsin regiments, which contained a high percentage of German and other immigrants, Lincoln received 82 percent of the votes.[33]

The Hungarian immigrant who edited the *Chicago Tribune,* Josef Medill, opined that "Mr. Lincoln has continued to have not only the confidence but the love of the masses of the people. Everybody has his own little fault to find with him. . . . But never were the people of a great nation more unanimous in favor of sustaining any public officer."[34] The French military observer, Colonel De Chenal, also thought the election victory was an endorsement of Lincoln's insistence on continuing the war until victory was achieved: "The people of the Union . . . knew that a peace which was not the result of victory would be only a truce and would be followed by unending wars. They were unwilling to leave to their children the duty of revenging the defeat of a cause which they themselves deserted."[35]

In the 24th Illinois, Captain Charles Lucas rejoiced at the election results because they indicated that "the majority of the people are determined to overthrow the rebellion." The Belgian immigrant wrote that "there will still be much blood spilled, but I have complete confidence in the ultimate success of our army."[36] Private James Horrocks, a British immigrant in the 5th New Jersey Battery, assured his brother in England that "the federals will eventually be successful. . . . The Southern Confederacy is a gone goose. . . . The resources of the North are too much superior to those of the South. . . . There is too much at stake for the North to leave off fighting." But he acknowledged that "the Confederates have everything to lose and nothing to gain by giving in. So . . . a great deal of fighting is to be expected."[37]

Chapter 23

AMERICA HAS FELT HER STRENGTH

International Issues: 1863–1865

Although concern in the North about the possibility of official British recognition of the Confederate independence waned after Gettysburg, resentment of unofficial British support for the Confederacy remained strong. Anti-British attitudes in the North were refueled during 1863 by the depredations of the two British-built Confederate commerce raiders, the *Florida* and the *Alabama*; by the prospect of attacks on Union ships and ports by two ironclad rams that were being built for the Confederacy at the same Liverpool shipyard where the *Alabama* had been built; and by the dominant British role in the extensive blockade-running system that was sustaining the Confederate economy and war effort.

"I hope . . . that mercenary war breeder of Liverpool, Mr. Laird, is not to be allowed to send out the rams," a British visitor, Henry Yates Thompson, wrote to his brother in September 1863. "I believe the Yankees would be made very savage and probably declare war on us. . . . I blush for my country when I think of the moral support we are giving these brutal slave owners."[1] Thompson wrote just before news reached America that the British government had acted to prevent the delivery of the rams to the Confederates.

But bitterness about the British-built commerce raiders and blockade-runners continued unabated in all sections of the Northern society. "If the South had not been so clandestinely supported by the tyrannical aristocratical merchants . . . of England and France," an English wool spinner wrote from Ohio, "the war would have been closed up long since. . . . If those rascally European merchants were prevented from lending them their aid by running the blockade, . . . [the

205

Confederates] would have been made to succumb before now."[2] A British officer noted that conversation about politics was "entirely tabooed" in New York society: "The only approach to them is to abuse England, which everyone is glad to do."[3]

In Britain, upper-class support of the South and criticism and misjudgment of the North remained unchanged. George Augustus Sala, correspondent for the *London Daily Telegraph,* noted that "there is a strong impression afloat that Mr. Seward hates England, and would like to bring about a war between his country and ours. . . . He has . . . written a great deal that is irritating and insulting to Great Britain, but . . . Seward has always done his utmost to dissuade the President and the rest of the Cabinet from coming to an open rupture with the British Government."[4] But Sala was only stating that it was the president, not the secretary of state, who wanted war with Britain. No British observer attempted to explain why an American president engaged in a great civil war would welcome a simultaneous war with the strongest nation in Europe.

In the first two years of the war, official British neutrality in the American conflict had been based primarily on the fear that British recognition and support of the Confederacy would lead to an unwanted war with the United States. During 1863, British neutrality was bolstered by two additional factors. The first was the growing realization in Britain—following the Union victories at Gettysburg and Vicksburg—that the Union might win the American war after all and that a victorious Union army would be a real threat to British colonies in North America. The second was the major though unacknowledged impact of the Emancipation Proclamation on British foreign policy.

Even before the Proclamation, some Britons had realized that Britain could not support the Confederacy without appearing to support slavery in the South. William H. Russell wrote to *The Times* late in 1861 that "if she raised the blockade of Southern ports and entered into direct relations with the Slave states for the supply of cotton, Great Britain would be presented to the world as the patron and protector of slavery."[5] While U.S. minister to Spain in 1861, Carl Schurz concluded that "as soon as the war becomes distinctly one for and against slavery, public opinion will be so . . . overwhelmingly in our favor that . . . no European Government will dare to place itself . . . upon the side of a universally condemned institution."[6] On his return from Spain in January 1862, Schurz urged Lincoln to consider an abolition policy. He recalled that Lincoln had clearly recognized the potential international impact of such a policy: "I cannot imagine that any European power would dare to recognize and aid the Southern Confederacy if it becomes clear that the Confederacy stands for slavery and the Union for freedom."[7]

Schurz stated in his memoirs that the international impact of the Emancipation Proclamation had been essentially as he predicted: "The great masses of the

English people, moved by their instinctive love of liberty, woke up to the true nature of our struggle. . . . Hundreds of public meetings were held all over Great Britain. . . . Thousands of the suffering workingmen of Lancashire . . . adopted an address . . . thanking the President for what he had done and was doing for the cause of human freedom. From that time on, the anti-slavery spirit of the British people . . . became a force which no British Government . . . would have lightly undertaken to defy. . . . When, in the eyes of the world, the war for the Union had become a war against slavery, foreign intervention against the Union became well-nigh impossible. . . . Neither the French emperor nor the British aristocracy could safely venture to defy the enlightened opinion and the moral sense . . . of the best part of their own subjects or constituencies . . . by giving open and effective support to human slavery."[8] These conclusions are essentially those in my earlier book, *One War at a Time*, on the reactions of European governments to the Civil War.[9]

Although there was great frustration that British recognition had been so long delayed, Confederates persisted in the belief that European recognition was still possible and would, if given, end the war. In a September 1863 letter to William Gregory, a leader of the Confederate lobby in the British Parliament, Francis Lawley quoted Confederate Secretary of State Judah P. Benjamin: "There has never been a moment since the Second Manassas when simple recognition by England and France would not have ended the war. It would at once pull out the lynch pin of the Yankee chariot. It would be a solemn declaration that enlightened spectators pronounce the Yankee job hopeless. They would grumble and threaten for a month, and then would succumb."[10] "Although the Confederates think that they have been very unhandsomely and unfairly treated by the British Government," a British visitor wrote in January 1864, "they appreciate very highly the sympathy of Englishmen, which they believe to be entirely with them, . . . and believe the people of England to be misrepresented by their present Foreign Secretary."[11]

Most Confederates thought slavery was the only major barrier to European recognition of Confederate independence. In a document dated January 2, 1864, the highest ranking Irishman in the Confederate army, Major General Patrick Cleburne, proposed the use of blacks in the Confederate army after emancipating them and their families. He thought the elimination of slavery in the South would transform European attitudes toward the Confederacy: "England and France . . . cannot assist us without helping slavery, and to do this would be in conflict with their policy for the last quarter of a century. . . . But this barrier once removed, . . . we may expect from them both moral support and material aid. . . . As soon as the great sacrifice to independence is made and known in foreign countries, there will be a complete change of front in our favor of the sympathies of the world."[12] At that time Jefferson Davis was not ready to consider such radical ideas, and he suppressed Cleburne's memorial.

The French occupation of the Mexican capital in the summer of 1863, accompanied by reports that Archduke Maximilian of Austria had been invited to become emperor of Mexico, stirred interest in Mexico in both North and South. The French intervention was viewed in the North as a dire threat to democracy in the Americas and to American influence in the western Hemisphere. Confederate leaders thought the French intervention provided an opportunity for a valuable alliance with France.

Carl Schurz described the French emperor's reactions to the American civil war: "He harbored . . . schemes of aggrandizement, the execution of which would have been much facilitated by the dismemberment of the United States. He would, therefore, have been glad to break our blockade of the Southern ports and even to interfere directly in our struggle in favor of the Southern Confederacy, could he have done so without running contrary to a strong public opinion in his own country and also without the risk of entangling himself, single-handed, in a conflict of such magnitude that it might compromise the position of France among the powers of Europe."[13]

Schurz, U.S. minister to Spain in 1861, recalled Spain's continuing interest in her troubled former colony: "Mexico had been the prey of revolutionary disturbances. . . . Commerce and industry languished, . . . there being little . . . security for life or property. . . . The government suspended all payment of the public debt for two years, and that debt was held in greatest part abroad. . . . Foreign claims had accumulated to enormous magnitude. . . . I concluded that . . . Spain would watch her chance to use her power to the end of erecting a monarchy in Mexico with a Spanish prince on the throne. . . . Spain . . . appeared first on the field of action with a strong force of ships and soldiers. . . . But . . . Louis Napoleon's own scheme to erect a throne for the Archduke Maximilian came to the fore, and Spain and England withdrew from the enterprise."[14]

At any other time, the United States would have strongly opposed the French invasion of Mexico as a violation of the most important principle of U.S. foreign policy, the Monroe Doctrine. This doctrine, proclaimed by President James Monroe and expanded by President James K. Polk, opposed any extension of European influence or territorial control in the Western Hemisphere. The Germans in the North, reflecting the old hostility between Germans and French, strongly condemned the French intervention. Carl Wittke wrote that the "French invasion of Mexico, at a time when the Union was fighting for its life, aroused the entire German press, and many editorials condemned the President for indecisiveness and tardiness in dealing with so flagrant a violation of the Monroe Doctrine."[15] The French in the North and South said little about the French intervention in Mexico.

Lincoln was determined to avoid any risk of entrapment in a Mexican quagmire, but he wanted the French to think there was a real possibility of U.S. intervention in Mexico on the side of the Mexican republicans.[16] Three French journalists in America commented on this possibility. Ernest De Hauranne thought the French intervention in Mexico had given the Americans "a pretext to come forward as liberators and to work for their own interests in the name of outraged Mexican sovereignty. . . . Today . . . they show strong brotherly feelings toward those good neighbors whom they shot down in their own capital not so long ago."[17] Auguste Laugel worried that the French invasion of Mexico would lead to a war with the United States: "The grand policy which governs us . . . is quite capable eventually of converting traditional sympathy . . . into sentiments of genuine hostility. . . . America has felt her strength, and will want to make use of it like the bird that feels its wings."[18] The Marquis of Chambrun wrote his wife that, according to Senator Sumner, Lincoln thought "America was in a position which allowed her to speak firmly, and, though desirous of avoiding complications with France, my country had behaved so badly that America's duty was to make France feel this. The Secretary of State spoke in the same terms."[19] Lincoln's policy of steady diplomatic pressure on the French to withdraw from Mexico, coupled with the implied threat of American intervention in support of the Mexican republicans, was continued by Seward as Andrew Johnson's secretary of state after the war and contributed to Napoleon III's ultimate decision to withdraw his troops in 1867.

Confederate leaders were not very interested in the French role in Mexico but were still very interested in obtaining European recognition and support for the Confederacy. During the last two years of the war Confederate authorities attempted on four occasions to use Europeans who were in the South—two Prussian officers, a French immigrant, and a volunteer French officer—as envoys to convince French or British officials to support the Confederacy.

Three of the missions were to Paris. In the fall of 1863 Captain Justus Scheibert—the Prussian engineer whose crucial contribution to the escape of Lee's army after Gettysburg is described in Chapter 15—was preparing to return to Prussia via Paris. Jefferson Davis asked him to seek an audience with Napoleon III: "If the Emperor will free me from the blockade, . . . I guarantee him possession of

Mexico. We forced [Mexico] into submission with about 12,000 men. . . . The dispatch of a corps of some 12,000 to 20,000 men would by no means be difficult for us in return for the advantages of lifting the blockade, which is gnawing at our vital nerve."[20] Scheibert promised to "do all within his power to help," but he recalled in 1902 that his visit to Paris had been very brief and he was ordered back to Prussia before he could "make all the diplomatic arrangements Davis had requested."[21]

The idea that the Schiebert mission was a serious diplomatic initiative is supported by Davis's anti-Mexican attitudes in the 1840s and 1850s, by his apparently positive reaction in early 1865 to a suggestion of a joint North-South expedition to Mexico following a negotiated settlement of the American civil war, and by his evident misunderstanding of the reasons for French and British neutrality. Given his limited interest in foreign affairs, he may not have considered the appropriateness of using a Prussian officer as an envoy to a French emperor in a period of great Franco-Prussian tensions that would lead to a war between the two countries in 1870.

Two of the missions using Europeans as envoys were initiated by Confederate commanders in the trans-Mississippi region. They hoped for an early French occupation of Matamoras, the Mexican port near the mouth of the Rio Grande, since the French blockade of the mouth of the river interfered with Confederate exports through Matamoras. In January 1863 the Confederate commander in west Texas, Brigadier General H. P. Bee, sent a French immigrant identified only as A. Superviele to contact French officials in Mexico. When he arrived in the environs of Puebla, which was besieged by the French, he assured the diplomatic adviser to the French commander, A. Dubois de Saligny, that "the conduct of the Emperor from the beginning of our struggle had gained all the sympathies of our Government and people and that we looked upon France as our natural ally." Saligny replied that, although all his sympathies were with the Confederacy, all available French troops were needed for the siege of Puebla and the expected subsequent occupation of the Mexican capital. But Saligny promised that Matamoras would be occupied as soon as possible.[22]

In September 1863 the commander of the trans-Mississippi region, General Edmund Kirby Smith, wrote to the Confederate commissioner in Paris, John Slidell, urging him to press Napoleon III for an early occupation of "both banks" of the lower Rio Grande. Superviele was given a copy of the letter and instructed to take it first to Mexico, where he might show it to an appropriate French official, and then take it to Slidell in Paris. This may have been a backup mission, in case the courier bearing the letter to Slidell was unable to get through the blockade. Superviele showed the letter to a French admiral in Mexico in late December. *The Times* in London reported early in 1864 the arrival in Paris of "a M. Superviele, who had sailed from Vera Cruz in a French steamer, as a special envoy to secure recognition for the Confederacy."[23] No information is available on Superviele's activities in Paris.

During 1864 it became evident in Richmond that the French government had no intention of recognizing or supporting the Confederacy. In June, following strong U.S. pressure, the French government prohibited the release of two ironclad corvettes that had been built for the Confederacy at a French shipyard. But the isolated Confederate officials west of the Mississippi may not have known of this French decision. At the beginning of 1865, the trans-Mississippi commander made another effort to obtain French support.

Major General Polignac, the highest ranking Frenchman in the Confederate army, asked for six months leave to return to France. The French prince convinced General Smith that through his acquaintance with the Emperor's half-brother, the Duke of Morny, he could make a strong case to the French government for recognition and support of the Confederacy. "It cannot be too strongly impressed upon the Emperor of the French," General Smith wrote to Slidell on January 9, "that the security of his empire in Mexico and the interests of his own Government all demand immediate interference to restore peace and establish firmly the nationality of the Confederate States." He added that "in the great slave districts of this department nineteen-twentieths of the planters would at this time willingly accept any system of gradual emancipation to insure our independence as a people."[24] It is not clear whether Smith knew that a few weeks earlier Jefferson Davis had authorized an offer of gradual emancipation of the slaves in return for British recognition.

A German immigrant in Texas heard rumors in February that Polignac had gone to Europe "to make proposals to France as well as England that they recognize us."[25] When Polignac arrived in Paris in March, he learned that the Duke of Morny had died. Polignac had a short and unproductive audience with Napoleon III, who said he had made two unsuccessful proposals to the British for joint recognition of the Confederacy and that France could not act alone."[26]

During the winter of 1864–65, the Confederate government in Richmond sent two more men to Europe, one of whom was a European. Late in 1864 Colonel Heros Von Borcke accepted a "mission for the Government to England" which he said was urged by General Hampton, General Lee, and President Davis.[27] The Prussian cavalryman's book contains no hint of the nature of the mission. It may have been connected to the simultaneous assignment of Duncan F. Kenner, who was bearing to London the Confederate offer of gradual emancipation of the slaves in exchange for British recognition of Confederate independence. Because of rumors of a Union attack on Wilmington, Kenner traveled incognito through the North and took a packet from New York to England. He was to give secret verbal instructions to

James Mason, the former Confederate commissioner in London, who was now living in Paris. Von Borcke, who had impressed Mason in London in 1862, may have been a backup messenger who was to deliver the message to Mason in case Kenner was apprehended by the Yankees. Kenner reached Mason without difficulty, and Mason reluctantly went to London. But aristocratic friends told him it was much too late for a reconsideration of British neutrality. It was indeed too late; his report to Benjamin was written the day the Confederate government evacuated Richmond.

A second possibility is that Von Borcke was sent to England as a propaganda agent. Soon after his arrival in London, his diary in German was converted into a series of articles for a prestigious British magazine by a Richmond journalist, John R. Thompson, who had come to London to assist the Confederate propaganda agent, Henry Hotze. The story of the gallant Prussian cavalryman who nearly lost his life in the Confederate service and was honored by the Confederate Congress would have been very effective Confederate propaganda, had it been published before the Confederate surrender.

The four Confederate diplomatic missions given to Europeans (Scheibert, Superviele, Polignac, and Von Borcke), as well as the Kenner mission, were based on misunderstanding by Confederate leaders of the reasons that no European government had recognized Confederate independence. The Confederates thought slavery was the only major barrier to European recognition. They knew that Lincoln and Seward had said that recognition by any European power would lead to war with the United States, but they thought the Union leaders were only bluffing. They did not realize that the Union threat had had a serious restraining effect on British and French policies toward the American conflict.

As Britons began to realize during 1864 that a Union victory in the Civil War was likely, they began to worry that the victorious Union armies might be used for a conquest of Canada. In fact, Americans gave very little thought to Canada during the war until late in 1864, when they discovered that the Confederates were using Canada as a base for subversive activities in the United States and for forays across the border. On October 18–19, twenty Confederates secretly crossed the border from Canada into Vermont, proceeded in small groups to the small town of St. Albans near Lake Champlain, and stayed that night in several hotels. The next morning they robbed several banks of more than $200,000, set fire to several buildings, and, when residents fired on them, returned the fire and killed several residents before fleeing back across the border on stolen horses. Twelve of the raiders were captured in Canada, but were released on a technicality by a Canadian court in November.

Three French visitors noted that the St. Albans raid and its aftermath had greatly intensified American resentment of Britain. De Hauranne recorded that anti-British sentiment was "rising with unexpected and threatening vigor, accusing England of making its colonies the headquarters of rebel outlaws."[28] "I found great irritation against England . . . in all grades of the army," Auguste Laugel wrote. "I recall a young officer from Vermont . . . saying 'I have served my . . . three years in the army . . . and I hope never again to draw the sword. But, sir, if war were declared against England . . . I would not wait a day to enter a regiment.' "[29] The Marquis of Chambrun wrote his wife that several English officers were staying at his hotel in New York: "Three or four Americans . . . said to the English: . . . 'Now that we are the first nation in the world, thanks to our army and our navy, we shall go over to England and punish you all for the harm you have been doing us during the last four years.' "[30]

U.S.–British relations would remain strained for seven years after the Civil War. During this period the U.S. public and government insisted that the British government accept responsibility and pay reparations for a complex package of damages—known collectively as the "Alabama claims"—resulting from actions by Britons and the British government during the war. A settlement of these claims was reached via the treaty of Washington in 1871 and an international tribunal established at Geneva in 1872 pursuant to the treaty. This settlement marked the end of a century of hostility between Britain and America and cleared the way for U.S.–British alliances and cooperation in the twentieth century.

Chapter 24

A THUNDERCLAP
FROM THE BLUE SKY
Atlanta *to* Appomattox: 1864–1865

A week after Lincoln's reelection, General Sherman began his audacious "march to the sea." "In the original plan conceived by General Grant," recalled General Regis de Trobriand," Atlanta was to be the base of an expedition across Georgia, supposing that Hood's army should continue to fall back in that direction. But . . . the rebels turned back to the North, in order to force Sherman to retrace his steps on the long line of communication he had to defend as far as Chattanooga. . . . Sherman . . . conceived the bold idea of . . . leaving the protection of Tennessee to General Thomas and himself advancing through the heart of Georgia, independent of all base of operations and supplies."[1]

"Sherman cut loose from Atlanta," Francis Lawley reported to *The Times* in late November, "darting with five army corps and a large cavalry force into the heart of Georgia. . . . Sherman must have with him at least 40,000 men. His force is probably the finest army which the federals have ever had in the field. . . . The earnestness and zeal of the Georgians as Confederates have been wonderfully stimulated by the savage and ruthless spirit which Sherman and his men have everywhere exhibited. . . . Men are not to be coaxed back into the Union by burning their barns and houses, stealing their horses, cattle, poultry, hogs, slaves, provisions and wagons."[2]

For weeks there was no authentic news of Sherman's progress. Just before Christmas Charles Mackay reported from New York that "General Sherman . . . has reached the seacoast and . . . captured Savannah." He provided details on December 28: "General Hardee having but 15,000 men to defend

Savannah against the attack of 50,000 under General Sherman and by a cooperating fleet, crossed over the Savannah river on the 20th . . . and on the following day General Sherman took possession. Sherman found in the city . . . no less than 25,000 bales of cotton . . . which, with the city of Savannah itself, he presented as a 'Christmas gift' to the Yankee nation."[3]

Meanwhile, on Christmas Eve, Union forces attempted to capture Fort Fisher, the Confederate fort that protected blockade-runners in the Cape Fear River near Wilmington. "For five weary hours upon the 24th the iron hailstorm . . . descended upon or around the fort," Lawley reported. "About 4 in the afternoon of Sunday, December 25th, several surf boats were lowered from the transports and ferryboats. . . . These boats landed three brigades of Federal troops. . . . It seems to have been the impression of the federals that after such a bombardment . . . the resistance to an attack could not have been otherwise than feeble. . . . But . . . immediately that the federals saw the defenders of Fort Fisher swarming over the parapet and rushing forward with undiminished heart and in unabated numbers, . . . all vigour and hope departed from the assailants and the fort was saved."[4]

Lawley wrote a quite different report on the second Union attack on Fort Fisher in mid-January: "Upon the 13th and . . . the 14th, while the federal monitors maintained an unintermitted fire, federal transports were engaged in landing troops upon the beach. . . . A line of federal sharpshooters approached Fort Fisher, sunk rifle pits in the sandy beach, and picked off the Confederate gunners as they served their guns. . . . Most of the garrison, worn down by sleeplessness, hunger, and the strain of a bombardment ceaselessly sustained for more than 60 hours, shrunk within the bombproofs. . . . Suddenly a shrill steam whistle is heard, and in an instant every gun is hushed. . . . A large body of marines dashes swiftly out of the smoke. . . . After a short and bloody struggle, the assailants are driven headlong back along the beach. But while the attention of the garrison is engaged, . . . a body of soldiers dashes forward . . . and occupies the sallyport which enters the fort."[5]

"After a hard struggle which lasted seven hours," wrote T. D. Jones, the Welsh chaplain of the 117th New York, "our men took Fort Fisher. There fell into our hands over 1900 unwounded prisoners and 250 wounded, not counting the dead of whom there were hundreds. We also took 500 guns of every kind in perfect condition. . . . Among these was one huge gun, a six barreled Armstrong. . . . It is said that it was a gift from merchants in Liverpool to the people of Wilmington. . . . The port of Wilmington has been closed and we have dealt the South the heaviest blow of the war, for it was through Wilmington that they were receiving the major portion of their supplies from foreign countries."[6]

The events of December and January finally dampened Lawley's persistent optimism: "In addition to the fall of Fort Fisher and the triumphal march of Sherman to Savannah, there was much to abate the characteristic hopefulness of Richmond and Virginia. . . . At no previous stage of the war have I felt so painfully impressed by the dark uncertainty of the future."[7]

Soon Charleston, the last of the Confederate ports, fell to Union troops. The transatlantic lifeline had been cut, and only a fragile rail line connected Lee's army with the shrinking Confederate territory to the south. Lee's effort in early April to protect the rail lifeline gave Grant an opportunity to end the long siege of Petersburg. "Grant had detached Sheridan's cavalry and two corps of infantry (about 25,000 men in all) to act against the south-side railroad," Francis Lawley wrote in *The Fortnightly Review* a few months later. "Lee had despatched . . . about 17,000 men to meet the attack. . . . But in sending away these 17,000 men, Lee had so weakened his lines before Petersburg that there was but one Confederate left to every fifty yards. . . . Grant . . . threw a very heavy column . . . consisting chiefly of Gibbon's corps, upon the weakest spot. . . . Five times Gibbon's corps surged up and around Fort Gregg, five times, with dreadful carnage, they were driven back. . . . Fort Gregg fell about seven o'clock in the morning of the 2nd. . . . The Federals swept onwards in the direction of Petersburg."[8]

"Lee saw immediately that the evacuation of Petersburg, and consequently of Richmond, was inevitable," Lawley reported to *The Times*. "He telegraphed at once to Richmond, . . . announcing that the enemy would probably take possession the following morning. . . . President Davis was occupying his accustomed seat during morning service in the Church of St. Paul's. . . . Suddenly the sexton . . . handed to him a paper. . . . Rising from his seat with singular gravity and deliberation, Mr. Davis left the church. . . . During the long afternoon and the feverish night, . . . the exodus of officials and prominent citizens was unintermitted. About 8 in the evening President Davis, accompanied by all the members of his Cabinet except General Breckenridge, started by an express train for Danville. . . . The glare of vast piles of burning papers turned night into day. . . . At the first streak of dawn, . . . tremendous explosions seemed to shake every building in Richmond to its foundations. . . . About half an hour after my eyes rested for the last time upon the dingy old Capitol, . . . the Stars and Stripes floated in triumph from its rebellious roof. . . . Never might Prospero's words 'Hell is empty, and all the devils are here,' have been more appositely spoken."[9]

Lee retreated to the west, hoping to find rations for his starving army at various rail depots. "Delayed by the necessity of guarding an ammunition train of from thirty-five to forty miles in length, enfeebled by hunger and sleeplessness," Lawley wrote in the *Fortnightly Review*, "the retreating Confederate army was able to make only ten miles each night. This delay enabled the active Sheridan to get ahead with his cavalry, and to destroy the depots of provisions along the railroad. . . . Upon the 5th many of the mules and horses ceased to struggle. It became necessary to burn hundreds of wagons. . . . Hundreds of men dropped from exhaustion and thousands let fall their muskets from inability to carry them any further. . . . Many hearts . . . quailed in the presence of starvation, fatigue, sleeplessness, misery, . . . and hopelessness. . . . At Amelia Court House Lee found not a ration. . . . It became necessary for Lee to break nearly half his army up into foraging parties, to get food. . . . The foraging parties . . . were taken prisoners by wholesale. . . . Those foragers who returned to Lee brought little or nothing with them. The suffering of the men from the pangs of hunger has not been approached in the military annals of the last fifty years."[10]

General De Trobriand, a brigade commander with Grant's pursuing army, described the "grand chase": "We advanced by three columns, picking up all that were left behind by the Confederate army. This remnant was breaking up more and more, leaving its stragglers in the woods, in the fields, and along the roadside. Animals and men were yielding to exhaustion. The wagons were left in the ruts; the cannon abandoned. . . . We pushed forward, 'on a hot trail,' like hounds who are coming upon their quarry. . . . Sheridan . . . had dismounted his men, and deploying them in heavy line of skirmishers, contested the ground foot by foot, falling back slowly until the infantry of General Ord came into line behind him. Then all the cavalry, running to their horses, formed at a gallop to charge the enemy in flank at the instant when the Army of the James attacked him in front. . . . The circle of steel had closed about it."[11]

"At daybreak on the 9th," Lawley recorded, "a courier from Gordon announced to Lee that . . . Sheridan's cavalry was across the road at Appomattox Court House. . . . Lee had at this moment less than 8,000 men with muskets in their hands. The fatal moment had indisputably come. Hastily donning his best uniform and buckling his sword which it was never his fashion to wear, General Lee turned sadly to the rear to seek the final interview with General Grant."[12]

"All at once a tempest of hurrahs shook the air along the front of our line," General De Trobriand recalled. "General Meade is coming at a gallop from Appomattox Court House. He has raised his cap and uttered a few words: LEE HAS SURRENDERED! . . . Mad hurrahs filled the air like the rolling of thunder, in the fields, in the woods, along the roads, and are prolonged in echo amongst the trains. . . . General Meade leaves the road and passes through my division. The men swarm out to meet him, surrounding his horse. . . . Those who witnessed the explosion of that scene of enthusiasm will never lose the remembrance of it. . . . No description can induce the electric thrill of the occasion in the soul of the reader."[13]

The Marquis of Chambrun recorded Lincoln's reactions to Lee's surrender: "It was impossible to discover in Lincoln any thought of revenge or feeling of bitterness toward the vanquished. His only preoccupation was to recall the Southern States into the Union as soon as possible. . . . The policy of pardon, in regard to those who had taken a principal part in the rebellion, appeared to him an absolute necessity. Never did clemency suggest itself more naturally to a victorious chief. We were with him when he received the despatch from General Grant announcing that the final surrender of the whole Army of Virginia could be foreseen. . . . Grant added: 'Perhaps at the same time we can even capture Jefferson Davis and his cabinet.' This announcement greatly troubled Mr. Lincoln, who forcibly pointed out the difficulty and embarrassment in which the Government would be placed by this untimely capture. . . . One of those present . . . exclaimed: 'Don't let him escape. He must be hanged.' The President replied very calmly by repeating the phrase he had used in the Inaugural Address: 'Let us judge not, that we be not judged.' "[14]

On April 10, Chambrun heard Lincoln's speech at the White House window on reconstruction of the Union: "It was . . . a remarkable discourse, in which the President underlined his political conceptions and offered to moderate between the opposing parties. This solution does not seem to please a large majority." Afterward, Chambrun spoke with Lincoln: "He spoke at length of the many struggles he foresaw in the future and declared his firm resolution to stand for clemency against all opposition. . . . The President's address called forth violent reactions. On Thursday, a veritable campaign against him was launched." On Friday, Chambrun met Senator Sumner, returning from a Cabinet meeting, who told him that Lincoln "spoke with utmost firmness to all the secretaries present, for the most part hostile to his views, insisting upon the necessity of an attitude of clemency and pardon on the part of the victors." At eleven that night Chambrun was told that Lincoln had been assassinated.[15]

"A thunderclap from the blue sky could not have struck us more unexpectedly and frightfully," Carl Schurz wrote to his wife. "Our good, good Lincoln! . . . The murderer who did this deed has killed the best friend of the South. It is really patricide. The people of the South may thank God that the war is over. If this army had been obliged to march once more upon the enemy, not a single house would have been left standing in their path. The soldiers sat about their campfires, first in gloomy consternation; then you might everywhere have heard the words, 'We wish the fight were not over yet.' . . . If the war were continued now, it would resemble the campaigns of Attila."[16] "The South will suffer for it," De Trobriand wrote to his daughter, "and the mad fanatics who committed or connived in that atrocious crime will be made to pay for it. I suppose that in the North the people are furious and exasperated. No more so, at any rate, than in the army."[17] Carl Ketzler, a German immigrant in the 37th Illinois, was shocked by the assassination of "our beloved president." "Words cannot express the sadness and also the fierceness engendered against the Rebels by this news."[18]

Chambrun thought the assassination had transformed Lincoln's place in American memory: "Lincoln is now the greatest of all Americans. The tragic prestige which assassination lends its victims has confirmed upon him a superiority over Washington himself."[19] Colonel L. L. Zulavsky, a Hungarian immigrant, told his brigade of Negro troops that Lincoln would be remembered for "his great and undying services for his country, his noble efforts in the cause of freedom and humanity, and his noble qualities as a just and wise ruler of the nation through her most imminent peril."[20]

An English immigrant in Illinois, John Griffiths, wrote his brothers in England of the momentous events in America: "We . . . were contending for our Constitutional liberty against a Slaveholding Aristocracy. . . . There have been great sacrifices made to preserve the life of the nation. But thank God it is safe and the victory is won and Liberty is triumphant and slavery is dead. But in dying it . . . killed some of the noblest champions of liberty that ever lived, and amongst them our Beloved President Abraham Lincoln, a man that was loved more than any other man in the nation. But though his body has fallen, his Spirit lives in the hearts of the people. . . . We were rejoicing over our victory when the sad news reached us of the sad calamity and cast a gloom over the whole nation. There never was such a mourning on the continent of America as last Wednesday. There was funeral sermons preached in almost all the churches in the free states and large processions. So now we have a free country to offer to the oppressed of all nations, the home of the free and the land of the brave. . . . Thanks be to the Lord . . . that he has slain the monster slavery."[21]

Chapter 25

CONCLUSIONS

Virtually all of the four million European immigrants in America in 1860 had come to "the blessed place of freedom" in search of freedom and an opportunity for a better life. During the Civil War, thousands of immigrants enlisted in the Union or Confederate army to protect and enhance the freedom they had found in America. Most immigrants in the North thought their newfound freedom was endangered by the Confederate attack on the Constitution and the Union. Immigrants in the South usually accepted the Confederate assertion that they were fighting for freedom from intolerable Yankee oppression.

Enlistment decisions by immigrants in both North and South were also strongly influenced by peer and community pressures, by the desire to enhance their own status in the eyes of native-born Americans, and by enlistment bonuses and/or the prospect of steady pay.

Most immigrants were primarily concerned with maintaining their own freedom, rather than with freedom for the slaves. The majority of the immigrants in the North were unenthusiastic about Lincoln's policies on slavery and emancipation, and voted for his opponents in 1860 and 1864. Although the majority of the immigrants in the South were near the bottom of the economic ladder, most of them supported the "Southern way of life" that gave them a status distinctly superior to that of the slaves.

Although ethnic authors usually convey an impression of unanimity and solidarity within immigrant groups during the war, there was substantial disaffection and major efforts to evade military service among the Irish, the Germans, and the British in both North and South.

The reactions of the Irish in both regions were strongly influenced by their fear that emancipated blacks would compete with Irishmen for low-paying jobs. Although many Irish fought valiantly in the Union army, there was more opposition to the war and greater effort to avoid military service among the Irish in the North than in any other immigrant group. The Irish in the South supported the Confederate cause with greater unanimity than the Germans or the British, but desertion rates were high in predominantly Irish companies in the Confederate army.

The Germans in the North supported the Union cause in greater numbers and with greater devotion than any other major immigrant group. Some of the Germans—especially the "Forty Eighters" who had fought in the unsuccessful revolution in Germany in 1848—were strong advocates of the emancipation of the slaves, but abolition was opposed by at least half the German immigrants. There was more opposition to the Confederate cause and more attempts to avoid or escape from military service among the Germans than in any other immigrant group in the Confederacy.

While many British immigrants served with valor in the Union or Confederate army, a large number of British residents in both North and South attempted to avoid military service by claiming that they were still loyal subjects of Queen Victoria.

Although there are no statistics on the number of foreign-born in the Union or Confederate armies, the available information suggests that immigrants accounted for 18 percent to 20 percent of the men in the Union army—even though they represented only about 15 percent of the population of the Union states—and that the percentage of immigrants in the Confederate army was somewhat below the proportion (about 4 percent) of immigrants in the Confederate population.

Immigrants played an important but not decisive role in each army. The North would still have had a huge manpower advantage over the South even if there had been no immigrants in the Union army. The South would still have had a great manpower deficit even if there had been several times as many immigrants in the Confederate army. But immigrants and volunteers from Europe provided badly needed skills and experience—especially as artillerymen, engineers, and doctors—in both armies. The participation of immigrants in the war contributed significantly to their postwar assimilation and acceptance in both North and South.

The number of officers arriving from Europe during the war to join each army reflected the predominant attitudes toward the American conflict in the ruling classes of each country. A large number of British officers served as foreign volunteers in the Confederate army. They were usually on the staffs of Confederate generals and rarely served as line officers. A smaller number of nonimmigrant Britons served in the Union army; several of them held brigade or higher commands. Quite a few officers from Prussia and other German states arrived in 1861 or later for service in the Union Army. Several of these German officers were senior commanders. Only a handful of volunteer officers from Germany joined the Confederate army. The available evidence suggests that hopes of enhancing their military careers through active service in America were more important motives for most of the volunteer officers from Europe than attachment to the Union or Confederate cause.

Appendix I provides biographic information on fifty-nine men born abroad (including both immigrants and nonimmigrants) who commanded Union brigades, divisions, and corps, plus a list of seventy men born in Germany who commanded Union regiments. Appendix II has biographic data on twenty-six Confederate regimental and higher commanders who were born abroad.

A majority of the European civilian and military observers during the Civil War were upper-class Britons who arrived with well-developed preconceptions and prejudices about America. Most of these visitors were very skeptical about the political and social institutions in America. They preferred the somewhat aristocratic political system in the South to the rule of the "mob" in the North, thought Lincoln was a country bumpkin unfitted for national leadership, reacted negatively to the Emancipation Proclamation for various reasons, were skeptical of the effectiveness of volunteer armies consisting of untrained citizens, and believed that the Union would never be able to win the war.

Despite long-standing British opposition to slavery, British visitors to the South recognized but rarely admitted that British commercial and imperial interests were better served by continuation of the existing system of cotton production in the South than by the chaos that they assumed would follow emancipation of the slaves. On their return to Britain, many of these observers wrote articles and books that were highly critical of the North and very sympathetic to the South and its institutions. British opinions generated or sustained by these reports contributed substantially to very strained U.S.–British relations for a decade until 1872. Several French observers arrived with much more sympathetic attitudes toward American freedoms and institutions, and their reports from America were much more sympathetic to the Union cause.

The reactions of Europeans who were in America during the war—and indeed of most Europeans at home—were strongly influenced by their previous experience and attitudes and by their perceptions of the impact of the war in America on their personal interests and prosperity and on their homelands. For the great majority of the European immigrants, their new homeland was the part of America in which they lived. The reactions of visitors and volunteers from Europe were shaped primarily by their preconceptions of America and by their perceptions of the impact of the war on the interests of their nation and class in Europe.

EUROPEAN-BORN COMMANDERS IN THE UNION ARMY

BRITONS

Edward D. Baker was born in London in 1811, and was brought to America at age four. He was a lawyer in Illinois, and became a close friend of Abraham Lincoln. He was colonel of the 4th Illinois in the war with Mexico and served a term in Congress from 1849 to 1851, taking the seat previously occupied by Lincoln. Baker moved to Oregon before the Civil War and was elected to the U.S. Senate from Oregon in 1860. In 1861 Lincoln offered him an appointment as brigadier general, but he declined the federal appointment—which would have required him to give up his seat in the Senate—and accepted a state appointment as commander of the 71st Pennsylvania. He was killed on October 22, 1861, while commanding a brigade at the battle of Balls's Bluff.

Leonard Currie, a Londoner, had fought in the Crimea with the 19th Foot and was on leave in America in 1861. He resigned his British commission and after some months as a staff officer, became colonel of the 133rd New York, a regiment consisting mainly of New York policemen. In 1864 he commanded brigades in the Red River campaign and in Sheridan's campaign in Virginia

John Fitzroy De Courcy had been a major in the British army and commanded a Turkish regiment in the Crimean war. Early in the Civil War he trained American volunteers, who found him an excessively strict disciplinarian. Later he commanded Union brigades in Kentucky and Louisiana.

John Fraser was born in Cromarty in Scotland in 1827 and came to America in the late 1840s. By 1861 he was professor of mathematics and astronomy at Jefferson College in Canonsburg, Pennsylvania, and enlisted 100 former students in the 140th Pennsylvania. He commanded the regiment at Chancellorsville and Gettysburg, was wounded while leading a frontal attack at Spotsylvania, and was captured while commanding a brigade at Petersburg. In a Confederate prison in Charleston, he diverted the minds of the starving prisoners by reciting from memory scenes from the works of Shakespeare. Released in a prisoner exchange, he rejoined the army, and ended the war as a brigadier general. After the war he was chancellor of the University of Kansas, state superintendent of schools in Kansas, and professor at the institution that became the University of Pittsburgh.

John W. Fuller was born in 1827 in Harston, Cambridgeshire, and came to Oneida County, New York, with his family in 1833 when he was only six. Before the war he had been a publisher, city treasurer, and militia officer. He commanded the 27th Ohio at Island No. 10, a brigade at Corinth, and divisions in Rosecrans's army and in Sherman's campaign for Atlanta.

David Ireland, colonel of the 137th New York, was born in Scotland. He led his regiment at Fredricksburg, Chancellorsville, and Gettysburg. William F. Fox wrote that at Gettysburg the 137th New York was in a brigade that "alone and unassisted, held Culp's Hill during a critical period of that battle against a desperate attack of vastly superior force."[1] Ireland later commanded brigades in Thomas's army in Tennessee and Sherman's army in the campaign for Atlanta. He died of dysentery in Atlanta, just a week after its capture.

John McArthur was born in Erskine in Scotland in 1826, came to the United States in 1849 at age twenty-three; he managed an iron works in Chicago before the war. His Civil War career began as captain of a militia unit, the Chicago Highland Guards. He was colonel of the 12th Illinois in 1861, a brigade commander at Forts Henry and Donelson, a brigadier general in 1862, and a division commander at Shiloh, Corinth, Vicksburg, and Nashville.

Edward L. Molineux was born in England and came to America at an unknown date. He was colonel of the 159th New York in 1862 and a district commander in Louisiana in 1863. He commanded brigades with General Banks in the Red River campaign in Louisiana early in 1864 and with Sheridan in the Shenandoah valley that summer. He was appointed a brigadier general in October 1864 and commanded a brigade with Sherman in Georgia and South Carolina in late 1864 and the spring of 1865.

Joshua T. Owen, born in 1821 in Caermarthen in Wales, had been a Philadelphia schoolmaster, lawyer, and politician before the war. In 1861 he was colonel of the 24th Pennsylvania and later the 69th Pennsylvania, a regiment consisting mainly of Irishmen. He was with McClellan on the Peninsula and commanded brigades at Antietam, Fredericksburg, and Chancellorsville. His first appointment as brigadier general, in November 1862, expired due to inaction in the Senate, but he was reappointed in 1863. He was a brigade or division commander at the Wilderness, Spotsylvania, and Cold Harbor. In the Cold Harbor battle he was accused of failing to support a neighboring brigade and was mustered out in July 1864.

William H. Powell was born in Pontypool in Wales and settled in Ohio. He joined the 2nd [West] Virginia Cavalry in 1861–62, won a Medal of Honor at Sinking Creek, and was colonel of the regiment by May 1863. Powell was wounded and captured in 1863 but was exchanged for a Colonel Lee. He led a brigade in Sheridan's campaign in the Shenandoah Valley in 1864 and was promoted to brigadier general that October.

Thomas Stevens, who had been in the Queen's Life Guards, emigrated to Wisconsin in 1840. He commanded the 2nd Wisconsin Cavalry in Missouri and Arkansas in 1862, led two cavalry expeditions into Mississippi in late 1862 and early 1863, and commanded a brigade at Vicksburg.

Percy Wyndham was the son of a British colonel. He was in the student corps in Paris during the revolution of 1848, an ensign in the French navy, an officer in the British artillery, a captain in the Austrian Lancers, and a colonel in Garibaldi's army in Italy. In 1861 Wyndham was appointed colonel of the lst New Jersey Cavalry. He was captured while commanding a cavalry brigade in Virginia in June 1862 but was exchanged a few months later. In 1863 he led a Union cavalry brigade at the battle of Brandy Station, the most important cavalry battle of the war. Although wounded in that battle, he continued to command the 1st New Jersey Cavalry until the end of the war. In 1866–67 he was again on Garibaldi's staff in Italy.

FRENCH

Gustave Paul Cluseret was born in Paris in 1823. He graduated from the French military academy at Saint Cyr and served as an artillery officer, but he was relieved of duty after criticizing Napoleon III. He rejoined the army to fight in Algiers and the Crimea but resigned in 1858. In 1861 he was with Garibaldi in Italy. Cluseret came to America in 1862, was on McClellan's staff for a while, then joined Fremont in western Virginia and was promoted to brigadier general in October 1862 after gallant service at Cross Keys. After Fremont resigned, Cluseret quarreled with his new superiors and had to resign in March 1863. Early in 1864 he became the editor of a Fremont newspaper, *New Nation;* his radical editorials frequently attacked Lincoln's policies. After a while, Cluseret returned to France.[2]

Regis De Trobriand was born in Rouen in 1816, the son of a general. After his father died in 1840, he became the Comte de Trobriand. He spent a year in New York, where he met a banker's daughter whom he subsequently married in Paris in 1843. By 1854 they had settled permanently in New York, where he was an assistant editor of a French-language newspaper and a writer on art and music. He was elected colonel of the 55th New York in July 1861. De Trobriand and his regiment were in the Penninsula campaign in 1862; he commanded a brigade during most of 1863. He was promoted to brigadier general in 1864 and was a brigade commander in Grant's army at Petersburg and in the campaign leading to Appomattox. A French journalist who met De Trobriand in 1864 noted that "despite his long residence in America, he had lost none of his French manners or attitudes."[3] His memoir on the war, *Four Years with the Army of the Potomac*, was published in Boston in 1889.[4]

Alfred Napoleon Alexander Duffie was born in Paris in 1835, the son of a French count. He graduated from St. Cyr in 1854, served in the French cavalry in Algiers and Senegal, and won four decorations in the Crimea. After a wound at the battle of Solferino against the Austrians, he came to America on a leave of absence. When the Civil War began, he resigned his French commission and joined the 2nd New York Cavalry. By mid-1862 he was colonel of the 1st Rhode Island Cavalry. After distinguished service at Kelly's Ford in March 1863, he was promoted to brigadier general. Duffie commanded a cavalry division at Chancellorsville, in part of the Pennsylvania campaign, and in Sheridan's campaign in the Shenandoah Valley in 1864. He was captured by the Confederates in October 1864, paroled, and was still awaiting exchange when the war ended.

GERMANS

Ludwig Blenker was born in 1812 at Worms, was the revolutionary commander of Ludwigshafen in 1848, and fled to America in 1849. He recruited the 8th New York, commanded a brigade of four German regiments at the first Bull Run, and subsequently commanded a division assigned to General Fremont in western Virginia. Blenker was fond of fancy uniforms and European-style drill. He was criticized for appointing German aristocrats to his personal staff, and his aristocratic views were resented by some of the "Forty-Eighters" in his command. He was relieved of his command in June 1862.

Henry Bohlen, born in Germany in 1810, came to America as a boy and was in the Mexican war. In 1861 he was colonel of the 75th Pennsylvania and later a brigade commander in Blenker's division. He was appointed brigadier general in April 1862 and was killed while commanding a brigade at Cross Keys.

August Valentine Kautz, born in Germany in 1828, came to America before 1846 and served in the war with Mexico. Afterward he gradated from West Point and fought Indians on the frontier. He was a captain in the 6th U.S. cavalry in 1861, then colonel of the 2nd Ohio Cavalry. He was promoted to brigadier general in 1864, and commanded a cavalry division in Virginia and North Carolina. After the war he remained in the regular army, retiring as a brigadier general in 1892.

Karl Leopold Matthies, born in Prussia in 1824, was in the Prussian army before coming to America in 1849. He was a captain in the 1st Iowa at Wilson's Creek, a lieutenant colonel at Island No. 10, a colonel at Corinth, and a brigadier general commanding a brigade in the Vicksburg campaign. He began the Atlanta campaign but had to resign due to ill health.

Peter Osterhaus was born in the Rhineland in 1823. After service in the Prussian army, he came to America in 1849. He commanded Missouri volunteers at Wilson's Creek and a brigade at Pea Ridge; he was appointed a brigadier general in 1862 and a major general in 1864. Osterhaus commanded Union divisions in the Vicksburg and Atlanta campaigns and the XV Corps in Sherman's march to the sea. After the war, he was a U.S. consul in France and in Germany.

Prince Felix Salm-Salm was the scion of one of the oldest princely houses in Germany. He had served in the Prussian cavalry in the Schleswig-Holstein War. Prince Salm-Salm was colonel of the 8th New York in 1862, was out of the service for about a year, and was then commander of the 68th New York in the overland campaign in 1864 and a brigade commander in Sherman's march through Georgia. After the war he went to Mexico, where he joined the imperial army of the short-lived Emperor, former Archduke Ferdinand of Austria.

Frederick Salomon was born in 1826 in Prussia, fought in the revolution in 1848, and then fled to America with brothers Edward (later lieutenant governor of Wisconsin) and Charles (later colonel of the 9th Wisconsin). Frederick was a captain in the 9th Wisconsin at Wilson's Creek, colonel of the regiment in November, a brigadier general in 1862, a brigade commander in early 1863, and a division commander for the last two years of the war.

Alexander Schimmelfennig got his star because Lincoln liked the sound of his name, but he had more military experience than most of the Germans joining the Union army. Born in 1824 in Prussia, he attended a military school and joined the Prussian army at sixteen; he fought in the Schleswig-Holstein War of 1848 but later joined the revolutionary army in the Palatinate. After he came to America in 1853, he worked as a military engineer for the war department in Washington and published a book on the Russian-Turkish War. He commanded the 74th Pennsylvania in 1861 and a brigade at the second Bull Run. At Chancellorsville, Schimmelfennig's brigade resisted the onslaught of Stonewall Jackson's men until they were compelled to retreat. He was wounded on the first day at Gettysburg and hid in a stable for three days to avoid capture. In 1864 and early 1865 he was a brigade commander on the Carolina coast.

Carl Schurz was born in Prussia in 1829. He was a student at the University of Bonn in 1848 and a lieutenant in the rebel militia. After the revolution failed, he fled to Switzerland, England, and France, and emigrated to the United States in 1852. During the 1860 election he organized a band of German and other immigrants who spoke for Lincoln to groups of immigrants. Lincoln appointed him U.S. minister to Spain in 1861; by 1862 Schurz was bored with diplomacy, and Lincoln made him a brigadier general and later a major general. Schurz was a division commander at the second Bull Run, Chancellorsville, Gettysburg, and Chattanooga and was a corps commander for brief periods. Despite his initial military inexperience, Schurz was well respected by his officers. Major Frederick Winkler of the 26th Wisconsin wrote that "to mental endowments of the first order he added the kindest disposition, a stern integrity, and unquestionable honor."[5] Captain Frederick Otto von Fritsch noted that "by reason of his superior mentality, personal bravery, and sound judgment, he largely overcame his inexperience as a commanding officer."[6] In 1864 he resigned his commission to campaign for the reelection of Lincoln. After the war, Schurz was U.S. Senator from Missouri from 1869 to 1872 and U.S. Secretary of the Interior from 1877 to 1881.

Edward Siber had served in the Prussian army and then in the patriot army in Schleswig Holstein. When the Civil War began, he was serving as a military instructor in Brazil. He was colonel of the 37th Ohio, a German regiment, in western Virginia—where he also commanded a brigade in 1862—and in the siege of Vicksburg. He was discharged for medical reasons in 1863.

Franz Sigel was born in 1824 in Baden, fought with the revolutionary army in the Palatinate in 1848, and subsequently fled to America. In 1857 he was a teacher at a German-American school in St. Louis; in 1860 he was director of the city's schools. Sigel was colonel of the 3rd Missouri in May 1861, a brigade commander at Wilson's Creek in August 1861, and a division commander at Pea Ridge in 1862. Although he was not particularly distinguished as a combat commander, "I fights mit Sigel" became a rallying cry among the Germans. In March 1862 he was promoted to major general of volunteers; he commanded a corps at the second battle of Bull Run. From September 1862 until February 1863 he commanded the XI Corps but gave up the command due to ill health. In 1864 he commanded the Department of West Virginia for several months but was relieved due to an insufficiently aggressive performance.

Leopold Von Gilsa, a former Prussian officer, fought with the patriot army in Schleswig-Holstein in 1847–48 and came to America in the early 1850s. He was in

Blenker's Division at Cross Keys, with Pope in western Virginia in 1862 and was Sigel's chief of staff at the second Bull Run. He was a brigade commander at Chancellorsville and at Gettysburg, and was later in the siege of Charleston.

Baron Adolph Wilhem August Von Steinwehr was born in Brunswick in 1822, the son of a lieutenant general in the Prussian army. He came to America in 1847 to serve in the war with Mexico, was in a regiment of Alabama volunteers, and participated in the postwar survey of the new U.S.-Mexican boundary. He was colonel of the 29th New York at the first Bull Run and at Cross Keys. After appointment as brigadier general, he commanded a brigade in Blenker's division in the Shenandoah Valley and led Union divisions at the second Bull Run, Chancellorsville, Gettysburg, and Chattanooga.

August Willich was born in 1810 in Braunsberg, Prussia, attended a military academy, and was a lieutenant and captain in the Prussian army. He fought with the revolutionaries in 1848, fled thereafter to New York, worked as a carpenter in the Brooklyn Navy Yard, and after 1853 edited a radical German labor newspaper in Cincinnati. In 1861 he organized a German regiment, the 9th Ohio. After distinguished service at Shiloh and Corinth, he was appointed a brigadier general. He was captured at Murfreesboro, exchanged in May 1863, and led brigades at Chickamauga, Chattanooga, and in the Atlanta campaign. A rifle ball in the shoulder at Resaca ended his career as a field commander.

German Regimental Commanders

Fritz Anneke (34th Wisconsin)

Valentine Bausensetin (58th Ohio)

Adolf Becker (46th New York)

Gottfried Becker (28th New York)

Franz Blessing (74th Pennsylvania)

Louis Blenker (8th New York)

Henry Bohlen (75th Pennsylvania)

Lorenz Cantador (27th Pennsylvania)

Joseph Conrad (15th Missouri)

George W. Deitlzer (1st Kansas)

Christian F. Dickel (4th New York Cavalry)

Franz Endelmayer (32nd Indiana)

Paul Frank (52nd New York)

Augustus Funk (39th New York)

Joseph Gerhardt (46th New York)

Otto Harhaus (2nd New York Cavalry)

Frederick Hecker (24th Illinois)

Wilhelm Heine (105th New York)

Otto Hornhaus (2nd New York Cavalry)

William H. Jacobs (26th Wisconsin)

Gastave Kammerling (9th Ohio)

Peter Karburg (17th Missouri)

Konrad Krez (27th Wisconsin)

Eduard Kapff (7th New York)

William C. Kuffner (149th Illinois)

Bernhard Laiboldt (2nd Missouri)

George Limburg (108th Ohio)

Charles Matthies (1st Iowa)

Augustus Mersy (9th Illinois)

Seraphim Meyer (107th Ohio)

Theodore Meumann (3rd Missouri)

George Mindel (27th New York)

F. Nazer (4th New York Cavalry)

Elias Peissner (119th New York)

August Poten (17th Missouri)

Julius Raith (43rd Illinois)

Benjamin Ringold (103rd New York)

Prince Felix Salm-Salm (8th and 68th New York)

Charles Saloman (9th Wisconsin)

Edward Saloman (82nd Illinois)

Frederick Saloman (9th Wisconsin)

Frederick Schaefer (2nd Missouri)

Alexander Schimmelfennig (74th Pennsylvania)

Louis Schirmer (15th New York Artillery)

Phil Schopp (8th West Virginia)

Nicholas Schuettner (4th Missouri)

Christian Schwarzwaelder (5th New York Militia)

Albert Sigel (5th Missouri Militia)

Franz Sigel (3rd Missouri)

Gustav Sniper (185th New York)

Klemens Soest (29th New York)

Marcus Spiegel (120th Ohio)

George Von Amberg (45th New York)

Frederick Von Egloffstein (103rd New York)

Leopold Von Gilsa (41st New York)

Ernst Von Holmstedt (41st New York)

Rudolf Von Rosa (46th New York)

George Von Schack (7th New York)

Adolph Von Steinwehr (29th New York)

Gustav Wagner (2nd New York Artillery)

Louis Wagner (88th Pennsylvania)

Charles Walter (17th Connecticut)

George Walther (35th Wisconsin)

Max Weber (20th New York)

Francis Weiss (20th New York)

Karl Wetchky (1st Maryland Cavalry)

Joseph Wiedermeyer (40th Missouri)

August Willich (34th Indiana)

Frederick C. Winkler (26th Wisconsin)

Louis Zahn (3rd Ohio Cavalry)

HUNGARIANS

Alexander Sandor Asboth was born in 1811 in Keszehely in the Hungarian county of Zala. After service in the Austrian army, he was trained and worked as an engineer and then was adjutant to Kossuth, leader of the Hungarian revolution of 1848. Asboth came to America in 1851. He was appointed a brigadier general in March 1862, commanded a division at Pea Ridge, was a district commander in Kentucky and Florida, and was a brigade commander in 1864. After the war, Asboth was U.S. minister to Argentina and Uruguay until his death in Buenos Aires in 1868.

Julius Stahel was born in 1825 in Szeged, Hungary. Before 1848 he was an associate of Hungary's leading publisher and bookseller. After serving as a lieutenant in the revolution of 1848, he lived for a while in London and Berlin and came to New York in 1859. For two years he worked for a German-language newspaper in New York. In 1861 he helped to recruit the 8th New York. Stahel was a lieutenant colonel at the first battle of Bull Run and was appointed a brigadier general in November 1861. He was a brigade commander in Blenker's division in the Shenandoah valley campaign, commanded a division at the second Bull Run, and commanded the cavalry protecting Washington. After promotion to major general in March 1863, he commanded a cavalry division in the Shenandoah Valley and West Virginia with an assignment to curb the raids of the Confederate cavalry leader, John Singleton Mosby. In June 1864 a severe wound ended his career as a field officer. After the war, he joined the U.S. consular service, serving in Yokohama, Tokyo, and Shanghai. He developed a friendship with the U.S. consul in Hong Kong, John Singleton Mosby.

IRISH

Richard Busteed was born in 1822 in Cavan, Ireland, presumably came to America in the late 1840s, and was a newspaperman, lawyer, and politician in New York in the 1850s. He organized an artillery battery in 1861 but resigned in November. In August 1862 he was appointed a brigadier general, but the nomination was never sent to the Senate. But Busteed was nonetheless a brigade commander for several months at Yorktown. In September 1863 he was appointed a federal district judge.

Richard Byrnes, born in Ireland, had been an enlisted man in the U.S. Army before the war and a lieutenant in the 5th U.S. Cavalry during the Peninsular campaign. He was appointed colonel of 28th Massachusetts by the governor of Massachusetts after Antietam to end squabbling among volunteer officers. He led the 28th at Gettysburg and was killed while commanding the Irish Brigade at Cold Harbor in June 1864.

Patrick Connor was born in Ireland in 1820 and came to America in 1840. He was in both the Mexican war and Seminole war. In 1861 he raised and commanded the 3rd California and spent the war dealing with Mormons and Indians in the west. He was promoted to brigadier general in 1863.

Michael Corcoran was born in 1827 in Carrowkeel, County Sligo, son of a captain in the British army; he was an officer in the Irish Constabulary before emigrating to New York in 1849. There he joined the 69th New York, an Irish militia regiment, and was appointed colonel in August 1859. When the Prince of Wales visited New York in 1860, Corcoran refused to lead the 69th in the parade for the prince as a protest against British rule in Ireland. The state of New York initiated a court-martial, but it was forgotten when the Civil War began. Corcoran led the 69th New York militia at the first Bull Run, but was captured there and was a prisoner in the Confederacy for over a year. After he was exchanged, he was promoted to brigader general, recruited a brigade of four regiments known as "Corcoran's Irish Legion," and was a division commander for most of 1863. Corcoran was killed in December 1863 when a horse fell on him.

William Gamble, born in Ireland in 1819, commanded the 8th Illinois Cavalry in the Peninsular campaign and a cavalry brigade in Virginia in 1863.

Richard Henry Jackson came to America from Ireland as a teenager. He was a private in the Seminole war in 1851 and a lieutenant in the regular army when the Civil War began. He served in the siege of Charleston, was at Drewry's Bluff and New Market, and ended the war in Virginia as a brigadier general and division commander.

Patrick Henry Jones emigrated from Ireland as a child. He commanded the 154th New York at Fredricksburg and Chancellorsville and brigades in the Atlanta campaign, Sherman's march to the sea, and the Carolinas. He was promoted to brigadier general in December 1864.

Patrick Kelly was born in Castlehacket, County Galway. He commanded the 88th New York in the Irish Brigade at Fredericksburg and Chancellorsville and assumed command of the Irish Brigade for a period in 1863 that included Gettysburg. He resumed command of the Brigade again at Cold Harbor, after Colonel Byrnes was mortally wounded. Kelly was killed in June 1864 while leading a charge at Petersburg.

James L. Kiernan was born in 1837 in County Galway, came to America, studied medicine, and published a medical journal. In the first two years of the war he served as a surgeon with the 69th New York at the first Bull Run and with the 6th Missouri Cavalry at Pea Ridge, resigning in May 1863. He was appointed a brigadier general in August 1863 and commanded the Union post at Milliken's Bend near Vicksburg until February 1864, when he resigned due to ill health.

Michael K. Lawler, born in Ireland in 1814, reached America in time to serve in the war with Mexico. In the Civil War, he commanded the 18th Illinois in Tennessee and was a brigade commander in various corps from December 1862 until the spring of 1864.

Stephen McGroatry was born in Ireland in 1830. He was colonel of the 62nd Ohio by September 1862 and then commander of the 82nd Ohio. He commanded brigades in the half-German XI Corps in Virginia and Georgia, receiving twenty-three wounds during the war and losing an arm.

Thomas Francis Meagher was born into a wealthy family in Waterford in 1823. After a speech in Dublin advocating the violent overthrow of British rule in Ireland, he was condemned to death but the sentence was commuted to banishment for life to a penal colony in Tasmania. He escaped from Tasmania in a small boat and arrived in the United States in 1852. He eventually became the editor of an Irish newspaper and was an important Irish-American political leader. He was at the first Bull Run with Corcoran's regiment, the 69th New York, but later took the initiative in forming the Irish Brigade. He was appointed brigadier general in February 1862 and commanded the Irish Brigade at Yorktown, Seven Pines, Seven Days, the second Bull Run, Antietam, Fredricksburg, and Chancellorsville. More books and articles have been written about the Irish Brigade and Meagher than about any other ethnic unit or foreign-born commander. Two recent articles have contained critical remarks about Meagher. John T. McCormack wrote that "Meagher . . . made himself unpopular with the other high-ranking officers in the army by his constant political speeches and activities. It was also generally believed that he regarded the brigade more as an independent symbol of Irish glory than an effective unit of the army."[7] Gary Glynn commented that Meagher "demonstrated a lifelong propensity for making enemies and creating public furor."[8] After Chancellorsville, Meager wanted to take the Brigade back to New York and recruit replacements, but the administration refused. Meagher was indignant and resigned. He returned to the army only late in 1864, occupying an administrative post in the last months of the war.

Robert Nugent, born in Kilkee in County Down, was the last commander of the Irish Brigade. He commanded the Brigade's 69th New York at Fredericksburg but was badly wounded and resigned his field command. During the draft riots in New York in July 1863, he was provost marshal in charge of the draft in New York; his house was burned by the Irish mob. He later returned to active duy, took command of the Irish Brigade in November 1864, and led it to Appomattox and in the victory parade in Washington after Lee's surrender.

Robert Patterson was born in Ireland in 1792, was in the Pennsylvania militia during the war of 1812, and was a major general of volunteers in Mexico in 1846–47. He served again as major general for a few months in 1861 but was criticized for his inactivity at the first Bull Run and the sixty-nine-year-old general was mustered out soon thereafter.

James Shields was born in Altmore, County Tyrone, in 1810 and came to America in 1826 at age sixteen. He was a lawyer, politician, and judge in Illinois but was also in the Seminole and Black Hawk wars; he was a brigadier general in Winfield Scott's army that captured the Mexican capital in 1847. He was senator from Illinois from 1849 to 1854 and senator from Minnesota from 1858 to 1862. In 1862 he commanded a division under General Banks in the Shenandoah valley. Shields resigned from the army in 1863.

Thomas Alfred Smyth was born in Ballyhooley in 1832 and came to America in 1854. He gained paramilitary experience with a filibustering expedition in Nicaragua. Beginning as a captain in an Irish regiment, the 24th Pennsylvania, he was promoted steadily; Smyth commanded brigades at Gettysburg, the Wilderness, Spotsylvania, and Cold Harbor—including the Irish Brigade from February to May of 1864—and a division in the Appomattox campaign. He was killed on April 9, 1865, the last Union general to die in the war.

Thomas William Sweeny, born in Cork in 1820, emigrated to America in 1833 at age thirteen. He was a volunteer officer in the Mexican war and then joined the regular army. When the Civil War began, he quickly rose from captain in the 2nd U.S. Infantry to brigadier general of Missouri volunteers at Wilson's Creek. He commanded the 52nd Illinois at Fort Donelson, a brigade at Shiloh, and, after a period of garrison duty, a division in the Atlanta campaign in 1864. After the war he played a key role in planning an abortive invasion of Canada by Irish nationalists, the Fenians, who hoped to use Canada as a bargaining chip to force Britain to give Ireland its independence.

ITALIANS

Luigi Palma Di Cesnola was born in 1832 in Rivarola in the Italian Piedmont. He received a military education, served for several years in the Sardinian cavalry, and was on the staff of the Sardinian commander in the Crimean war. On arrival in New York in the later 1850s he established a military academy and trained many young Italians who later served in the Union army. In 1861 and 1862 Cesnola was colonel of the 14th New York Cavalry. In the cavalry battle at Brandy Station, he commanded a brigade in the Union cavalry division headed by a Frenchman, General Alfred Duffie. He received a Medal of Honor for gallantry in leading a charge at Aldie, Virginia, on June 17, 1863; he was seriously wounded at Aldie and was taken prisoner by the Confederates. The conditions of his imprisonment in Libby Prison in Richmond were described by another New Yorker: "Nine hundred and twenty-two are now in four badly ventilated rooms, . . . without decent food, with no changes of clothing, covered with vermin, and in an atmosphere which has destroyed the lives of some of the strongest of them in four days. Many of them are sick, all of them are emaciated, heartsick, and dispirited."[9] By May 1864 Cesnola had been exchanged and was back in command of the 14th New York Cavalry. That summer he commanded a brigade in the Shenandoah Valley. After the war, Cesnola was the first director of the Metropolitan Museum of Art in New York.

Enrico Fardella commanded the 101st New York in the Peninsula campaign in 1862. When Fardella protested a report by his division commander, Brigadier General Phil Kearney, that the 101st broke and ran when attacked, Kearney admitted his mistake and noted that Fardella was "a noble and brave old soldier" whose "only difficulty is that he does not speak English fluently." In late 1863 and early 1864, Fardella commanded the 85th New York on the North Carolina coast. He was captured by the Confederates in June 1864. The *Charleston Mercury* soon announced that a number of Union prisoners, including Fardella, had been brought to Charleston to "share the pleasures of the bombardment" during the Union siege of the city.[10] Fardella survived the bombardment and was exchanged in September 1864.

Eduadro Ferrero was born in 1832 of Italian parents in Spain and was brought to New York as an infant. In October 1861 he was appointed colonel of the 51st New York. He was with Burnside's expedition to the North Carolina coast in 1861–62 and commanded brigades at the second Bull Run, Antietam, and Fredericksburg. His promotion to brigadier general in September 1862 lapsed in March 1863 due to inaction by the Senate, but he was reappointed later that year. He served in the Union siege of Vicksburg and the battle of Knoxville. Ezra Warner wrote that "at the celebrated battle of the Crater on July 30, 1864, Ferrero's men were supposed to follow Ledlie's forces in the assault on the Confederate line after the explosion. But Ledlie and Ferrero remained in a bombproof shelter some yards in the rear, passing a bottle of rum back and forth, while the assaulting troops became a leaderless mass of humanity in the huge excavation. . . . A court of inquiry . . . found that Ferrero was culpable for 'being in a bombproof habitually, where he could not see the operation of his troops.' "[11]

Francesco Spinola, a member of the New York Senate from Brooklyn, had been a foe of Republican policies and of Lincoln. But when the war began he aroused the patriotism of fellow Italian-Americans in a speech in describing the U.S. flag as "my flag, which I will follow and defend." In May 1862 he applied to Lincoln for permission to raise a brigade; Secretary of War Stanton wrote the governor of New York that "the President would be very much gratified if you would grant him the permission."[12] Spinola was commissioned as a brigadier general; his "Empire Brigade"included many Irish and Germans as well as some Italians. He was with the Union force on the North Carolina coast in late 1862 and early 1863 and was then sent to the Army of the Potomac with a number of "nine months men" whose enlistment was about up. General Halleck, general-in-chief of the army, wrote General Meade just after Gettysburg that "the nine months men told me that they were willing to serve through this crisis under anyone but General Spinola, but would not serve under him, as they regarded him as worthless. You are authorized to relieve him and send him away."[13] This abrupt judgment by Halleck suggests a prejudice against foreign-born officers. Spinola kept his command until the spring 1864 and was praised by two superiors for his conduct in battle, but he was relieved from command during Meade's reorganization of the Army of the Potomac in preparation for the "overland" campaign of 1864.

Norwegians

Hans Christian Heg recruited and commanded a Scandinavian regiment, the 15th Wisconsin, pointing out to Norwegians the need to prove that they were just as patriotic as the Germans and Irish. The men of the regiment, 90 percent of whom were Norwegians, elected him colonel. The rest were Swedes and Danes. The 15th Wisconsin was in twenty battles. Colonel Heg was killed at Chickamauga.

Poles

Joseph Karge, an immigrant from Poland, commanded the 1st New Jersey Cavalry in eight actions in Virginia in 1862, including the battle of Fredericksburg. Later in the west he commanded the 2nd New Jersey Cavalry, a cavalry brigade in Thomas's army, a cavalry division on an expedition into Mississippi, and a cavalry brigade in the forces operating against Mobile in March 1865.

Wladimir Krzyzanowski was born in 1824 in Raznova, Poland. After participation in revolutionary activities in Poland, he came in the 1840s to New York, where he was a civil engineer. In 1861 he recruited and commanded the 58th New York, sometimes called the Polish Legion. He was with Fremont at Cross Keys and in Schurz's division at the second Bull Run. Colonel Krzyzanowski commanded brigades at Chancellorsville, Gettysburg, and Chattanooga. When Kryzyzanowski was reburied at Arlington National Cemetery in 1937, President Franklin D. Roosevelt called him "an honored son of Poland who faithfully served the country of his adoption" and "the embodiment of the Polish ideal of liberty."[14]

Albin Francisco Schoepf was born in 1822 in Podgorz, Poland, of an Austrian father and a Polish mother, but he is listed as a Pole by Ezra Warner in *Generals in Blue*. He was a captain in the Austrian army but joined the revolutionaries in Hungary in 1848 and arrived in America in 1851. He was appointed a brigadier general in 1861 and commanded a division of Buell's army at Perryville. His rigid European-style discipline was unpopular with American volunteers. During the latter part of the war he held positions of secondary importance, including the command of a prison.

Swedes

Charles Stohlbrand, born in 1821 near Kristianstad, Sweden, was an officer in the Swedish army and served in the Danish-Prussian War before emigrating to America. He commanded artillery units at Vicksburg and Chattanooga and was chief of artillery of the XV Corps in the Atlanta campaign. Although captured in May 1864, he escaped from Andersonville in time to participate in Sherman's march to the sea and the campaign in the Carolinas. In February 1865, Stohlbrand was appointed a brigadier general.

Ernst Mattias Peter von Vegesack was born in 1820 in Gottland, Sweden, was a captain in the Swedish army by 1857, and served in the Danish army during the war in Schleswig-Holstein. His two years with the Union army included periods as a staff officer for Brigadier General John Wool, Brigadier General Joseph Mansfield, and Major General George B. McClellan. He was colonel of the 20th New York; a brigade commander at the second Bull Run; again commander of the 20th New York at Antietam, Fredericksburg, and Chancellorsville; and adjutant to General George G. Meade at Gettysburg. Von Vegesack returned to his former command in Sweden in August 1863.

SWISS

Herman Lieb, a Swiss immigrant from Thurgau, commanded the 5th U.S. Colored Heavy Artillery and ended the war as a brigadier general in charge of the Union artillery west of the Mississippi.

John Eugene Smith was born in Bern in 1816 and settled in Illinois. He recruited and commanded the 45th Illinois and served with it at Forts Henry and Donelson, Shiloh, and Corinth. He was appointed a brigadier general in November 1862 and commanded a brigade and then a division in the Vicksburg campaign. He was a division commander at Missionary Ridge, in the Atlanta campaign, and in Sherman's march to the sea. After the war he served in the U.S. army in the west, resigning only in 1881.

Appendix II

EUROPEAN-BORN COMMANDERS IN THE CONFEDERATE ARMY

BRITONS

William M. Browne was born in a English family in Dublin in 1823. He served in a British regiment in the Crimean war and then emigrated to America. He was editor of pro-Buchanan newspapers in Washington in the late 1850s and went south in 1861. Although Davis appointed him a colonel of cavalry, he served on Davis's personal staff for some time and was an assistant secretary of state during the period when the office of secretary of state was filled by two men in succession who knew little of foreign affairs. Later he was commandant of conscripts for the state of Georgia and a brigade commander at Savannah just before General Sherman arrived there. Davis appointed him a brigadier general on November 11, 1864, but the nomination was rejected by the Confederate Senate in its last session.

James Duff was born in 1828 in Perthshire, Scotland, and arrived in America in 1848. He enlisted in the U.S. Army, fought Indians on the frontier, deserted, was court-martialed and then pardoned, and finished his five-year enlistment as a sergeant. In 1862 Captain Duff was appointed provost marshal in the Texas Hill Country inhabited by thousands of German farmers who were mostly Unionists. "Duff came to be viewed by German Unionists as a butcher who ran a virtual reign of terror," Rodman L. Underwood wrote in a book on the Germans in Texas. "Duff . . . brutalized many citizens of the Hill Country by arrests, burning crops and homes, and hanging and shooting dissidents."[1] Later in the war, Duff commanded the 33rd Texas Cavalry.

Collett Leventhorpe, the only English regimental commander in gray, was born in 1825 in Devonshire and served in British colonial posts for some years with the

14th regiment of foot. By 1861 he was living in North Carolina and was elected colonel of the 34th North Carolina. Later he commanded the 11th North Carolina. After service in several engagements in North Carolina, he was wounded and captured while in Pettigrew's brigade at Gettysburg. After nine months in prison, he was exchanged. Jefferson Davis appointed him a brigadier general on February 3, 1865, but he declined the appointment

Peter Alexander Selkirk McGlashan was born in Edinburgh in 1831, the son of a veteran of Waterloo. His family came to America in 1848; by 1861 he had settled in Georgia. He enlisted as a private in the 50th Georgia and was its colonel by 1863. He was with Longstreet in Tennessee in late 1863 and with Lee in Virginia in 1864. He was wounded in both thighs at New Market, returning to duty in time to command a Georgia brigade briefly and then led the 50th Georgia again at Sayler's Creek, where he was captured. Just before fleeing from Richmond, Jefferson Davis signed a commission appointing McGlashan a brigadier general, but it never reached him. After the war McGlashan was mayor of Thomasville, Georgia.

Robert Alexander Smith, born in 1836 in Edinburgh, was the son of a textile manufacturer. He joined his elder brother in Jackson, Mississippi, in 1850, at age fourteen. He had enlisted before the war in a militia unit, the Mississippi Rifles, and was soon captain and then colonel of the 10th Mississippi Rifles. He survived the battle of Shiloh but was killed while leading a charge at Munfordsville, Kentucky, on September 14, 1862.

GERMANS

August Carl Buchel was born at Mainz in 1813, attended a military academy at Darmstadt, and was a lieutenant in a Hessian regiment. He then attended a French military academy, was a lieutenant in the French Foreign Legion, and served for some years as a military instructor in the Turkish army. After killing a man in a duel, he came to Texas. In the war with Mexico (1846–48), Buchel was a captain in a Texas regiment and later an aide to General Zachary Taylor. President Taylor appointed him collector of customs at Port Lavaca on the Texas Gulf Coast. In 1861 he organized and commanded the 1st Texas Cavalry, which served on the Texas coast until the spring of 1864. Buchel was killed at Pleasant Hill in Louisiana during the Red River campaign.

John P. Emerich was commander of the 8th Alabama in 1864 and in the Appomattox campaign in 1865.

Benjam F. Eschleman, a German from Louisiana, rose to the command of the Washington Artillery, a four-battery battalion from New Orleans which was in battles at Bull Run, Antietam, Gettysburg, the James River, and the Appomattox campaign.

B.W. Frobel had been a militia officer in Georgia before the war. He was chief of artillery in Hood's division at Antietam, commanded artillery at Fort Fisher in 1863 and early 1864, rejoined Hood in Georgia in 1864, and was chief engineer at Savannah just prior to its capture by Sherman.

Gustav Hoffmann, born in Prussia in 1817, served in the Prussian army, was one of the early German settlers of New Braunfels, Texas, and the city's first mayor. Although many of the New Braunfels Germans were Unionists, Hoffmann raised a Confederate cavalry company from surrounding Comal County; it joined the 7th Texas Cavalry. He was wounded in the assault on Fort Butler in 1863 but was promoted to colonel of the cavalry regiment in 1864.

August Reichard, a former Hannoverian officer, New Orleans cotton exporter, and Prussian consul, attempted to unite several German militia companies in the city and form a German regiment. But the 20th Louisiana ultimately consisted of about 600 Germans in six German companies and 400 Irishmen in four Irish companies. Reichard became its colonel and later brigade commander. The regiment fought at Shiloh, Mufreesboro, Chickamauga, Atlanta, and Nashville.

John A. Wagener was the only German in the South to wear a general's star. He was born in Bremen and had emigrated to Charleston by 1835, when he a joined a militia unit, the German Fusiliers. By 1847 he was commander of a German artillery battery; in 1859 he was major of the 2nd battalion of the First South Carolina Artillery. His grandson, William Y. Wagener, wrote that "in spite of the fact that he was attached with his whole soul to the Union and regretted the desire for separation, he rallied to the support of the state which had become his most intimate home."[2] He was appointed colonel of the South Carolina artillery; he and his German troops built Fort Walker on Hilton Head island. On November 7, 1861, the fort was attacked by a Union fleet of 75 ships supported by 10,000 soldiers. The Germans held out for four hours, until half the defending force was killed or wounded, and then the fort was occupied by Union forces commanded by another German, Brigadier General Alexander Schimmelfenning. Wagener was later a brigadier general commanding all the state troops during the siege of Charleston.

Colonel Waldeck, son of Count Waldeck, commanded a Texas cavalry regiment at Bentonville in 1862 and was killed during the Red River campaign in 1864.

Leon Von Zinken, a former Prussian officer and son of a Prussian general, was wounded at Shiloh and commanded the combined 13th and 20th Louisiana regiments at Chickamauga.

IRISH

Patrick Ronayne Cleburne was the highest ranking Irishman in the Confederate army and one of two foreign-born Confederate major generals. Born in 1828 near Cork, the son of a doctor, he enlisted in the British army's 41st infantry regiment at age seventeen, rising to the rank of corporal. After three years' service, he emigrated to America. He settled in Arkansas, where he studied and practiced law. When the war began he rose quickly from colonel of the 14th Arkansas to a brigade command at Shiloh, the command of two brigades in Kentucky, appointment as major general in December 1862, and the command of divisions at Murfreesboro, Chickamauga, and Chattanooga, in the Atlanta campaign, and at Jonesboro and Franklin. He told a visiting British officer in 1863 that he ascribed his advancement in the Confederate army mainly to "the useful lessons which he had learned in the ranks of the British army."[3] His proposal to use freed slaves as soldiers was suppressed by Jefferson Davis. He was killed at Franklin on November 30, 1864.

Joseph Finnegan, born in 1814 in Clones, came to America when in his twenties. Before the war he was a lumber miller, railroad builder, lawyer, and judge. Finnegan was a brigade and district commander in Florida from 1862 to early 1864, and commanded a brigade at Cold Harbor and Petersburg.

James Hagen was born in County Tyrone in 1822 and went to Philadelphia while still young. He was a cavalryman in the Mexican war, then moved to Mobile. In the Civil War he was commander of the Mobile Dragoons, major in the 1st Mississippi Cavalry at Shiloh, colonel of the 3rd Alabama Cavalry with Bragg in Tennessee, and commander of a brigade of cavalry with General Joseph Wheeler.

Walter Paye Lane, born in County Cork in 1817, was brought to Texas in 1821 at the age of four. At age eighteen he fought for Texas independence at the battle of San Jacinto. A decade later he was the captain of a company of rangers in the war with Mexico, and then he became a gold miner in California. In 1861 Lane was elected lieutenant colonel of the 3rd Texas Cavalry. He fought at Wilson's Creek, Pea Ridge (Elkhorn Tavern), in various battles in Indian territory, and in the Red River campaign in 1864. Early in 1865 he commanded a cavalry brigade in Texas; he was confirmed as brigadier general by the Confederate Senate on March 17, 1865, the last day it assembled.

Patrick T. Moore, born in Ireland in 1821, grew up in Canada until his father was appointed British consul in Boston. Moore was wounded while commanding the 1st Virginia at the first Bull Run and was on Longstreet's staff during the Peninsula campaign. In 1864 he was a brigadier general in charge of a reserve brigade in Virginia.

FRENCH

Raleigh Edward Colston was born in France in 1821 and was adopted by a Virginia physician living in France. He came to America in 1842 at the age of twenty-one, attended the Virginia Military Institute at Lexington, and remained there until the war as professor of French. He was colonel of the 16th Virginia and then a brigade commander during the Peninsular campaign and in Stonewall Jackson's corps. He was in Beauregard's command during the defense of Petersburg. After the war, Colston was a colonel in the Egyptian army.

Xavier B. Debray was born in 1818 in Epinel, graduated from the French military academy at St. Cyr, and served for a while in the French diplomatic service. By 1852 he had resigned due to his republican views and moved to Austin, Texas, where he edited a Spanish newspaper, was a translator for the General Land Office, and then established a school. During the war he was successively major of the 2nd Texas Infantry, colonel of the 26th Texas Cavalry, commander of Galveston Island, and a regimental commander in the Red River campaign in the spring of 1864. As a result of his participation in the battles of Mansfield and Pleasant Hill, the Confederate commander in the trans-Mississippi region, General Kirby Smith, appointed Debray a brigadier general, but the appointment was never confirmed by Jefferson Davis. Nevertheless, when captured in Virginia by Sheridan's army in April 1865, he was commanding a brigade consisting of three Texas cavalry regiments.

Aristide Gerard had been an editor at a French-language newspaper in New Orleans. He was badly wounded while commanding the 13th Louisiana at the battle of Farmington. A court-martial acquitted him of charges of disobedience of orders while in command of Fort De Russy in Louisiana in April 1863. He had been ordered to evacuate the fort but to save its guns, and had been unable to do so.

Victor Jean Baptiste Giradey was born in France but was brought to Georgia at the age of five and was educated in New Orleans. Giradey was repeatedly commended for his skill, bravery, and efficiency as a staff officer for several generals. For his role in organizing the Confederate counterattack at the battle of the Crater in 1864, he was promoted to brigadier general. He was killed a few weeks later near Richmond, while commanding a brigade that was resisting a Union attack.

Paul Francis de Gournay, Marquis of Marcheville, had been a large landowner in Brittany, managed his father's estates in Cuba for a while, and then came to New Orleans where he was a newspaper editor. In 1861 he equipped an artillery battery at his own expense and commanded it in Virginia. He was responsible for the construction of breastworks used by Confederates in the Seven Days battle. In the spring of 1863 Lieutenant Colonel de Gournay commanded the Confederate artillery during the Union siege of Port Hudson, a key Confederate post on the Mississippi River. He was wounded by a shell fragment, was captured, and spent the rest of the war as a prisoner. After the war, he was French vice consul in Baltimore for seven years.

Antoine-Jacques-Philippe de Mandeville de Marigny had been an officer in the French cavalry. In July 1861 he organized the 10th Louisiana, a polyglot regiment made up of men from twenty-three countries. The regiment was in the siege of

Yorktown in the spring of 1862. By the time it saw its first major action at Malvern Hill in July 1862, Colonel de Marigny had resigned.

Camille Armand Jules Marie, Prince de Polignac, was born in 1832 at Millemont, Seine-et-Oise. His mother was English; his father had been president of King Charles X's council of ministers. Polignac was a lieutenant in the 4th Chaussers in the Crimean war but resigned his commission in 1859 and was studying plants in Central America when the Civil War began in America. He was appointed a lieutenant colonel and was chief of staff to General Beauregard. His brigade commander, Colonel Preston Smith, reported enthusiastically on Polignac's performance at the battle of Richmond, Kentucky, in August 1862: "Though not born on our soil, . . . he has freely exposed himself to all the dangers of warfare, leading the gallant little band of which he was temporarily in command through the thickest of the fight and cheering them on to victory. He deserves the thanks of this country."[4] By January 1863 he was a brigadier general commanding a Texas brigade in Louisiana. His valor at the battle of Mansfield during the Red River campaign in 1864 led to a promotion to major general. Polignac and Patrick Cleburne, an Irish immigrant, were the only two foreign-born major generals in the Confederate army. Polignac returned to France early in 1865, on a mission to promote French recognition and support of the Confederacy. The mission is reviewed in Chapter 23.

NOTES

Chapter 1   Decisive Elements in the Coming Struggle

1. Miller, 315.
2. B. B. Sideman and L. Friedman, eds., *Europe Looks at the Civil War* (New York: Orcon Press, 1960), 262.
3. Dicey, *Spectator*, 170–71.
4. Schurz, *Reminiscences*, II, 65–66.
5. Anbinder, 106.
6. Maureen Harrison and Steve Gilbert, eds., *Lincoln in His Own Words* (New York: Barnes and Noble, 1994), 15.
7. David Herbert Donald, *Lincoln* (London: Simon and Schuster, 1995), 170.
8. Schurz, *Papers*, I, 24–25.
9. Villard, I, 92.
10. Paul M. Angle, ed., *The Lincoln Reader* (New Brunswick: Rutgers University Press, 1947), 246–47.
11. Anbinder, 267.
12. Rowan, 112–13.
13. Schurz, *Papers*, I, 116–17.
14. Schurz, *Reminiscences*, II, 197–98.
15. Kune, 84–88.
16. Ella Lonn, "The Forty-Eighters in the Civil War," in Zurcher, 183–84.
17. Joseph Shafer, "Who Elected Lincoln?" in Luebke, 61.
18. James M. McPherson, *Battle Cry of Freedom* (New York: Ballantine Books, 1988), 223.

19. William E. Gienapp, "Who Voted for Lincoln?," in John L. Thomas, ed., *Abraham Lincoln and the American Political Tradition* (Amherst, Mass.: University of Massachusetts Press, 1986), 73–74.

20. Shirley Blumenthal and Jerome Ozer, *Coming to America* (New York: Delacorte Press, 1980), 117–18.

21. Kohl, 8.

22. Burton, 6.

23. James Hennessey, *American Catholics: A History of the Roman Catholic Community in the United States* (New York: Oxford University Press, 1981), 145.

24. Villard, I, 155.

25. Ibid., I, 143–46.

26. Rappolt, 189.

27. Villard, I, 158.

28. Beckett, 13–14.

29. Schurz, *Reminiscences*, II, 223.

30. Villard, I, 161.

31. De Trobriand, 138.

32. Dicey, *Spectator*, 77.

33. Ibid., 296.

34. Russell, *Diary*, 186.

35. Fisch, 163.

36. Villard, I, 161.

37. Joinville, 14–15.

38. Ferri-Pisani, 72.

39. ORN, ser. II, vol. 3, 454.

40. ORA, ser. II, vol. 3, 483.

41. Woodrow Wilson, *Division and Reunion, 1829–1889* (New York: Longmans, Green, and Co., 1905), 163.

42. Lincoln to Lorenzo Montuntar, April 24, 1862, *Collected Works of Abraham Lincoln*, V, 198.

Chapter 2   Show Yourselves Worthy of Freedom

1. Kaufmann, 111.

2. Library of Congress American Memory web site.

3. Rowan, 180.

4. Lonn, *Union*, 71–72.

5. Leonard Streiff to *Louisville Journal*, June 11, 1861, in Frank Moore, ed., *The Rebellion Record* (New York: G. P. Putnam, 1861–62), I, 377.

6. Walter D. Kamphoefner et al., *The Westfalians: From Germany to Missouri* (Princeton: Princeton University Press, 1987), 402.

7. Rowan, 147–48.

8. Lonn, *Union*, 51.

9. Grebner, 68.

10. Ibid., 5.
11. *Louisville Anzieger,* October 24, 1861.
12. Maury Klein, *Days of Defiance* (New York: Vintage Books, 1999), 168.
13. Ibid., 218.
14. Lonn, *Union,* 67.
15. German-American Corner web site.
16. Streiff, see note 5 above.
17. Rowan, 203.
18. Chambrun, 64–65.
19. Dicey, *Spectator,* 234.
20. Lonn, *Union,* 72.
21. Kamphoefner et al., see note 6 above, 402–03.
22. Von Fritsch, 66.
23. Grebner, 195.
24. Loeffler, 180.
25. Martin Kuehn, "Wofuer kaempften die 48er?," conference paper, Rastatt, Germany, October 1999.
26. Schurz, *Reminiscences,* III, 37–38.
27. Lonn, *Union,* 659.
28. Zurcher, 269.
29. Engle, xv.
30. Zurcher, 115–16.
31. Loeffler, 180.
32. Burton, x.
33. Grebner, 128.
34. Germans in the Civil War web site.
35. Engelhart, *Zu den Waffen,* 61, 66.
36. De Trobriand, 81.
37. ORA, ser. I, vol. 12/3, 352.
38. Lonn, *Union,* 649.
39. Irene M. Franck, *The German American Heritage* (New York: Facts on File, 1989), 109.
40. Kaufmann, 78.
41. Levine, 257.
42. Franck, see note 39 above, 109.
43. Joseph R. Reinhart, "Indiana and Kentucky's German-Americans in the Civil War," 6th Kentucky web site.
44. ORA, ser. I, vol. 4, 581.
45. ORA, ser. I, vol. 8, 482.
46. ORA, ser. I, vol. 13, 86.
47. ORN, ser. II, vol. 3, 454.
48. Sala, III, 373.
49. Levine, 257.

50. Sala, II, 373.
51. Domschke, 43–44.
52. Kauffmann, 256–337.
53. Engelhart, *Zu den Waffen*, 66, 97–99.
54. Carl Sandburg, *Abraham Lincoln, The War Years* (New York: Harcourt, Brace, and Co., 1939), II, 60.
55. Tim Englehart, "Unter fremde Fahne: Deutscher Adel in Amerikanischen Buergerkreig," (article for *Magazine fuer Amerikanistik*, Hamburg, Germany), 2001.
56. Von Fritsch, 8.
57. Loeffler, 77.
58. Lonn, *Union*, 281.
59. Ibid., 291.
60. Kaufmann, 98.
61. Lonn, *Union*, 650.

Chapter 3   Plant That Flag on Fort and Crag

1. Lonn, *Union*, 43.
2. Egan, 24–25.
3. Conyngham, 253.
4. Kohl, 66–67.
5. Lonn, *Union*, 550.
6. Kohl, 10.
7. Lonn, *Union*, 42–43.
8. Conyngham, xv.
9. Ibid., 61.
10. Egan, 24–25.
11. Kohl, 65–66.
12. Mulholland, v.
13. Lonn, *Union*, 43.
14. Kohl, v.
15. Burton, 188.
16. Ibid., 69.
17. Conyngham, xvi.
18. Lonn, *Union*, 647–48; Burton, 153; De Trobriand, 81.
19. Conyngham, 8–9.
20. Lonn, *Union*, 646.
21. De Trobriand, 81.
22. Burton, 112–54.
23. Irish Word web site.
24. Kevin Kenny, *The American Irish* (New York: Longmans, Green, and Co., 2000), 123.
25. Lonn, *Union*, 646.

26. Conyngham, 8.
27. Gould, 27.
28. Fox, IX, 9.
29. James M. McPherson, *Battle Cry of Freedom: The Civil War Era* (New York: Ballantine Books, 1989), 606–67.
30. Kenny, see note 24 above, 125.
31. Brogan, 113–14.
32. Lawrence, 12.
33. Brogan, 113–20.
34. Daly, 246.
35. Brogan, 113–20.
36. Daly, 249–251.
37. Carl Sandburg, *Abraham Lincoln: The War Years* (New York: Harcourt, Brace, and Co., 1939), II, 366.
38. Kohl, 115.
39. De Chenal, 60.
40. Kenny, see note 24 above, 126.
41. De Trobriand, 536.
42. ORA, ser. I, vol. 43/1, 481; ORA, ser. III, vol. 3, 383, 510, 511, 552, 567, 1008.
43. ORA, ser. IV, vol. 3, 694.
44. ORA, ser. IV, vol. 3, 825, 1012.
45. C. Vann Woodword, ed., *Mary Chestnut's Civil War* (New York, Book of the month Club, 1981), 661.
46. ORA, ser. IV, vol. 3, 1083.

Chapter 4   Putting Down This Awful Rebellion

1. Charlotte Erickson, *Invisible Immigrants: The Adaptation of English and Scottish Immigrants in the Nineteenth Century America* (London, 1972).
2. James M. McPherson, *For Cause and Comrades* (New York: Oxford University Press, 1997), 22–23.
3. Erickson, see note 1 above, 350–51.
4. T. G. Hunter collection, Department of Welsh, University of Wales at Cardiff.
5. James M. McPherson, "Lincoln and the Millennium," Abraham Lincoln Online web site.
6. Van Vugt, 146.
7. Carnegie, 96.
8. Blackett, 51.
9. Watson, 395.
10. Conway, 173.
11. T. G. Hunter, University of Wales, to author, August 21, 2001.
12. Lewis, 23.

13. ORA, ser. III, vol, 2/1, 563.
14. Barnes, 295.
15. Lonn, *Union*, 441.
16. Barnes, 320.
17. Ibid., 331.
18. *Foreign Relations*, 1864, II, 254.
19. Gould, 27.
20. Fox, IX, 62.
21. Lonn, *Union*, 577–79.
22. Fox, X, 210.
23. Burton, 165.
24. *Daily Mail*, London, June 3, 1998.
25. Russell, *Diary*, 24.
26. Allen Thorndike Rice, ed., *Reminiscences of Abraham Lincoln* (New York: North American Publishing Co., 1888), 229.
27. Russell, *Pictures*.
28. Brogan, 8.
29. James M. Perry, *A Bohemian Brigade: The Civil War Correspondents* (New York: John Wiley and Sons, 2000), 185.
30. E. D. Adams, 176n.
31. Leslie Stephen, *The "Times" on the American War: A Historical Study* (London: W. Ridgway, 1865), 22.
32. Dicey, *Spectator*, ix–x.
33. Perry, see note 29 above, 174–75.
34. Ibid., 254.
35. Brayton Harris, *Blue and Gray in Black and White: Newspapers in the Civil War* (Washington: Batsford Brassey, 1999), 284–85.
36. Holland, I, 48.
37. Barnes, 341, 455n.
38. Ibid.
39. Gideon Welles, *Diary of Gideon Welles* (Boston, Houghton Mifflin, 1911), I, 496–97.

Chapter 5   A Fine Appearance

1. 5th New York web site.
2. Burton, 166.
3. De Trobriand, 83.
4. Ibid., 81.
5. Lonn, *Union*, 280.
6. Conyngham, 174.
7. Burton J. Hendrick, *Statesmen of the Lost Cause: Jefferson Davis and His Cabinet* (New York: Literary Guild, 1939), 253.

8. Louis Philippe Albert d'Orleans, Count of Paris, *History of the Civil War in America*, 4 vols. (Philadelphia: Jas H. Coates, 1875–88).
9. ORA, ser. I, vol. 5, 23.

Chapter 6 For the Sake of Right and Freedom

1. Hungarians in the Civil War web site.
2. Nicholas Perczel, *Naplom az emigraciobol* (Budapest, 1977), translation by Stephen Beszedits.
3. Stephen Beszedits, ed., *The Libby Prison Diary of Colonel Emeric Szabad* (Toronto: Band L. Information Services, 1999).
4. Hungarians in the Civil War web site.
5. *The Times*, London, February 9, 2000.
6. David Herbert Donald, *Lincoln* (London: Simon and Schuster, 1995), 412.
7. *Foreign Relations*, 1862, 567.
8. Mahin, 204–05.
9. Lonn, *Union*, 59.
10. Ibid., 78.
11. Hokanson, 68.
12. Ibid., 22–23.
13. Allyson McGill, *The Swedish Americans*, (New York, 1980), 45; Hokanson, 194.
14. *Foreign Relations*, 1861, 330.
15. Ibid., 1861, 337.
16. Hans Rudolf Guggisberg, "Das ungewoehnliche Amerika-Erlebnis der Schweizerischen Bundesrates Emil Frey," *Baseler Zeitschrift fuer Geschichte und Altertumskunde*, vol. 85, 1985, 130.
17. Ibid., 131.
18. Ibid., 141.
19. Aschmann, 24–25.
20. Ibid., 29.
21. ORA, ser. I, vol. 11/2, 467.
22. ORA, ser. I, vol. 29/1, 760.
23. Burton, 103.
24. Ferdinand Lecomte, *The War in the United States: Report to the Swiss Military Department* (New York: D. Van Nostrand, 1863).

Chapter 7 The Replenishing Stream

1. John M. Taylor, *William Henry Seward: Lincoln's Right Hand* (Washington: Brassey's, 1991), 201.
2. Lonn, *Union*, 419–20.
3. Hokanson, 27n.
4. ORA, ser. III, vol. 2, 359.

5. Basler, vol. 7, 40.
6. Phillip Shaw Paludan, *A People's Contest* (Lawrence, Kans.: University of Kansas Press, 1996), 181.
7. Basler, vol. 7, 36.
8. ORA, ser. 3, vol. 4, 456.
9. Basler, vol. 8, 141.
10. Katz, 103–104.
11. Kaufmann, 80.
12. Ibid.
13. *Foreign Relations*, 1861, 40.
14. Loeffler, 77.
15. *Foreign Relations*, 1862, 546.
16. ORA, ser. III, vol. 3, 19.
17. *Foreign Relations*, 1862, 544.
18. Otto Von Corwin, *Errinerungen aus meine Leben* (Leipzig, 1880), 283–85.
19. Gannon, 322.
20. B. B. Sideman and L. Friedman, eds., *Europe Looks at the Civil War* (New York: Orcon Books, 1969), 121–22.
21. O'Grady, 147.
22. *Foreign Relations*, 1863/2, 131.
23. William D'Arcy, *The Fenian Movement in the United States* (Washington: Catholic University Press, 1947), 63.
24. Miller, 359-60.
25. Ibid.
26. *Foreign Relations*, 1863/1, 255.
27. Lonn, *Confederacy*, 74.
28. ORN, ser. II, vol. 3, 994–95.
29. Web site of the Sons of Confederate Veterans, Sterling Price Camp.
30. ORN, ser. II, vol. 3, 949–50.
31. Mahin, 212.
32. Lonn, *Confederacy*, 80.
33. *Foreign Relations*, 1864/1, 247–54.
34. Ibid., 1864/2, 14.
35. Ibid., 1862, 87.
36. Ibid., 1863/2, 1365.
37. Hokanson, 77.

Chapter 8   The Seeds of Discord Had Been Thickly Sown

1. Lonn, *Confederacy*, 481.
2. Russell, *Diary*, 106.
3. Lonn, *Confederacy*, 4.
4. Ibid., 481.
5. Ripley, 58.

6. Russell, *Diary*, 99.
7. Schurz, *Papers*, I, 124.
8. Watson, 66.
9. Fisch, 151–53.
10. Watson, 96.
11. Watson, 114–15.
12. Jews in the Civil War web site.
13. Day, I, 23–24.
14. James M. McPherson to Civil War newsgroup, August 16, 1996.
15. Dicey, 123.
16. Watson, 122.
17. Russell, *Diary*, 234.
18. Watson, 116–17.
19. Hokanson, 96.
20. Egan, 251.
21. Corsan, 94.
22. ORA, ser. IV, vol. 1, 908.
23. Watson, 345–48.
24. Bonham, 118.

Chapter 9   Friends, Brothers, and Neighbors

1. Maury Klein, *Days of Defiance* (New York: Vintage Books, 1999), 8–9.
2. Beckett, 19.
3. Bright, 100–104.
4. Lonn, *Confederacy*, 420.
5. ORA, ser. I, vol. 22/1, 83.
6. Lonn, *Confederacy*, 45.
7. Andreas Dorpalen, "The German Element and the Issue of the Civil War," in Luekbe, 70.
8. Rosen, 31–32, 35, 50.
9. Ibid., 54.
10. Kaufmann, 81.
11. Living History web site.
12. Lonn, *Confederacy*, 153.
13. T. R. Fehrenbach, *Lone Star: A History of Texas and Texans* (New York: Macmillan, 1968), 346.
14. Underwood, 121–145.
15. Lonn, *Confederacy*, 415.
16. Fremantle, *Three Months*, 43.
17. Robert L. Kerby, *Kirby Smith's Confederacy: The Trans-Mississippi South, 1863–1865* (Tuscaloosa: University of Alabama Press, 1972), 93.
18. Rudolf L. Biesele, "German Attitude toward the Civil War," Handbook of Texas On Line web site.

19. Donald S. Fraser, *Blood and Treasure: Confederate Empire in the Southwest* (College Station, Tex.: Texas A and M University Press, 1995), 230.
20. Kaufmann, 330.
21. Ibid., 333.
22. Ibid., 284.
23. ORN, vol. 22, 124.
24. Kaufmann, 81.
25. Watson, 89.
26. Lonn, *Confederacy*, 114.
27. Kaufmann, 81.
28. Lonn, *Confederacy*, 234.
29. ORA, ser. I, vol. 6, 620.
30. ORN, ser. I , vol. 18, 462.
31. Lonn, *Confederacy*, 238.
32. Kaufmann, 82.
33. Bright, 87.
34. Wust, 222.
35. Ibid.
36. Ibid., 220.
37. Andrea Mehrlaender, "Deutsche in de Diensten der Konfoederation," Technical University of Berlin web site.
38. W. Y. Wagener, "General John Andreas Wagener" (Ph.D. dissertation, University of South Carolina, Columbia, 1937), 61–62, in George B. Shealy, *Gen. John A. Wagener: Charleston and South Carolina's Foremost German-American, Founder of Walhalla* (Walhalla, S.C.: Alexander's Office Supply, 2001), 119.
39. Loeffler, 186.
40. George B. Shealy, *Walhalla: The Garden of the Gods* (Seneca, S.C.: Blue Ridge Arts Association, 1990), 64.
41. Ibid.
42. ORN, ser. I, vol. 16, 7.
43. Bright, 98.
44. ORA, ser. I, vol. 35/2, 243.
45. ORA, ser. I, vol. 34/2, 227.
46. ORA, ser. I, vol. 7, 524.
47. Kaufmann, 299.
48. Carl Schurz, *Lebenserrinerungen* (Berlin, 1906–12), II, 205–206.
49. ORA, ser. I, vol. 27/2, 711.
50. ORA, ser. I, vol. 51/2, 859.
51. ORA, ser. I, vol. 42/2, 1174.
52. Von Borcke, 447–48.
53. William S. Hoole, introduction to Scheibert, *Seven Months*, iii.

54. Hoole, Lawley, 55.
55. Ross, 195.

Chapter 10 They Caught the Spirit of the Community

1. Lonn, *Confederacy*, 28.
2. Crawford, 71.
3. Lonn, *Confederacy*, 28.
4. Niehaus, 47–48.
5. McLeod, 40.
6. Mahone, 65, 77.
7. Maguire, 546.
8. Joslyn, 54.
9. Gannon, xi.
10. Gleeson, 121.
11. Ibid., 163.
12. Web site of Sons of Confederate Veterans, Sterling Price Camp.
13. ORA, ser. I, vol. 8, 300.
14. ORA, ser. III, vol. 2, 731.
15. O'Grady, vii–viii.
16. Niehaus, 158.
17. O'Grady, xvii; Gleeson, 154, 230.
18. O'Grady, 247–59.
19. Fremantle, *Three Months*, 185.
20. Maguire, 578.
21. Ibid., 585.
22. ORA, ser. I, vol. 7, 244.
23. ORA, ser. I, vol. 10/1, 441.
24. Gannon, 42.
25. Ibid., 320.
26. Gleeson, 125.
27. Ibid., 157.
28. Egan, 251.
29. ORA, ser. I, vol. 7, 524.
30. Richard S. West, *Lincoln's Scapegoat General; A Life of Benjamin F. Butler, 1818–1893* (Boston: Houghton Mifflin, 1965), 168.
31. ORA, ser. III, vol. 3, 766.
32. Burton, 70.
33. ORA, ser. II, vol. 5, 240.
34. Gleeson, 167.
35. Works Progress Administration, *New Orleans City Guide* (Boston: Houghton Mifflin, 1938), 356–57.
36. Gleeson, 169.

Chapter 11　Duty to Cause and Country

1. Lonn, *Union*, 662.
2. Bonham, 137.
3. Russell, *Pictures*, 63.
4. Russell, *Diary*, 136–137.
5. Bonham, 178.
6. ORA, ser. II, vol. 3, 689.
7. Bonham, 113–14.
8. Ibid., 81, 104.
9. Ibid., 81–82.
10. ORA, ser. IV, vol. 2, 239–40.
11. Fremantle, *Three Months*, 68.
12. Berwanger, 114.
13. Bonham, 142–44.
14. Mahin, 210–11.
15. ORA, ser. II, vol. 4, 300.
16. Lonn, *Confederacy*, 493; Bonham, 79.
17. Bonham, 91.
18. Ibid., 118.
19. Russell, *Pictures*, 34.
20. Richard B. Hartwell, ed., *Confederate Reader* (New York: Barnes and Noble, 1992), 32.
21. Stanley, 109.
22. Watson, 122–23.
23. Johnson, 91–92, 98–99.
24. Watson, 122–23.
25. [Anon], *Battlefields of the South*, xii–xiii.
26. Lonn, *Confederacy*, 33.
27. Ibid., 56.
28. Ibid., 33.
29. Lonn, *Confederacy*, 33.
30. Starr, Stephen Z., 224–25.
31. Ibid., 266.
32. Lonn, *Confederacy*, 190–93.
33. C. Vann Woodward, ed., *Mary Chesnut's Civil War* (New York: Book of the Month Club, 1981), 148.
34. Scheibert, *Seven Months*, 103.
35. Hoole, *Lawley*, 19.
36. Lonn, *Confederacy*, 361; Day, 293–94.
37. Von Borcke, 220–21.
38. G. Moxley Sorell, *Recollections of a Confederate Staff Officer* (Wilmington, N.C.: Broad Foot Publishing Co., 1991), 116.

39. Lonn, *Confederacy*, 364–65.
40. James A. Rawley, introduction to Wolseley, x–xiii.
41. ORA, ser. I, vol. 6, 725; Richard S. West, *Lincoln's Scapegoat General: A Life of Benjamin F. Butler, 1818-1893* (Boston: Houghton Mifflin, 1965), 19; ORA, ser. III, vol. 2, 130–31.
42. Beckett, 57.
43. Watson, 370.

Chapter 12   Until the Land Is Blessed with Peace

1. Jews in the Civil War web site.
2. Russell, *Diary*, 129.
3. Lonn, *Confederacy*, 101–106.
4. ORA, ser. I, vol. 26/1, 362.
5. Lonn, *Confederacy*, 457.
6. ORA, ser. I, vol. 15, 480; ORA, ser. II, vol. 2, 722.
7. French Guard web site.
8. ORA, ser. III, vol. 2, 728–29.
9. ORA, ser. III, vol. 2, 722–23.
10. Ibid.
11. ORA, ser. I, vol. 6, 58.
12. ORA, ser. I, vol. 6, 595.
13. ORA, ser. I, vol. 6, 553.
14. ORA, ser. I, vol. 25, 463.
15. ORA, ser I, vol. 15, 497.
16. ORA, ser. I, vol. 15, 550.
17. ORA, ser. III, vol. 2, 722–23.
18. ORA, ser. III, vol. 2, 569.
19. ORA, ser. III, vol. 2, 567–68.
20. Russell, *Diary*, 144.
21. Jews in the Civil War web site.
22. ORA, ser. I, vol. 25, 428.
23. ORA, ser. I, vol. 26/1, 690.
24. ORA, ser. IV, vol. 2, 366.
25. ORN, ser. II, vol. 3, 1243–44.
26. ORA, ser. I, vol. 20/1, 533.
27. ORA, ser. II, vol. 7, 609.
28. ORA, ser. III, vol. 4, 779.
29. ORA, ser. I, vol. 42/3, 694.
30. Jews in the Civil War web site.
31. ORA, ser. IV, vol. 2, 100.
32. Lonn, *Confederacy*, 471–72.
33. ORA, ser. II, vol. 5, 240.

34. ORA, ser. IV, vol. 3, 625.
35. ORA, ser. I, vol. 16/2, 751–52.
36. John Garibaldi letters, Virginia Military Institute web site.
37. ORA, ser. I, vol. 42/2, 794.
38. ORA, ser. I, vol. 42/3, 694.
39. 10th Louisiana web site.
40. Gannon, 393.

Chapter 13   To Ogle the President

1. De Hauranne, II, 350.
2. Russell, *Diary*, 22.
3. Dicey, *Spectator*, 91.
4. Sala, II, 129.
5. Carnegie, 97.
6. Chambrun, 99–100.
7. Dicey, *Spectator*, 91.
8. Carnegie, 98.
9. Lord Charnwood, *Abraham Lincoln* (New York: Henry Holt and Co., 1917), 235.
10. Chambrun, 22.
11. Kune, 98.
12. De Hauranne, II, 350.
13. Harold Holzer, ed., *Lincoln as I Knew Him* (Chapel Hill: Algonguin Books, 1999), 95.
14. Dicey, *Spectator*, 92.
15. Chambrun, 100.
16. Hudson Strode, *Jefferson Davis* (New York: Harcourt Brace and Co., 1964), 171.
17. Dicey, *Spectator*, 90–91.
18. Holland, I, 43.
19. Sala, II, 129.
20. Wolseley, 48, 55.
21. Lawrence, 31.
22. De Hauranne, II, 231–32, 350.
23. Chambrun, 100–103.
24. Schurz, *Papers*, I, 251.
25. De Trobriand, 150–51.
26. Russell, *Diary*, 93–94.
27. Day, I, 235.
28. Fremantle, *Three Months*, 267–68.
29. Hoole, *Lawley*, 34.
30. Joinville, 19.

31. Fremantle, *Blackwood's*, in "Books on the American War," *Blackwood's Edinburgh Magazine*, vol. 94 (December 1863), 767.
32. Russell, *Diary*, 142.
33. Day, I, 255.
34. Fremantle, *Three Months*, 123.
35. Scheibert, *Seven Months*, 127.
36. Conolly, 47–48.
37. Fremantle, *Blackwood's*, 767.
38. Wolseley, 76.
39. Beckett, 123.
40. Watson, 452.

Chapter 14 A Head Capable of Managing Great Armies

1. Villard, I, 178–79.
2. De Trobriand, 68.
3. Russell, *Diary*, 93.
4. Ibid., 199–200.
5. De Trobriand, 68.
6. Aschmann, 88–89.
7. Russell, *Diary*, 245.
8. Day, II, 1–2.
9. Ibid., 250.
10. Schurz, *Reminiscences*, II, 334–36.
11. Conyngham, 103–104, 125.
12. Paris, Count of, II, 45.
13. Post, 358.
14. Paris, Count of, II, 248–49.
15. Von Borcke, 109.
16. Ibid., 127.
17. Villard, I, 336.
18. Wolseley, 32–33.
19. De Trobriand, 321.
20. Von Borcke, 260–61.
21. Wolseley, 33.
22. De Trobriand, 320–23.
23. Galwey, 40–46.
24. Von Borcke, 162.
25. De Trobriand, 326.
26. Von Borcke, 162.
27. Ibid.
28. Wolseley, 33.
29. Villard, I, 336.

30. McCarter, 63–64.
31. Galwey, 52–53.
32. McCarter, 68.
33. Galwey, 53.
34. Sala, I, 85, 284.
35. Wolseley, 33.
36. Paris, Count of, II, 558.
37. Winston Churchill, *The Great Democracies* (New York: Dodd, Mead, and Co., 1958), 209.
38. Wolseley, 67, 112.
39. G. F. R. Henderson, *Stonewall Jackson and the American Civil War* (London: Longmans, Green, and Co., 1903), x, 40.
40. Schurz, *Reminiscences*, II, 334.
41. De Trobriand, 348–49.
42. Nicholas Perczel, *Napolm az emigraciobol* (Budapest, 1977), 188, translation by Stephen Beszedits.
43. Villard, I, 338, 350.
44. McCarter, 68.
45. Von Borcke, 313.
46. McCarter, 226.
47. *Irish American,* New York, January 3, 1863, 69th New York web site.
48. McCarter, 178, 183.
49. ORA, ser. I, vol. 21, 278–79.
50. 69th New York web site.
51. McCarter, 184.
52. Von Borcke, 313.
53. Ross, 182.
54. Conyngham, 351–52.
55. 69th New York web site.
56. Ibid.
57. McCarter, 173.
58. Ibid., 229.
59. Von Borcke, 313.
60. Conyngham, 351–52.
61. Villard, I, 390–91.
62. Beckett, 88–89.
63. Hirst, 100.
64. Galwey, 81–82.
65. Beckett, 75–76; Hoole, *Lawley,* 31.
66. Hoole, *Lawley,* 116; Lawley, *Fortnightly Review,* 1–2.
67. Wolseley, 29.
68. Fremantle, *Blackwood's,* 375.
69. Scheibert, *Seven Months,* 38–39.
70. Paris, Count of, II, 77.

71. Watson, 370.
72. Beckett, 77–78.
73. Von Borcke, 408.
74. Harris, see Chapter 4, note 35, 264–65.
75. McCarter, 60n.
76. Beckett, 79.
77. Fremantle, *Three Months*, 190.
78. Von Borcke, 22–32.
79. Dawson, 129–30.
80. [Anon], "Books on the American War," *Blackwood's Edinburgh Magazine*, December 1863, 766.
81. Beckett, 36–37.
82. Watson, 363.

Chapter 15   The Valley of the Shadow of Death

1. Villard, I, 347.
2. Galwey, 81–82.
3. Scheibert, *Seven Months*, 65.
4. Schurz, *Reminiscences*, II, 423.
5. De Trobriand, 443.
6. Samito, 188.
7. Stephen W. Sears, *Chancellorsville* (Boston: Houghton Mifflin, 1996), 270.
8. Martin, 134–35.
9. Germans in the Civil War web site.
10. 26th Wisconsin web site.
11. Ibid.
12. Martin, 134–35.
13. Fox, Part VIII, 87.
14. ORA, ser. I, vol. 27/1, 721.
15. ORA, ser. I, vol. 27/1, 728.
16. Aschmann, 116–18.
17. Fremantle, *Three Months*, 207.
18. Von Fritsch, 85.
19. Gannon, 393.
20. Von Fritsch, 85.
21. Schurz, *Reminiscences*, III, 24–25.
22. Aschmann, 193–95.
23. Schurz, *Reminiscences*, III, 24–25.
24. Fremantle, *Three Months*, 207–208.
25. Justus Scheibert to J. Wm. Jones, November 21, 1877, Gettysburg Discussion Group web site.
26. Count of Paris to J. Wm. Jones, January 21, 1877, Gettysburg Discusssion Group web site.

27. Brogan, 128–32.
28. Hirst, 149–50.
29. Brogan, 128–32.
30. Galwey, 116–18.
31. Scheibert, *Seven Months*, 115.
32. Galwey, 116–18.
33. Hirst, 149–51.
34. Brogan, 128–31.
35. Fremantle, *Three Months*, 212–14.
36. Pula, *Krzyzanowski*, 49.
37. Dawson, 98.
38. Hirst, 182.
39. Brogan, 131.
40. Aschmann, 112.
41. Schurz, *Reminiscences*, III, 37–38.
42. Brogan, 132.
43. Ross, 81.
44. Dawson, 98.
45. James A. Kegel, *North with Lee and Jackson* (Mechanicsburg, Pa.: Stackpole Books, 1996), 364.
46. Lonn, *Confederacy*, 452–53.
47. Scheibert, *Seven Months*, 119–20.
48. Shelby Foote, *Stars in Their Courses: The Gettysburg Campaign* (New York: Modern Library, 1994), 283.
49. John W. Schildt, *Roads from Gettysburg* (Shippensburg, Pa.: Burd Street Press, 1998), 74.
50. John O. Casler, *Four Years in the Stonewall Brigade* (Girard, Kans.: Appeal Publishing Co., 1906), 179.
51. Egan, 125–27.
52. Galwey, 124–27.
53. 26th Wisconsin web site.
54. Von Fritsch, 89–90.
55. *Richmond Dispatch*, April 15, 1896, in Gettysburg Discussion Group web site.
56. Fremantle, *Three Months*, 220.
57. Ross, 75–76.

Chapter 16   Vicksburg Has Fallen!

1. B. B. Seidman and L. Friedman, eds., *Europe Looks at the Civil War* (New York: Orcon Press, 1960), 86.
2. Kaufmann, 115.
3. Ripley, 60.
4. Kune, 10.
5. Villard, I, 273.

6. Stanley, 135.
7. 6th Kentucky Infantry web site.
8. Watson, 350–51.
9. Conway, 153–54.
10. Watson, 366.
11. Fletcher, *Cornhill Magazine*, VII, 499.
12. Hoole, *Lawley*, 49.
13. De Trobriand, 560.
14. Cadwallader, 87–88.
15. Belgians in the Civil War web site.
16. John G. Jones letters, National Library of Wales, Aberystwyth.
17. Belgians in the Civil War web site.
18. Watson, 369.

Chapter 17   The Zeal and Bravery of Citizen Soldiers

1. Lawrence, George A., 274.
2. Wolseley, 38.
3. George F. R. Henderson, *The Civil War: A Soldier's View* (Chicago: University of Chicago Press, 1958), 119n.
4. Lawrence, George A., 231.
5. Fletcher, *Cornhill Magazine*, VII, 507.
6. Lecomte, 95.
7. Russell, *Diary*, 177.
8. Holland, I, 44.
9. Lecomte, 94.
10. Trollope, 430.
11. Dicey, *Spectator*, 140.
12. Ferri-Pisani, 136.
13. Lecomte, 98.
14. Joinville, 15.
15. Russell, *Diary*, 209.
16. Joinville, 52–53.
17. Dicey, *Macmillan's*, 16–29.
18. Dicey, *Spectator*, 141.
19. Lecomte, 53–54, 73–74.
20. Von Borcke, 195–96.
21. Von Fritsch, 17.
22. Joinville, 96.
23. Jay Luvaas, *The Military Legacy of the Civil War* (Chicago: University of Chicago Press, 1959), 43.
24. De Chenal, 228.
25. Luvaas, see note 23 above, 97.
26. Wolseley, 40

27. Beckett, 67–68.
28. Fremantle, *Three Months*, 97n.
29. Scheibert, *A Prussian Observes*, 195, 200.
30. Henderson, see note 3 above, 143.
31. Joinville, 19.
32. Harris, 34.
33. Day, I, 126.
34. Watson, 359
35. Ibid., 453, 135.
36. Ibid., 347–48.
37. Schurz, *Reminiscences*, III, 70.
38. Domschke, 109–10.
39. Day, I, 97.
40. Ferri-Pisani, 127.
41. Beckett, 79.
42. *Charleston Mercury*, February 5, 1863.
43. Scheibert, *Seven Months*, 78–79.
44. Brogan, 93.
45. Stanley, 110–11.
46. Wolseley, 31, 63.
47. Stanley, 135.
48. Ross, 60.
49. De Chenal, 26.
50. De Trobriand, 538.
51. De Chenal, 26–27.
52. Aschmann, 58.
53. De Trobriand, 548.
54. De Chenal, 40, 231.
55. Russell, *Diary*, 199–200.
56. John G. Jones letters, National Library of Wales, Aberystwyth.
57. Dawson, 54–56.
58. Scheibert, *Seven Months*, 321.
59. Fremantle, *Three Months*, 246.
60. De Trobriand, 90.
61. Beckett, 67–68.
62. Von Borcke, 25.
63. Scheibert, *A Prussian Observes*, 71–72.
64. Hoole, *Lawley*, 83.
65. Lawrence, George A., 32–33.
66. Russell, *Diary*, 199.
67. Luvaas, see note 23 above, 333, 337–38.
68. Galwey, 170.
69. De Trobriand, 90.

70. Ibid., 338.
71. Lecomte, 73.
72. Scheibert, *Seven Months*, 49.
73. Ibid., 113.
74. Hoole, *Lawley*, 95.
75. Luvaas, see note 23 above, 4–5.
76. Colonel William Vossler, "The European Heritage of the American Civil War," lecture at U.S. Army Military History Institute, February 18, 1998, 23.
77. Luvaas, see note 23 above, 46.
78. Ross, 33, 91.
79. Von Borcke, 301–302.
80. Scheibert, *A Prussian Observes*, 63.
81. Fremantle, *Three Months*, 126.
82. Ibid., 284–85.
83. Ross, 81.
84. Edwin B. Coddington, *The Gettysburg Campaign: A Study in Command* (New York: Simon and Schuster, 1997), 65.

Chapter 18   A Bold and Daring Enterprise

1. Ivan Musicant, *Divided Waters: The Naval History of the Civil War* (New York: Harper Collins Publishers, 1995), 56.
2. Ibid., 59; Gideon Welles, *Diary of Gideon Welles* (Boston: Houghton Mifflin, 1911), II, 121, 129.
3. Still, 55.
4. Ibid.
5. Still, 86–87.
6. Ibid.
7. ORN, ser. I, vol. 15, 108.
8. Still, 84.
9. C. S. S. Alabama web site.
10. Arthur Sinclair, *Two Years on the Alabama* (Boston: Lee and Shepard, 1895), 37.
11. Summersell, xii.
12. ORN, ser. I, vol. 3, 73.
13. Sinclair, see note 10 above, 22.
14. Summersell, xiii.
15. Ibid., 138, 171.
16. Dawson, 26–27.
17. Summersell, 23.
18. Ibid., xxii.
19. Maguire, 613.
20. Paris, Count of, II, 650–51.
21. Welles, see note 2 above, II, 67, 70.

22. Civil War Medals of Honor web site.
23. Fremantle, 161.
24. Corsan, 64–65.
25. Scots in the Civil War web site.
26. Paris, Count of, II, 643.
27. Hoole, *Vizetelly*, 112–13.
28. Hobart-Hampden, 2.
29. Day, I, 218.
30. Beckett, 122.
31. Hobart-Hampden, 2.
32. Beckett, 97–98.
33. Ross, 205.
34. Cochran, 71–72.
35. Lonn, *Confederacy*, 310.
36. Corsan, 64–65.
37. Francis Lawley to William Gregory, September 16, 1863, Gregory Papers, Emory University, Atlanta, Ga.
38. Corsan, 55.
39. Ross, 209.
40. Fremantle, *Three Months*, 161.
41. Ross, 149–51.
42. Hoole, *Lawley*, 99–100.
43. Calvin Coolidge, May 29, 1926, Library of Congress American Memory web site.
44. Joinville, 30.
45. Coolidge, see note 43 above.
46. Hokanson, 188.
47. Joinville, 30.
48. Hokanson, 189–90.
49. Dawson, 38–41.
50. Hokanson, 188.
51. Coolidge, see note 43 above.

Chapter 19   Will Europe Ever Recognize the Confederacy?

1. Russell, *Diary*, 205.
2. Conyngham, 381.
3. Barnes, 251.
4. Kohl, 103.
5. Russell, *Diary*, 25, 30, 36.
6. Trollope, 237.
7. Watson, 120.
8. Russell, *Diary*, 69, 78.
9. Ibid., 69, 78–9, 98, 112, 137, 157.

10. Bourke, 762.
11. Trollope, 418, 10.
12. Dicey, *Spectator*, 113, 127, 117.
13. Ibid., 115–116.
14. Trollope, 7–8.
15. Lawrence, G. G., 56.
16. Russell, *Diary*, 19.
17. Dicey, *Spectator*, 97.
18. Sala, 129–30.
19. Dicey, *Spectator*, 97–98.
20. Schurz, *Papers*, 186–88.
21. Wolseley, 48.
22. Lawrence, G. G., 12.
23. Lierley, 125–29, 174.
24. Blackett, 155.
25. Russell, *Pictures*, 33.
26. Lonn, *Confederacy*, 470.
27. Hoole, *Vizetelly*, 52–53.
28. Wolseley, 47.
29. Hoole, *Lawley*, 30.
30. Wolseley, 41–42.
31. Daly, 148.
32. Kohl, 62.
33. Schurz, *Reminiscences*, II, 302.
34. Russell, *Diary*, 260–61.
35. Trollope, 237.
36. ORA, Ser. II, vol. 2, 1106–08.
37. Lawrence, G. G., 8.
38. Taylor, 13–14.
39. Lierley, 125–29.
40. Trollope, 333–34.
41. Sala, I, 33.
42. Beckett, 42.
43. Schurz, *Reminiscences*, II, 310.
44. Taylor, 14.
45. Dicey, *Spectator*, 97.
46. Fremantle, *Three Months*, 165–66.
47. Beckett, 42.
48. Schurz, *Reminiscences*, II, 310.
49. Beckett, 42.
50. Dicey, *Spectator*, 114.
51. Wittke, 245.
52. D'Arcy, see Chapter 7, note 23, 21.

53. Day, II, 311.
54. Schurz, *Reminiscences*, II, 275–76.
55. ORN, ser. II, vol. 3, 293.
56. Conway, 150.
57. Starr, Louis M., 120–21.
58. Corsan, 93–94.
59. Wolseley, 41.
60. Hoole, *Lawley*, 52–53.
61. Ibid., 47.
62. Fremantle, *Three Months*, 154, 165–66, 169.
63. Dicey, *Spectator*, 299–300.
64. William H. Russell, *Army and Navy Gazette*, June 6, 1863, in E. D. Adams, II, 166.
65. Paris, Count of, III, 404.
66. Dicey, *Macmillan's*, 19.
67. Dicey, *Spectator*, 299–300.
68. Ibid., 303.

Chapter 20   This Abominable Institution

1. Joslyn, 176.
2. Web site of Sons of Confederate Veterans, Polignac Camp.
3. Jews in the Civil War web site.
4. Ferri-Pisani, 132.
5. Seymour, 399.
6. Holland, I, 45.
7. Lecomte, 9.
8. Trollope, 356.
9. Dicey, *Spectator*, 289–91.
10. De Hauranne, I, 105.
11. Jews in the Civil War web site.
12. Day, I, 20.
13. Bourke, 757.
14. Ross, 109, 147, 236.
15. Jews in the Civil War web site.
16. Holland, I, 52.
17. Ferencz A. Pulsky, *White, Red, and Black: Sketches of Society in the United States* (New York: Johnson Reprint Company, 1968), 201–202, 212.
18. Russell, *Diary*, 101, 120.
19. Wolseley, 8
20. Fremantle, *Three Months*, 162.
21. Trollope, 359–60, 420.
22. Day, II, 38.
23. Wolseley, 60.

24. Bourke, 767.
25. Thompson, 25.
26. Dicey, *Spectator*, 293.
27. Holland, I, 45.
28. Beckett, 69–70.
29. Ibid., 85–86.
30. Dicey, *Spectator*, 292.
31. Lecomte, 139.
32. Beckett, 85–86.
33. Ibid., 76.
34. Russell, *Pictures*, 27.
35. Dicey, *Spectator*, 293.
36. Chambrun, 59.
37. Laugel, 30.
38. Niel Johnson, "William Paul Esbjorn and the Battle of Lexington, Missouri," Missouri Valley History Conference, March 1862: L. P. Esbjorn Papers, Augustana College, Rock Island, Illinois.
39. T. G. Hunter, University of Wales at Cardiff, to author, August 29, 2001.
40. Conway, 172.
41. 15th Wisconsin web site.
42. Ibid.
43. James Hennesey, *American Catholics: A History of the Roman Catholic Community in the United States* (New York: Oxford University Press, 1981), 149.
44. Spiegel, 114–15.
45. Goodell and Taylor, 161.
46. Bell Irvin Wiley, *The Life of Billy Yank: The Common Soldier of the Union* (Indianapolis: Bobbs-Merrill, 1952) 109.
47. Todd, 70.
48. Spiegel, 204.
49. Carl Sandburg, *Abraham Lincoln: The War Years* (New York: Harcourt Brace and Co., 1942), III, 204.
50. Ella Lonn, "The Forty-Eighters in the Civil War, in Zurcher, 184.
51. Spiegel, 226, 230.
52. Ibid., 244.
53. Ibid., 261.
54. Ibid., 316.
55. Ibid., 321.
56. Daly, 179.
57. Hudson Strode, *Jefferson Davis* (New York: Harcourt Brace and Co., 1964), 323.

Chapter 21   With the Sublimity of Genius, or of Madness

1. Hoole, *Lawley*, 68.
2. Virginia Military Institute web site.

3. Laugel, 15–16.
4. ORA, ser. I, vol. 30/2, 223.
5. 15th Wisconsin web site.
6. Grebner, 152.
7. Laugel, 15–16.
8. 15th Wisconsin web site.
9. Von Fritsch, 98–99.
10. Schurz, *Reminiscences*, III, 77.
11. ORA, ser. I, vol. 31/2, 305.
12. ORA, ser. I, vol. 31/2, 435.
13. Von Fritsch, 100–101.
14. Laugel, 16.
15. Dawson, 114–116.
16. Laugel, 17.
17. Beckett, 234–45.
18. Ross, 218, 221.
19. Beckett, 142.
20. Laugel, 18–19.
21. Beckett, 144–45
22. Ibid., 142–43.
23. 15th Wisconsin web site.
24. Thomas Tucker web site.
25. 26th Wisconsin web site.
26. Thomas Tucker web site.
27. 26th Wisconsin web site.
28. Thomas Tucker web site.
29. De Chenal, 194.
30. Thomas Tucker web site.
31. De Chenal, 194–95.
32. De Trobriand, 646.
33. ORA, ser. I, vol. 43/1, 508.
34. Dawson, 121.
35. Domschke, 46, 68–69.
36. Hobart-Hampden, 43.
37. Hoole, *Lawley*, 101.

Chapter 22   This Turbulent Democracy

1. Laugel, 45.
2. 26th Wisconsin web site.
3. De Hauranne, I, 113, 117.
4. Grant, 176.
5. Schurz, *Reminiscences*, III, 103.

6. John C. Waugh, *Reelecting Lincoln: The Battle for the 1864 Presidency* (New York: Crown Publishers, 1997), 282.
7. Laugel, 48.
8. De Chenal, 237.
9. Schurz, *Reminiscences*, III, 105.
10. Beckett, 147.
11. De Trobriand, 671.
12. Belgians in the Civil War web site.
13. Laugel, 53.
14. Daly, 302.
15. 26th Wisconsin web site.
16. Laugel, 45–47.
17. Wittke, 246.
18. Ibid.
19. Levine, 261.
20. De Chenal, 237.
21. Laugel, 47.
22. Katz, 146–47, 149.
23. Schurz, *Papers*, I, 238–39, 246.
24. Goyne, 147.
25. Wittke, 248.
26. Zornow, 211.
27. De Hauranne, II, 30.
28. Waugh, see note 6 above, 354.
29. James M. McPherson, *For Cause and Comrades* (New York: Oxford University Press, 1997), 176.
30. Beckett, 151–152.
31. Zornow, 208.
32. John G. Jones letters, Collection of Welsh Americana, National Library of Wales, Aberystwyth.
33. John Mertens, "The Second Battle: A Story of Our Belgian Ancestors in the American Civil War, 1861–65," unpublished manuscript, Green Bay University, Green Bay, Wisconsin.
34. Waugh, see note 6 above, 358.
35. De Chenal, 237.
36. Belgians in the Civil War web site.
37. Horrecks, 105, 107.

Chapter 23   America Has Felt Her Strength

1. Thompson, 82–83.
2. *Rochdale Observer*, April 4, 1863.
3. Ross, 219.

4. Sala, 129–30.

5. Beckett, 42.

6. Schurz, *Papers,* II, 186–88.

7. Schurz, *Reminiscences,* II, 310.

8. Ibid., II, 302, 325.

9. Mahin, 139–41.

10. Francis Lawley to William Gregory, September 16, 1863, Gregory Papers, Emory University, Atlanta, GA.

11. Ross, 201.

12. Purdue, 455–57.

13. Schurz, *Reminiscences,* II, 277.

14. Ibid., II, 288–300, 318

15. Wittke, 245.

16. Mahin, 218–238.

17. De Hauranne, I, 373.

18. Laugel, 322–23.

19. Chambrun, 53–54.

20. Justus Scheibert, *Mit Schwert und Feder: Errinnerungen aus mein Leben* (Berlin: Mittler, 1902), 154.

21. William S. Hoole, introduction to Scheibert, *Seven Months,* vii.

22. ORA, ser. I, vol. 26/2, 140–50.

23. Lonn, *Confederacy,* 86–88.

24. ORA, ser. I, vol. 48/1, 1319–20.

25. Goyne, 160.

26. Kinard, 181.

27. Von Borcke, 447.

28. De Hauranne, I, 487.

29. Laugel, 321–22.

30. Chambrun, 8.

Chapter 24   A Thunderclap from the Blue Sky

1. De Trobriand, 697.

2. Beckett, 154–55.

3. Ibid., 159–60.

4. Ibid., 157–59.

5. Hoole, *Lawley,* 110–11.

6. Conway, 169–73.

7. Beckett, 165–67.

8. Lawley, 1.

9. Brogan, 166–69.

10. Lawley, 5–6.

11. De Trobriand, 745, 749.

12. Lawley, 8.

13. De Trobriand, 750–51.
14. Chambrun, 84–85.
15. Ibid., 94–95.
16. Schurz, *Papers*, II, 326.
17. Post, 331.
18. Illinois Greyhounds web site.
19. ORA, ser. I, vol. 49/2, 833–34.
20. Chambrun, 100–103.
21. Erickson, 200–201.

Appendix I

1. Fox, Chapter X, 233.
2. Philip M. Katz, *From Appomattox to Montmartre: Americans and the Paris Commune* (Cambridge, Mass.: Harvard University Press, 1998), 4–10.
3. De Hauranne, II, 379.
4. Regis De Trobriand, *Four Tears with the Arm of the Potomac* (Boston: Tichnor and Company, 1899).
5. 26th Wisconsin web site.
6. Von Fritsch, 32.
7. John F. McCormack, "Never Were Men So Brave," *Civil War Times*, December 1998.
8. Gary Glynn, "Meagher of the Sword," *America's Civil War*, March 2000, "America's Civil War" web site.
9. ORA, ser. II, vol. 6, 605.
10. ORA, ser. I, vol. 35/2, 145.
11. Warner, *Generals in Blue*, 150–51.
12. ORA, ser. III, vol. 2, 104.
13. ORA, ser. I, vol. 27/1, 91.
14. Gettysburg Discussion Group web site.

Appendix II

1. Underwood, 39–40.
2. W. Y. Wagener, "General John Andreas Wagener," (Ph.D. dissertation, University of South Carolina, Columbia, 1937), 56, in George B. Shealy, *Walhalla: A German Settlement in Upstate South Carolina* (Seneca, S.C.: Blue Ridge Art Association, 1990), 27.
3. Fremantle, *Three Months*, 122–23.
4. ORA. ser. I, vol. 15/1, 948.

BIBLIOGRAPHY

Primary Sources

[Anon], *Battlefields of the South from Bull Run to Fredericksburg . . . By an English Combatant, Lieutenant of Artillery in the Field Staff* (New York: Time-Life Books, 1984).

Aschmann, Rudolf, *Memoirs of a Swiss Officer in the American Civil War* (Bern: Herbert Lang, 1972).

Barnes, James J. and Patience P., eds., *Private and Confidential: Letters from British Ministers in Washington to the Foreign Secretaries in London, 1844–67* (Selingsgrove, N.J.: Susquehanna University Press, 1993).

Basler, Roy P., ed., *Collected Works of Abraham Lincoln* (Abraham Lincoln Association web site).

[Bourke, Robert], "A Month with 'The Rebels,'"*Blackwood's Edinburgh Magazine*, vol. 90 (December 1861), 757–67.

Cadwallader, Sylvanus, *Three Years with Grant* (New York: Alfred D. Knopf, 1955).

Carnegie, Andrew, *Autobiography of Andrew Carnegie* (Boston: Northeastern University Press, 1924).

Chambrun, Marquis Adolphe, *Impressions of Lincoln and the Civil War: A Foreigner's Account* (New York: Random House 1952).

Conolly, Thomas, *An Irishman in Dixie: Thomas Conolly's Diary of the Fall of the Confederacy* (Columbia, S.C.: University of South Carolina Press, 1988).

Conyngham, David P., *The Irish Brigade and Its Campaigns* (New York: Fordham University Press, 1994).

Corsan, W. C., *Two Months in the Confederate States: An Englishman's Travels through the South* (Baton Rouge: Louisiana State University Press, 1996).

Crawford, Martin, ed., *William Howard Russell's Civil War* (Athens, Ga.: University of Georgia Press, 1992).

Daly, Maria L., *Diary of a Union Lady, 1861–65* (Lincoln, Nebr.: University of Nebraska Press, 1994).

Dawson, Francis W., *Reminiscences of Confederate Service, 1861–65* (Baton Rouge: Louisiana State University Press, 1993).

Day, Samuel Phillips, *Down South, or an Englishman's Experiences at the Seat of the American War*, 2 vols., (London, 1862; New York: B. Franklin, 1971).

De Chenal, Francois, *The American Army in the War of Secession* (Fort Leavenworth: U.S. Army, 1894).

De Hauranne, Ernest Duvergier, *A Frenchman in Lincoln's America*, 2 vols. (Chicago: Lakeside Press, 1975).

De Trobriand, Regis, *Four Years with the Army of the Potomac* (Boston: Tichnor and Company, 1899).

[Dicey, Edward], "Washington during the War," *Macmillan's Magazine*, VI (May 1862), 16–29.

Dicey, Edward, *Spectator of America* (London, 1863; Chicago: Quadrangle Books, 1971).

Domschke, Bernhard, *Twenty Months in Captivity: Memoirs of a Union Officer in Confederate Prisons* (Teaneck, N.J.: Fairleigh Dickinson University Press, 1987).

Egan, Michael, *The Flying, Gray-Haired Yank* (Philadelphia: Edgewood Publishing, 1888).

Ferri-Pisani, Camille, *Prince Napoleon in America, 1861: Letters from His Aide-De-Camp* (Paris, 1862; Port Washington, N.Y.: Kennikat Press, 1973).

Fisch, George, *Nine Months in the United States* (London: J. Nisbet and Co., 1862).

[Fletcher, Henry Charles], "A Run through the Southern States," *Cornhill Magazine*, VII (April 1863), 495–525.

Fletcher, Henry Charles, *History of the American War*, (London: 3 vols., R. Bentley, 1865).

Foreign Relations of the United States ("Papers Related to Foreign Affairs Accompanying the Annual Message of the President"), (Washington: Government Printing Office, 1861–1865).

Fox, William F., *Regimental Losses in the American Civil War, 1861–1865* (Albany, 1889), in *The Civil War CD-ROM* (Carmel, Ind.: Guild Press of Indiana, 2000).

[Fremantle, James Arthur], "The Battle of Gettysburg," *Blackwood's Edinburgh Magazine*, September 1863, 365–94.

———, *Three Months in the Southern States* (Lincoln, Nebr.: University of Nebraska Press, 1991).

Galwey, Thomas F., *The Valiant Hours: Narrative of "Captain Brevet" and Irish Americans in the Army of the Potomac* (Harrisburg, Pa.: Stackpole Books, 1961).

Goodell, R. C. and Taylor, P. A. M., eds., "A German Immigrant in the Union Army: Selected Letters of Valentine Bechler," *Journal of American Studies*, vol. 4 (1971), 145–62.

Gould, B. A., *Investigations in the Military and Anthropological Statistics of American Soldiers* (New York: U.S. Sanitary Commission, 1869).

Goyne, Minnetta Altgelt, *Lone Star and Double Eagle: Civil War Letters of a German-Texas Family* (Ft. Worth: Texas Christian University Press, 1982).

Grebner, Constantine, *We Were the Ninth, A History of the Ninth Regiment, Ohio Volunteer Infantry, April 17, 1861, to June 7, 1864* (Kent, Ohio: Kent State University Press, 1987).

Hirst, Benjamin, *The Boys from Rockville: Company D, 14th Connecticut Volunteers* (Knoxville: University of Tennessee Press, 1998).

Hobart-Hampden, Augustus, *Never Caught: Personal Adventures Connected with Twelve Successful Trips in Blockade Running during the American Civil War, 1863–1864* (Carolina Beach, N.C.: The Blockade Runner Museum, 1967).

Horrecks, James, *My Dear Parents: An Englishman's Letters Home from the American Civil War* (London: Gallanez, 1982).

Johnson, Terry A., Jr., ed., *Him on the One Side and Me on the Other: The Civil War Letters of Alexander Campbell, 79th New York Infantry Regiment, and James Campbell, 1st Carolina Battalion* (Columbia, S.C.: University of South Carolina Press, 1999).

Joinville, Prince of, *The Army of the Potomac: Its Organization, Its Commander, and Its Campaign* (New York: A. D. F. Randolph, 1862).

Kohl, Lawrence, ed., *Irish Green and Blue: The Civil War Letters of Peter Welsh, Color Sergeant, 28th Massachusetts Volunteers* (New York: Fordham University Press, 1960).

Kune, Julian, *Reminiscences of an Octogenarian Hungarian Exile* (Chicago: The Author, 1911),

Laugel, Auguste, *The United States during the War* (Bloomington, Ind: University of Indiana Press, 1961).

[Lawley, Francis], "The Last Six Days of Secessia," *The Fortnightly Review*, vol. 2, August 15, 1865, 1–10.

Lawrence, George Alfred, *Border and Bastille* (London: Tinsley Brothers, 1863).

Lawrence, G. G., *Three Months in America in the Summer of 1863* (London: Whittacker and Co., 1864).

Lecomte, Ferdinand, *The War in the United States: Report to the Swiss Military Department* (New York: D. Van Nostrand, 1863).

Lewis, A. S., ed., *My Dear Parents: An Englishman's Letters Home from the American Civil War* (London: Gallanez, 1982).

Maguire, John Francis, *The Irish in America* (London, 1868; New York: Arno Press, 1969).

McCarter, William, *My Life in the Irish Brigade* (Campbell, Calif.: Savas Publishing Co., 1996).

Mulholland, St. Clair, *The Story of the 116th Regiment, Pennsylvania Volunteers in the War of the Rebellion* (New York: Fordham University Press, 1995).

Official Records of the Union and Confederate Armies in the War of the Rebellion (ORA) (Washington, 1880–1900).

Official Records of the Union and Confederate Navies in the War of the Rebellion (ORN) (Washington, 1894–1914).

Paris, Count of, *History of the Civil War in America*, 4 vols., (Philadelphia: Jas H. Coates, 1876–88).

Rappolt, Hedwig, ed., *An American Apprenticeship: The Letters of Emil Frey, 1860–1865* (New York: P. Lang, 1986).

Ross, Fitzgerald, *Cities and Camps of the Confederate States* (Urbana: University of Illinois Press, 1997).

Rowan, Steven, ed., *Germans for a Free Missouri: Translations from the St. Louis Radical Press* (Columbia, Mo.: University of Missouri Press, 1983).

Russell, William H., *My Diary North and South* (New York: Harper and Brothers, 1954).

———, *Pictures of Southern Life, Political and Military* (New York: J. G. Gregory, 1861).

Sala, George A., *My Diary in America in the Midst of War* (London: Tinsley Brothers, 1865).

Samito, Christian G., ed., *Commanding Boston's Irish Ninth: The Civil War Letters of Colonel Patrick R. Guiney* (New York: Fordham University Press, 1997).

Scheibert, Justus, *Seven Months in the Rebel States during the North American War, 1863* (Tuscaloosa: Confederate Publishing Company, 1958).

———, *A Prussian Observes the American Civil War: The Military Studies of Justus Scheibert* (Columbia, Mo.: University of Missouri Press, 2001).

Schurich, Hermann, *The German Element in Virginia* (Baltimore, 1898–1900; Baltimore: Heritage Books, 1977).

Schurz, Carl, *Reminiscences of Carl Schurz*, 3 vols. (New York: McClure and Company, 1907–1909).

———, *Speeches, Correspondence, and Political Papers of Carl Schurz* (New York: G. P. Putnam's Sons, 1913).

[Seymour, Edward A.], "Ten Days in Richmond," *Blackwood's Edinburgh Magazine*, vol. 92 (October 1862), 391–402.

Spiegel, Marcus M., *A Jewish Colonel in the Civil War* (Lincoln, Nebr.: University of Nebraska Press, 1995).

Stanley, Henry M., *Sir Henry Morton Stanley, Confederate* (Baton Rouge, Louisiana State University Press, 2000).

Summersell, Charles G., ed., *The Journal of George Townley Fullam* (Tuscaloosa: Confederate Publishing Company, 1973).

Taylor, Thomas E., *Running the Blockade* (London: John Murray, 1896).

Thompson, Henry Yates, *An Englishman in the American Civil War: The Diaries of Henry Yates Thompson* (London: Sidwick and Jackson, 1971).

Todd, William, *The Seventy-Ninth Highlanders: New York Volunteers in the War of Rebellion, 1861–1865* (Albany: Brandow, Barton, and Co., 1886).

Trollope, Anthony, *North America* (New York: Alfred A. Knopf, 1951).

Villard, Henry, *Memoirs of Henry Villard, Journalist and Financier, 1835–1900*, 2 vols. (Boston: Houghton Mifflin, 1904).

Von Borcke, Heros, *Memoirs of the Confederate War for Independence* (Nashville: J. S. Sanders Company, 1999).

Von Fritsch, Otto, *A Gallant Captain in the Civil War, Being the Extraordinary Adventures of Frederick Otto Baron von Fritsch* (New York: F. Tennyson Neely, 1902).

Watson, William, *Life in the Confederate Army* (Baton Rouge: Louisiana State University Press, 1995).

Wolseley, Field Marshall Viscount, *The American Civil War: An English View* (Charlottesville: University Press of Virginia, 1964) including reprint of "A Month's Visit to the Confederate Headquarters," *Blackwood's Edinburgh Magazine*, XCIII, January 1863.

Principal Secondary Sources

Adams, E. D., *Great Britain and the American Civil War* (London: Longmans, Green, and Co., 1925).

Anbinder, Tyler, *Nativism and Slavery: The Northern Know Nothings and the Politics of the 1850s* (New York: Oxford University Press, 1992).

Beckett, Ian F., *The American Civil War: The War Correspondents* (London: Grange Books, 1997).

Berwanger, Eugene A., *The British Foreign Service and the American Civil War* (Lexington, Ky.: University of Kentucky Press, 1994).

Bilby, Joseph G., *The Irish Brigade in the Civil War* (Conshohocken, Pa.: Combined Publishing, 1997).

Blackett, R. J. M., *Divided Hearts: Britain and the American Civil War* (Baton Rouge: Louisiana State University Press, 2001).

Boatner, Mark M., *The Civil War Dictionary* (New York: Vintage Books, 1991).

Bonham, Milledge L, *The British Consuls in the Confederacy* (New York: Columbia University Press, 1971).

Bright, Erich W., "Nothing to Fear from the Influence of Foreigners: The Patriotism of Richmond's German-Americans during the Civil War" (Master's thesis, Virginia Polytechnic Institute, 1999), Virginia Polytechnic Institute web site.

Brogan, Hugh, *The Times Reports the American Civil War* (London: London Times Books, 1975).

Burton, William, *Melting Pot Soldiers: The Union's Ethnic Regiments* (New York: Fordham University Press, 1998).

Cochran, Hamilton, *Blockade Runners of the Confederacy* (Indianapolis: Bobbs-Merrill, 1958).

Conway, Alan, "Welshmen in the Union Armies," *Civil War History*, vol. 4 (1958), 143–74.

Engelhart, Tim, *Zu den Waffen: Deutsche Emigranten in New Yorker Unionsregimenten waehrend des Amerikanischen Burgerkrieges 1861–65* (Zella-Mehlis, Germany, 2000).

Engle, Stephen D., *Yankee Dutchman: The Life of Franz Sigel* (Fayetteville, Ark.: University of Arkansas Press, 1993).

Erickson, Charlotte, *Invisible Immigrants: The Adaptation of English and Scottish Immigrants in the Nineteenth Century America* (London: London School of Economics and Political Science, 1972).

Gannon, James P., *Irish Rebels, Confederate Tigers; A History of the 6th Louisiana Volunteers* (Mason City, Iowa: Savas Publishing, 1998).

Gleeson, David. T., *The Irish in the South, 1815–1877* (Chapel Hill: University of North Carolina Press, 2001).

Grant, Alfred, *The American Civil War and the British Press* (Jefferson, N.C.: McFarland and Co., 2000).

Hokanson, Nels, *Swedish Immigrants in Lincoln's Time* (New York: Harpers, 1942).

Holland, Bernard, *The Life of Spencer Compton, Eighth Duke of Devonshire* (London: Longmans, Green, and Co., 1911).

Hoole, William Stanley, *Vizetelly Covers the Confederacy* (Tuscaloosa: Confederate Publishing Company, 1957).

———, *Lawley Covers the Confederacy* (Tuscaloosa: Confederate Publishing Co., 1964).

Joslyn, Mauriel Phillips, ed., *A Meteor Shining Brightly: Essays on Maj. Gen. Patrick R. Cleburne* (Macon, Ga.: Mercer University Press, 1998).

Katz, Irving, *August Belmont: A Political Biography* (New York: Columbia University Press, 1968).

Kaufmann, Wilhelm, *Germans in the American Civil War* (Carlisle, Pa.: John Kallmann, 1999).

Kinard, Jeff, *Lafayette of the South: Prince Camille de Polignac and the American Civil War* (College Station, Tex.: Texas A and M University Press, 2001).

Latimer, Jon, "Along with the Irish and Scots, the Welsh also played a significant role in the Civil War," *America's Civil War*, May 2000, 16–17.

Levine, Bruce, *The Spirit of 1848: German Immigrants, Labor Conflict, and the Coming of the Civil War* (Urbana, Ill.: University of Illinois Press, 1992).

Lierley, Joyce M., *Affectionately Yours: Three English Immigrants, the American Civil War, and a Michigan Family Saga* (New York: Making History, 1998).

Loeffler, Michael, *Preussens und Sachsens Bezeihungen zu den USA Wahrends des Sessessionskrieges, 1860–1865* (Berlin: Free University of Berlin, 1999).

Lonn, Ella, *Foreigners in the Union Army and Navy* (Baton Rouge: Louisiana State University Press, 1951).

———, *Foreigners in the Confederacy* (Gloucester, Mass.: P. Smith, 1965).

Luebke, Frederick, ed., *Ethnic Voters and the Election of Lincoln* (Lincoln, Nebr.: University of Nebraska Press, 1971).

Mahin, Dean B., *One War at a Time: International Dimensions of the American Civil War* (Washington: Brassey's, 1999).

Mahone, Kathryn Lynn, "The Irish Community in Antebellum Richmond, 1840–1860" (Master's thesis, University of Richmond, 1986).

Martin, David G., *Carl Bornemann's Regiment: The 41st New York Infantry (DeKalb Regiment) in the Civil War* (Hightstown, N.J.: Longstreet House, 1987).

McLeod, Norman C., "Not Forgetting the Land We Left: The Irish in Ante-bellum Richmond," *Virginia Cavalcade*, Winter 1998, 37–46.

Miller, Kirby A., *Emigrants and Exiles: Ireland and the Irish Exodus to North America* (New York: Oxford University Press, 1950).

Niehaus, Earl F., *The Irish in New Orleans, 1800–1860* (New York: Arno Press, 1976).

O'Grady, Kelly J., *Clear the Irish Way: The Irish in the Army of Northern Virginia* (Mason City, Iowa: Savas Publishing, 2000).

Post, Marie Caroline, *The Life and Memoirs of Comte Regis de Trobriand* (New York: Dutton, 1910).

Pula, James S., *The French in America* (New York: Oceana Publications, 1975).

———, ed., *Memoirs of Wladimir Krzyzanowski* (San Francisco: P and E Research Associates, 1978).

Purdue, Howel and Elizabeth, *Pat Cleburne, Confederate General: A Definitive Biography* (Hillsboro, Tex.: Hillsboro Junior College Press, 1983).

Rippley, La Vern J., *The German-Americans* (Boston: Twayne Publishers, 1976).

Rosen, Robert M., *The Jewish Confederates* (Columbia, S.C.: University of South Carolina Press, 2000).

Starr, Louis M., *Bohmenian Brigade: Civil War Newsmen in Action* (New York: Alfred A. Knopf, 1954).

Starr, Stephen Z., *Colonel Grenfel's Wars: Life of a Soldier of Fortune* (Baton Rouge: Louisiana State University Press, 1971).

Still, William N., Jr., et al., *Raiders and Blockaders: The American Civil War Afloat* (Washington: Brassey's, 1998).

Underwood, Rodman L., *Death on the Nueces: German Texans, Treue de Union* (Austin: Eakin Press, 2000).

Van Vugt, William E., *Britain to America: Mid-Nineteenth-Century Immigrants to the United States* (Urbana: University of Illinois Press, 1999).

Warner, Ezra J., *Generals in Gray: Life of the Confederate Commanders* (Baton Rouge: Louisiana State University Press, 1959).

———, *Generals in Blue: Lives of the Union Commanders* (Baton Rouge: Louisiana State Universite State, 1964).

Wittke, Carl, *Refugees of Revolution: The German Forty-Eighters in America* (Philadelphia: University of Pennsylvania Press, 1970), 245.

Wust, Klaus, *The Virginia Germans* (Charlottesville: University Press of Virginia, 1969).

Zornow, William F., *Lincoln and the Party Divided* (Norman, Okla.: University of Oklahoma Press, 1954).

Zurcher, A. E., *The Forty-Eighters* (New York: Columbia University Press, 1950).

Internet Web Sites

Abraham Lincoln, Collected Works, Abraham Lincoln Association web site: http://www.hti.umich.edu/l/lincoln

Abraham Lincoln Online: http://www.netins.net/showcase/creative/lincoln.html

Belgians in the Civil War: http://users.swing.be/sw03210/index.htm

Civil War Medals of Honor: http://www.army.mil/cmh-pg/mohciv.htm

C.S.S. Alabama: http://www.csa-dixie.com/Liverpool_Dixie/crew.htm

French Guard roster: http://www.geocities.com/Area51/Lair/3680/cw/french/cwb.html

German-American Corner: http://www.germancorner.com

Germans in the Civil War: http://www.geocities.com/Athens/Atlantis/2816/germans/units.html

Gettysburg Discussion Group: http://www.gdg.org

Hungarians in the Civil War: http://www.interlog.com/~silbert/civilwarhung.html

Illinois Greyhounds: www.ketztle.com/diary

Irish Word: http://hometown.aol.com:80/IrishWord/page/index.htm

Jews in the Civil War: http://www.jewish-history.com/salomon/salo05.html

Library of Congress American Memory web site: http://memory.loc.govt/ammem/hdlpcoop/tml

Living History (Germany): http://www.gtg1848.de

Official Records, Union and Confederate Navies (Cornell Univesity): http://library5.library.cornell.edu/moa/browse.monographs/ofre.html

Scots in the Civil War: http://www.scots-in-the-civil-war.net
Sons of Confederate Veterans, Polignac Camp: http://rampages.onramp.net/
~jtcreate/polignac.htm
Sons of Confederate Veterans, Sterling Price Camp:
http://www.geocities.com/~sterlingprice/kelly.htm
Technical University of Berlin: http://www.tu-berlin.de/tui/95jan/de
Texas On Line, Handbook of: http://www.tsha.utexas.edu/handbook/online/
Thomas Tucker web site: http://www.etuckers.com/ttucker/journal/
1863/November.html
Virginia Military Institute: http://www.vmi.edu/archtml/ms284014.html
Virginia Polytechnic Institute: http://scholar.lib.vt.edu/theses/available/
etd-041999-15176
6th Kentucky: http://www.geocities.com/reinhart_us/hund.htm
10th Louisiana: http://www.interlinks.net/rebel/10th/10th.htm
5th New York: http://www.zouave.org
69th New York: http://www.69thnysv.org
15th Wisconsin: http://www.15thwisconsin.net
26th Wisconsin: http://www.agro.agri.umn.edu/~lemedg/wis26/26pgmain.htm

INDEX

ABOUT THE AUTHOR

Dean B. Mahin is a veteran of forty years' service for American international agencies, including the U.S. Department of State, the U.S. Information Agency, and the U.S. Agency for International Development. He has previously written *One War at a Time: The International Dimensions of the American Civil War* and *Olive Branch and Sword: The United States and Mexico, 1845–1848.* He lives in Charlotte, North Carolina.